A HISTORY OF THE HISTORY-MAKING
(IN THE WORLD'S MOST INFLUENTIAL "MINING CAMP")

TOMBSTONE
Arizona Mystique

Don Chaput &
David D. de Haas, MD

Caxton Press

ISBN# 978-087004-648-3

First Edition

Library of Congress Control Number: 2023948070

Cover and book design by Jocelyn Robertson
Cover artwork by Gary Zaboly

Printed in the United States of America
CAXTON PRESS
Caldwell, Idaho

This book is dedicated to our families

Don dedicates this book to Antoinette Chaput and our sons Ben and Ed.

David dedicates this book to Mary de Haas; our children Lindsay, Heather, and Lance; our grandchildren Ethan, Jacob, Asher and, since our last book, now little Levi; and to my brothers Darryl and Dirk de Haas.

Praise for Tombstone, Arizona Mystique

Tombstone, Arizona Mystique is fact-filled and interesting in terms of mining matters, and I learned much about how important water was to the industry and how flooding crippled it. The authors build a good case as to why the town of Tombstone was certainly different from other boomtowns and had a mystique all its own. I really like the history of the town being divided into "eras." It adds structure and important reference points for readers keen to understand more fully how the town handled the ups and downs associated with silver mining.

In my opinion, the biographies are the real strength of the work, and would be an excellent reference point for any student of the eras covered in them, and an invaluable research source. I am a sucker for timelines, so, as a reader, I am always glad to see a thorough one included in a work of this size. It helps the reader understand the temporal relationships and importance of certain events and acts; once again, a great reference tool for all researchers.

In summary, I was glad to read this truly extensive work, and I learned much about the many and varied people who influenced Tombstone from 1877 until 2023. It contains information that will be invaluable to future scholars.

– Peter Brand, Tombstone/Earp researcher and author,
The Life and Crimes of Perry Mallon; The Story of Texas Jack Vermillion: Wyatt Earp's Vendetta Posse Rider, and Doc Holliday's Nemesis: The Story of Johnny Tyler & Tomstone's Gamblers' War

Tombstone had it all; a rags-to-riches story of a down-on-his-luck prospector named Ed Schieffelin, who was warned he'd find nothing in that desolate, Apache-infested country but his own tombstone; the rise of a boomtown that attracted some of the most famous and infamous gamblers, gunslingers, good-time girls, hustlers, con men, entertainers and entrepreneurs in the West. The Chiricahua Apache were a constant threat; stagecoach robberies plagued Cochise County; outlaws were as thick as fleas and roamed the streets at will; cattle rustlers were brazenly stealing livestock in broad daylight; and a friendly county sheriff conveniently overlooked their transgressions as "boys just having fun." The public at large accepted their bad behavior because they spent their ill-gotten money freely in town. The upper-crust citizens, movers and shakers demanded law and order to attract outside investment, while the working-class citizens preferred a laissez-faire, "live and let live" town; oh yes, there were Democrats versus Republicans and there was an alleged love triangle between a beautiful woman, the county sheriff and the brother of the town marshal. Last and certainly not least, the "most famous gunfight in the West" was fought on the streets of Tombstone.

Does this sound like a 1940s B Western movie? But it's all true and it all happened in Tombstone. All the other boomtowns from Montana, Deadwood and Dodge City to Virginia City and the California Mother Lode were basically one-dimensional. Their story is mostly about mining or cattle. Tombstone had both, and much, much more. Hollywood has attempted many times to capture the true essence of the Tombstone story, and up to now has not been successful. Chaput and de Haas, the authors of *Tombstone, Arizona Mystique*, have carefully and thoroughly dissected the above-mentioned events and personalities of the denizens who fashioned those events and have given researchers, historians, and aficionados an in-depth tome of the Old West's most famous town.

– Marshall Trimble, Arizona State Historian, author of twenty-nine books on Arizona and the West and *True West* magazine's monthly column, "Ask the Marshall;" winner, Arizona Veterans Hall Column of Fame 2004 and Arizona Music and Entertainment Hall of Fame 2011; recipient of two television Emmys; Vice President Emeritus, Wild West History Association

Francis Austin, Charles and Samuel Calhoun, Mary Jane Evans, Hale McCormick, May Woodman, Charlie Brown (no, not that cartoon character), Manuel Corella, T.J. Drum, Alfred Emanual. Names that may not be familiar—even to folks who know a bit about Tombstone and southeast Arizona. But these and so many others contributed to the Tombstone mystique: a touch of history, legend and myth that carries on more than 140 years after a certain gunfight in an empty lot off Fremont Street.

Tombstone, Arizona Mystique does a great service to the "Town Too Tough to Die" as well as the Old West field. It fills in a lot of blank spaces with characters, big and small, who impact-ed the area (and vice versa). And it takes the story well beyond the severe limitations of the town heyday between 1878 and 1882. Tombstone has had a dizzying number of highs and lows over the decades, and those periods are covered as well.

This is beyond just storytelling. *Tombstone, Arizona Mystique* is a remarkable reference book that is a "must" for any Tombstone aficionado. You will learn things and be enter-tained. And you'll marvel at the mystique that seems to grow with every year.

Then there's the story of this Charlie Brown fellow...

– Mark Boardman, Editor, *The Tombstone Epitaph;*
Features Editor, *True West* magazine

Tombstone, Arizona Mystique is not only a wonderful overview of the town's history, but also an in-depth look at the mystery and mystique of the place. The authors have taken the time to do great research and provide the history, then offer-ing up their take on how and why Tombstone is forever a place of legend and lore.

Take, for instance, the so-called feud between the Earps and the Cowboys. This is part of the mystique of Tombstone. While the Earp brothers and Doc Holliday disliked the Clan-tons and McLaurys, there was really more of a feud between Sheriff Behan and Wyatt Earp, which may or may not have led to the fight behind the O. K. Corral. It's a long story, one the au-thors flesh out in great detail. And the O. K. Corral gunfight? Actually, in an alley behind the O. K. Corral.

Much of this mystique comes from Hollywood and the authors do a great job in wrestling fact and fiction apart to give the reader the real, not reel, story. I really liked it. Great con-cept! This is a fascinating read, not only about the mystique, but the history of a wild west town we all have come to love: Tombstone.

– Linda Wommack, author and historian; contributing editor, *True West* magazine; columnist, *Wild West* magazine; contributing writer, *The Tombstone Epitaph* newspaper; member Wild West History Association, Women Writing the West; Women Writing the West DOWNING Journalism Award creator and chair; three-time winner, Will Rogers Medallion Award; winner, Carolyn Bancroft Colorado History Award for Best Biography

TABLE OF CONTENTS

Lifting the Illusion

I whisper abracadabra—a word that means I will create as I speak—and pull a radiant red flower out of the space between my ribs. I hold its dazzling beauty before your gaze, and you believe that, embodied in those pretty petals, I have spoken all the words inside my chest into existence. Yes, that's right: watch this flower and don't notice that I conjure in my second hand concealed behind my back, abracadabra, the power of a magician's sleight of hand...

– Michelle Izmaylov, MD,
Vanderbilt University Medical Center, Nashville, Tennessee[1]

FOREWORD
John Boessenecker

"You'll find your tombstone."

THAT IS WHAT U. S. SOLDIERS TOLD PROSPECTOR ED Schieffelin in Arizona Territory. They were not exaggerating the danger posed by roving bands of Apache warriors, but Schieffelin ignored their warnings. As a result, when he struck silver in 1877 in the isolated hills seventy miles southeast of Tucson, he named his first mine Tombstone. More big silver strikes followed, and miners and adventurers flocked to the region and founded the boomtown of Tombstone. It quickly became a typical rowdy western mining camp, populated by miners, gamblers, cattlemen, desperadoes, and adventurers of every stripe.

Most notable of those settlers were the Earp brothers: Jim, Virgil, Wyatt, and Morgan, who were later joined by their younger brother Warren. The Earps took an active part in Tombstone's business life, investing in real estate and mining claims and running gambling games in saloons. But to modern Americans, they are best known as gunfighters and lawmen who took on the Cowboys, the old west's biggest outlaw gang. In the inaptly named "gunfight at the O.K. Corral," which actually took place in a vacant lot behind Tombstone's O.K. Corral, Wyatt, Virgil, and Morgan Earp, accompanied by their friend John H. "Doc" Holliday, shot and killed three of the leaders of the Cowboys. In retaliation, the Cowboys assassinated Morgan Earp and tried to assassinate Virgil, wounding him and leaving him with a useless arm. Wyatt then began his famous vengeance ride when he and his partners tracked down and killed Curly Bill Brocius and other members of the Cowboys. That effectively broke up the gang and ended organized outlawry in southern Arizona.

Those dramatic events kept Tombstone in the public eye ever after. As early as the 1920s, when Wyatt Earp and many other Tombstoners were still alive, books began to appear that dramatized the exploits of the Earp boys. Then, in 1932, the

1

film *Law and Order* was released, and thus became the first motion picture to feature the "gunfight at the O.K. Corral." Hollywood's fascination with Tombstone never ceased. *Frontier Marshal* came out in 1934 and was remade five years later with the same title, and starred Randolph Scott as Wyatt Earp. In 1942 came *Tombstone, the Town Too Tough to Die*, and naturally featured Wyatt Earp and Doc Holliday battling Ike Clanton and Curly Bill Brocius.

My Darling Clementine, starring Henry Fonda and directed by John Ford, hit the theaters in 1946. It was a huge commercial success and many film critics have lauded it as one of the best Westerns ever made. Unfortunately, movie critics tend to know very little about the Old West. The only connection this film had to the Tombstone saga is that it featured characters called Wyatt Earp and Doc Holliday. Yet it made the Earps and Tombstone even more famous.

Gunfight at the O.K. Corral, released in 1957, featured Burt Lancaster as Wyatt Earp and Kirk Douglas as Doc Holliday. The film had a highly skilled cast, but, like *My Darling Clementine*, it contained barely an authentic moment. The personalities, the costumes, the dialogue, the sets, and the scenes were wrong in every detail. But this film, along with the hugely popular television series, *The Life and Legend of Wyatt Earp*, which ran from 1955 to 1961, and *Tombstone Territory* (1957-1959), contributed incalculably to the fame of Tombstone.

During the 1960s, Tombstone remained in the public eye. *Hour of the Gun* (1967) starred James Garner as Wyatt and Jason Robards as Doc. Its director was John Sturges, who had also directed *Gunfight at the O.K. Corral* ten years earlier. *Hour of the Gun* was presented as a more accurate portrayal of the events in Tombstone. An opening title reads, "This picture is based on fact. This is the way it happened." That was hardly true. But the filmmakers at least tried to replicate reality, providing a heavily fictionalized account of the street fight near the O.K. Corral, the shootings of Virgil and Morgan Earp, and Wyatt's vengeance ride that followed. *Hour of the Gun* proved popular with critics and audiences alike.

It would not be until 1993 that Hollywood produced what is by far the best film about Tombstone and the Earp saga. It was aptly titled *Tombstone*, starring Kurt Russell as Wyatt Earp and Val Kilmer as Doc Holliday. The first five minutes and the last fifteen minutes contain fabricated, overwrought blood-baths that have no relation to reality. But in between those opening and closing scenes, a viewer will see what may well be the finest western ever filmed. The costumes, language, and attention to historical detail are extraordinary. Much of *Tomb-stone's* success was attributable to its historical accuracy, which in turn was a result of the superb screenplay by the late Kevin Jarre and the expertise of technical consultant Jeff Morey, a leading authority on Wyatt Earp.

Those who love film depictions of Tombstone are sure to love what appears in the pages that follow. The authors, Don Chaput and David D. de Haas, are both authorities on the history of the Old West. The first section of *Tombstone, Arizona Mystique* provides sketches of many of the most colorful—though largely forgotten—pioneers of Tombstone. The first, in alphabetical order, is Ah Lum, a Chinese businessman who operated popular restaurants, owned mines, and battled racial bigotry. The last is Conrad Zulick, a prominent mine owner who became Arizona's governor in 1885. In between are dozens of colorful characters, such as the ruffian and gunman Jerry Barton; Jack Crabtree, brother of the famous entertainer Lotta Crabtree; Fred Dodge, a gambler who later claimed—falsely—to have been a Wells Fargo undercover agent in Tombstone; Tom Fitch, the once-famed frontier lawyer who represented the Earp boys; Camillus Fly, the pioneer photographer of the Southwest; Joe Goldwater, great uncle of U. S. Senator Barry Goldwater; Tom Jeffords, "blood brother" of the Apache leader Cochise; and Lou Rickabaugh, a popular gambler and friend of the Earps.

Nor are the women of Tombstone forgotten. Included here are Big Nose Kate, the paramour of Doc Holliday; Addie Bourland, a dressmaker who was one of the principal witnesses to the O.K. Corral fight; Clara Brown, a journalist whose reports from Tombstone remain important to this day; Nellie Cashman, the "angel of Tombstone;" Samantha Fallon, a hotelkeeper and reputedly the paramour of Ed Schieffelin; Lizzie Gallagher, a "soiled dove" who stabbed a soldier to death; "Red Emma" Parker, a hard-fisted prostitute and madam; Minnie Rafferty, a saloonkeeper's daughter and shopkeeper who was prominent in Tombstone's social events; Mary Tack and Mary Toomey, both of whom were boarding-house owners and successful businesswomen; and finally, May Woodman, who shot and killed her lover in front of the Oriental Saloon.

This volume does not end with the dramatic era of the late 1870s to the mid-1880s. The succeeding section deals with the years up to 1900 and includes Tombstone biographies of everyone from lawman-turned-train robber Burt Alvord to Owen Wister, who went on to become the best-selling author of the classic Western novel *The Virginian*, published in 1902. The ensuing chapters of this volume describe the most significant and colorful Tombstoners up to the modern era.

This book is plainly a labor of love by Don Chaput and David de Haas, and their enthusiasm for Tombstone is contagious. Even the most diehard fans of the Wild West are sure to learn something new in *Tombstone, Arizona Mystique*.

PREFACE
David D. de Haas, MD

AS MANY NINETEENTH-CENTURY OLD WEST AND MINING scholars have come to realize, Tombstone, Arizona was a distinctive place in the grand scheme of things, and not just another North American "mining camp." As Wild West/ Tombstone/Earp authority and historian/author extraordinaire Lee A. Silva so aptly put it in his *Wyatt Earp: A Biography of the Legend (Volume II, Part 1: Tombstone Before the Earps)*:

> ...Tombstone was unique in so many ways other than just its name...Apaches, stage robbers...it was a major risk just getting to or leaving Tombstone in the early days...the surrounding rich grasslands...brought cattlemen...and cattle rustlers...to the area even before silver was discovered, giving Tombstone a double dose of good (or bad) fortune as a cattle boomtown as well as a silver boomtown that attracted twice as many "bad guys" to it as other boomtowns might have...

Silva went on to describe Tombstone's early years as "...a town that still did not have an inkling that the truth about its roaring existence would soon be obliterated by myth and legend that would be as voluminous as the millions of dollars of silver that was just beginning to pour from the bowels of its mine shafts..."

In 1917 historian George Wharton James asked:

> How do certain towns, cities, or mining camps become famous easier or readier than others?...There is a psychology in names that is often as baffling as it is fascinating to study. Tombstone, however, is one of the mining camps of Arizona that seemed to achieve fame at once. The very singularity of its name attracted attention. Writers in the public press throughout the country...rendered it the butt of their wit, and because in the days of its founding there were many...wild and wooly

5

things occurring in the West, it was easy to hang them all on to the convenient peg called Tombstone. [2]

In his 2004 *Tombstone, Arizona: "Too Tough to Die"* book, author Lynn Bailey quotes Arizona W.P.A. researcher, journalist, and publicist Pat H. L. Hayhurst as having asserted:

> The difference (from otherwise similar frontier mining towns) lies in the wild…conditions of the country surrounding (Tombstone) for miles…But, as one Tombstoner once said to me after I pointed this fact (that there were as many killings in the Bisbee region in the 1880s as in Tombstone) out, "The rest of the country didn't boast about its killings as much as we have." The curious name, Tombstone, the fact that it was the capital of a *cimarron*—a wild country, that caused a lot of publicity to be written about it.

And, long before all this (and the unremitting newspaper/magazine articles, books, television shows, and movies which were subsequently to follow), on December 29, 1879, future O.K. Corral Gunfight trial Judge, Wells Spicer, had already written from/about "new" Tombstone, A.T., during its embryonic stage, demonstrating the mystique of the place was already blossoming from its very foundation:

> "…the prevailing idea that people abroad too often have of (Tombstone)…(is they) consider it a dry, sandy, herbless, waterless desert, without vegetation, and where life, with the best the country affords, would be without comforts, much less luxuries-in fact, a burden….a far off country, that can only be approached at risk of life; a barren waste of trackless desert, unexplored and impassable, of which little is known; where the herbs and flowers are without scent; where the vegetation has no juice; where every bush or sprig has a thorn; where every man is a thief and every woman a prostitute…." [3]

On June 22, 1929, the *Tucson Daily Citizen* newspaper (reprinted in the *Tombstone Epitaph* newspaper on June 27, 1929), in a commentary in anticipation of Tombstone's proposed upcoming 50th ("semi-centennial") anniversary of its founding (what became known as its "Helldorado" celebration), wrote:

> It (Tombstone) lives in the mellow light of romance, not only for its dwellers but for its wandering sons. These were formerly so many, so adventurous, and so widespread that each week Bill Hattich was enabled to announce some sensational feat accomplished by a "former Tombstoner." Every telegraphed news story telling of an unusual accomplishment...was susceptible to localization, for all adventurers it was suspected, must have tarried at Tombstone. Thus "old Tombstoners" each week brought to (former; 1895 - 1915) Editor and Publisher (of the Tombstone Daily Prospector and Weekly Epitaph newspapers) Bill Hattich rich cargo of sensation and amazement; the news mines of the wide world poured a steady stream of griat (sic; grist) into the Epitaph's hopper.

As this 1929 *Tucson Daily Citizen* analysis points out, there were such extraordinarily exceptional people who spent time in Tombstone in its formative years, and even to this day one might add, that the preliminary working title of this book was *The Folks From Tombstone: They Made a Mark*, but we *never* intended that be the definitive title, as this book is not about "the folks," or actually even about Tombstone; it is about Tombstone's "mystique," and a big, but by no means exclusive, part of that, was its diverse folks. What made the place so extraordinary/different and set it apart from every other seemingly similar "mining camp" which came before or after it? To make our point, though, and contemplate and understand this "history of the history-making," one must first take a step back and appreciate the folks who spent time there and the history of the town itself. We make the argument that, each in their own special way, "the folks" who were attracted to Tombstone and its environment were a remarkably unique and, in many instances, immensely talented (or cunning), group of individuals. Many went on to significant and noteworthy accomplishments (or colossal failures) in Tombstone and/or later in life; so much so that, when all has been considered, Tombstone, with its milieu, became the most impactful town in American (and the world's) mining history. The list of names of those who spent time there is simply remarkable, some of the most famed (and infamous) of the late nineteenth and early twentieth centuries. Many of them made a mark and name for themselves, and received national and even worldwide attention (both good and bad), either before, in, or after leaving Tombstone.

This work is also distinct in that for the first time, it categorizes the Tombstone story into definitive quantifiable "eras," and covers much more than just Tombstone's Earp/the Cowboys years. It embraces its entire exceptional history, focusing not only on its mining saga and glory/bonanza times, but on the bust/borrasca years, and those gifted individuals who, sometime during its 145-year history, called it home for a period of time. It concerns only those who actually spent time living in Tombstone itself, as opposed to all of Cochise County, and emphasizes persons who had a great impact and helped make it such a distinctive place. These individuals, its location, circumstances, and extraordinary peripheral events combined to bring Tombstone what seemed like nonstop national attention and worldwide news coverage (both flattering and undesirable; the Tombstone notoriety being a perfect example "no such thing as bad publicity") during its glory years, continuing on well thereafter, even to this day. There is no other boomtown in history which can make such a claim. When all has been considered, one may well make the assertion, as we do here, that Tombstone was the most wide-reaching and influential "mining camp" the world has ever known. A unique place indeed, with unrivaled impact and significance on so many levels.

For those Tombstone scholars and historians who have passionately studied its comprehensive history, and then stepped back and taken a bird's eye view, it becomes readily apparent that there were actually five distinct boom-bust cycles ("eras") and four separate and diverse "bonanza periods," in Tombstone's history, which make its story so fascinating and exceptional, finally clarifying why and how it still flourishes to this day:

> First Era (1877-1885) – *The legend-making years (the original bonanza period)*
> Second Era (1886-1900) – Era of the *"chloriders" (borrasca/ bust)*
> Third Era (1901-1910) – *The first revival (second bonanza)*

Fourth Era (1914-1923) – *Manganese and World War I (the second revival/third bonanza)*
Fifth Era (1927-2023) – *Living on the legend (the final revival/greatest bonanza)*

In composing this story, we have endeavored to tie the Tombstone mystique all together in one place for the first time, so future scholars may more readily assimilate the temporal relationships and then grand scheme of things. Why is Tombstone still thriving, and so significant, to this day? In its early beginnings, this specific miniscule mining town was surrounded by ominous bandits (both American "cowboys" and Mexican "bandidos" and smugglers from south of the border), and intimidating Apache Indians. It was and is located in the middle of a treacherous desert, with dangerous topography and unbearable heat/cold, monsoons and haboobs (wind, rain, sandstorms), menacing insects (tarantulas, scorpions), poisonous snakes, Gila monsters, shortage of water to drink or use for irrigation, and of wood to build shelters and provide warmth at night or cook with; filled with spined vegetation, threatening wildlife, disastrous fires, and flooded mines. Yet it *is* still thriving more than ever, and still significant. How and why did this so aptly named "Town Too Tough to Die" survive and flourish when so many comparable others of its day and age did not, and were destined to become "ghost towns," never to be reminisced about again? Of course, the fact that the most famous gunfight of the Wild West occurred in town plays no small part. Add to that its renowned participants, including celebrated frontier Marshals Wyatt and Virgil Earp and notorious gunfighting dentist John Henry "Doc" Holliday, and their nemesis cowboy gang members, the Clantons and McLaurys, and you have the formula for a legend in the making. Hopefully, this totally new take on the world-wide impact of Tombstone, Arizona, and "the folks" who made it all happen in its renowned glory years (1877 to approximately 1922) and beyond (now modern-day), is thought-provoking; and enthusiasts will learn new information about the Wild West as well as intriguing mining, Tombstone, and more generally important historical facts, and thus be better able to organize their thoughts and assimilate the big picture.

Tombstone, a mining center in the desert, in deep trouble because the mines had too much water. Tombstone, with law enforcement officers Virgil and Wyatt Earp taking care of things at the legendary "Gunfight at the O.K. Corral." Tombstone, with such exotic remarkable characters as Buckskin Frank Leslie, Nellie Cashman, Sheriff "Texas" John Slaughter, John "Doc" Holliday, Johnny Ringo, "Curly Bill" Brocius, Ike Clanton, and lawman/train robber Burt Alvord. The West's most famous "surgeon to the gunfighters," Dr. George Goodfellow, earned his reputation in Tombstone. In the early 1890s, Lewis Aubury began experimenting with cyanide, and by 1893 was getting paid in silver from the leased Mayflower Mine by using his cyanide process, one of the first in the United States. He began working on Tombstone's waste dumps with these methods to make them (waste) pay once again; such success enhanced an "era of chloriding" there and subsequently led to his appointment as state mineralogist of California. One of the West's most famous lynchings took place here, when John Heath swung for all to view (and indeed the world, due to the morbid, extensively circulated iconic photo), to the town's delight. Tombstone in 1901-1910 (its third era) had a significant mining revival, two decades after its first bonanza; few Western mining towns ever had such a second chance, let alone a third chance (during era four) and fourth (during era five). For more than ninety years now, annually in October, Tombstone commemorates its first era with Helldorado Days, bringing to residents and tourists some of the excitement associated with life in that nineteenth century silver-mining center. This, too, indicates some of the interest, the vitality, not shown by many other former mining centers. The townsfolk had no way of realizing at the unveiling of this special event that they were also ushering in their final, and by far most significant and enduring era: number five.

On a personal note, I would like to share an anecdote that, for the interested reader, may help clarify the circumstances that ultimately led to my own personal fascination/obsession with this story. In mid-1994, I began a shift in the emergency department at Saint Bernardine's Medical Center in San Bernardino, California, where I served as the assistant medical director. It was quiet at that time as it was early in the morning, and the daily mad rush hadn't yet begun. I got to conversing with Barbara Brown (RIP), one of the many wonderful ER nurses I had worked with there for many years, who was just arriving for her morning shift, too. I told her our family had all watched the Tombstone movie the night before, and asked her if she herself had seen it. She said no, but that "there was an Earp in that bed right over there yesterday evening" (about the same time our family was watching the Tombstone movie, it turned out), and pointed just across from where we were sitting.

My first reaction was *no way*; I couldn't believe it! To me, although I had heard of them nearly my entire life and knew better, Doc Holliday and Wyatt Earp were pretty much just mythical cartoon characters, portrayed in western movies, not real people. Tombstone itself, like Dodge City, was just an iconic movie-set, western-town fantasyland that didn't actually exist in the real world, only in the theaters and on TV. In fact, if one "googles" the town of Tombstone to this day, a question immediately appears and is answered: "Is Tombstone a real town?"

And thus began my thirty-year fascination with everything Tombstone, O.K. Corral, Earp, and Doc Holliday. I then made the effort to learn as much as I possibly could about the real townspeople and events in those days before the ubiquity of computers and the internet. I quickly discovered that the Earps actually had lived for quite some time in the San Bernardino area surrounding the hospital where I had been working for years. It was the family's home base. I was even more amazed to also soon discover that not only was Wyatt's brother James buried adjacent to the hospital, in the Mountain View Cemetery, but so were their sister Adelia and sister-in-law Allie Earp (wife of famous frontier lawman Virgil Earp), right alongside him. I then discovered that Wyatt's mother was buried in the "Pioneer Cemetery" just a couple miles south of the hospital, right next to James's wife Bessie. Younger brother Morgan, who was a participant in the legendary Tombstone O.K. Corral Gunfight, and subsequently murdered in ambush by members of the cowboy gang while playing pool in a Tombstone saloon, was buried in Colton, just a few miles west of there. I visited all these graves and then was really off and running.

I next endeavored to delve into the Tombstone legend and learn just how this small town became a household word, known pretty much the world over, and especially to the young child I once was. This book most definitely answers that question once and for all. I wish something comparable had been available when I first began my quest, as it would have saved me the thirty years it has taken to finally piece it all together; the questions I am certain countless others besides myself have also pondered through the years, finally all answered in one place. By breaking the story up into "eras," as we have done, everything now all becomes readily apparent, falling into place, and so much easier to grasp the big picture, for the casual reader and the intense Tombstone scholar alike. Here is the legend-making, the mystique, the history of the history, of the most iconic and renowned frontier/Wild West mining camp the world has ever known—Tombstone!

PROLOGUE

IN THE ANNALS OF AMERICAN HISTORY, WHAT HAPPENED IN Tombstone may seem comparatively exaggerated, mythical, or downright fiction. Yet in that place there were many larger-than-life events and men and women of unusual character, living in an isolated frontier desert environment for half a century; and well beyond that, even into the current day, but for very different reasons. The saga of the Western community of Tombstone is not an amalgam of pretend scenarios, nor a creation of Hollywood show business needs; it was real life, and contained much of what we have come to consider as the fabled "American West," owing to its peculiar unique mystique.

Mystique; "a fascinating aura of mystery, awe, and power surrounding someone or something. An air of secrecy surrounding a particular activity or subject that make it impressive or baffling to those without special knowledge. Magic, charm, appeal, allure, romance, charisma, mysteriousness, glamour…"—that's Tombstone, Arizona![4]

THE FIRST ERA, 1877-1885
The Legend-Making Years: The Original Bonanza Period

ONLY ONE TOMBSTONE

INTEREST AND USE OF METALS IN THE NEW WORLD WERE NO different from that of Europe. Metals were rare, often attractive, had a variety of uses, and were associated with wealth and the good life. Explorers, prospectors, and miners in the Spanish and Portuguese sections of the New World were successful in finding major deposits, especially of gold and silver. Nothing of great significance was found to the north, in the British and French parts of North America.

This was to change, as in the early 1800s paying gold deposits were located in North Carolina, and even larger, richer deposits were found and worked in Georgia by the late 1820s. The Georgia gold deposits were so promising that a mint was erected at Dahlonega. Yet, it was not the precious metals of gold and silver that led to extensive mining development in the new United States. Lead was discovered in the Missouri area in the late 1700s and was in major production by the middle of the 1800s. The Wisconsin lead district, especially around Mineral Point, got off to a good start by the late 1830s, and was a decent producer for decades.

Even larger and more significant were the native copper deposits of Michigan's Upper Peninsula. By the late 1840s, thousands of men were prospecting and working the south shore of Lake Superior, getting masses of native copper; this production would continue for another one hundred years. These gold, lead, and copper developments in the first half of the nineteenth century were the highlights of the metals industry, but were about to be almost forgotten when the exploration and prospecting in the American West erupted following the discovery of gold in California in 1848.

In the American metal mining past, the time from the California Gold Rush of 1848-49 until the era of World War I formed a distinct period. There were discoveries and exploitation after that, but new technologies and markets determined that those mining activities would be far different from what transpired earlier. And, although there was some metal mining in the East, such as the significant iron production of Alabama, the overwhelming amount of metal production in the United States would be in the trans-Mississippi West. The metals would be primarily gold, silver, copper, and lead. The regions include not only Alaska, but also the Klondike/Yukon gold experience; the mining equipment, personnel, even the transportation in this Canadian zone were most closely connected to Seattle and San Francisco.

Communities small and large arose, grew, and declined around the business of metal mining. It is our premise that the silver mining settlement of Tombstone, Arizona Territory had such a variety of events and personalities associated with its past that it has had a greater historical, technological, and image-creating impact than that of any other mining center, not only of the American West, but the entire world. This does not mean it was the most productive, the wealthiest, or the longest in production; but Tombstone, and its thousands of residents who later took their backgrounds and talents to other parts of North America and indeed the world, had a measurable impact unmatched by any other mining community.

Considering some of the reasons that Tombstone has earned such recognition, one must first compare it to a hundred or more other such important mining centers in the American West, to name just a few (in alphabetical order):

Angels Camp, CA
Bodie, CA
Cripple Creek, CO
Grass Valley, CA
Joplin, MO
Kennecott, AK
Leadville, CO
Nevada City, CA
Pioche, NV
Rough and Ready, CA
Tonopah, NV
Wallace, ID

Bingham, UT
Butte, MT
Deadwood, SD
Jerome, AZ
Juneau, AK
Klondike, Canada (Yukon)
Mariposa, CA
Nome, Alaska
Placerville, CA
Telluride, CO
Virginia City, NV

Seeing these names, researchers, historians, and the casual reader will have some immediate responses, such as the town's location, its decade of most production, its important transportation links, or perhaps a special personality or so associated with that mining environment. That is not the case with Tombstone. There are a few dozen reasons why the name Tombstone brings to mind many more unusual events and unique personalities. The very name itself, "Tombstone," creates considerably more interest than names like "Jerome," "Pioche," or "Bingham."

The name of the mine and the community is said to have a confused origin, but not if you read the several accounts provided by its discoverer, Ed Schieffelin. The versions have a few details added here and there, but it all started in March 1877, when Schieffelin was in northern Arizona. A detachment of Indian Scouts of the U. S. Army was heading south to Fort Huachuca (then Camp Huachuca, until 1882), for campaigns against "hostile Apaches." Schieffelin accompanied them, rather than travel alone.

Using Camp Huachuca as his base for supplies, Schieffelin wandered in various directions on his prospecting trips. Often, when he returned, the soldiers would ask if he found anything, and he would report no luck. Their common reply was, "You'll find your tombstone if you don't stop running through the country all alone," referring, of course, to an Apache threat. The big silver discoveries by Schieffelin and party took place in the summer and fall of 1877, and his first location, made in the spring of 1878, he named Tombstone.[5]

What we are presenting in these pages is not a history of Tombstone. That community, and its significant mining past, has already been well chronicled by Lee Silva and Lynn Bailey; William B. Shillingberg's book is also very useful.[6] This book is the "beyond and after" Tombstone, examining how the mining, the milling, and the many fascinating people of the area had a wide impact on other communities in the West and around the world. Aside from the mining personnel, the inhabitants of the town—the doctors, lawyers, judges, merchants, gamblers, saloon keepers, cowboys, teachers, clergymen, accountants, prostitutes—these people typically eventually went elsewhere, and the Tombstone past and traditions were part of the transfer, unfolding from San Diego to Nome, from Seattle to Santa

Fe. The Tombstone mystique went with them. When Sol Israel, Tombstone bookseller, died in Los Angeles in 1931, his death notice contained the words: "Tombstone papers please copy."

The Tombstone legacy was a package of great deeds, fantastic bonanzas, important mining and milling innovations, and a rich cast of characters from many walks of life, over a prolonged period (146 years, now) of time. Their great doings, and their low-life counterparts, became main ingredients in what later generations would think was the American West. This would not be the legacy of Jerome, Joplin, Butte, Cripple Creek, or Juneau. These places may have been significant, but they lacked the combination of factors that made Tombstone such a Western icon.

TOMBSTONE, ABBREVIATED

AFTER THE IMPORTANT SILVER DISCOVERY, ED SCHIEFFELIN went to Tucson, where he filed his claim on August 1, 1877. To his chagrin, there was no assayer in Tucson. A few months later, Schieffelin arrived at the Signal Mill in Mohave County, Arizona Territory, where his brother Albert worked as a laborer. Also at the mill was Dick Gird, an engineer and an assayer. Gird was no novice. Aside from his assaying knowledge, he had produced the first official map of Arizona Territory, in 1865, and was very familiar with the topography and terrain of much of the territory. Gird looked over the samples, was very impressed, and they cemented the trio of Ed and Al Schieffelin and Dick Gird, who would launch one of the more successful mining ventures of the American West.

The trio, and a few others who followed them, returned to the site; then, early in 1878, in Tucson filed specific claims, whose names would soon become known widely: Tombstone; Graveyard No. 1; Lucky Cuss, and a few more. On April 9, 1878, the Tombstone Mining District was recorded in Tucson, Pima County, and by then, newspapers in Arizona and California were abuzz with the tales of silver riches.

With the silver value known, the Schieffelin team then found strong financial backing in ex-Governor Anson Safford, and John Vosburg, a Tucson gunsmith who had also been an officer in the territorial government. Within months, work was started on the mines where Tombstone would evolve and mill sites were chosen, with construction beginning along the San Pedro River a few miles west of the mines. The year 1878 was the birth of the Tombstone mining and milling empire.

The important development of Tombstone would not be overseen by the five men most responsible for its existence. Neither of the Schieffelin brothers took much of a role in the new community; Ed would soon be off prospecting in Alaska. Dick Gird took quite an interest for a year or so, and was especially concerned with development of the mills along the San Pedro River. Vosburg, too, was financially interested in the milling aspect, but after a year or so began to spend the good life among his orchards in Southern California. The other great financier, Governor Anson Safford, would exchange the Tombstone desert for the tropics of Florida.

The mines of greater Tombstone developed rapidly, and soon practically every promising inch was part of a mine, prospect, or claim. One report indicated that by 1881 there were several dozen producing mines, including the well-known Grand Central, Lucky Cuss,

Ed Schieffelin, who discovered the Tombstone silver, was a photographer's and casting director's delight. Library of Congress.

Head Centre, Sulphuret, Vizina, Way Up, Girard, Sunset, Boston & Arizona, and the Tombstone Mill & Mining Company.[7]

Ore needs milling, and the nearest water for power was a few miles to the west on the San Pedro River. The milling presented some challenges, as the ores were a variety of silver types that needed special treatment. Some of the key geologists and metallurgists of the era either worked on and planned these mills, or later visited, examined, and wrote of the construction, problems, and output. W. P. Blake and John A. Church,

Richard Gird was a partner and confidant of the Schieffelin brothers of Tombstone fame. *Out West*, July 1907.

nationally prominent educators and metallurgists, were closely connected with the mills, from Charleston to Contention.[8]

What evolved into the community of Tombstone had origins in several places, known as Goose Flats, Richmond, Old Tombstone, and eventually the Tombstone of history, with its Allen, Toughnut, Fremont, Third, Fourth, and Fifth being some of the better-known street names. The best early visual of the place is Frank Ingoldsby's *Map of the Tombstone Mining District*, using specifics compiled by the city surveyor of Tombstone, Michael Kelleher, and civil engineer Martin Ruter Peel; this was a lithograph produced in San Francisco in December 1881. Early street scenes, humble homes and stores, as well as views of nearby mines and mills are shown, all set within a framework of a hundred or so named mining properties. In July 1881, Kelleher had previously produced a street map, *Map of the City of Tombstone*, which is notable, as it is the first to depict Tombstone's (third) cemetery, subsequently (in 1884) known as the "Old Cemetery," and now known worldwide as the notorious Boothill, in its current location just northwest of town. The *Arizona Quarterly Illustrated* of Tucson, in 1880-81, published several issues with illustrations of prominent Tombstone buildings and streets, as well as such pioneers as "Buckskin Frank" Leslie and John Clum.[9]

The heyday or bonanza period of Tombstone was 1877 to approximately 1885 (the first era), and the population may have reached as high as six thousand. Many of these residents were miners and their families, but Tombstone in its throbbing days had dozens of lawyers and speculators, merchants galore, prostitutes, saloon keepers, churches, a school, courthouse, liveries, restaurants and hotels, the Mining Exchange, and anywhere between fifty and one hundred saloons or places of entertainment.[10]

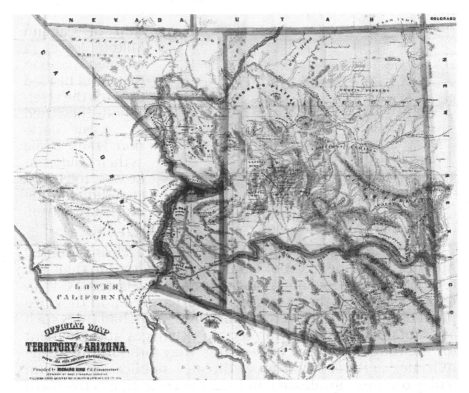

In 1865 Richard Gird published the first official map of Arizona Territory. Library of Congress.

Consideration of the "Apache threat" or the U. S. Army in Tombstone was never a pressing problem in town. Contrary to what has been presented in some movies and fiction, the residents of Tombstone were never barricaded in their homes, dodging Apache arrows. There were no incidents of such danger, as Tombstone was a huge settlement, with hundreds of armed single men. Apache bands were not that foolhardy or ignorant. There was, though, for a decade, a decided Apache threat outside of town, and single travelers, even small groups, could be waylaid.[11]

There were occasions when renegades from the San Carlos Reservation did create havoc in the rural areas, and on both sides of the Arizona-Mexico border. But these affairs were the responsibility of the U. S. Army. In early 1883, when the San Carlos Apaches did have some wandering braves seeking adventure, a meeting was held in Tombstone. At least sixty resident would-be heroes signed up for the Tombstone Rangers, under the leader-

21

This building served as the Richard Gird home as well as the office of the Tombstone Mill and Mining Company. *Out West,* July 1907.

ship of Captain Milton Joyce (a talented saloon man) and headed towards the reservation. They tried to recruit Buckskin Frank Leslie as their guide, but he was "too busy," and didn't think much of the venture anyway.

The Tombstone Rangers intended to "clean out" the Apaches, but General Crook's biographer referred to their "intemperate behavior," and that their campaign lasted less than ten days because their whiskey was exhausted and they "expired of thirst."[12] They were important fellows, had titles such as "captain," and asked for certain privileges and payment for the tough jobs they were doing. They did nothing of significance to lower any frontier threat. A publication by Lynn Bailey on these Tombstone heroes, *The Valiants*, has the word "frivolities" as part of the subtitle.[13] In other words, Tombstone and Apaches were never in any kind of conflict. This did not prevent authors and screenwriters from depicting the savage hordes from invading Tombstone, burning down the town, and despoiling the women. Therefore, the "Apache threat" became part of the Tombstone aura, even though such events never occurred.[14]

Another part of movie interpretation has groups of soldiers hanging around the saloons of Tombstone, drunk, causing problems with civilians, and so forth. This never happened. Any soldier, or group of them, would be walking into a room filled with miners and cowboys, often armed, who would have looked with disdain on the uniformed fellows. Furthermore, Fort Huachuca was thirty miles to the southwest, not a quick trip for a whiskey. The only incident of note regarding the army occurred during some labor troubles in Tombstone in the summer of 1884. The Secretary of War authorized a company of twenty-three soldiers to go to Tomb-

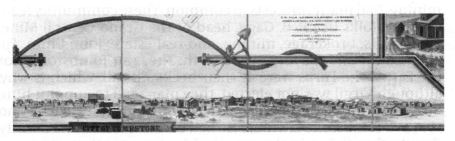

Tombstone in its early phase as a bonanza mining camp. Ingoldsby, *Map of the Tombstone Mining District*, 1881. Library of Congress.

stone until the troubles ceased; they were to report to Sheriff Ward. The soldiers had no involvement in the labor events of August-September.[15]

One aspect of the Tombstone saga that has rightfully received considerable attention is the Earp-cowboy "feud." (Authors' note: Sometimes the word "cowboy" will be capitalized, as it can refer to what was sometimes called "the Cowboy Gang," a loose affiliation of rural ranch hands, etc.) This is a simple phrase not suitable for that era. It implies that the Earps were an independent force trying to tackle the unruly cowboys. The Earps were not in charge of much. Even Virgil Earp, who was a U. S. deputy marshal as well as the chief of police, had so little public backing that he was defeated as the candidate for chief of police, receiving the position by appointment of the town council in October 1880.[16]

Not only was Tombstone a new community, but Cochise County had only been split from Pima County in 1881. The years 1881-82 were the time of the "troubles," which climaxed in the legendary Gunfight at the O. K. Corral.

In this new town and new county, political, social, business, and financial groups were jockeying for power and positions. The ineffective governor, John C. Fremont, had given the sheriff's appointment to John Behan. Within months, Sheriff Behan moved much closer to the cowboy or rural crowd; he was closely tied in with the Dunbar brothers, whose livery and stock business were also mainly rural, farm, and ranch.

Greater Tombstone existed because of the silver mines, and those who owned and operated the mines and mills, as well as the lawyers, judges, and merchants connected with mining, had many interests in common. These community leaders were folks like E. B. Gage, head of the Grand Central Mine; J. V. Vickers, brokerage, mining, and real estate; John Clum, *Epitaph* editor and mayor; and so forth. They ran Tombstone, not the Earps. The Earps were at their beck and call, which is why, although Virgil was not elected, they managed to appoint him. Brother Morgan was deputized by Virgil, but Wyatt Earp had no role as a Tombstone lawman. He had earlier been a Pima County deputy sheriff, but in the new Cochise County, Wyatt Earp was mostly a faro dealer at the Oriental Saloon.

The rural or cowboy crowd were quite independent, floating all over Cochise County. They were, indeed, tough customers. William "Billy the Kid" Claiborne rubbed out a fellow in Charleston, Curly Bill caused havoc in Galeyville, and the Clantons, the "Old Man" as well as his sons, were "active" in many places. There were frequent claims along the Arizona/Mexico/New Mexico border that the Clantons had possession of cattle that were not their own.

There were rustling charges, allegations that the cowboys were selling stolen cattle to Tombstone butchers, gun play, pranks, and all sorts of behavior that disgusted the Tombstone authorities and "better citizens." Other cowboys of note were Pete Spence, Frank Stilwell, Johnny Ringo, "Indian Charley," and the McLaury brothers. These fellows, because of some of their behaviors, and their acquaintances, were branded "cowboys," which in that area and era was loaded with negative connotations. ("Cowboys" also became the name for a loosely-affiliated gang of outlaws and trouble makers.)

Comments about the "town people," as opposed to the "cowboy crowd" must be digested with the knowledge that the Cochise County sheriff, Johnny Behan, was more than "thick" with the cowboys. One of the most troublesome and raucous of their gang was Curly Bill Brocius. The cowboy-Behan relationship was such that his deputy sheriff, Billy Breakenridge, once "deputized" Curly Bill to help him collect taxes in Galeyville.[17]

The culmination of this intermingling sequence of situations led to what is without doubt the most famous event in Tombstone's long history, the street shootout of 1881. This is one of the iconic sagas of frontier history. The invasion of Sicily, the Battle at the Pass of Thermopylae, William Tell's bow-and-arrow prowess, or Paul Revere's ride are mere footnotes when compared to the fortunes publishers and movie and television studios have dedicated to some gunplay near the O.K. Corral on October 26, 1881. Because of the massive amount of attention this even has received, one must contemplate how it all meshes into the overall Tombstone saga.

The basics of the story took place from 1879, when the Earps first arrived in town, until early 1882, when they departed as a result of it all. Upon their appearance in November 1879, they were already part of the law-and-order group, as experienced lawman Virgil Earp had just been appointed a deputy U. S. marshal.

THE SHERIFF OF TOMBSTONE AND HIS CONSTITUENTS.

John Behan, right, the first sheriff of Cochise County, the job Wyatt Earp wanted. *Harper's Monthly,* March 1883.

Very soon Wyatt would become a deputy sheriff of Pima County, and Wyatt and Morgan would both be connected with Wells Fargo. In the coming period, Virgil would also be town marshal of Tombstone, and he frequently appointed brother Morgan as one of his deputies; Morgan had earlier served as a policeman in Butte, Montana. The Earps were unquestionably veteran lawmen.

This was primarily the town and mining environment. Even after Wyatt was no longer a deputy sheriff, Tombstone was his base, where in addition to having a role in the gambling scene and at the faro tables in the Oriental Saloon, he and his brothers were heavily involved in the mining world. They bought and sold more than a dozen claims and had dealings with some of the leading players in town. They leased a tract to Remi Nadeau, the West's leading freighter, who had a hauling contract for some of the larger mines. Wyatt was also in a mining partnership with Gus Bilicke, owner of the Cosmopolitan, the largest hotel in town. And in the "doings" of the day, they were closely associated with Dr. George Goodfellow, George Parsons, a mining engineer, and John Clum, *Tombstone*

The Earp nemesis and the instigator of the famous shootout near the O. K. Corral was Ike Clanton, prominent in the cowboy crowd. Library of Congress.

Epitaph editor. These, and many of that ilk, were the solid middle strength of Tombstone.

When John Behan arrived in the area in 1880 he would immediately curry favor with the out-of-town types. Behan (and many others) was pushing to create a new county sliced off the southeastern part of Pima County, and aiming to become the new sheriff, allying himself with many ranchers, cowboys, and farmers. All of these people, depending upon where/how they lived, had different occupations and aspirations than the residents of Tombstone, and Behan knew his contingency. He was one of the most well-known persons in the territory, having already served as sheriff of Yavapai County. He had also been in the territorial assembly and held a half-dozen posts in greater Prescott.

When Cochise County was created in 1881, it was Behan, not Wyatt Earp, who was appointed its first sheriff. Furthermore, Behan reneged on his promise to appoint Wyatt as his deputy if Wyatt let him run unopposed, deceiving him afterwards and turning elsewhere. These arrangements also created bitterness between Wyatt and Ike Clanton. They had had an agreement to capture and turn in a few murderous (Cowboy gang) stage robbers and rustlers, so Wyatt could take credit and win back the lucrative sheriff appointment, but Ike backed out of the deal at the last moment, fearing his cowboy friends would chastise him if/when they learned of his betrayal of the gang for his own personal profit.

There would be a half dozen Earp-cowboy incidents in this era, emphasizing the town-rural split. The Cowboys as a gang were notorious for causing trouble from Galeyville to the San Pedro River mill towns, for raucous behavior, for shooting up the town, and were often blamed for missing mules, horses, and cattle. One of these events involved the McLaury boys, accused by Wyatt of "removing" some U. S. Army mules. On another occasion, when Curly Bill Brocius, a well-known cowboy "sport," killed Fred White, the Tombstone town marshal, Wyatt was promptly on the scene, bashed Curly Bill's skull with a revolver, and humiliatingly visibly shepherded him to jail, first in Tombstone and then Tucson.

One doesn't have to pile up incidents. This cowboy-bad guy image of Cochise County was so widespread that details were known by the U. S. marshal of Arizona Territory, and were also discussed, with proposed legislation, in the U. S. Congress.

Another layer of the animosity concerned the personal lives of Wyatt Earp and Johnny Behan. In Tombstone, Behan had a living arrangement with a young "actress," Sadie Mansfield (aka Josephine, "Josie" or "Sadie" Marcus). Although the details are slim, most investigators agree that Sadie and Wyatt began seeing one another. One can imagine what that did to the relations between the two men. This was not a dalliance on Wyatt's part; he and Sadie would remain together for nearly fifty years until his death in 1929.

The spark that set the flames of the famous street fight was a night of gambling and drinking in Tombstone, and an angry Ike Clanton the next morning, October 26, deciding that he had had enough of the Earps. In spite of an ordinance prohibiting the carrying of firearms in town, Ike, with rifle and revolver and drunken courage, headed down Fremont Street, threatening the lives of the Earps. He was waylaid by Marshal Virgil Earp, who clobbered him upon hearing of the threats. Subsequent events involved a justice of the peace and harsh words from Wyatt Earp, who then buffaloed and knocked to the ground Tom McLaury, after he, too, foolishly threatened and challenged Wyatt. Upon the arrival in town of his contentious older brother Frank McLaury, who, along with Billy Clanton, witnessed the aftermath of this all and the manhandling of their brothers, they began buying up ammunition at Spangenberg's Gunshop, where they were all once again confronted by Wyatt, who ushered their horses off the sidewalk. The ever-inefficient Sheriff Behan was present but carried little influence with ei-

This was also the site of the Wells Spicer Hearings following the famous street shootout of October 1881. Ingoldsby, *Map of the Tombstone Mining District*, 1881. Library of Congress.

ther of the parties who both disrespected and ignored him.

The gunfight occurred as the Earp party headed up Fremont Street for the Clantons and McLaurys, who were behind and just west of the O. K. Corral, in a vacant lot next to Fly's Photography Studio. The Earps intended to disarm the other men, as they were in violation of the firearms ordinance, but the result was instead the shootout, followed in the coming days and weeks by the well-known Wells Spicer hearings. When the cowboys didn't get the result they wanted there, they resorted to the ambush and back-shooting (and serious maiming) of Virgil Earp, and subsequently of Morgan Earp, who died shortly thereafter of his wounds. In their national newsworthy, mythical, avenging "Vendetta Ride," Wyatt Earp, Doc Holliday, Texas and Turkey Creek Jack, and party ended the lives of several of the Cowboy gang members responsible for the cowardly shootings.

The gunfight and consequent vendetta, usually emphasized as the "Tombstone story," was really the culmination of serious town and rural differences; political in-fighting between Wyatt Earp and John Behan; rustling and other criminal charges against the cowboy faction; and a romance gone wrong.[18]

In mining law, also, Tombstone provided fuel for much of the West. The Mining Law of 1872 contained the apex, or extralateral concept. This means that if your claim has the lode at or near the surface, you can work that lode, even if it crosses or "invades" an adjacent claim. This led to scores of legal suits throughout the Western states and territories, including early Tombstone.

A case in 1882 brought some sense to the matter, at least in Arizona Territory. The Tombstone Mill & Mining Company sued the Way Up Mining Company. They believed that the ore the Way Up was removing (from the old Good Enough claim) was infringing on their rights. High-powered experts and witnesses spewed forth, with claims of limestone layers, cheating on measurements, and a dozen or so other complicated mineral and legal issues. The case did, though, contain some prose easy enough to follow: Viewed from the standpoint of facts, the case is no new one. It is simply the case of one party owning a rich and valuable mine, and working and developing it in the manner permitted to him by law; of the other party, beginning by casting envious eyes upon his neighbor's luck, and ending breaking into that neighbor's mine, through his wall, like a burglar—in the dark.

In addition to the above jobs, Spicer was also a justice of the peace, a writer, a mining investor, and conducted the hearings following the famous street shootout of October 1881. *Arizona Quarterly Illustrated*, October 1880.

The Arizona Supreme Court not only ruled in favor of the Way Up Mining Company but used such strong language about the extralegal clause that it would be almost forty years before a similar case would reach the higher court. In those decades, Dr. James Douglas of Bisbee, a national authority on metal mining and processing, wrote widely on how and why adjacent mining companies should cooperate in order to avoid these legal quagmires. In this almost half-century, the Tombstone Mill-Way Up case was often cited as common sense being applied to mining law.[19]

The Tombstone of good times, the first bonanza era, the celebrations, was in the years 1877-1885. Several events combined in the next few years to set Tombstone on a decline that would continue into the twentieth century.

The first of these problems was water, too much of it, an unusual circumstance in a desert environment. The depth of the water table varies throughout the world, usually depen-

Grand Central Mill and Mining Company

The Grand Central was the most well-known Tombstone mining property. Ingoldsby, *Map of the Tombstone Mining District*, 1881, Library of Congress.

dent on geological factors such as type of rock and soil, local upheavals, volcanic action in the past, and so forth. By 1883 major producers, such as the Grand Central, were working into or below the water table, trying to pump it out in order to get at the paying ore.

The answer to the water problem? There was none. Mining and scientific experts from New York to San Francisco were called in and could not solve the problem of water in the Tombstone mines. The technology of the era wouldn't provide the pumping machinery capable of keeping up with the surge of water. In at least ten periods between 1883 and 1886, "new pumps" were proclaimed; they were new, but still inadequate. E. B. Gage of the Grand Central gave tours to visiting experts, to no avail. At one point it was established that some water pumped from the mines "actually finds its way back into the mines whence it was pumped at great expense."[20]

In these "water" years there was a constant call for new technology to get rid of the excess water. The *Arizona Daily Star* of January 1, 1886, was blunt, using the word "retarded" when referring to Tombstone's economy, blocked by excess water in the mines.

Throughout the world, a sound generalization is that in precious metal mines, as one goes deeper, the richness of the ore gradually thins out. The ore was still "rich enough" at the Grand Central and other leading Tombstone mines when they reached the water table; however, the working miners were in a constant struggle with rising levels. The Grand Central paid its miners $4 a day for this work, as opposed to the standard $3 daily wage. This was a hefty increase, but not enough to stop the rising water.[21]

In this same period, 1883-84, the Tombstone miners began to agitate for better working conditions and wages and formed a union. This was most likely related to the water problems in the mines, but the two factors were seldom mentioned at the same time. Things came to a head in August of 1884. Mobs of men gathered, marches were held to the Grand Central and Head Centre, threats exchanged, and in mid-August, after a rally and arguments about a wage cut to $3, over a hundred shots were fired, mostly in anger, as there were no casualties. Foremen and managers such as Charley Leach and Christopher S. Batterman held firm against the union.

E. B. Gage was the dominant Tombstone personality during the original era 1 glory years as well as in the era 3 revival of the early 1900s. *Successful American,* March 1903.

At one point, Leach stated that the Grand Central needed 150 men, but only non-union need apply. On one day, at Schieffelin Hall, there were three union meetings, all rallying against the mining companies. A troop of soldiers sent to town from Fort Huachuca stood by, but took no important role in the mine-labor conflict. The whole messy episode came to an end when the union admitted defeat and disbanded. That this was serious business was obvious from comment in the *Tucson Citizen* of August 23, 1884, stating that Charles Leach of the Grand Central was rebuilding his house, "which mysteriously burned itself up a few weeks ago."[22]

The double curse of water in the mines, and a serious but losing miners' strike in 1884, led to the end of the original Tombstone bonanza period. Silver ore was still down there, but at a cost that was prohibitive to mine. From the end of 1884 onwards, a trickle, then almost a flood, of mining people left town, and accompanying them were merchants, lawyers, gamblers, and other types not interested in living in a down-turning economy. The high point of Tombstone population was almost six thousand in 1882; by 1884 it was down to four thousand, and a few years later, three thousand. This means that the

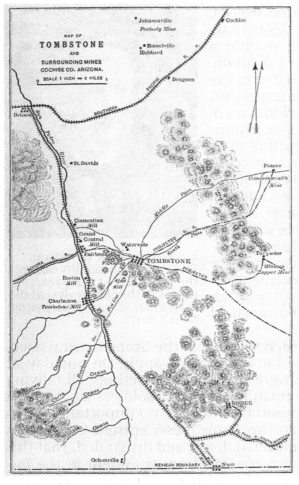

The mills and smelters were developed on the San Pedro River to handle silver ores from the Tombstone mines. *Transactions, American Institute of Mining Engineers*, 1903.

near collapse of the silver mining had halved the town population in seven years.

There was still mining, as several dozen Tombstone properties still had some ore above the water table; probably not the richest, but still worth working. This meant smaller crews, less work for the mills on the San Pedro River, and fewer customers and clients for the lawyers, newspapers, and merchants of Tombstone.

The key measure of success or degree of activity in a mining camp is the number of men employed in the mines. In greater Tombstone in 1881, a key year of the bonanza era, there were around 650 men on payrolls in the leading mines. Even in 1885, when the decline had begun, quite a few men were still employed, such as at the Toughnut (130); Esmeralda (75); Grand Central (70); and Contention (60). Add to this various assayers, ore transportation workers, and other mine types and one can appreciate the impact their wages could have on the local groceries, barber shops, saloons, and law offices.[23]

The history of Tombstone, its rich silver deposits, the

importance of water and the water table, and the demise of Tombstone as a vital mining center has led to considerable confusion and contradictory summaries. Yet, there are a few bold, significant statements that should be made here.

From 1878 and for five or six years after, the San Pedro River workings were essential underpinnings for Tombstone's greatness. Ore is practically useless unless it can be worked (improved), and water is the essential ingredient. This holds for most of the world's great gold, silver, copper, and lead operations. Water is needed for the gravity flow in the mills, to stamp or "reduce" the ore, and to use in the various milling processes that separate the silver from its waste. Tombstone was pretty much without water, but a few miles to the west was the San Pedro River, and within two years huge milling plants were erected at Millville, then north at the Boston Mill, further north at the Grand Central Mill, and at Contention City. Hundreds of men worked in these facilities, and the places had their share of streets, homes, stores, saloons, even justices of the peace and men of the law. Daily freight wagons arrived from the Tombstone mines with the ore to be processed. Following this milling, the resultant bullion would be sent to such places as El Paso or San Francisco for its final treatment prior to marketing.

The above scenario operated during the bonanza era, but everything began to change in 1881 when water was first struck in the Sulphuret Mine. By December, water was being hit in other Tombstone mines. The Girard Mill was completed in Tombstone, the first of several local mills which would spell the eventual doom of Millville and Contention City. Soon, Tombstone, the place without water, had enough to run its own mills. And, it also soon had so much water that it could not operate its mines in order to run its mills. This is the simple dual water tragedy of Tombstone.[24]

Many of the leading events in the history of greater Tombstone must be viewed against this water backdrop: The huge freight wagons of Remi Nadeau carrying ore to the river mills, Dick Gird running his successful plant at Millville, Johnny-Behind-the-Deuce arrested at Charleston and taken to Tombstone and almost lynched, the emergence of Fairbank as Tombstone's supply center on the San Pedro, Ike Clanton running a store in Millville-Charleston, and on and on.

On January 24, 1885, the *Arizona Weekly Citizen* (Tucson)

reported that James Coyle, Tombstone chief of police, had ordered "out of that city all who have no visible means of support," which, it reported, "…makes the place look like a grave yard." The overall picture was clearly presented by the Tombstone Mill and Mining Company in 1886, explaining how the ore was no longer very rich, and all that remained on the San Pedro property were slimes and mediocre ore that was awaiting treatment. The San Pedro milling era was indeed finished.[25]

In the following biographical sketches, most are of personalities who left Tombstone for other locales. Whether they were miners or mill men, merchants or attorneys, laborers or saloon keepers, barbers or prostitutes, they took their Tombstone experiences with them. A few returned to their native Connecticut, Ohio, or Missouri, but the vast majority of these temporary Arizonans opted for the West, and their life and spirit of Tombstone would be passed on to other Western mining camps, small towns, and urban centers. Their years in Tombstone had an impact, but the folks adjusted, or tried to fit in wherever they settled.

There were others, of course, those Tombstoners who had found their niche right there in greater Tombstone. For some, Tombstone was the promised land, whereas others may have remained out of apathy. To a few, the belief was always that "the mines will come back," and they remained around for fear of missing and not participating in the further glory days to come.

To help better elucidate their temporal relationship to one another, and their contributions to the town/mystique itself, our "Tombstoners" are listed alphabetically by "era." Not necessarily the one in which they first arrived in Tombstone, or even spent the most time, but the era in which they made their biggest impact, gained their notoriety or fame – left their "mark."

Whether these Tombstone folks went elsewhere, or remained in this unique mining center, they were all part of a 146 year plus slice of life that was unlike any other Western mining camp. Their brief life stories detail some of the experiences of these Tombstoners, and demonstrate how in so many cases, what happened in Tombstone and the lessons gained there carried much more impact and significance than similar events had in other Western settlements; this impact was passed on by these distinct individuals who spent time and lived in this incredibly special "mining camp," indeed the most influential mining camp history has ever known. They made a mark!

THE "FIRST ERA" FOLKS FROM TOMBSTONE:
THEY MADE A MARK

AH LUM Born in China in 1859, Ah Lum was operating one of the Can Can restaurants in Tombstone by 1882. His long career in Tombstone and vicinity ended with his death there on May 3, 1931.

His half-century was filled with all the positive and negative stereotypes common on the frontier. In spite of Anti-Chinese League talk, and persistent acts of prejudice, Ah Lum and a few other Asians managed to maneuver their way through decades of Tombstone doings. However, he participated in the life, had some mining interests, operated or worked in ten to twenty restaurants and other businesses, and was seen from time to time gambling in the Crystal Palace. Ah Lum also worked restaurants at Pearce and other nearby mining camps, but Tombstone remained his base. He married at least three times, had several children, and was known as a reliable fellow, frequently helping or grubstaking prospectors.

Things didn't always go his way, such as the incident in 1920 when he was arrested for receiving opium via the U. S. mails. At his funeral in 1931 were Tombstone's leading cattlemen and merchants, most of whom had known Ah Lum for years. His fifty local years are an interesting corrective to the typical tales of Chinese on the Western frontier.[26]

ALLEN, JOHN B. This fellow's brief career in Tombstone was noteworthy. He was from Maine, lived in Arizona Territory in the 1850s, and became a major figure in Tucson, serving several terms as mayor; and had also been territorial treasurer. Because of his merchandizing work he was often referred to as "Pie" Allen. These were the dried apple pies he sold which were apparently immensely popular. Allen lost no time in shifting to Tombstone, where he opened the first store (on the southwest corner of Fourth and what would become Allen Street, which was named after him), and quickly became a major merchant and man-about-town, yet by the end of 1879 he was out of business. Allen moved to several other local mining communities, large and small, and almost always held positions of trust.

He eventually moved back to Tucson, dying there in mid-June 1899, having had a long public career in Arizona Territory. And his Tombstone period? In a detailed obituary in the *Arizona Republican* of June 18, 1899, Tombstone gets no mention. Strange legacy for a town pioneer, a leading merchant, the fellow who built the first house in Tombstone, and who is the namesake for the community's leading street, as well as an entire district/neighborhood in Tucson.[27]

ALVORD, CHARLES E. Alvord is usually ignored in Tombstone accounts because of the notoriety of his son Burt, the lawman-turned-train-robber, yet he had some presence there.

Charles was a New Yorker early in the California gold fields. He was a mechanic and liveryman, was in Lassen County for a time, then in Santa Barbara County. In these places, he usually filled positions of trust such as justice of the peace, assessor, or tax collector. He arrived in Tombstone in 1880 and would work at his trades as well as serve as a local justice of the peace for almost two decades. Because of his background, he was able to place young Burt as an employee at the O.K. Corral.

The career of Justice Alvord in Tombstone was at best mediocre, with the typical small claims business, a marriage here and there, some land contracts to sign, and so forth. The various grand jury reports had neither praise nor condemnation for Justice Alvord. It should be noted, though, that Judge Barnes and a few other local citizens were friendly with and believed Alvord was a decent fellow.

Justice Alvord retired in the mid-1890s and moved in with his son Burt, who was serving as a constable in Willcox. Alvord died there on February 9, 1898, fortunately before his lawman son went on a crime spree.[28]

AUSTIN, FRANCIS B. Frank was a miner and inventor, but when he entered the Tombstone world it was as a merchant in 1881. He opened the Papago Cash Store at 324 Fremont Street, which became one of the better-known places of business, and was immortalized in history, as both the Earp/Holliday and the Cowboy parties walked right past it en route to their legendary gunfight. Austin supposedly handled "fine groceries," but all sorts of dry goods, tools, etc., could be found at the Papago.

As the town declined, Austin looked elsewhere, tried Tempe for a time in the early 1890s as a farmer and as a merchant. A few years later, apparently anticipating a Tombstone rebirth, he returned and opened the Pioneer Store at Fremont and Fifth. In spite of an actual revival happening, things went downhill for Frank, and poor health and other worries led him to suicide in 1905. His Papago Cash Store and Pioneer Store have become symbols for many of Tombstone.[29]

BABCOCK, NEWTON JARVIS
Born in Virginia in 1833, Babcock was in the Midwest for some years, then tried the California gold fields in the 1850s. He came onto the Arizona stage around 1879, to the Tucson area.

Long before Virgil Earp arrived wearing the badge of a deputy U. S. marshal in December 1879, there had been law and order in Tombstone. Babcock had already been named Pima County deputy sheriff on June 4, 1879 (the second earliest lawman in the

Tombstone district, replacing Shibell appointee William A. Harwood—appointed circa September 1878, and resigning May 22, 1879), and he spent many months of that year and of 1880 patrolling the budding town of Tombstone and environs. The man in overall charge was Sheriff Charles Shibell of Pima County; it was also Shibell who later appointed Wyatt Earp a deputy sheriff. On July 11, 1879, Babcock was credited in the Tucson *Arizona Weekly Citizen* newspaper as the "efficient" arresting officer of the Hicks (July 6, 1879) murderer. It was Babcock, along with deputy sheriff Adolph Buttner, who in November 1879 (just before the Earps arrived and became active on the scene) were the lawmen who transported J. Van Houten's accused murderers (including Cowboys Frank Stilwell and Pete Spence) from Charleston to the Tombstone jail.

Babcock's role ended with the creation of Cochise County, but he did not immediately leave the area. In 1881-82 he was in Galeyville, the Cowboy outlaw hangout, running a primitive saloon. It was in Babcock's Saloon that on May 19, 1881, Cowboy leader Curly Bill Brocius, while leaving, was shot in the neck by known rustler cohort Jim Wallace after an argument.

The remainder of Babcock's life was in Pima County, and he was usually identified in voting and census records as a miner, a resident of Tucson. One exception to this was the census of 1900 where he was listed as a bartender in the Silver Bell District. Babcock died in Tucson, and in his obituary the *Arizona Daily Star* of February 24, 1901, mentioned a few facts about his pioneering days, without mentioning his lawman efforts in early Tombstone.[30]

Tombstone area mining and milling, and quite active with some Huachuca Mountains claims.

Baron was well known and respected in the district, and for some time was a director of the First National Bank of Tombstone. He died at the Copper Queen Hospital in Bisbee on December 8, 1913, and is buried in Tombstone. Neither a loudmouth nor a shrinking violet, Baron was a mid- to top-level mining manager familiar with all aspects of Tombstone silver production.[31]

BARON, AUGUST Gus Baron's Tombstone career was indeed unusual. He was a German immigrant who started near the top and remained there for three decades. He was not just early on the scene, he knew the Schieffelins and Gird even before the silver discovery. In 1879 he received orders from Schieffelin to take charge of the works, which he did until Superintendent Church took over in 1881. In the following years Baron was a foreman, manager, or superintendent at many local properties, including the Lucky Cuss, the Sulphuret, and the Contention. He also prospected, invested, and in general was involved in all aspects of

BARTON, JERRY This is one of the truly hard cases of Western history. Information on his activities, his "career," can be found in a variety of sources. He was probably a New Yorker, spent time in Texas, was in Phoenix in the late 1870s, then hit Tombstone in the early phase of the bonanza. He fought, peddled, boozed, killed, and eventually served time in the territorial prison in Yuma. He may have been a constable at Charleston for a time, could have killed as many as twelve men, and in general was what folks thought of when thinking of Western hard cases.

The activities and reputation of Barton come through

in this notice of December 3, 1887, in the *Mohave County Miner*: "Jerry Barton, who killed E. Swift at Tombstone a few months ago with a blow of his fist, was found guilty of manslaughter and sentenced by Judge Barnes to three years in the territorial prison."

At one time, in a court situation, when asked how many men he had killed, he wondered if that included Mexicans. This fellow "finalized" in Yavapai County, Arizona, in the summer of 1904, and in an obituary it was pointed out that this fine specimen of humanity, at the end of his life, was a wreck.[32]

BATTERMAN, CHRISTOPHER S. Here is another of the lucky few who start at the top and remain there. He was born in Placerville, California, in 1859. His father would become General Christopher C. Batterman of the Confederacy. Later, General Batterman was superintendent of the Gould & Curry Mine on the Comstock. Young Chris was raised there, then graduated in engineering from the University of California. He was working in Carson City at the time of the census of 1880, then left for Tombstone.

He was an expert witness at suits involving the Conten-tion, Tranquility, and Head Centre mines, and once the cases were settled, he was appointed superintendent of the Head Centre, which became one of the more successful Tombstone mines during the bonanza era.

Batterman was involved in several community and business affairs of interest. For more than a year he did survey work and planning, trying to get the community interested in a railroad connection to Fairbank. In early 1882 he joined Dr. Goodfellow, Dr Matthews, and other Tombstoners in organizing a microscopical society. In 1883 he was an expert witness in the case of the Copper Prince vs. Copper Queen, where he so vigorously disagreed with the Copper Queen expert, Dr. William P. Blake, that there were charges of lying, throwing someone out of a window, and so forth.

His greatest local challenges were in 1884, with the severe water problems in the mines and the labor troubles of that year. He was threatened and pressured to leave town, but held firm; the miners eventually backed down on their threats, and the union disbanded.

Other forces were at work, and in 1886, with changes in ownership of the Tranquility and the Head Centre, Batterman was forced out. He soon left with a few dozen men for a mining project in Sonora. From this point on, Batterman became a major force in Western mining, as he was frequently called in as an expert witness in cases in California, Nevada, and Montana. His last major venture, which lasted for some years, was in Montana. He was a prominent figure in Amalgamated Copper, and was also president of the Boston & Montana Copper Company. Batterman died in Butte in October 1901, and his obituaries appeared in the country's leading newspapers as well as in the professional journals. The *Butte Miner* of October 9, 1901, reported the community's flags were at half-mast. His start on the path towards this national reputation was with the Tombstone silver mines.[33]

BAUER, APOLLINAR Bauer was a German who tried the Illinois and California systems, but early on opted for the new town of Tombstone, trying to get in on the beginning of the good life. He was a butcher, but like most folks in the area, tried to plug in to the mining life; and bought and sold many claims. Bauer had a meat-cattle deal with Henry Hooker, which helped him in providing for the food needs of Tombstone. This was formalized as early as 1880, with the organization of Hooker & Bauer, on Fremont (318) between Third and Fourth Streets, behind the O. K. Corral, and a few lots east of the future gunfight site.

Although he had already sold his butcher shop to Matthew and Jacob Everhardy (who renamed it the "Fremont Street Market") in March 1881, Bauer was an eyewitness to, and a court witness (testified) following, the famous street fight between the Earp and cowboy faction in October 1881. The fire of 1882 [34] devastated Bauer, but he recovered, not only in his butcher activity, but also in his mining claims, especially in the Dragoon Mountains. In the coming years Bauer was active in the meat business as well as mining, and in 1896 shifted to Bisbee, certainly more promising than Tombstone.

Bauer continued in both trades, meat and mining, for many years, having a reasonable measure of success in both. His dozens of claims in the Mule Mountains were at least moderately successful. He died in Bisbee in March 1914. The Bauer family was an important part of the Tombstone story. His daughter Bertha, born in Tombstone in 1887, published "I Love You, Arizona," in 1917, a song popular for years. She recalled her family's past in a memoir in the Phoenix *Arizona Republican* of April 12, 1922.[35]

BEHAN, JOHN H. Johnny Behan had one of the longest lives in public service of any Westerner, starting in 1864 as clerk of Arizona's first territorial legislature. He was later sheriff and many other things in and around Prescott and Yavapai County. Behan found his way early on to Tombstone, Pima County, and with political pull (envied by Wyatt Earp), became the first sheriff of newly created Cochise County in 1881.

Johnny's name is widely known in Western history, largely due to his connections with the rural or cowboy crowd, as opposed to the miners and residents of Tombstone proper. The names Behan and Earp were at opposite ends of several Tombstone realities. Behan had many jobs: census taker, part-owner of a stable, tax collector, supervisor of town and country road contracts, and so forth.

The Behan career as sheriff and man-about-town can be measured in his inactions rather than actions. The famous gunfight in October 1881 between the Earp faction and the Clantons and McLaurys is just one example of Johnny-not-on-the-spot. On posse work, or in general tracking criminals, it was usually U. S. Deputy Marshal Virgil Earp making things happen.[36] Behan, because of his multiple roles, his interest in saloon life, and his political connections, was as well-known as anyone in this part of Arizona. As a lawman, he was less than mediocre.

The Behan years after Tombstone would take pages merely to list his various positions: Yuma prison warden, tax collector, El Paso border inspector; he even claimed to have been in China during the Boxer Rebellion. Behan worked for some time as an inspector at Nogales, later at El Paso, and for a few years at the patent office in Washington, DC. He died at the age of sixty-seven at St. Mary's Hospital in Tucson on June 7, 1912, of "Artero Sclerosis" and syphilis, and was buried there, in the Holy Hope Cemetery.

The paper trail for the Behan career is indeed deep, covering tons of positions and many parts of the American West. The most appropriate closing for this fellow's life appeared in *Cochise County Stalwarts*:

> Wherever Behan appeared, one could count on several things. He would be popular, would get a job (by election or by appointment), and during or after that service, there would be investigations, charges, and most likely court action. This was what happened in his fifty years in Arizona Territory and was certainly born out in his decade in Cochise County.[37]

BERRY, GEORGE A. B. (Augustine Byron) A native of Maine, Berry was a Mexican War veteran, and he and several brothers mined in California before the Civil War. George later mined in Yavapai and Mohave Counties and arrived in Tombstone by 1880. In January 1882, his mining expertise (along with that of another knowledgeable mining local, U.S. Deputy Marshal J. H. Jackson, who had recently been appointed to replace the Earps) was tapped by George Hearst, who was touring mining investment opportunities in the Winchester district, northeast of the Tombstone.

Berry is noted in most Tombstone literature for the night he spent in Hatch's saloon and billiard place. On March 18, 1882, when an assassin (Cowboys Frank Stilwell, *et al*) took shots at Wyatt and Morgan Earp through a window, one shot missed and entered Berry's leg. Another hit its mark, killing Morgan Earp; while a third narrowly missed Wyatt Earp's head), as he was sitting nearby observing the game. In late 1882, although in poor health, Berry took the election tickets to Galeyville for that precinct and developed a "cold," dying there in November.[38]

BIG NOSE KATE There are too many challenges in pinning a name on this person—aka Mary Katherine Harony, Kate Elder, Kate Fisher, Mary Katherine Cummings.[39] She was born in Hungary on November 7, 1849, and was in Iowa in the 1860s where her father was a physician; she was soon orphaned. Kate first met Doc Holliday in 1872 in St. Louis and they would have off-and-on relationships for the next fifteen years. By 1877 she was in Fort Griffin, Texas (with Doc). She was a hanger-on in the saloon world, loving the gambling environment, and frequently worked as a prostitute. When Holliday decided to join the Earps in the bustling silver camp of Tombstone, Kate followed.

Kate figured in a few events in Tombstone. Once, supposedly while drunk, she tried to convince the (Earp adversary) authorities that Doc Holliday robbed stages. She also claimed to have seen the main events of the shootout of October 1881. Then and later in life, she provided considerable detail about those stirring times, but few historians grant her any credibility. Kate's time in Tombstone was brief—a year or so at most—and what she did has been written about and distorted by many.

Her post-Tombstone career was indeed long and didn't have much to do with Doc Holliday. She lived in Globe and Bisbee for some years, was married, and later took up with a fellow near Dos Cabezas where she kept house and did gardening. Later in life she convinced the state of Arizona that she deserved a place at, and was thus admitted to, the Pioneers Home in Prescott, in 1931; dying there on November 2, 1940.

There is a large, confusing, literature on Kate's life. A worthwhile capsule was provided by Lynn Bailey in *Cochise County Stalwarts*: "Born in Hungary, introduced to the flesh pots of Kansas, working the saloons and vice dens of Tombstone, traveling the West for years with Doc Holliday, then spending thirty years peeling pears and picking lettuce, and ending her stay on earth by putting in a decade in the Pioneer Home—if a screen writer came up with such a story line he would be fired."[40]

ALBERT C. BILICKE.

A mining partner and close friend of the Earps, Albert Bilicke operated leading hotels in Tombstone (Earp hangout the Cosmopolitan) and Los Angeles. *The H. M. M. B. A. in California,* 1896.

BILICKE FAMILY German immigrant Carl Gustavus and son Albert C. Bilicke were Western hotel operators, running a place in Florence, Arizona, when the Tombstone strike was in its infancy. In mid-1879 they started work on their Cosmopolitan Hotel, which would be a major center in Tombstone for a few years. The Bilickes were part of the in-group, investing in mining and in close relationships with John Clum, E. B. Gage, Virgil Earp, George Parsons, Dr. Goodfellow, and other town leaders. During the shootout "troubles" and aftermath in 1881-82, the Cosmopolitan was the refuge of choice for the Earp faction.[41] A fire in May 1882[42] destroyed the Cosmopolitan, and the Bilickes moved on to several places in California.

In 1893 they settled in Los Angeles, soon took control of the Hollenbeck Hotel, and within a few years Albert C. Bilicke was one of the leading hoteliers in Southern California; father Carl died in Los Angeles in 1896. The Hollenbeck became known as a "Western-er" hotel, and the Earps, John Clum, and many other figures from Arizona and Nevada made it their stopping place. Still reeling from the devastating loss of their Tombstone Cosmopolitan Hotel to the 1882 fire, Albert helped design and construct the luxurious and "fireproof" Alexandria Hotel in downtown Los Angeles in 1906, just a few blocks south of the Hollenbeck. Albert had other hotel and mining and industrial interests, made several tourist trips to

Europe, and was one of the more successful personalities of Southern California. This was all snuffed out in May 1915. Bilicke and wife Gladys were passengers on the *Lusitania* when it was hit and sunk by a German torpedo, one of the precursors of World War I; Albert perished, but Gladys was one of the survivors.[43]

Los Angeles Hollenbeck, usual choice for the Earps and other visiting Arizonans, was owned by the Bilicke family. David D. de Haas, MD, Collection.

BLACKBURN, LESLIE F. Blackburn was a native of New York State and first came to notice in front of the Crystal Saloon on the Comstock, where in 1868 he drilled a fellow who was drawing on him. He went to California, and from that time forward was a "public man," practically always holding some type of government job. He appears in Tombstone around 1880 and was there for about four years in the first bonanza (the first era).

In Tombstone he had contact with anyone who was anyone. Sheriff Shibell named him a deputy sheriff for the Tombstone area, and Crawley Dake named him a deputy U. S. marshal for the same region; he shared an office with justice of the peace Wells Spicer. Blackburn was also intricately linked in social and business affairs with Johnny Behan. For a time, 1882-83, Blackburn was also part owner of the Senate Saloon. A few years later Blackburn, a figure in Republican politics, was appointed a clerk in the territorial assembly. He was active with one of the hose companies and very well known in Tombstone. In spite of Blackburn interfacing with all figures of note in Tombstone and Cochise County, he was never a leader, or in on major decisions. He was there seemingly always in a secondary role.

Moving back to California and again holding a host of government jobs, he served two terms as clerk of the California senate in the late 1890s. Blackburn lived in Oakland, and by the time of the 1910 census was unemployed, living on "own income," a status usually reserved for those who had few worries. During much of his public life he was described as "a former Tombstone law officer." Blackburn died in Oakland, California on January 22, 1913, and his death notice in the *San Francisco Call* of January 23, 1913, referred to him as "a daring peace officer."[44]

BLINN, LEWIS W. This native of Maine was in the lumber business for a few years in San Francisco, then opted for the possibilities of Tombstone in 1880. He opened a lumber yard on Toughnut Street, and a few years later opened the Cochise Hardware and Trading Company at the corner of Allen and Fourth. During this decade, Blinn was one of the leading merchants in town, even running for mayor (he lost). By 1890, though, Blinn had linked with E. B. Gage, Dr. Goodfellow, and a few other investors and bought major property in the Phoenix area. Although this venture was extraordinarily successful, he shifted to the Los Angeles area, starting with a lumber business in San Pedro.

Within fifteen years Blinn was the leading lumberman in Southern California, owning outright or in part many dozens of firms, especially in Los Angeles, San Bernardino, and Ventura counties. He was a major business figure, and along with George Parsons, another interesting Tombstoner, was one of the powers that dictated that the port of Los Angeles would be in San Pedro rather than Santa Monica.[45] Lewis lived for years on Flower Street in Los Angeles and died there on November 12, 1928. He is buried in the Hollywood Forever Cemetery.[46]

LEWIS W. BLINN.

Tombstone lumber dealer Blinn would become the largest lumber merchant in Southern California. *Los Angeles Herald,* April 25, 1906.

BOURLAND FAMILY William A. Bourland and wife Addie, of Arkansas origins, were Tucson merchants when they opted for the boom in Tombstone in 1879. There Bourland operated a "store," sometimes identified as a cigar store. Mrs. Bourland was also in business, variously described as a milliner or a dressmaker at 523 Fremont Street.

Addie Bourland is a name well-known in Western history, as her shop was across the street from the photo studio of C. S. Fly and O. K. Corral. In her Spicer hearing testimony, she stated, "I live on the opposite side of Fremont Street from the entrance to Fly's lodging house." As she looked out her window on that day in October 1881, she witnessed the opening phase of the legendary Earp-Cowboy gunfight. She would not only testify at the hearings held by Justice Wells Spicer, but was one of the few witnesses who was recalled for elaboration.

What happened to Addie Bourland in subsequent years is not known, although her husband, usually known as W. A. Bourland, remarried in El Paso in 1899. Bourland was a true Western wanderer. For several periods he ran a business in Tucson, opened a store in Phoenix which lasted less than a year, and headed for a new Colorado gold strike in 1892. He finally grounded in El Paso, for a few decades owned his own grocery store, and died in there in November 1925.[47]

BOYLE, NED Edward C. Boyle (if that was his name) was a Western figure with years in Comstock and Sacramento. By 1880 he was in Tombstone. He was a laborer and also worked at the Oriental Saloon, and thought highly of Wyatt Earp. On the fateful day of October 26, 1881, Boyle heard Clanton conspiring against the Earps and went to Wyatt's lodging and told him so. This is a fellow who had quite a past. He had been part of the inquest during the Mike Killeen affair (the Buckskin Frank Leslie shooting), and later played the organ at Marshal White's funeral, after White had been drilled by Curly Bill). Boyle was later quoted as saying, "I shall only speak of one of them, Wyatt Earp; he is one of the partners of the firm I work for, and a more liberal and kind-hearted man I never met."

Details are lacking, but in 1886 he was a night guard at the territorial prison at Yuma, but resigned and moved to Tucson. Newspaper accounts

of that year are not fulsome with praise for his actions there.[48]

W M Breakenridge

A Cochise County deputy sheriff in the early days, William Breakenridge went on to a long career as a lawman and detective. *Portrait and Biographical Record of Arizona*, 1901.

BREAKENRIDGE, WILLIAM "BILLY" MILTON This Wisconsin native early shifted to Colorado, where he had some military service, worked on railroad and telegraph projects, freighted into Montana and Wyoming, and was a wagon master. In later years, Breakenridge took great pride in having been a participant in what became known as the Sand Creek (John Chivington) Massacre in Colorado. At the time, he was in the 3rd Colorado Cavalry, when on No-

47

vember 29, 1864, they killed hundreds of Cheyenne and Arapahoe, mostly women and children. History does not share the Breakenridge pride, and the location is now the Sand Creek Massacre National Historic site. By 1877, he was in Maricopa County, Arizona doing surveying. He served for a time as a deputy sheriff, then in January 1880, arrived in Tombstone.

After some prospecting, in 1881 he was appointed a deputy sheriff of the newly created Cochise County, and beholden to Sheriff John Behan, who had close links to the rural or cowboy faction. Breakenridge had a busy two years as a deputy sheriff, most of his work being in and around Tombstone. He was not a welcome presence to Marshal Virgil Earp or brothers Wyatt and Morgan.

In 1885 Breakenridge was appointed a deputy U. S. marshal, working out of Phoenix. In the following years he did some surveying, helped crack down on the illegal selling of liquor to the local Indians, and participated in posses after train robbers. He shifted to Tucson in 1891, worked on irrigation projects, and was a special officer to the Southern Pacific Railroad. Breakenridge was variously referred to af-ter 1900 as a detective, special agent, and claims agent. Some of his work for the Southern Pacific took him into Sonora, Mexico. In 1910, one account mentioned that he had a race-horse which he kept stabled in Phoenix. His memoir, *Helldorado: Bringing Law to the Mesquite*, published in 1928, wherein he attempted to portray Wyatt Earp in a bad light, is a frequently consulted book on Southwestern history. He died in Tucson in January 1931.[49]

BROCIUS, WILLIAM "CURLY BILL" This was Curly Bill, whose name may have been Graham, and he was probably from Texas, or Illinois, or Colorado. By 1878 he was working with cattle at the San Carlos Reservation, Arizona, and by 1880 was scrambling around Cochise County as part of the cowboy crowd. He figured in a few key episodes of Tombstone history.

In the early hours of October 29, 1880, being tipsy and shooting at the moon, he was confronted by Marshal Fred White. In a confused scuffle, Curly's revolver "went off," fatally wounding Marshal White. On the scene quickly was Pima County Deputy Sheriff Wyatt Earp, who bashed in ("buffaloed") Curly's skull with a revolver borrowed from Fred Dodge. Earp later escorted Curly Bill to the jail in Tucson. He was exonerated, as the dying marshal stated that Curly Bill had shot him by accident. The event was a double dose of bad news for the Cowboys, as not only had Wyatt Earp manhandled and publicly humiliated Curly Bill, one of their leaders, but the replacement town marshal would be their nemesis, Virgil Earp.

A few months later, in January 1881, Curly Bill and friends created havoc in the mill towns of Charleston and Contention, shooting up a few saloons and apparently making a preacher (and parishioners) dance to revolver shots.

The last event in Curly Bill's saga was the Vendetta Ride of the Earp posse, who were on the prowl following the ambush/wounding of Marshal Virgil Earp, and subsequent backshooting killing of Morgan Earp while playing billiards in the Campbell & Hatch Saloon. The posse caught up with the Cowboys on March 24, 1882, in what has become known as the "Battle at Iron Springs." The Cowboys were surprised at breakfast and amid considerable action, Wyatt later claimed to have had his saddle horn shot out from under him and described how he killed Curly Bill. Doc Holliday, who was there, corroborated it all in a newspaper interview he gave in Denver a few months later (May 1882), which would have been extremely foolish to do if it hadn't been true.

The above chapters in the life of Curly Bill have been covered in articles, books, and movies, most of the information loaded with speculation and wish-fulfillment. The best local information was provided by the Tombstone newspaper fraternity. In an attempt to embarrass Wyatt and his posse, the *Nugget,* often labeled the "cowboy organ," denied their claims and offered $1,000 to anyone who could prove that Curly Bill was actually dead. On the other hand, the pro Earp *Epitaph* of April 19, 1882, countered with an offer of $2,000 to any charity if Curly Bill would present himself, which never happened. Anything following that was based on rumor or humor.

The above events were of more than"loca' Interest. The Cowboy actions, and the Earp posse, were followed in much of the Western press. Both the *Los Angeles Times* and the *Los Angeles Herald* of March 26, 1882, on page one, featured articles about the killing of Curly Bill.[50]

BRONK, ANDREW G. Bronk had one of those unusual name combinations that are relatively easy to follow in the literature: Andrew Garrison Bronk. He was a New Yorker, and along with his father was in California in the 1850s. Bronk served two years during the Civil War with the 2nd California Cavalry. He later farmed in the Marysville area, was arrested for illegal gambling in Sacramento in 1876, then moved on the Prescott in Arizona Territory. There he served as a night watchman with Virgil Earp. When Virgil was deputized as a U. S. marshal and headed to Tombstone in 1879, Bronk soon followed.

Andrew was at first listed as a miner, at other times was active in mining claims and in a census was identified as a speculator. In 1881-82, though, he served as a policeman under his old buddy Virgil Earp, who was now town marshal. In Bronk's few years as a Tombstone policeman, he had a reputation as sufficiently tough and reliable.

He stayed in Tombstone a few years, was sued for debt in 1886, and shortly thereafter was in Santa Barbara operating a saloon. He married in Santa Barbara in 1889, but that was also the year his saloon was in receivership. Bronk was sued in Santa Barbara in 1892, and died in Skagway, Alaska on February 17, 1899 (a gambler who left a widow and children in Placerville, California). In 1907 in Sacramento, his wife Mary was listed as a widow employed in an orphanage.[51]

BROOKS, FRED E. Does crime pay? Maybe it is an aid in beginning a career. Fred Emerson Brooks, born in New York State in 1850, was by 1881 a deputy recorder in Cochise County, and when John Clum was criticized in his role as Tombstone postmaster, he was replaced by Fred Brooks. For two years there was confusion and disaster in the Tombstone post office; at one-point Brooks demanded a government relief package for some goods stolen on his watch. However, prompt investigations by postal authorities led to the dismissal of Brooks. Brooks was a crook, and his bondsmen Herring, Goodrich, Ritter, Blinn, and Emanuel found out they had backed the wrong man. It was determined that Brooks had faked the box rents, overcharged others, was deficient in his accounts, and had a

Roderick Hafford's place was a frequent stop for the Earp faction and Browns Hotel was Tombstone's first. *Arizona Quarterly Illustrated*, October 1880.

collection of duplicate keys. Goodbye, Brooks.

Did he go quietly? Maybe, but he was busy. Shortly after his dismissal in 1884, he was arrested in San Francisco for interfering with the mail and was sent to Phoenix for further examination of this case.

In less than a decade, Fred Emerson Brooks was a household name for greatness, and in geography much wider than Arizona or California. He became a poet-humorist, wrote for leading magazines, and gave hundreds of patriotic speeches in dozens of cities throughout the West. He praised Yosemite, gloried in the heroism of Civil War battlefields, wrote at least fifteen books, and got space in the nation's press for years, with nary a word about his unusual Tombstone background. As an example of his reputation, the *Marin Journal* on December 7, 1916, headed an article on Brooks as "America's Greatest Poet Humorist."

The luster and high reputation of Brooks followed him into his retirement community of Berkeley, California, where he died on June 1, 1923.[52]

BROWN, CHARLES R. Brown, an Ohio native, had a long Western career involving storekeeping, mining, hotel operations, steam boating, and so forth, from California to Idaho to Nevada, Oregon, and Arizona. The Brown Hotel on Fourth Street, a massive structure, was a Tombstone landmark; he also was part owner of the Grand Hotel on Allen Street. For a few years, Brown and his hotel were among the Tombstone success stories. He was part of the law-and-order crowd, put up a bond for Virgil Earp when he became police chief, and posted bond for Wyatt Earp following the big shootout.

Charles was married to Carolina Ghilati in Tombstone on March 17, 1880, by Justice of the Peace Thomas J. Bidwell, with Al Schieffelin as a witness. Brown was in for the long haul, except that his fine building burned in the 1882 fire, and he was out of business. He farmed for a time in Anaheim, then took charge of the Planter's Hotel there. In the mid-1890s he moved to Alaska, possibly Nome. In the 1900 census, the couple was living in Alameda County, California, and Charlie was retired.[53]

BROWN, CLARA SPALDING
Clara Brown was living in San Diego in 1880 when her husband Theodore wrote to her from Tombstone; she was to come at once as his mining ventures were promising. He had some moderate success in working his claims and in investing. Clara, meanwhile, used her time by getting to know Tombstone, its residents, and its surroundings. She made arrangements with the *San Diego Union* and became their local correspondent. Her columns for almost two years covered all aspects of local life: Elections, mining and milling news, visiting entertainers, attempts at education, fires, and other local disasters; even the occasional gunplay received her attention and was forwarded to her San Diego audience. She was also fairly accurate in her comments about the famous gunfight in October of 1881.

However, writings on Tombstone, and their life there, ended in 1882 when they moved back to California. The remainder of her life was filled with travel from New Jersey to California. She became a well-known author of dozens of books and articles, both fiction and nonfiction. Although having little audience today, during her lifetime she had a modest literary reputation and for some time was an officer in the Southern California Women's Press Association. She died in July, 1935. Her varied career can be followed in Lynn Bailey's *Tombstone from a Woman's Point of View* (Tucson, 1998).[54]

CALHOUN, CHARLES and SAMUEL R. For reasons not clear, these brothers are seldom mentioned in histories of Tombstone. They were noteworthy for their successes and for their disturbing, disrupting personalities. They were Pennsylvanians and were in Arizona by the mid-1870s. Sam was in Gillett in 1878 and was drunk when he walked by a saloon window and shot (and killed) a fellow he didn't like. Brother Charles was also in town, having just arrived from Globe. He made a few court appearances regarding some of the doings of Jack Swilling. Word of the wonders of Tombstone arrived in Gillett, and the brothers headed for the excitement.

In 1879 they hit the jackpot, filing claims on what became the Mountain Maid mining property. Not the greatest silver around, but this was the land that became an important part of Tombstone. The brothers became rich, getting hundreds of dollars for lots, putting the squeeze on what became the Tombstone Townsite crowd, and in general letting folks know they were important. On one occasion, in September of 1879, fearing a steal of one of his Allen Street lots, Charlie Calhoun fired a few shots of warning into the air before he was arrested.

For a few years the brothers were important because of their new wealth and their ability to command attention. Another incident of note occurred in September 1880 when Charlie Calhoun and Ed Peacock were really plastered, "talking loud, using violent and riotous language," and a crowd of more than one hundred gathered for the entertainment. Policeman J. W. Bennett and Deputy Sheriff Wyatt Earp came to the scene, arrested them, and they were taken to the court of Justice of the Peace James Reilly. Wyatt Earp and Charlie Calhoun were not strangers; Calhoun was an owner of the Mountain Maid, and the Earp brothers owned its North Extension.

The Calhouns apparently feared no man. In 1881, for several months, attorney Tom Fitch published summons for the district court, trying to get the Calhoun brothers to clear some debts. Soon thereafter the they left the area, but not leaving pleasant memories in Tombstone. Samuel's tracks are hard to follow, but Charlie headed to several mining camps, working as a carpenter or millwright.

In 1895 near Flagstaff, Charlie was a bum, riding in the baggage car of a passenger train when the car went off the rails; and with broken arm and other injuries, he was taken to the Flagstaff hospital. "He claims to have been one of the founders of the town of Tombstone," one report read. That may have gotten a laugh, but it was indeed true.

The next three decades for Charlie Calhoun were tough. He worked in and around Congress Junction for years, was always broke, and several times tried to get placed on Yavapai County relief rolls. Finally, in 1918 he was admitted to the Pioneers' Home in Prescott, where he died on September 1, 1925.[55]

CALISHER, DAVID Calisher, born in San Bernardino in 1860, was in Tombstone by 1880, operating a boot and shoe shop on Allen Street. This was in part the business of his father, M. (Maurice; Morris) Calisher, a merchant of Nevada and California, who first sent David to Tombstone. David was in business for a few years, and folks familiar with this phase of Tombstone history have seen his name in print. His business sign can be prominently seen in a renowned 1880s photo of Allen Street. One of his big brushes with fame came when he served on the coroner's jury following the famous gunfight of October 1881.

What is not generally known is that Morris Calisher was married to the sister of Lionel and Barron Jacobs, the Tucson businessmen who opened Tombstone's first bank (the Agency Pima County Bank), thereby creating an important business alliance. There are many letters in the Jacobs Collection from Tombstone, where young David was writing to his "Dear Uncle" in Tucson.

In March 1882, the Calisher store was in flames, but with quick thinking and good luck, the fire was extinguished and a major portion of Tombstone was saved. However, too many thought Calisher was a bad actor, and a few witnesses thought his business had tanked. He was taken before a justice court on an arson charge, and at once sent to a higher court. Days of testimony were inconclusive, but it was the general feeling of Tombstoners that Calisher was guilty of arson. He was released, and left town.

Calisher had a long life ahead of him, as he died in the Pioneers Home in Prescott (as did Doc's Big Nose Kate and John Behan's son Albert) on January 31, 1932. The "in-between" years were mixed. He

54

This was a branch of a Tucson bank. Calisher was a leading merchant, and Smith the bank manager. David D. de Haas, MD Collection.

sold boots and shoes in Nogales and Yuma, had some mining property in Chihuahua, sold some defective stoves in a few Arizona towns, tried to operate a casino in Nogales, and so forth. Once, later in life, he applied for a veteran's pension, claiming service as a scout with an Arizona infantry unit in the 1890s. In March 1921, Calisher was again in court, this time in a federal system, charged with fraud in dealing with Eastern merchandisers. Such was the half-century career of an ex-Tombstoner.[56]

CAMPBELL, JOHN HENRY Campbell, an Illinois native, arrived in Tombstone in 1880 and went to work as a miner, but the world of saloons would be his focus for the next few decades. He was a partner in the Palace Saloon for a time, then teamed up with Bob Hatch in what was known as the Campbell & Hatch Saloon and billiard parlor on Allen Street. If this sounds familiar, it is because it is mentioned in hundreds of books and articles (and movies) about Tombstone. This is where Wyatt and Morgan Earp went one night for a quiet game of pool. On March 18, 1882, an assassin (Frank Stilwell and company) fired shots through a window, narrowly missing Wyatt, but Morgan was fatally wounded. Miner George A. B. Berry (please see his entry) was also struck with a stray bullet but survived.

Campbell remained in Tombstone for some years and for a time operated the Pony Saloon. He was also active as a volunteer fireman and served on the town council.

Around 1890, Campbell left Tombstone and headed for Seattle. There in his normal environment he rose, by 1893, to become president of the Liquor Dealers Association. By 1900, Campbell and wife Julia were living in Los Angeles, where he worked as a bartender.[57]

CARR, JOHN Born in Ireland in the 1820s, Carr tried Illinois for a time, then around 1850 found himself in northern California. Over the years he would be a miner, blacksmith, carriage maker, and merchant. Most of these years were in Eureka, Humboldt County. Around 1880, in Tombstone, Carr opened a carriage repair and blacksmith shop on Allen Street.

In December 1881, Carr soundly defeated L. W. Blinn for the post of Tombstone mayor and was re-elected two years later. These years saw the aftermath of the famous Earp-Cowboy shootout, the labor strike in the mines, and the beginning of the economic downturn in the Tombstone district.

Given these facts, lovers of Tombstone history are delighted to find that in 1891, John Carr published his *Pioneer Days in California*. Opening this book, one finds that Tombstone left little impression on Carr, who gave the town a one-sentence comment. He returned to Eureka in the late 1880s, was still a merchant and blacksmith, but was mostly known for serving as the local police judge until his death there in May 1896. Of the five or six obituaries of this pioneer, only a few mention Tombstone, as though it was less than a footnote in his career.[58]

CASHMAN, NELLIE (ELLEN) Escaping the potato famine in Ireland, Fanny Cashman and daughters Nellie and Fanny headed for Boston, where they lived for some years. They arrived in San Francisco in 1866, where there was a substantial Irish community. They were in the midst of things related to mining, and in the early 1870s, Nellie and her mother went to the mining camp of Pioche, Nevada, where they operated a boarding house. In the mid-1870s, Nellie was in the Stickeen River country of British Columbia, where she had her first brush with fame. In the midst of a severe winter, she carried provisions to some starving miners. She opened a restaurant in Tucson in 1880, but the lure of a throbbing Tombstone attracted her attention.

Nellie's Tombstone years, 1880-86, are very well known, as she was a prominent public figure. She ran a restaurant and a boarding house (on the northwest corner of Fifth and Toughnut), invested in many mining properties, was the leader in several fund drives for a church and a hospital, and when things became a bit dull, she led a team of prominent men from Tombstone on a prospecting trip to Baja California.

The following decades were filled with drama and travel.

For a few years she was at Dawson in the Klondike country, mining as well as operating a restaurant. The last twenty years of her life were mostly in the Koyukuk District of Alaska, above the Arctic Circle, working the Midnight Sun Mining Company. In ill health, she managed to find her way to Victoria, British Columbia. She died among the Sisters of St. Ann on January 2, 1925, in the very hospital she had helped to found decades earlier. In 1994, a "Legends of the West" twenty-nine cent stamp series was issued, and Nellie was one of those featured, along with Wyatt Earp and Bat Masterson.[59]

Boomer, miner, restaurant operator, doer of good works, Nellie Cashman was in Tombstone for the glory years. Her last decades were spent north of the Arctic Circle. *Sunset Magazine*, May 1921.

CHURCH, JOHN ADAMS This is the top of the heap. There is mining, Tombstone, education, international reputation, and on and on, and there is Professor Church. This fellow, born in Rochester, New York in 1843, was the first graduate of the Columbia University School of Mines; and later a professor there. He arrived in Tombstone in October 1880, studied the geology and mining practices, became an executive (superintendent of the Tombstone Mill and Mining Company; one of the local giants) for four years beginning in 1881, married Jessie Peel, the daughter of Judge Bryan L. Peel (on July 30, 1884), and wrote some of the significant studies of the great silver camp. Along the way he had a noted rival, that other expert, Professor William Phipps Blake.

Aside from Tombstone, Church had a fantastic career, writing a key work on the famous Comstock Lode in Nevada, and making breakthrough studies in geology in China and Mongolia. He had other major roles in his life, such as being on the U. S. Geological Survey, and teaching geology at Ohio State University. Church, a major figure in nineteenth-century mining and geology, was one of those who thrust Tombstone into a memorable place in the history of those disciplines. He eventually retired in Manhattan and died in New York City on February 13, 1917.[60]

CLAIBORNE, WILLIAM (aka Arizona's "Billy the Kid") Claiborne was a native of Mississippi, born there in 1860, and in the 1870s was part of the Texas cowboy contingent that went to Arizona with John Slaughter. In Tombstone, Charleston, and the San Pedro milling areas, Claiborne worked with cattle and did some mining, but was mostly a troublemaker. He killed a man during a shooting in Charleston in 1881, and received a few newspaper notices for other questionable actions.

Claiborne was at the gunfight at the O.K. Corral in October of 1881, but he and Ike Clanton had the presence of mind to run, quickly, before they would become participants in that bloody encounter.

The real claim to fame of Arizona's "Billy the Kid" came in his encounter with Buckskin Frank Leslie on November 14, 1882. Buckskin was in the Oriental Saloon, talking to a few fellows, and Claiborne several times tried to barge in on their conversation. Buckskin did his best to get Claiborne to leave, as he was a distraction. Once outside, at a fruit stand, Claiborne readied his rifle and taunted Buckskin Frank. So Buckskin walked out and tried to dissuade Claiborne, but after he fired his rifle at Frank, Frank returned fire with a revolver shot; and a few minutes later, "Billy the Kid" Claiborne was dead. There were many witnesses to this affair, and Tombstone diarist George Parsons commented that Buckskin Frank was so calm "he didn't lose the ash of his cigar."

This event is one of the keystones of Western frontier history. With names like "Tombstone," "Oriental Saloon," "Buckskin Frank," and "Billy the Kid" involved in a street shooting, that's a lot to think about. Too bad that this "Billy the Kid" was an inadequate replacement for the legendary New Mexico (William H. Bonney) original.[61]

CLANTON, JOSEPH ISAAC "IKE" The Clanton family is one of the better-known in Arizona history. They had farmed in California, moved to Arizona and did some farming and cattle raising, then in the early 1880s were in Cochise County, in and around Tombstone mostly. They were part of the cowboy crowd, and although frequenters of Tombstone's gambling and drinking places, were usually considered a bit apart from these town folks.

The rivalry, then bitterness, between the Clantons and the law-and-order types is well documented. The obvious is that Marshal Virgil Earp and brother Wyatt had half a dozen reasons to force the Clantons and McLaurys out of town. When the Earp faction tried to do so, this led to the famous gunfight near the O.K. Corral. Two McLaurys were killed, along with Billy Clanton. Ike Clanton, apparently unarmed, was saved from similar destruction by fleeing the scene as the fighting commenced. This event and the aftermath incidents were among the most publicized and bloodiest in Western history, and included the Wells Spicer hearings, the ambush of Virgil Earp, the assassination of Morgan Earp, and the punitive Wyatt Earp Vendetta Ride.

Ike Clanton's subsequent years were not noted for good deeds. He and brother Phin Clanton had a habit of borrowing other people's cattle. They were wanted for rustling in Apache County in 1877, and on June 1, near Springerville, Arizona, Deputy Sheriff Al Miller and Detective Jonas "J.V." Brighton caught up with Ike. Although Ike spotted them and drew his rifle, Brighton was faster and pumped two shots, and Ike Clanton was dead within minutes. The dignity of his end was well described by Marshal Trimble: "Ike's body, along with his spurs and pistol, was wrapped in a piece of canvas and buried at the Wilson ranch."[62]

CLAPP, MILTON B. Clapp, a New Yorker, was working in a bank in San Francisco that went under in 1880. He and fellow employee George Parsons decided to move on to that new silver camp, Tombstone. Both men were fairly successful for a few years.

Clapp was associated with Hudson & Co. Bank, a branch of the Tucson firm. He variously advertised as notary public, conveyancer, and fire insurance salesman. He was also the bank cashier. Tombstone became a troubled place in 1884, with water in the mines and a serious labor union situation. On May 10, Hudson & Co. suspended operations. Relevant detail was provided by the *Arizona Weekly Citizen* of May 17. The grand jury report stated that Cashier Milton Clapp was seen leaving the bank, three hours before suspension, "with a valise in hand…little money will be found in the vaults." There was so much unrest and anger at Clapp in Tombstone that George Parsons packed a few things for Mrs. Clapp and drove her to the train station at Fairbank.

Such shenanigans didn't seem to affect the Clapp career; by 1889 he was again in San Francisco, secretary of the Title Insurance and Trust Company. He left to operate an insurance company in Los Angeles. Yet by 1891, Clapp was said to have a wandering mind, probably mental problems. He was given treatment in Los Angeles and San Diego, but things got out of control. He went to a hotel in Pacific Grove, and on July 22, 1892, following bouts with morphine and whiskey, committed suicide. Although the *Los Angeles Times* in a detailed obituary on July 28 referred to his Arizona years, there was no mention of his absconding from Tombstone with a valise full of cash.[63]

CLARK, DICK A Civil War veteran of the 1st Colorado Cavalry, Clark tried the gambling venues of Abilene, Dodge City, and Ellsworth, Kansas before he landed "home" in Tombstone in 1880. Here, he and folks like Napa Nick would dominate the tables for years. Early on, at the Oriental Saloon, the table fellows were Lou Rickabaugh, Wyatt Earp, and Dick Clark.

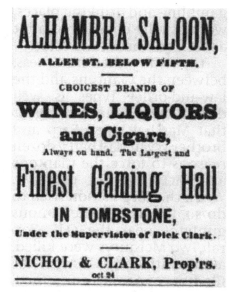

ALHAMBRA SALOON,

ALLEN ST., BELOW FIFTH.

CHOICEST BRANDS OF

WINES, LIQUORS and Cigars,

Always on hand. The Largest and

Finest Gaming Hall

IN TOMBSTONE,

Under the Supervision of Dick Clark.

NICHOL & CLARK, Prop'rs.

oct 24

This was a major gathering place, operated by Napa Nick (Nichol) and Dick Clark. *Tombstone Epitaph ads,* 1882.

Clark was also involved in the Huachuca Mountains in mining claims and water rights with Wyatt Earp, Jim Leavy, and Doc Holliday.

For the rest of the decade, Clark owned or controlled the Crystal Palace, the Alhambra, and the Elite, and also wandered to gambling action in Bisbee, Tucson, Phoenix, and a few New Mexico locales. Expanding his interests, he became active in Republican politics, bought a ranch in the San Pedro Valley, and served as an officer in the Stock Grower's Association with folks like J. V. Vickers, Fred Herrera, and Dr. Goodfellow. He enjoyed going to cattlemen's conventions (good faro action). He had married Louisa d'Agincourt in Tombstone in 1883, and they adopted a daughter; their home was at First and Toughnut.

Saloon life, alcohol, and drugs took their toll. Clark went to Chicago for treatment, but died at Albuquerque on October 28, 1893, en route to Tombstone. The *Tombstone Prospector* of November 1, 1893, referred to him as "a whole-souled man and had a host of friends all over the Southwest."[64]

CLARK, JAMES S. Interested in real estate in Western mining camps? Look into the career of Clark. In San Francisco in the 1870s, this fellow believed that the Tombstone silver strike presented an investing opportunity. He threw in his money, and his investment led to many Tombstone adventures, bad dreams, bad memories, and tons of litigation. He was *the* man in the period 1880-1882, but "Townsite Clark," a nickname gained due to his attempts at taking control of others' lots in Tombstone, would experience a bad press, local fires, and a fiasco of regional legal nightmares. He was bombed out, castigated, and should have regretted his interest in this Cochise County location.

Litigation, lawyers' fees, and horrible memories were all that could be derived from the Tombstone sojourn of James S. Clark. For years he hired a battery of attorneys to "make right" his Tombstone years. He took his cause to Washington, DC, and beseeched numerous legislators. But when he died there on October 3, 1889, most of the newspapers would report he perished in "abject poverty."[65]

CLUM, JOHN Not many folks have Western credentials as varied and interesting as Clum. He was an Easterner who went West in the 1870s and served a few years as an Apache agent at the San Carlos Reservation. He was subsequently an editor in Tucson, then a founder of and worked on the *Tombstone Epitaph* newspaper in Tombstone for the vital years of that community's life. In the first part of the 1880s he was a Tombstone journalist, mayor, postmaster, and was plugged in to the personalities that mattered in this vibrant town. He mostly backed the law-and-order or Earp faction in the rural-town rivalry, and in many senses was the most public figure of Tombstone. To follow the

Clum activities during this era is to know what was going on in Tombstone.

The town "gave out" for him though, and by the late 1880s he was in San Bernardino, California peddling real estate and fruit. This did not work out well, but fortunately, Clum was well connected, and received an appointment as postal inspector and administrator in Alaska. While there in the early 1900s he met up once again with Wyatt Earp, George Parsons, Nellie Cashman, and other former Tombstoners. John almost became governor of Alaska Territory, but lacked the local clout. In the following years he was a major speaker-lecturer in the United States, focusing on his days as an Indian agent, Tombstone editor, and his work in Alaska.

The influence of Tombstone on Clum can be seen in Los Angeles on June 16, 1930, when his granddaughter Marjorie A. Clum (daughter of his son Woodworth, 1878- 1946), "prominent socialite," married real estate investor Carl A. Bilicke (born approximately 1908), the son of Albert C. Bilicke, the preeminent Tombstone and Los Angeles hotelier who died on the Titanic. They divorced in 1933. Marjorie died in 1985.

Clum was one of the honorary pallbearers for Wyatt Earp (after having spoken with him the day before his death) in Los Angeles in 1929. He himself died in Los Angeles on May 2, 1932. At his funeral was George Parsons, a close associate from the Tombstone days of the early 1880s. [66]

In 1900 Tombstoners Wyatt Earp and John Clum met in the new mining district of Nome, Alaska. *Alaska State Museum.*

COMSTOCK, SYLVESTER B. Born in Rhode Island in 1837, Comstock was in San Francisco by 1853 and in the following decades spent time investing, prospecting, gambling, and in business in Alaska, Montana, and Arizona. He was one of the early Tombstone arrivals, elected as a councilman in

1880, and was co-owner of the Grand Hotel, one of the Tombstone landmarks which was on Allen, between Fourth and Fifth Streets. The Grand Hotel was a total loss in the big fire of 1882.[67] Comstock did not rebuild, but erected a large structure to house several business establishments. He was a leader in the local Democratic Party, was interested in the "sporting life," and was a strong backer of the Earp faction during the troubles of 1881-82. Sylvester had also served on the coroner's jury following the gunfight of October 1881.

Comstock figured in quite a few mining ventures in his few years in town. He, all three of the Earp brothers, Uncle Bob Winders, and A. S. Neff bought and sold and did a bit of development work in or near the Comstock, Long Branch, Grasshopper, and Mountain Maid properties. They even convinced Senator John P. Jones of Nevada to join them; this became the Senator Jones Claim, near the Charleston Road southwest of town.[68]

Comstock was a wanderer, looking for excitement and new deals. He headed for Texas in 1884, and was in various Arizona spots in the next decade; in some voting registers he identified himself as a spec-ulator. In the summer of 1899, in Yuma County, as head of the Colorado River Fiber Company, he tried to get financing for this hemp business from investors in Denver and Chicago. The *Scientific American* of May 11, 1901, published a blurb that Comstock, of La Colorado, Mexico, had invented a gaming table, allowing for proper flow of dice, etc. In 1907, Comstock was regaling listeners in Phoenix and Tucson of the glory days of Tombstone and the Grand Hotel. He is last noticed in Prescott in 1908 in the voting registers, a native of Rhode Island, age seventy-two.

COOK, BENJAMIN Cook, from Massachusetts, was in California and all over the West prospecting and mining, before he arrived in Tombstone in 1878, a true pioneer of the community. He mined with J. M. Vizina, successfully, and they put up one of the earliest, substantial buildings in Tombstone at Allen and Fifth.

Cook would remain in Tombstone for the rest of his life, with forays to other parts of Cochise and Pima counties for mining. In the early 1900s he served as Tombstone's fire chief. He had substantial land holdings, was active in the fire department, and also owned property and buildings in Los

Angeles. Cook died in Tombstone on October 30, 1915, having centered his life there for almost thirty years.

By the time of his death, Cook had long carried the honorific of "Captain," and was frequently noticed in the Arizona press. In an obituary in the *Bisbee Daily Review* he was praised for his pioneering work, and was an "intimate friend of Ed Schieffelin."[69]

COOLEY, LEWIS W. Cooley was born in Illinois in 1854, gradually shifted West, and was an early Tombstone arrival; as early as 1879, he was driving a stage there. Cooley would remain in Tombstone for a decade, but not doing many of the things attributed to him. According to some accounts he was a major gunfighter, involved in many incidents, including the death of John Ringo. None of these events can be documented. What is certain is that Cooley was there, was known to many of the leading folks around, and for a few years was close to E. B. Gage, the Tombstone leading light; he often drove him on major errands.

Cooley left the area, and in the 1900 census was listed as living with wife and son Lester in Benson, where he raised cattle. Lester died in Oakland, California, in September 1912, and a fellow named Louis Cooley died there on May 31, 1914; this was most likely his father.

Lou's life and career in greater Tombstone has been complicated by many writers who place him as a secret Wells Fargo operator, a major local hit man, a fellow behind important financial takeovers, and a man to help the leading mining men in their corporate takeovers. The fact that he sued John Behan for $5,000 because of false arrest is just one actual event that suggests some of the intrigue associated with Cooley may have been accurate.[70]

CORBIN BROTHERS The brothers Philip, Andrew, Elbert, Frank, and George figure in a major way in the first few years of the Tombstone saga. By the late 1870s, the Corbins were important in many New England industries from their Connecticut base. They also had some California and Arizona mining interests. They were early invited to participate in the Tombstone financing and did so in a major way. They all spent some time in San Francisco and in Pima County, arranging for the planning, financing, and installation of what became the Corbin Mill, as well as of several mining projects. Much of their San Pedro River and Tombstone mining and milling projects were consolidated as the Tombstone Mill & Mining Company. They were forceful, successful pioneers in these projects, but Tombstone, as important as it was in Western mining, was a small part of the Corbin interests. Their hardware, lock, boiler, banking, and water projects in Connecticut and in the East in general received most of their focus. The leading brother, Philip Corbin, died in Connecticut in 1910.[71]

CORELLA, MANUEL M. His death by heart attack was one of the more dramatic events of the Tombstone bonanza era. Corella had been born in Sonora, Mexico, in 1839, was raised in California, and educated at the university in Berkeley. He became an instructor there in 1874. Among his later jobs was a stint as a correspondent for *La Cronica,* the Los Angeles newspaper. By early 1882 he was practicing law in Tucson and then headed southeast to Tombstone where, in late May, 1882, he was named Mexican consul.

By then he was well connected in mining and social circles. When George Hearst left Tombstone for a major prospecting trip to northern Sonora in February 1882, he would be a guest of Corella's nephew. Tombstone mining man George Berry, who was subsequently wounded in the Morgan Earp assassination attempt in March 1882, was amongst the Hearst party.

In early July 1882, Corella left his office in the Gird building, walked past the *Epitaph* office where he greeted the staff, and arrived at his rooms near Bruce and Second. By then, he was not feeling well. Two colleagues met him, and they engaged in a vigorous debate on some Sonoran political issues (agriculture, education, etc.). When told of some political moves in Sonora, Corella threw up his hands and said, "It cannot be, it cannot be!" and fell dead.

Naturally, such a dramatic ending led to many questions, and a battery of Tombstone's finest medical men were drawn in. Dr. Giberson gave his comments, and Dr. Goodfellow, after looking over the corpse, declared that Corella had died a natural death. The coroner's jury, which included George Berry, concluded that there was no funny business connected to his death; he just died.

Nothing about this affair was routine. A large funeral procession, led by Mayor Carr and a marching band, paraded down Allen Street. Corella was not just the Mexican consul resident in Tombstone. His wife Josephine, mother of three children, was then in Battle Creek, Michigan, where she had just given birth to a fourth child. Corella's father-in-law was Judge Charles Lindley, one of the codifiers of the first California laws. Judge Lindley, who lived in Tombstone with Major Frank Earle, superintendent of the Lucky Cuss Mine, was a major investor in several Sonoran gold mines. So Corella, only a Tombstone short-timer, had been plugged into the important mining and social life of the community.[72]

CORRIGAN, TOM This Irishman, raised in New York, is a good example of someone wanting to be only in exciting places. He was early on the scene in Tombstone, 1879, controlled claims there and near Tucson, and sold at the right time. By April 1880 he was a Tombstone businessman, fitting up his new place, the Alhambra Saloon. The bar, and Corrigan, soon became known as one of the flashiest places in town, and the saloon was the scene of many an interesting gathering during the wild early Tombstone years.

Yet, as early as 1884, Corrigan had been traveling, prospecting, and working a few miles from the mining camp of Trinidad, in Sonora, Mexico. In April of that year, rich specimens of gold from its Companero Mine were exhibited in Tombstone. For a few years, the Companero did very well, and Corrigan had two other Tombstoners in as partners, Smith Gray and Billy Caldwell. Corrigan also liked the Trinidad area, married into one of the best families, and settled down for the good life as a prosperous miner with wife Josefa and daughter Catalina.

It all unraveled on November 6, 1889. Details of any ownership quarrel are vague, but it is known that partner Smith Gray got very drunk, said he was going to gun down Corrigan as soon as he saw him, and he did just that, a few miles from Trinidad.[73]

COYLE, JAMES Born in Ireland in 1844, Coyle went to San Francisco for some years until 1879, then arrived in Tombstone. At once a substantial citizen, he served as superintendent at the Grand Central Mine, was city health officer, and a city policeman. It was Officer Coyle on duty in 1882 during the Buckskin Frank Leslie- William (Billy the Kid") Claiborne shootout,[74] and he testified at the coroner's jury.

In 1883, James became the Tombstone chief of police. Until his death in 1921, Coyle was always associated with law and order as well as mining.

He would join Wyatt Earp, Nellie Cashman, Charlie Shibell, and other bonanza seekers in Harqua Hala in 1889, but for most of 1886-1892 he was working mining property in New Mexico. Coyle owned land and mined around Gila Bend, Arizona, where he also served as a justice of the peace for some years. In 1895-96, James served as assistant warden in Yuma at the territorial prison. He died in Ajo in November of 1921, having spent around forty years in Arizona and New Mexico as a man of the law and mining.[75]

CRABTREE, JACK Here we have it, really big-time fame, except that the fame belonged to Jack's sister, Lotta Crabtree, one of the major singers and entertainers of the nineteenth century. The Crabtrees were born in England, but early on were in the United States. Jack was in Tombstone as early as 1880, working as a miner, but mostly trying to impress folks with the fame of his sister Lotta. Jack was known to many, but liked by few, as he was mostly a blowhard.

Nevertheless, the Crab-trees have considerable fame beyond Lotta's entertaining career. Though not generally well-liked, one Tombstone female liked Jack just fine, and she bore him a child. Lotta died in 1924, leaving a large estate up for grabs. This brought in Jack, the child born to his "woman" in Tombstone, and so forth. In a major trial in 1926, the claim of Jack and his descendants was turned aside. Yet, much testimony was provided which enlightens us about the doings of Tombstone in the 1880s. Wyatt Earp was interviewed in the case, and although the information he provided did not help Jack's heirs, he did contribute many tidbits about life in Tombstone, including the local interest in ice cream parlors.[76]

CROUCH, ROBERT "Sandy Bob" would be one of the most common names associated with the greatest days of pioneer Tombstone. He started a stage line between Benson and Tombstone in 1880, and for more than a decade, under a variety of company names, was the leader in local transportation. We should recall that in this era, Tombstone lacked a railroad, so it was firms like Sandy Bob's that moved people and some freight between Tombstone

Arizona Mail and Stage Line

TOMBSTONE, ARIZONA.

STAGE FOR FAIRBANK, connecting with eastern and western bound trains on Southern Pacific railroad leave at 9:15 o'clock, a. m. Stage leaves Fairbank upon arrival of Sonora train and leaves Tombstone to connect with train to Sonora at 8 o'clock, p. m.
Stage for Fairbank by way of Charleston, leaves Tombstone at 7 o'clock a. m., and returns upon arrival of Benson train.
STAGE FOR BISBEE leaves every morning at 6 o'clock, except Sundays.

406 Allen St., Under Occidental Hotel.
ROBT. CROUCH,
PROPRIETOR.

"Sandy Bob" Crouch was a leading transportation figure in southern Arizona. *Tombstone Daily Epitaph*, April 23, 1886.

and the outer world: Benson, Willcox, Fairbank, Charleston, and Contention, where there were rail connections. Sandy Bob also had a lucrative wood and freight contract with several Bisbee firms. By the mid-1880s Sandy Bob also owned a cattle ranch between Tombstone and Bisbee.

The decline of the Tombstone mining world by the 1890s was obvious to Sandy Bob, though he remained in business for a few years; he even sponsored and managed the Tombstone baseball club. However, Bob began to travel in Mexico and came to believe that his future was there. He moved to Mexico City, but any ventures there are unknown. Arizona newspapers announced his death in Guadalajara in early September 1908.[77]

DANNER, SAMUEL S. Danner was apparently born in South Carolina in 1825, but the first definite notice of him was peddling booze in Tombstone, even before there was a Tombstone. He and partner Billy Owens put up Danner & Owens Saloon, near what would become Tombstone, early in 1879. This was a tent where thirsty men gathered to drink, fight, and be entertained. John Hicks, possibly the first gunfight death in Tombstone, was fueled by Sam Danner's liquid. The account of this incident left by Davis Chamberlain of the Danner saloon, and its significance to local lore, is a classic of Western history.

As the three (or four) Tombstones sifted into one, Danner and Owens followed the flow, and in 1880, at 438 Allen Street, opened Danner and Owens Hall, which had a large auditorium, chandeliers, fancy seating boxes, even curtains. This became one of the better-known locales for the sporting types, even getting mentioned by Virgil Earp in his testimony at the Spicer hearings after the October 1881 shootout.

The Danner decision to go to Tombstone in 1879, so calculated, was not matched by his move in mid-1882. He left town and headed for the next bonanza, Total Wreck. There he would be similarly involved for a few years, active in the saloon world, serving as a local election official, and so forth. Yet, the Total Wreck never became an economic powerhouse like Tombstone, and Danner moved on to settle in Tucson.

He would remain in Tucson until his death in 1898. The few notices of him in these later years referred to him as "Colonel Danner," returning from a tour and prospecting around the Grand Canyon or being appointed road overseer for Greaterville and Pantano. Even more telling were the several brief obituaries or death notices, using language like "a quiet and unassuming gentleman," with no hint of his previous prominence. This was the fellow who had pretty much inaugurated the drinking, vomit, violence, humor, and the sporting life that would become a hallmark of Tombstone in its bonanza days.[78]

DODGE, FRED This Californian, born in 1854 in Butte County, arrived in Tombstone (from Sacramento) in August 1880, nine months after the Earps had arrived. They became very close for a time; Fred even took a room with Morgan. The Earps would move on after a few years, but Dodge stayed the decade. In the 1880s, no one in Tombstone or in Cochise County saw as much action as Fred Dodge. He gambled, ran a saloon, and was a constable for many of these years. He was in, or quashed, numerous brawls, witnessed and participated in several gunplay events, led several different posses, and from time to time had to clamp down on unruly court witnesses. To scrutinize Fred Dodge's Tombstone years is to see the most exciting aspects of frontier living.

This was a fantastic, varied, often violent life. Although Fred Dodge was up to it, and did yeoman work, as a raconteur or historian he was abysmal. In 1969 Carolyn Lake (daughter of Wyatt Earp's biographer Stuart Lake) put together *Under Cover for Wells Fargo: Unvarnished Recollections of Fred Dodge*. This is an oft-quoted work but is as unreliable as a book of fairy tales. He was no more an undercover agent than John Dillinger was a scout master. Most of his dates are wrong, he gets confused on the participants, forgets what the motives were, and usually arrives at the wrong conclusion. A great history of Tombstone during the 1880s could be written by following the Fred Dodge career, so long as you avoided the Fred Dodge version. Fred left around 1890, spent some years in Tucson, then in California locales, and was eventually taken on by Wells Fargo as an investigator. Much of the last decades of his life were working out of the Houston office as investigator, detective, or liaison with local law enforcement agencies. He had a solid, recognized, Wells Fargo career. He retired to his ranch at Boerne, Texas, and died there on December 16, 1938.[79]

DOLING, JACK This native of Maine operated a stage express company and a saloon in Greenwood, Mohave County, Arizona, in the 1870s. The news from Tombstone caused his immediate shift there and in 1880 he first showed up on the census. For nearly a decade he was one of the more prominent merchants in town. Although he operated a saloon on Allen Street, the Doling name is usually best remembered for its association with horse racing. The Doling Driving Park was on Contention Road just southwest of town, with its first races in the summer of 1880, and for a few months of each year, this was the center of much frivolity, betting, and good times. There were also dog races, foot races, and the town's baseball games held here. In the years 1880-1882, the Earps, Johnny Behan, and many other Tombstone stalwarts were regular attendees. Because the good times ended, in 1888 Doling shifted to Clifton, Arizona, where he ran a saloon for a time, then tried northern California for a few years. A short spell in Cochise County was followed by a return to Mohave County, where he had started his Arizona years.

The exciting part of frontier living was again evident in July 1898, when he was shot in the ribs during a quarrel in White Hills, in the Cerbat Range of Mohave County. Doling died in Chloride, Mohave County, in February 1904.[80]

DRUM, T. J. Thomas Jerome Drum was an Illinois native who in the early 1870s was practicing law in San Francisco. He looked around Arizona in the summer of 1876, working in Prescott and later in Tucson for some time. T. J. was one of the many lawyers who flocked to Tombstone in the early days and received an appointment as a U. S. commissioner.

Drum would be in Tombstone about five years, and although involved in many legal activities, two of them were prominent. After the O. K. Corral gunfight in October 1881, in the Spicer hearings, Tom Fitch ran the legal defense team for the Earp faction; Virgil, Wyatt, and Morgan. It was decided to have a special counsel for Doc Holliday, and that was Drum's role. However, where Tom Fitch was, that was the center of power, and in the hearings and in subsequent accounts of that event, little attention is given to Drum.

His other brush with fame was in 1884, after the Bisbee Massacre, when John Heath was strung up in Tombstone and his cohorts went to trial. Drum was one of the attorneys challenged with getting these fellows acquitted. It didn't work out, as Heath was lynched and the other five convicted and subsequently the first to be legally hanged in Tombstone.

Following these Tombstone years, Drum opened an office in Denver, where he was in business until his death in September 1899. He had a famous death, as his name and condition were splashed across the nation's newspapers. He was rushed from Denver to Chicago for an operation, where his tongue, palate, and tonsils were sliced away. The account in the *El Paso Daily Herald* of September 5, 1899, was typical of the coverage: "STRONG CIGARS: Caused Man's Death From Cancer."

Irony of ironies: When Doc Holliday passed on in Glenwood Springs in 1887, nobody knew of the event. When his attorney died in 1899, the news was flashed coast to coast. Current accounts, though, are filled with images of the shotgun-wielding Doc Holliday fighting the vicious Cowboy faction in Tombstone, while the Drum name remains unknown. [81]

DUNBAR, JOHN Dunbar and brother Thomas were from Maine and were early on the scene in Tombstone. In 1881, John was appointed the first Cochise County treasurer, and would be a very active citizen of Tombstone for most of the 1880s. He and his brother, along with Sheriff John Behan, operated a successful Tombstone livery stable for a few years, and John Dunbar embarked on a long, recognized career in journalism. In Tombstone he was associated with the *Nugget, Epitaph,* and *Republican* newspapers, and was later associated with newspapers in Benson, Dos Cabezas, and Globe.

John Dunbar found his home in Phoenix, where for years he published the *Dunbar's Weekly*, and he died there on February 1, 1923. Some measure of his local reputation appeared in the *Phoenix Tribune* of February 3, which praised his attack on the Ku Klux Klan.[82]

EARP FAMILY Some of the Earps were in Tombstone, mostly from 1879 to 1882. The leader was Virgil, who after a law position in Prescott was named a deputy U. S. marshal, and assigned to the new Tombstone area in Pima County in 1879. Soon Wyatt came over from his Kansas and New Mexico doings, as did James; and Morgan came down from Montana, where he had been a policeman. Young Warren Earp came over from the family home in Colton, California. What happened in 1881 and 1882, with a few confrontations, a vendetta, an assassination, and so forth, can be found in multiple sources—

publications, movies, television, interviews, and so on.

The after-Tombstone days of the Earps has also been well documented. Young Warren got himself obliterated in a bar shootout in Willcox in 1900; he had been working as a teamster in Cochise County. Virgil, after a stint as a town marshal in Colton, California, later mined in Yavapai County, then went to the boomtown of Goldfield, Nevada, where he was a deputy sheriff of Esmeralda County; he died there in 1905. James from 1901 through 1907 pushed drinks ("blind pigs") and illegal gambling in Sawtelle, California, adjacent to the Old Soldiers' Home, and just east of Santa Monica and west of Los Angeles, California. There his veteran father

A SKETCH OF WYATT EARP.

Wyatt, heading to Goldfield, Nevada, to join brother Virgil. *Los Angeles Record*, January 12, 1905.

Nicholas and brother Newton had both retired and were living at the time. Afterwards, James moved to San Bernardino, where he lived until a year before his death in 1926. He died in the home of Allie Earp's grandniece Hildreth Halliwell (where Virgil Earp's wife Allie was also residing at the time) in Los Angeles. Wyatt's career included memorable stops in Idaho, California, Nome, and Nevada, then back to Southern California, where from around 1904 until his death he mostly worked marginal copper and gold properties in the Whipple Mountains near the Colorado River, living in Los Angeles during the sweltering desert summer months. He died in Los Angeles in 1929.

The Earp family time in Tombstone had been brief, less than three years, but stands as one of the better-known periods in the history of the Wild West.[83]

PIONEER AND YOSEMITE DISCOVERER DIES AT 81

Robert A. Eccleston, pioneer, Indian fighter and father of prominent Oakland man, who passed away Wednesday night.

Tombstone pioneer Robert Eccleston had previous fame. *San Francisco Call*, February 3, 1911.

fore he moved to Tucson. The locals were not familiar with the unusual background of Robert. He was in Tombstone around fifteen years, moved to Oregon for a few years, then permanently settled in Oakland in 1900. When he died in California early in 1911, his biography and photos were splashed across the newspaper pages, listing his significance as the "Finder of Yosemite," not a small achievement for which to be remembered.[84]

ECCLESTON, ROBERT and JAMES Y. Robert and son James were in Tombstone for a few interesting years in the early 1880s. Robert was treasurer of the Tombstone Mining Exchange and had several other local interests, and James operated a harness and saddle shop for some years be-

EMANUEL, ALFRED H. This fellow was one of Tombstone's long-stayers. A native of Philadelphia, Emanuel arrived in San Francisco in 1850, and in the 1860s was so experienced in mining that he served as a foreman at the famous Gould & Curry Mine. For many years he operated a livery and

Mining pioneer A. H. Emanuel later served several terms as Tombstone mayor. Ben Traywick Collection.

freighting business among several Nevada mining camps. Emanuel shifted to Arizona in the late 1870s and hit Tombstone in its early days. In 1880 he bought and sold some of the claims of Wyatt and Virgil Earp that were decent, and by the end of the year was superintendent of the Vizina Consolidated works.

His career was too long, varied, and mostly successful to be presented here, though there is detailed information in *Cochise County Stalwarts*.[85] Even when the decline hit, Emanuel overcame the situation, becoming politically active and for years serving as clerk in the district court. In the 1890s he developed a highly successful wagon, carriage, and blacksmith shop, and was indeed "Mr. Tombstone," elected mayor in 1896 and subsequently re-elected several times. From 1902 to 1904, during the important rebirth of local mining headed by E. B. Gage, Emanuel had much to do with the legal machinations and his business did very well with the new mining and milling needs.

Emanuel finally lost out in a mayoral contest, but for a time hung around, fascinated by what was going on in this new Tombstone. On the other hand, he also looked elsewhere. In 1905, Emanuel had railroad construction contracts in Globe, and even moved his office furniture there. After 1910, he finally moved on, shifted to Los Angeles, and died there on March 9, 1915. Because he arrived in Tombstone in 1880 and remained through 1910, he was the most important, successful personality who saw the beginnings and the ends of both of Tombstone's rich mining eras.[86]

ENGLISH, ALLEN Tombstone represented quite a geographical shift for English. He was born in Saginaw, Michigan, in 1858, where his father was a shipbuilder on Lake Michigan, and he would spend the last forty-five years of his life in Cochise County. Allen arrived in Tombstone in 1880 as a miner, read law, became a justice of the peace, and would be a legal force in this part of Arizona for more than twenty years. He became district attorney in 1887 because of a vacancy, then was elected to the post for several terms.

English was more than a known quantity in legal circles; he was an accomplished, vigorous speaker, and his courtroom appearances were like public events that seldom disappointed his audience.

English handled hundreds of cases, sending teams of those convicted to the awaiting cells of the territorial prison at Yuma. He figured in some of the most dramatic legal events in the area, including the trial of William Greene, and the trial and public hanging of the Halderman Brothers in 1899-1900.

The flaw in the English saga was the bottle. He started to lose his edge, moved to Bisbee in 1907, and the downward slide became precipitous. He died in Douglas on September 7, 1927, and was buried in Bisbee using funds provided by well-wishers.[87]

ESCAPULE, JOHN E. Escapule was a French Basque, born in 1856, and in the American West by the mid-1870s. He was a reporter and arrived at Fort Huachuca in 1877 while researching a story on the capture of Geronimo for the *San Francisco Chronicle*. While there, Escapule met and befriended prospector Ed Schieffelin and spent time with him at Brunckow's cabin, even before he (Schieffelin) went on to discover the claims that became Tombstone as we know it today. With Schieffelin's assistance, Escapule came to have vast land holdings in and about Tombstone, including ranches in the Dragoon Mountains as well as the Huachucas, with the main family ranch located on the west edge of town. Escapule became a mill man just west in Charleston, and in 1879, took an interest in the State of Maine Mine and opened an assay office near the O. K. Corral.

Escapule died in Tombstone on October 11, 1926, at his ranch. He and his family represent the greatest continuity of any others with a Tombstone past. He lived mostly in town, but had land and mining interests, and for many years operated a successful cattle ranch. His death, far from ending any Escapule influence locally, was but one event in the family's long concern with local mining, cattle raising, and public affairs.
He subsequently donated the land (his "New Year's Gift" mining claim) which became the Tombstone city cemetery (where he himself was interred after his death) with the stipulation that all Tombstone townsfolk (who had lived there for at least one year) could be buried for free.

To this day, Tombstone and Cochise County continue to have many Escapule descendants, engaged in many of the same activities as John was in the 1880s. In the early 2020s, Dusty Escapule (a great-grandson of John) was still serving as mayor (an office he has held for seven terms) of Tombstone.

As a very interesting aside, and adding even more to the Tombstone mystique, it is John Escapule's photo that was misidentified as Doc Holliday by an author many years ago (first uncovered by then-Tombstone town historian Ben Traywick), and still to this day incorrectly labeled and universally believed to be Doc in books and magazines, and on everything from t-shirts to postcards to soda cans, and on and on. [88]

EVANS, MARY JANE In 1947, when "May" died in Riverside County, California, at the age of ninety, few locals knew of her unusual background. She figured in two of Tombstone's nastiest events. She had married Mike Killeen, but in the Tombstone of 1880, she fell for the flirting smile of Buckskin Frank Leslie. Leslie "rubbed out" Killeen in a bit of treachery, which led to one of the longest trials in Arizona Territory's history. Buckskin Frank was "cleared" of all charges, and almost at once, he and May entered matrimony through the magic words of Justice James Reilly.

Wedded bliss never arrived, and soon Buckskin was using May as a punching bag; some legends go further in reporting on his cruel ways with her. A divorce and departure from Tombstone followed for May. She was the lucky one, as Buckskin's next "true love," Mollie Williams, was killed by him.

Somewhere in Arizona, May met and married Alexander Durward, and in 1894 they moved to Banning, California. In this community they had a small almond orchard and expanded that to include a profitable fruit farm. It was in this peaceful environment that May spent the last half century of her life, probably trying not to think of the wild year she had endured in Tombstone.[89]

EVERHARDY, JACOB Prussian-born, Everhardy arrived with his family when he was still a child. The Everhardys had a substantial cattle and beef business in Kansas, but Jacob aimed for more Western projects. In 1878-79 he was in Oregon and Wyoming purchasing cattle, bringing some to Tombstone in 1880. In March 1881, Jacob purchased (from Apollinar Bauer) a butcher shop in Tombstone on the south side of Fremont Street, and almost immediately also procured a ranch near town. His shop burned down in the devastating May 1882 Tombstone fire, but he reopened once more on the opposite side of the street, between the American Hotel and the San Jose House. Everhardy always had the big picture in mind, and this was when Tombstone was in bonanza. For a few years he expanded his interests to Benson as well as to places in Sonora, Mexico.

However, the decline of Tombstone was obvious to him, and in 1887 Jacob moved to Los Angeles where for a time he was in the wholesale meat business. The following year, however, Everhardy moved to the Anaheim area, purchased a large landholding, and within a few years was the largest beet producer in southern California. He died in early June 1908 and had an impressive funeral at St. Vibiana's Cathedral in Los Angeles. The Everhardy career was notable enough to warrant a substantial write-up in Guinn's *Historical and Biographical Record,* published in 1902. He is buried in the Calvary Cemetery near his wife.[90]

FAIRBANK, NATHANIEL K. The Fairbank presence in Tombstone was infrequent, yet his significance was tremendous. By 1880, Nathaniel was a leading Chicago industrialist, and his empire would include soap, animals, baking powder, and a massive production and marketing empire in at least five countries.

He plowed a fortune into Tombstone's Grand Central Mining Company, receiving more than a reasonable return. In his honor, the small railroad station/town on the San Pedro River was given the name Fairbank.

This had enormous geographical and strategic ramifications. Tombstone, a major national silver producing center of the 1880s, would only see a railroad connection after the 1900s. One cannot use the Tombstone literature without constantly seeing the place name "Fairbank." It was near the mills, the cartage center for freight and passengers to and from Tombstone, and also the site of some significant events in frontier law and order, such as gunfights and train robberies.

At the time of his death in Chicago on March 28, 1903, Fairbank was a leading player. He was a major patron of education and music and was particularly associated with the University of Chicago.[91]

FALLON, SAMANTHA An authentic Tombstone pioneer, Fallon arrived in 1879 and stayed for a vital few years. Born Samantha E. Steinhoff in Canada in 1858, she was indeed experienced in the ways of the world. In 1874 in Oakland she married John T. Monks, then in San Jose in June of 1877, she married Thomas Fallon, the big mogul (ex-mayor, etc.). Samantha filed for divorce from Fallon in October, 1878, and soon heard talk of Tombstone. She went there, and in 1879 opened Tombstone's third lodging place, the San Jose House, at the northwest corner of Fifth and Fremont, one of the key community landmarks. The place was attractive, had plants and a water fountain, and multiple functions.

Fallon and the San Jose House knew all the folks who mattered. It was apparently more than a rumor that she was beyond friendly with Ed Schieffelin, and Wyatt Earp used the San Jose House as a "holding" pen for miscreants. Doc Holiday stayed there for a time, as did Bat Masterson, and gambler Charlie Storms' body was brought there by Bat after he had lost a confrontation with Earp confidant and gambler/gunfighter Luke Short. The sheriff, business-

78

people, lawyers–everyone in town knew Samantha Fallon and the San Jose House. Early on, in 1880, she married Zachary Taylor, who operated a major livery in Tucson.

Much of what we know about Fallon, the San Jose House, and greater Tombstone came about because of the Lotta Crabtree estate controversy in the 1920s. Lotta, a major entertainer of the nineteenth century, died in 1924 and left an impressive estate. Her brother Jack had lived in Tombstone in the early 1880s, which is how Earp and Breakenridge figured in the estate settlement. Jack Crabtree and his paramour apparently used the San Jose House, and Wyatt Earp, William Breakenridge, and other early Tombstoners testified about the principals in the case and life in early Tombstone.

Although much is known about Fallon's years in Tombstone, it is often difficult to sift the rumor from the reality. She was an important, successful, well-known Tombstone personality of the 1880s. Her later life was also unusual, as she married several more times and lived mostly in southern California. One indication that she was not your average Western housewife were the entries in the 1910 census for San Bernardino. Her husband, Samuel Logie, was a contractor and builder. Samantha identified herself as "preacher, Free Methodist."

Her last years were in Glendale, California, where she died on March 16, 1931. The biography, *Tombstone Pioneer Samantha Fallon's Wanton Past*, contains many theories regarding her questionable history, but does present some solid, interesting evidence.[92]

FARISH, THOMAS E. Born in Tennessee in 1837 and arriving in California with his family in 1854, he had a distinguished career in mining around the Feather River, and also served in the California legislature. In 1880, with backing from San Francisco investors, Farish moved to Tombstone and took control of the Head Centre Mining Company. He had other Cochise County mining investments and was very active in politics for the Democratic party. His younger brother William, in mining in Colorado, was also interested in the Head Centre operations, but most of the decisions were handled by Thomas, who was on the spot.

Farish developed other interests, and for a few years had much to do with a few mining and milling projects in Sonora, still using Tombstone as his base. By the late 1880s, Farish was settled in Phoenix, and that would be his focus until his death. He had newspaper, mining, and political interests, and was a very public man. Farish had been associated with Conrad Zulick in the Sonoran ventures, and later became private secretary to Governor Zulick. Farish also served in the territorial legislature, was for a time territorial treasurer, and in 1913 was appointed Arizona state historian. His multi-volume *History of Arizona* is still a frequently-used source. Farish died in Los Angeles in October of 1919.[93]

FAY, ARTEMUS E. Fay was a Pennsylvanian who began his journalism career in the oil city of Titusville. From 1877 through 1879, Fay was in Tucson as editor of the *Star* newspaper. He was also a member of the territorial legislature, and there became a buddy of Earp adversary John Behan.

Fay hit Tombstone in the first big year, 1879, and started the town's first newspaper, the *Tombstone Nugget*. When John Clum's *Epitaph* appeared soon thereafter, the stage was set for Tombstone's vigorous debates, mostly centered around the differences between the rural interests and the mining-town folks. Clum was solidly behind the law-and-order or Earp crowd, and the *Nugget*, and Fay, usually favored the cowboy group, with which Sheriff Behan and the Dunbars were closely associated.

By 1883, though, Fay went on to a few other Arizona newspaper projects that led to nothing, and by 1884 was on the Pacific Coast. He was a printer, started the *Santa Monica Wave*, which had a short life, then moved on to Fresno, California, there having a long, solid career with the *Fresno Expositor*. Fay died in Fresno on February 10, 1906.[94]

FICKAS, BENJAMIN A. This Indiana native served in the Civil War, then lived in San Diego for a few years as a news editor, and also served in an abstract (land title) office. He moved to Arizona in 1876, shifted to Tucson, then in 1879 was the chief clerk in Prescott with the legislature. The Tombstone bonanza news caused him to immediately depart for that excitement.

There he was involved in a dozen major activities, even serving in the legislature for Pima County in the 1880 session. Fickas was a notary public, worked as a stage agent, and was in frequent demand because of his expertise in land titles and abstract work.

He was an officer with the local Democratic party, a member of the school board, and clerk of the district court. This is not a complete list of the Fickas public presence in Tombstone; his name will appear in documents covering a variety of Cochise County topics.

By 1887, however, more than the handwriting was on the wall for Tombstone, and Fickas headed to Phoenix. There he had a nice eighty-acre spread, worked as a newspaper business manager, even put in some time as the Maricopa County undersheriff. Fickas then organized the Valley Abstract Company in 1894. He died in Phoenix in May 1903, his career there pretty much resembling the active years he had spent in Tombstone.[95]

FITCH, TOM If one were to study the career of Tom Fitch, one would get an outstanding summary of Western legal, cultural, political, and social history. Only a fragment of this fellow's life concerns Tombstone, but it was noteworthy.

A New York City man who found fame, wealth, and success in the West, Fitch was a lawyer, as well as a legislator in California and Nevada, and practiced law there as well as in Arizona, Utah, and other locales. Fitch was probably the most well-known public speaker in the Western part of the country, his usual nickname being "the silver-tongued orator." More than six years prior to the legendary gunfight at the O. K. Corral, in July 1875 he was the featured speaker at the unveiling ceremony of the beautiful Pacific Ocean city of Santa Monica, California. That Fitch was well-known and well-connected can be seen in a partial list of his personal friends or business associates: Queen Liloukalani of Hawaii, Mormon leader Brigham Young, author Mark Twain, Governor John Fremont of Arizona Territory, and Senator Leland Stanford of California. He was also either elected or appointed to legislatures in four different states: California, Nevada, Utah, and Arizona; and was present at Promontory Point, Utah on May 10, 1869, when the Golden Spike was hammered to celebrate the completion of the country's first official transcontinental railroad. Fitch then rode on "the first train through" with other prominent dignitaries. The literature on his Western legal career abounds.

Fitch's intelligence, brashness, and loud mouth brought him attention wherever he went, and he favored exciting places. No wonder, then, that he left Tucson and headed for Tombstone in April 1881, where he opened an office. When the famous gunfight erupted in October of that year, followed by the lengthy Wells Spicer hearings, the Earp faction selected Tom Fitch to handle their affairs. He did so, and although a few other attorneys were also on board, it was known to all that Fitch ran the show. His role seems to have been fairly effective, as the conclusion of the hearings was that Virgil Earp and those he had deputized were acting as normal members of an official law enforcement entity.

Fitch left Tombstone the following year and went on to his typical, fantastic legal and journalistic career in California, Hawaii, and other places, until his death in California in November, 1923. Although he was known in his lifetime as an important speaker and as a major legislator, the typical mention in historical summaries refers to his defense of the Earps in the Tombstone hearings of 1881.[96]

FLY, CAMILLUS S. C. S. Fly and Tombstone should not be exclusively linked, as he was much more than that. This Missouri fellow began his Western career in Napa, California, learned some photog-raphy, then as early as 1879 arrived in Tombstone with wife Mary ("Mollie"). The Fly career was important; he was one of the West's most intriguing photographers, capturing the lives of mining camps, Apache patrols, earthquakes in Sonora, the surrender of Geronimo, and a dozen other fascinating events in Western history. Along with this, and with his being sheriff of Cochise County for a few years, it is hard to exaggerate the career, the success of Camillus S. Fly. The literature on his work, travels, and interests is extensive.

Like others, though, even Fly realized that the Tombstone glow would eventually dim. He shifted to Bisbee in 1899, trying to continue his photographic career. He did so, but alcohol was increasingly more important to him. He died in Bisbee on October 12, 1901, and was buried in Tombstone. His wife, Mollie, herself a talented photographer, carried on the business for some time, but in 1911 moved to Los Angeles. She arranged for the quality C. S. Fly materials to be sent to the Smithsonian Institution. Mollie died in Santa Ana, Orange County, California, on February 19, 1922, but is buried in Sunset View Cemetery, El Cerrito, in Contra Costa County, California.

It is impossible to exaggerate the career of the Fly team during their varied careers in Arizona, but like most Tombstoners, they realized that the bloom had wilted.[97]

FLYNN, JAMES Irishman Flynn, at around age thirty, was in Arizona Territory in the late 1870s. By 1880 he was in Tombstone, a partner with Jim Vogan, operating a saloon on Allen Street. Details are lacking on why there was an Earp connection, but in 1881 Marshal Virgil Earp named James as one of his policemen. He often held night duty, which is when the saloon world was very active.

Within months, Officer Flynn was very busy, walking the streets and bashing a head or two, and in general was considered to be doing a decent job. After the O. K. Corral gunfight of October 1881, Virgil Earp was pushed aside and Flynn was named acting chief of police, later running for the office, but withdrawing before the election was held.

Flynn had a further bit of excitement on January 17, 1882, when on Allen Street, Doc Holliday and Johnny Ringo engaged in a shouting match that got get serious. Officer Flynn intervened and took them both to court, where they were both fined.

The last heard about Flynn was in August 1885, when he was in Tucson operating a dive called Congress Hall. His old buddy James Vogan dropped in for a few drinks to "alleviate his sufferings," and fell dead in his chair.[98]

FORSYTH, WILLIAM B. ("W.B.") and ALICE CHANDLER Forsyth and brother-in-law Ira Chandler operated the Chandler & Forsyth Cash Store a few lots east of the Fremont Street exit from the O. K. Corral (and before that on Allen Street) by early 1882, and until their store burned down in the massive May 1882 fire. Although their days there were not protracted, they did claim to have witnessed the O. K. Corral gunfight. This had a tremendous influence on W. B.'s son Victor Clyde Forsythe (an "e" was later added to the last name), who became an influential Western artist and painter of the deserts. Clyde was born on August 24, 1885, raised and educated in Orange and Los Angeles Counties of California, and was fascinated with the Forsyth-Chandler days in pioneer Tombstone.

In 1904, Clyde left home for New York City, to study at the famed Art Students League. There he met a young unknown artist by the name of Norman Rockwell, and they ended up becoming the best of friends (Forsythe would later be Rockwell's best man at his wedding), sharing Frederic Remington's studio. It was Forsythe who helped Rockwell procure his most celebrated job, after introducing him to *The Saturday Evening Post*, where Rockwell had a prolonged and distinguished career. Forsythe himself had several interesting artistic jobs, then returned to the West. Over the decades he became a leading Western artist, especially popular for his renditions for *Desert Magazine* and other Pacific Coast publications. Clyde eventually produced (in 1952) what is considered to be one of the most authentic renditions of the Tombstone gunfight of 1881 (called "the closest thing we have to an actual photograph of the event"), largely based on information passed down from his father, mother, uncle, and their Tombstone pioneer friends, as well as on his own additional research, which included a visit to the town and surrounding areas in the early 1950s. He was close colleagues with Maynard Dixon, Frank Tenney Johnson (his Los Angeles Biltmore Hotel art studio mate), Ed Borein, Nico-

lai Fechin, John Hilton, Bill Bender, Olaf Wieghorst, and Jimmy Swinnerton; all were considered major artists who knew how to present the frontier West. He died in California in 1962 and is buried next to his wife in the San Gabriel Cemetery, not far from his studio partner, Frank Johnson.[99]

Forsythe (1885–1962) poses by one of his desert works.

Western artist Clyde Forsythe, born in California in 1885, was the son of a Tombstone merchant. David D. de Haas, MD, Collection.

FULLER, WESLEY Born in Oregon in 1855, Wes Fuller wandered down to Yuma, arriving in Tombstone in the early 1880s. He would be noticed in the courts and newspapers for a decade. Fuller was a hang-around-town type, sometimes mining and usually in trouble. In April, 1881, he was in court for drunkenness and obscene language, and on October 26, 1881, was one of the six Cowboys who greeted the (lawmen) Earp party in an empty lot on Fremont Street; this of course became forever thereafter erroneously known as "The Gunfight at the O. K. Corral." Of course, not staying too long, he and William Claiborne absconded (as did Ike Clanton, albeit a bit later) before the shooting actually started, leaving their friends (Frank and Tom McLaury, as well as Billy Clanton) to die in the street fight. Fuller (and Claiborne) would subsequently testify in the newsworthy Wells Spicer O.K. Corral hearings, gaining even a bit more infamy.

In 1883, Fuller shot up a saloon on Allen Street, and in 1889, while in a merry-drunken fracas, borrowed a revolver from Deputy Sheriff Burt Alvord, and killed a man. Similar events followed; in Willcox in 1890, he served fifty days for terrorizing the town.

The post-Tombstone decades for Fuller were mostly in and around Nogales, where for some years he worked on his father's farm. In the various censuses and voter registrations he was usually listed as a laborer, occasionally as a miner. The end came for Fuller on March 24, 1923; according to his death certificate, he died of a gunshot wound in his left breast. Newspaper accounts attributed this to an accident while cleaning his shotgun.[100]

GAGE, E. B. Eliphalet Butler Gage was born in New Hampshire in 1839, educated at Dartmouth, and in the mid-1870s was in Arizona as a mining-milling administrator. He was in Tombstone from the beginning and took control of the Grand Central, and in the vibrant years of Tombstone production was probably the most important person in the community. By the mid-1880s, Gage was reorganizing, restructuring, and doing what could be done to keep the economy vital. When that seemed dismal enough, he shifted to the Congress Mine in Yavapai County and made that a substantial producer.

During his years in Yavapai County in the 1890s, Gage and his right-hand man, William Staunton, made periodic trips to greater Tombstone, buying up abandoned and promising mining properties. He was still convinced that rich silver ore was available there and hoped that new technology would overcome the severe water problems. Also while at the Congress Mine, Gage recruited some of the best foreman and miners, and when the time was right took them south to Tombstone with him.

In Tombstone's third era, between 1901 – 1910, Gage, believing the deep water and other problems of Tombstone could be solved, spearheaded the revival of that community, one of the few times in Western history that a precious metals center had more than one life. That, too, petered out somewhere around 1909-1910. Gage's few remaining years were spent in Phoenix and San Francisco, where he died in May, 1913. Of all the developers, manipulators, and administrators of what went on in Tombstone for thirty years, Gage must be considered as the major player in this important Western saga.[101]

GALLAGHER, LIZZIE Lizzie Gallagher was sentenced to fifteen months in the Yuma Penitentiary on November 18, 1878, after being tried for murder and pleading guilty to manslaughter for stabbing to death James Moriarty, a soldier from Camp Grant, Arizona, "through the heart," on May 24, 1878; this for no apparent reason ("cold-blooded act") in "a house of ill-fame" in Yuma, Arizona. When he died,

the "soiled dove" from San Francisco became newsworthy and infamous as "Arizona's first Murderess." She was pardoned early on November 22, 1879, "on account of her youth and good conduct in prison, and because a marriage to a worthy man had been arranged immediately on her liberation." That "worthy man" was named Hood, who she first met and befriended during her trial. After her release, they married and moved to Tombstone, where the newlyweds opened the Star Restaurant. It did not last long and they "disposed of it" and pushed on to Santa Fe, New Mexico, shortly thereafter. There her husband, Mr. Hood, purportedly committed suicide, "driven to it by the infidelity of his (prostitute) wife." Not long after, Lizzie "was killed in a row." [102]

GALLAGHER, PATRICK J. This Catholic priest was born in Ireland in 1844, arrived in the States in 1871, and by the early 1880s was part of the Vicariate of Arizona, headquartered in Tucson. In 1881, Father Gallagher was assigned to Tombstone, where he would remain through 1884, the original bonanza years, becoming a vital part of the new community, coordinating with Nellie Cashman and others who were instrumental in building a church and hospital for Tombstone. He also sponsored and led various community and church activities and was a major participant in the dedication of the courthouse in 1882. A few years later (1884), he was a distraught clergyman who had to assist in the program that led to the public hanging in Tombstone of five of the convicted men who had caused the Bisbee Massacre the year before.

The fact that Father Gallagher and Nellie Cashman were Irish, by far the largest ethnic group in town, does not mean that all was smooth in the Tombstone Irish community. Father Gallagher and another Irishman, Justice James Reilly, got in such a disagreement over town affairs that the two got into a fistfight, caused primarily by Father Gallagher, in which the two combatants struggled from sidewalk to saloon, and supposedly a knife belonging to the priest fell to the ground. Father Gallagher yelled at Reilly, called him "vile names," and followed him through the streets of Tombstone, finally bashing Reilly in the face. Reilly then responded, gave the priest "a good drubbing" and had him arrested. In front of Justice of the Peace Charles Clark, Father Gallagher plead guilty, and the fine and costs totaled $71.00. The priest later sued Reilly for slander and asked for $10,000 (outcome unknown). There were probably not many frontier communities that had men of the cloth in a street fight with men of the law.

In the late 1880s, Father Gallagher returned to Ireland for a visit, and then spent at least three years as a priest in the Diocese of Nottingham. By the late 1890s, he had decided to return to the American West, mostly in the San Francisco area, where until 1907 he was the chaplain for St. Vincent's Orphan Asylum in nearby Marin County. This was a large, tough institution for boys, where someone of Father Gallagher's talents were needed. There were at least two occasions where the priest appeared in court action in San Francisco, as he aggressively took the part of educators whom he felt had been wronged. From 1907 to 1914, Fr. Gallagher served the Catholic parish at Oakdale near Modesto, California, retiring in 1914 and returning to County Donegal, Ireland, in 1915, where he died on April 26, 1918.[103]

GARDINER, THOMAS Born near Glasgow, Scotland, in 1826, Gardiner joined the rush to California in the early 1850s. Gardiner was a newspaperman in the widest sense, involved in writing, editing, and promotion of all types, and always eager to start another paper somewhere. In the West, Gardiner was a key newspaper player in Portland, Los Angeles, Victoria, Tucson, San Diego, and a few other locations.

Our concern with him is that in the time between 1880-1882, in Tucson, he established the *Arizona Quarterly Illustrated*. Although short-lived, this publication put before the world some of the most iconic Western biographies and illustrations. These images of the saloons and merchant houses of Tombstone, artistic representations of Buckskin Frank Leslie and others, and views of the early Tombstone mines and mills have been used and reproduced thousands of times. Gardiner was aided in this publishing venture by Wells Spicer, the justice of the peace who would preside over the hearings regarding the O.K. Corral gunfight. The dozens of illustrations of greater Tombstone in these few issues of the *Arizona Quarterly Illustrated* are some of the lynchpins in the history of Western frontier mining and marketing.

Just a partial listing of these illustrations makes the point: views of Dick Gird and the Schieffelin brothers; the Alhambra Saloon, based on a C. S. Fly photo; Sheriff Charles Shibbell; acting governor John Gosper; and exterior views of the Golden Eagle Brewery.

On May 11, 1881, Gardiner began publishing the *Tombstone Union* newspaper in town, but it didn't last long (a few weeks), owing to the intense competition from the local papers (the *Epitaph*; the *Nugget*) already there. This, though, was a mere stop on the route for him. He went to Los Angeles later in 1881, where he was a cofounder of the *Los Angeles Times* (first issue December 4, 1881; he had a short stay). Gardiner died in Oakland on June 10, 1899.[104]

GIRD, RICHARD ("DICK") Western careers do not get much more interesting or significant than that of Richard Gird. He was one of "the three" that made Tombstone possible. Ed Schieffelin with his brother Al tagging along hit some good stuff in southeastern Arizona, and by fortunate choice they convinced Gird to join them, look the area over, see what the possibilities were. Gird, a New Yorker, had been in South America, knew much of California, and was so familiar with Arizona Territory that he had surveyed much of the place and prepared its first decent map, published in 1865.

They located, assayed, and confirmed the rich silver deposits and in the spring of 1878, organized the Tombstone Mining District, which included such well-known properties as Lucky Cuss, Tough Nut, Contention, and Ground Hog. Huge profits were made by them and a few associates. The Schieffelins had little to do with the developing community of Tombstone, as prospecting and other projects were their interests.

Gird would remain in the area through 1881 and had some impact with setting up mining and milling systems, and was involved in local government and some social and cultural arrangements for a growing population. But Gird and strong Tombstone connections pretty much ended in 1881. This complicated, fascinating saga has been especially well-presented in books and articles by Lee Silva, Lynn Bailey, and William Shillingberg.

Gird became even more relevant after he left Tombstone. Richard Gird died in Los Angeles in 1910, but the thirty years between Tombstone and his death were filled with tremendous projects, major success, and setbacks. He became a major player in financial, mining, and industrial circles in southern California and Mexi-co. His massive ranching, real estate, railroad, and sugar beet empire at Chino was the largest such project in the United States. To this day, he is known as "the Father of Chino (California)," as his ranch became the city of Chino in ensuing years. His gold and silver operations in several districts in Mexico included many mines and mills.

The financial crisis that became the Panic of 1893 was the beginning of a gradual downturn for Gird's hopes, and by the early 1900s, his various empires were near collapse. He had been a shrewd businessman and used his mining profits from Tombstone judiciously, but he was mostly undone by financial and legal situations beyond his control. By the time of his death on May 29, 1910, sadly, his estate could handle funeral costs, but not much more.[105]

GOLDWATER, JOSEPH The Goldwater family from Prussia (western Poland at that time) arrived in San Francisco in 1852 and founded some of the most significant pioneer businesses in the West. Joseph and brother Michael were early on the scene for the La Paz-Ehrenberg gold rush on the Colorado River in the early 1860s, and this gave them a head start with building their

Joseph Goldwater, a Tombstone regular, operated a store in nearby Fairbank. Southwest Jewish Archives.

Goldwaters were Tombstoners. Joseph Goldwater died in Tombstone on August 31, 1889. He is buried in the Hills of Eternity Memorial Park, a Jewish institution in Colma, California. Interestingly, this is the same cemetery in which Wyatt Earp and his wife Josephine would later be buried, in her family plot. Joseph's tombstone proudly proclaims that he died in Tombstone.[106]

GOODALE, CHARLES W. Born at the top and remaining there throughout life, Goodale's was a prominent Massachusetts family. He was born in Honolulu in 1854, where his father was collector of customs for the Kingdom of Hawaii. Charles attended high school in Boston, graduated from MIT, then headed to Colorado where, in the 1870s, he was an assayer for the Black Hawk Mining Company in Gilpin County. He would later marry the great-granddaughter of United States president John Quincy Adams.

In 1880, Goodale was enticed to Tombstone, and appointed superintendent of the Boston & Arizona Smelting Company, usually referred to as the Boston Mill. This was on the San Pedro River, a few miles from Charleston. He was there through 1885, therefore in the center of the great

Arizona commercial empire, especially in Prescott and Phoenix.

Joseph had business interests in many parts of Arizona Territory, but by the 1880s was heavily invested in products and personnel in southeastern Arizona, especially in and around Tombstone and Bisbee. He was more than a frequent visitor to Tombstone. By the end of the 1880s, he had the leading business in Fairbank, which was operated by his sons. For most of the 1880s, Joseph registered as a resident of Fairbank. Fairbank, of course, was the Tombstone railroad center, which means that the

Tombstone silver craze during the first bonanza stage. Experts like Professor W. P. Blake could theorize about the origins of the complicated ores of greater Tombstone, but it was the few, like Goodale, who had to tinker, assay, experiment, plan, and build the systems that would break down the Tombstone ores.

Charles became the authority on the weird ores of the Lucky Cuss, Wedge, Knoxville, Luck Sure, and other local mines. One of his articles after he left the field was "The Occurrence and Treatment of the Argentiferous Manganese Ores of Tombstone District, Arizona."

After Goodale left Tombstone in 1885, he shifted to Butte, Montana, which for half a century would become a world leader in copper production. From his base in Butte, he built a reputation as an innovator in the treatment of precious and base metals, becoming president and serving on the board of directors of many firms; he was a member and officer of the leading chemical, mining, and metallurgical organizations; and a member of the leading national committees regarding metal research. Goodale died in Butte in April 1929 and was returned to Boston for burial.[107]

Dr. George Goodfellow, famed Western surgeon to the gunfighters, repairer of Earp body parts, and authority on gunshot wounds. Chaput, *Dr. Goodfellow*, 1996.

GOODFELLOW, GEORGE E. Goodfellow was born in 1854 in the gold mining camp of Downieville, California, where his father was a mine foreman. He went East for an education and graduated from medical school in Cleveland. After practicing medicine in Prescott between 1877 and 1879, the same era Virgil Earp roamed the streets as a lawman (and also chairing a lecture series there, which had as one of its guests the renowned future Earp-O.K. Corral attorney Thomas Fitch), Goodfellow arrived in Tombstone in 1880, at the beginning of its bonanza days.

The interesting life of this

fellow can be followed in Chaput's *Dr. Goodfellow, Physician to the Gunfighters, Scholar, and Bon Vivant* (Tucson, 1996). He was in Tombstone for a decade, and his experiences there led him to become one of the best-known medical personalities of the frontier West. Goodfellow was an outstanding surgeon, was favored by the leading mining companies, tended to the victims of major mining accidents, saloon shootings, and countryside medical situations, and was known for his bravery, intelligence, and skill. He provided the first solid data on the serious earthquake in northern Sonora in 1887, led a relief expedition there, and was praised for his actions by the president of Mexico.

Goodfellow left Tombstone in 1889 to become the leading surgeon for the Southern Pacific Railroad in Arizona, the Arizona Territory health officer, and the author of texts on medical subjects in the nation's best professional journals. During the Spanish-American War he was in Cuba as personal physician and consultant to the man in charge, General William Shafter. Dr. Goodfellow later developed a major practice in San Francisco, which was demolished by the earthquake of 1906. He then served as the leading surgeon for the Mexican branch of the Southern Pacific Railroad. Goodfellow contracted a serious disease in Sonora, returned to Los Angeles for treatment, and died there on December 7, 1910.

Goodfellow's years in Tombstone had seen the development of his combination of skills, accomplishments, and renown that would continue to flourish in the following decades in his work in other parts of Arizona, California, Cuba, and Mexico.[108]

GOODRICH BROTHERS Ben and Briggs Goodrich were well connected Texas lawyers who arrived in Tombstone in 1880. They were talented and active in political circles and their careers are easy to follow. Ben became county treasurer as well as district attorney, and his name was connected with dozens of important events in and around Tombstone. Goodrich & Goodrich were part of the legal team hired by Ike Clanton in the Wells Spicer hearings after the famous gunfight of October 1881. By the early 1890s, Ben was an acknowledged authority on mining law and had important contacts throughout the Southwest; he opened a Los Angeles office to serve this large base of clients.

With the revival of Tombstone mining in 1903, Ben returned was an important local force, and was elected to the Arizona Territorial Legislature. This revival sputtered, however, and Ben returned to Los Angeles as his center, but continued his important career as a mining legal expert. His major client over the years was Colonel William C. Greene, who headed the rich copper production in Cananea, Sonora. Ben Goodrich died in Los Angeles on February 22, 1923.

An authority on mining law, Ben Goodrich was a leading political and legal figure in Arizona Territory and Southern California. *Press Reference*, 1915.

Briggs Goodrich in Tombstone also developed a reputation for knowledge in mining, real estate, and tax law, and after a few years there moved on to Phoenix. His sharp legal talent was quickly realized and in early 1887, he was appointed attorney general of the Territory of Arizona. Such rapid advancement for a young man unfortunately ended in June of 1888 when he died of Bright's Disease.[109]

GRAY, MIKE This Tennessee-born pioneer had a dozen or so careers before arriving in Arizona. He was in the Texas Rangers, a Mexican War veteran (serving under his friend, General Sam Houston), a miner and county sheriff in California, later mining in Mexico and Colorado. When things looked lively in Tombstone, Gray was sent to the new Pima County community in 1879 as a justice of the peace. His imprint on the place was huge, but not always in a positive way. Gray was one of that small group who concocted the Tombstone Townsite business, which led to so much controversy and wrangling over the years regarding land ownership. Gray was well acquainted with all the early famed Tombstone characters, including the Earp brothers, Doc Holliday, Ed Schieffelin, Judge Stillwell, Johnny Ringo, and Curly Bill Brocius. Gray and his family later developed extensive land

and ranching interests in Cochise County. His sons John Pleasant and Richard "Dixie Lee" Gray (who was murdered along with "Old Man" Clanton and gang in August 1881), also became well-known Tombstone figures. Mike Gray also became an acquaintance of George Hearst, General Nelson Miles, Mickey Free, Tom Horn, and Leonard Wood in his Arizona years.

Gray sort of left Tombstone, but never got too far away. He was a public man, and in a series of elections over the years convinced the citizens of Benson, Rucker, and Pearce to send him to the territorial legislature. Age and poor health caught up with him, and he died of "senility" (after an arm amputation) in San Francisco, on September 8, 1906.[110]

HAFFORD, RODERICK F. Colonel Hafford (title most likely honorary) was a Massachusetts native who left home and changed his name (he was formerly Reuben F. Hafford). By 1860, he and relatives were in Sonoma County. For around twenty years, an R. F. Hafford, who seems to have been our man, was in San Mateo County, Donner Lake in Nevada County, and Elko County, Nevada, where he was county recorder. He arrived in Tombstone in 1879-1880 with backing from San Francisco investors, and quickly established himself, occupying the first floor in Brown's Hotel at the corner of Allen and Fourth as R. F. Hafford & Co., a leading wholesale dealer in liquor and tobacco. This location figured prominently in many events and was also a favorite haunt of the Earp faction. They gathered there on their way to the famous 1881 gunfight. In the subsequent Wells Spicer hearings later, Colonel Hafford was one of the key witnesses. He also served on the coroner's jury following the shootout.

As the years passed, Hafford became fascinated with the bird life of the region, began to travel widely, especially in the Huachuca Mountains, and soon had a display of stuffed birds in his place; after 1890, he even referred to it as a museum. He was an important contact for naturalists and was frequently consulted by the Smithsonian for advice as well as specimens.

The Tombstone decline caused him to look elsewhere, and in 1896 he moved to the new Randsburg Mining District in Kern County, California, opening a business and investing in and actually working mineral properties nearby and in the Slate Range. His store experienced a severe fire, and that setback, plus the work on his mining project, was too much for the elderly fellow. He died in a Bakersfield hospital on December 21, 1900. Hafford had been a participant in the good times of two of the West's most interesting bonanzas, Tombstone and Randsburg.[111]

HAGGERTY, HUGH Born in Ohio around 1843, Haggerty served two years in the Civil War in an Ohio infantry regiment, then moved West. He was in Pima County in the late 1870s and seems to have arrived in Tombstone in 1879, where he identified as a miner. In 1880, the board of supervisors appointed him as constable to work in Tombstone, working with Virgil Earp on several occasions, and in the few years on the job, he had his share of interesting times. He was a key witness in the Ziegler murder case, joined Chief Virgil Earp in breaking up a few fights, and was on hand several times when May Woodman (who killed her husband) tried to commit suicide. In September of 1882, Constable Haggerty was sued by the volatile Emma Parker, a local madam, who accused him of confiscating her property illegally. This was a fascinating legal suit, as two brash women (Emma Parker and Inez McMartin) were squabbling over goblets, kitchen chairs, wine glasses,

and silver spoons. As constable, Haggerty was caught in the middle of the dispute.

By 1884, Haggerty was an ex-constable, back working as a Tombstone miner. When he left Tombstone is not known, but he may have been the Hugh Haggerty who was quoted in a Klondike Rush report in 1897. By 1900, Hugh Haggerty was living in Los Angeles, again listed as a miner. In that same year, he was admitted to the Old Soldiers' Home in nearby Sawtelle. For the next twenty years, Haggerty was in and out of soldiers' homes in California, South Dakota, and Tennessee. His last stop was in the Los Angeles National Cemetery at the soldiers' home in Sawtelle, where he died on April 19, 1920; he is buried in section 40, row E, number 9.[112]

HART, SAMUEL L. Hart was a native of Wisconsin and served in an infantry regiment in the Civil War. He was a Tombstone pioneer, operating as a gunsmith as early as 1880; his shop was on north Fremont Street, just east of Schieffelin Hall, where Gordon Anderson's Larian Motel resides today.

After Spangenberg left town in 1882, Hart was the leading gunsmith in greater Tombstone. He was active in community affairs, served several times on a grand jury, and was noted for his hunting trips in the Huachuca Mountains.

Like many of the merchants and professional people in Tombstone, Samuel was more than casually interested in mining and speculation. Alone, or with partners, he was involved in more than a dozen claims and prospects, none of which was significant. Hart died in the summer of 1893; even the magic hands of Dr. Goodfellow were not sufficient to save him.[113]

HARWOOD, WILLIAM A. A Cornish seaman who arrived in California sometime in the 1870s, Harwood was in Mohave County in 1878 and joined the Schieffelin brothers in their Tombstone ventures. Harwood acquired the Mizzen Top Mine, as well as some key lots in Tombstone, eventually running a lumber yard. He became Pima County's first Tombstone district-based deputy sheriff in approximately September of 1878, having first been appointed by Pima County sheriff Charles Shibell in the Signal area in January of that year. He resigned on May 22, 1879, and was replaced by Newton Babcock on June 4, 1879.

Harwood also became Tombstone's first elected mayor in November 1879 and acted through January 1880, served in the territorial legislature, and over the years held many positions of responsibility in Tombstone and Cochise County. His home was on Fremont Street, just west of the lot behind the O. K. Corral, and is often mentioned in the accounts of the infamous gunfight.

He was on the board of supervisors and served often as the county assessor. By the time of the 1910 census, Harwood had retired. He died in Tombstone on March 5, 1913, and is buried in the local cemetery; one of the original Tombstoners, he never left the place in thirty-five years.[114]

HATCH, BOB A Civil War veteran, Hatch arrived in Tombstone in 1880, and would remain there for some exciting years. Robert Hatch was a prospector, ran a saloon, liked card games, and was plugged in to the early Tombstone exciting times. Hatch was a main witness to the famous gunfight in October 1881, and although not an Earp follower, was very familiar with that faction. It was in the Campbell & Hatch Saloon in March of 1882 that Morgan Earp was assassinated, while another shot coming in from the window barely missed Wyatt Earp.

From 1883 through 1886, Hatch was sheriff of Cochise County, and either witnessed or participated in dozens of fistfights, shootings, and other goings-on in the saloons and gambling halls of Tombstone. After his career as sheriff, he continued in the active Tombstone life, mostly running the Criterion Saloon.

However, there was life after Tombstone. He shifted to Yuma in approximately 1891, and had all sorts of responsible positions, working for a time at the territorial prison, serving as undersheriff, and even served a term in the territorial legislature. He was a village marshal and as a U. S. deputy marshal. Hatch died in Yuma in June, 1904, and was identified in his obituaries as a peace officer, a reasonable description of his many years in Cochise and Yuma counties.[115]

HATTICH, BARTHOLOMEW

Hattich, a Tombstone pioneer, had a solid reputation that only increased as his son Billy became the leading journalist/editor/publisher in Tombstone. Hattich was born in Switzerland, and after stops in Kansas and Colorado, arrived in Tombstone in 1880. He was a merchant tailor, with a shop

Tombstone saloon owner and County Sheriff, Bob Hatch later headed the guards at the Territorial Prison in Yuma. Lee A. Silva Collection.

at 528 Allen Street near the Bird Cage Theatre. The Hattich family opted for Tombstone even during the mining decline. After 1890, he had more to do with mining, as he became an investor, speculator, and owner, and facilitated the purchase of many local mining properties for Easterners.

By the turn of the century, Hattich was indeed a solid citizen, active in several fraternal lodges, member of a hose company, on the city council, and serving several terms as city treasurer. He gradually became interested in Tucson and by 1910, had considerable

For years Billy Hattich controlled both the Tombstone Epitaph and Tombstone Prospector newspapers; these papers merged on August 23, 1915. Photo taken on September 4, 1915, of a last gathering of original Tombstone mining camp pioneers with the old Modoc Stagecoach on North Fremont Street (just west of Fourth Street; photo looking east toward Schieffelin Hall). Ben Traywick Collection.

rental properties there. In 1913, Hattich and his son Billy moved to Tucson. By the time of his death there in October of 1916, he was well-known throughout Arizona as Colonel Hattich.[116]

HATTICH, WILLIAM HENRY
Billy Hattich was born in Kansas on October 4, 1872, and raised in Tombstone, after he arrived there in 1881 to join his father. In 1882, as a child, he witnessed the Oriental Saloon gunfight and killing of Billy Claiborne by Buckskin Frank Leslie. William went to Tombstone's first school and

worked as a newspaper boy for the *Epitaph*, later becoming a "printer's devil" there. In the 1890s, young Hattich, after first working for S. C. Bagg in Tombstone while still in his teens, went to L. A. to work for the *Los Angeles Herald* newspaper for a year. There he learned typesetting, returning home to purchase (from Bagg in 1895), edit, and publish the *Tombstone Prospector* and *Tombstone Epitaph* (actually living in the *Epitaph* building on the north side of Fremont) until 1915. Along the way, he wrote about his community, having known many of the people and events from his childhood, and was able to present immediacy not available to many writers. Probably his best publication was the 1903 pamphlet that the *Prospector* published at the beginning of the important Tombstone mining revival. In 1964, just before his death, his second book, *Pioneer Magic*, was published.

Hattich was not only a major figure in Arizona journalism; he was soaked in the ink and legacy of the business. The printing press used by the *Nugget* in 1879 and by the *Epitaph* in 1880 was the pioneer machinery of the profession and Arizona's very first; this press was originally used in Tubac's *Weekly Arizonian* in 1859 before it shifted to Tucson, then to the bonanza town of Tombstone. In the 1930s, Hattich arranged for the printing press to go to the Arizona Historical Society, where it is now a major artifact of Western journalism.

Hattich wrapped it all up in 1915 when he retired to Los Angeles. According to a very flattering editorial in the *Times* of September 5, 1915, he retired "with the good will of the whole State of Arizona," and hoped that the change in climate would give him some added years. People familiar with the history of Tombstone will know the name of Hattich because of his long association with the local newspapers. Yet, at the time of his death at age 93, on November 4, 1964, he had been a resident of Los Angeles for forty-eight years. Good friend and Earpiana historian/collector John Gilchriese labeled Hattich "a living encyclopedia of the history of Tombstone," and one of the last links to its past. After his passing Gilchriese, who served as University of Arizona field historian, would arrange a journalism scholarship to the university in Hattich's honor, for distinguished writing.[117]

HAYNE, MARCUS PETER Hayne was a district attorney of Newark, New Jersey in 1881, when he was invited to be city attorney in the mining bonanza town of Tombstone. He would remain only two years, but was involved with a major incident of frontier history.

One of his first important tasks was to work with the authorities in Prescott to obtain a village charter. But of much more significance, Hayne was the fellow who drafted/concocted the "firearms in town" ordinances that led to the gunfight at the O. K. Corral. It may not be clear as to the various voices and factions regarding these ordinances, but attorney Hayne turned them into reality. The ordinance regarding "deadly weapons" was adopted on April 19, 1881, and appeared in the *Tombstone Epitaph* of June 29, 1881, signed by V. W. Earp. It was cited that fateful day ("I want your guns") by Chief Virgil Earp as his reason for confronting the Cowboys.

From Arizona, Hayne moved to Minnesota, where he had an important career as a leading lawyer. He died in Minneapolis in January, 1899, and at that time had been president of the Minneapolis Baseball Club for some years.[118]

HEARST, GEORGE A native of Missouri, Hearst became a Western mining mogul, with his first successes in Nevada and California, and with the great gold production of the Homestake in Dakota Territory. His base was San Francisco, and he often entered projects with the other leading metal men of the West, especially James Ben Ali Haggin and Lloyd Tevis. All three were also speculators in another sense, owning some of the best racing horses in the country.

In early 1882, when Tombstone was in bonanza, he gave it a look, making several trips to the town, and also had his leading point man, John Sevenoaks, on the scene. The news accounts of the Hearst visits were enthusiastic, hoping, of course, that such a major player would become part of the silver boom. Yet Hearst never substantially believed in Tombstone mines. He bought, or at least invested in, some gold and copper properties in the Winchester District. He also bought the Contact claim towards the San Pedro River. This was supposedly promising because at one time, Dick Gird and the Schieffelin brothers owned the rights.

J. H. Jackson, an important local mining figure, and Heyman Solomon, a Tombstone banker, accompanied Hearst on some of the exploratory trips, even into New Mexico. The *Epitaph* would write of Hearst's third visit to Tombstone and of his "protracted stay among us," but Hearst never put big money into Tombstone-area projects. In the Hearst world, Tombstone was either not important enough, or else Hearst realized that it was too late to get the best properties.

Hearst became a U. S. senator a few years later, and until his death in 1891 was one of the best-known men in the country. His racing stable was outstanding, he was a senator from California, and, in the Homestake, owned the most successful gold mine in American history. His son, William Randolph Hearst, would carry on, and go on to remarkable accomplishments and worldwide notoriety in politics, newspaper publishing, and other businesses. [119]

HERRING FAMILY In the legal world, in nineteenth-century Arizona, this is the family that presents the most interesting, detailed life of the legal and mining events that led to the territory being so important in Western mining history. There is a tendency to think of William Herring, Bisbee, and copper as being the most important topics associated with this family. That will work, but to omit the important Tombstone events would miss a vital part of Arizona's' mining history. William, a New Yorker convinced of southeastern Arizona's significance and the future of silver and copper, and needing to handle the affairs of his recently-deceased brother Joseph (part owner of the Neptune mine in Bisbee), arrived on the scene in Tucson in early March 1880, and was in Tombstone by March 4, 1880. He was into what became the important silver and

Sarah Herring, daughter of a prominent lawyer and a product of the Tombstone schools, became a leading Western mining attorney. Public Domain.

copper deposits in Tombstone and Bisbee, which would lead to one of the most significant developments of this industry in the American West.

William became the attorney of note in Bisbee and Tombstone, and for a time the Herring & Herring firm of Tombstone was the firm of choice for those interested in the best legal representation. In the aftermath of the O. K. Corral Gunfight, Herring was in the area. It was Herring, acting on behalf of the Citizens Safety Committee, that persuaded Wyatt Earp to leave the territory so that things could settle down and the law could get things sorted. For around fifteen years, Herring kept offices in both Tucson and Tombstone. The George Parsons diaries for four or five years have hundreds of notices of the Herrings, as he was a frequent dinner and game guest at their home.

In one of the more bizarre arrangements in Western legal history, John Heath, mastermind of the "Bisbee Massacre," who was subsequently lynched by an angry Tombstone mob in 1884, gave his saddle and Colt revolver in payment to his attorney, William Herring.

Herring's son Howard Ford Herring, also an attorney and in practice with dad, died in a ridiculous dental episode on November 1, 1891, in Tombstone. Only twenty-seven years old, he was operated on by Dr. William Victor Ludwig Warnekros, and overdosed on the cocaine administered for the procedure. A grand jury dismissed the ensuing case against Warnekros, and he remained a career dentist, practicing in California in 1892, and also spending time in Hermosillo, Mexico. He returned to Tombstone to reconcile his affairs in May of 1893, and then shortly thereafter (1894), departed once again,

this time for good. In the ensuing two decades, Warnekros' brother, Paul, became greater Tombstone's largest holder of real estate. The Herring family didn't appear to hold any grudges against Paul, as their law firm subsequently represented him in several legal proceedings, including defending him in a defamation suit brought on by prominent rancher William C. Greene in January of 1898; this was dismissed in May of the same year. After being acquitted of the blatant murder of Justice James Burnett, Greene claimed Paul had defamed him in the newspapers.

Daughter Sarah Herring taught school in Tombstone, then studied law at New York University,, becoming the first female attorney in Arizona and one of the best-known mining attorneys in the Southwest. Her marriage to Thomas Sorin, a founder of the *Tombstone Epitaph*, did not hinder her reputation. Sarah and Thomas, although mostly associated with Tucson and that city's legal life, continued to live in Cochise County and were plugged in to the life of Tombstone and the many events there. Sarah was admitted to practice before the U. S. Supreme Court, becoming only the twenty-fourth female to do so. She died in Globe on April 30, 1914, at that time involved with an important mining case.

Another daughter, Bertha, spent most of the period from 1880 to 1900 in Tombstone. She attended the local school, and later taught there as well as in Tres Alamos. In 1894, she opened a notary public office in Tombstone, on Toughnut Street, which she operated for a few years. After 1900, the Herrings were mostly in Tucson, but it was constant business travel for Bertha and her father as they courted the Tucson-Tombstone-Bisbee clientele. After her father's death, Bertha moved to the Venice area of Los Angeles, where she died on October 13, 1925.[120]

HERRING, MARCUS F. No relation to the other Herring clan, Marcus Herring was a Kentuckian who was early in the West, served four years in the Civil War with the 5th California Infantry. By the mid-1870s, he was mining in Pima County. Herring had a bit of fame even before he arrived in Tombstone. In 1878, before there really was a Tombstone, he was one of the few prospectors and miners working around what would become Bisbee. According to leading pioneers of the era, it was Her-

ring who gave the name "Copper Queen" to what would become one of the country's leading copper mines.

By the early 1880s, Herring was in Tombstone, listed as a miner, and would remain throughout the decade. Herring may have had a position of foreman, or a boss of some sort, as from time to time he was buying and selling mining claims worth a few thousand dollars.

In 1891, Herring called it quits and moved to California, where he was admitted to the Old Soldiers' Home near Santa Monica. Shortly after 1900, his monthly pension was raised from $8 to $12, which is a good example of period values. He died at the Old Soldiers' Home on May 22, 1910, and is buried in section 17, Row F, Number 8; L. A. National Cemetery.[121]

HICKS, JOHN This fellow is important in Tombstone lore as one of the first to be killed in a shootout and said by some the first to be buried in Boothill, in July of 1879. Jerry McCormick, superintendent of the Lucky Cuss, was arguing with a man named Quinn, supposedly over a prostitute. The feud, fueled by whiskey from Danner & Owens Saloon, led to a fistfight. A few hours later, Quinn and friend John

Hicks saw McCormick, and the arguing was renewed. Hicks went, got his brother Boyce, and they returned with rifles.

Five shots were fired, Hicks was killed instantly, and his brother, at the time said to be "fatally wounded," actually survived but was blinded for life. Within minutes, Deputy Sheriff Babcock was on the scene, arrested folks, and an inquest was held over the dead body, in the saloon of Fatty Smith. The death was caused "by the hand of an unknown person." The working theory here is that McCormick, as a mining superintendent, had the law on his side.[122]

HOLLIDAY, DOC John Henry "Doc" Holliday needs little attention here, as his life and careers have been a staple of writing about the West for more than a century. The Georgia-born dentist may have gone West for his health, but if so, it was not worth the trip. A little dentistry in Texas and Kansas was mostly a sideline to gambling and drinking. His close association with Wyatt Earp stems from those days. Although he did not immediately follow the Tombstone-bound Earp party, remaining in the Prescott, Arizona saloons and gaming tables, Holliday finally rejoined them all in Tombstone on September 27, 1880, ten months after the Earps first arrived.

His Tombstone period was 1880-1882, and in that time, Holliday participated in some extraordinary frontier events. There was considerable gambling; shooting affrays and other confrontations (with the likes of Johnny Ringo, Ike Clanton, and the McLaurys); squabbles with Milt Joyce and other local notables; and finally, the famous street fight of October 26, 1881. When deputized by Marshal Virgil Earp, Holliday, Wyatt Earp, and Morgan Earp confronted the Clantons and McLaurys near the O. K. Corral.

The aftermath included the long Wells Spicer hearings, the revenge-filled vendetta, the bodies of Curly Bill, Morgan Earp, Frank Stilwell, and a few others, and with the ambush of Marshal Virgil Earp. By March of 1882, Holliday's Tombstone days were over, and Colorado would be the locale of his few remaining years.

He didn't make huge waves in the Colorado saloons and gambling halls, though he did wander here and there, leading up to a noteworthy stay in Leadville that included more gunplay. Alcohol was never far away, and he finally settled for the hot springs of Glenwood Springs, maybe hoping for a cure or at least something better. He got neither, and died there on November 8, 1887, only thirty-six years old. One can ignore the sensationalized movies and television portrayals of this unusual frontiersman, as well as most literature, and instead read Dr. Gary Roberts' heavily researched biography, *Doc Holliday: Life and Legend* (2006), which thoroughly examines and documents the entire career of this renowned character.[123]

HOOKER FAMILY Henry Clay Hooker, a New Hampshire-born Westerner, became one of the more important ranchers of the Southwest. His adventurous climb to success and his hard times in California and Arizona have attracted several historians, notably Lynn Bailey. His Sierra Bonita Ranch of Cochise County was a model of how to run a cattle operation.

Hooker's place was important by the late 1870s, precisely when Tombstone came into bonanza. Hooker was not a Tombstoner; however, as a major figure in the county, he was a frequent visitor to the community, for business and legal reasons. In the 1880s, there were usually ten to twenty merchants specializing in meat, and Hooker was usually the major provider for these businesses. As early as 1880, Hooker and butcher Apollinar Bauer established the meat market of Hooker & Bauer, at Fourth and Fremont near the back entrance to the O. K. Corral.

Because of who he was, Hooker was closely allied with the leading mining and political forces in town—men like E. B. Gage, J. V. Vickers, and John Clum. It is not surprising that the Earps, the law-and-order faction, were backed by Hooker. When they were roving the countryside tracking their Cowboy antagonists, Hooker gave them encouragement, as well as comfortable accommodations. He didn't do the same for Sheriff Behan and his cowboy posse.

The Hooker family gradually developed closer ties with Los Angeles, for schools, for vacations, and eventually for a place to live. Henry died in there in 1907. Another interesting connection with Tombstone was his daughter-in-law, Forrestine Hooker. She became a writer, worked for the *Los Angeles Examiner* newspaper for a time, and around 1919 interviewed Wyatt Earp for what she hoped would be the "inside story" of the Cochise County saga. She did finally produce something, but the result was garbled, fantasy Western history.[124]

HOWARD, JAMES G. This New Yorker began practicing law in Los Angeles in 1865 and within a few years was one of the most successful attorneys in Southern California. He was also a U. S. commissioner, and had dozens of high-profile cases, many of them controversial. Usually known as Colonel Howard, or "Big Jim" Howard, the fact that he went to Tombstone in 1880 is an indication of how attractive that town's prospects were; Howard was only one of a few dozen lawyers flooding the place. It is no exaggeration to mention that when James arrived in Arizona, he was being discussed as the replacement for Governor Fremont.

Much of his work was performed in the law office of J. W. Stump in the *Epitaph* building. The most newsworthy events of Howard's two years in Tombstone involved his connection with the Earp faction. By the time of the shootout, he was in partnership with Webster Street, and the Earp family had Howard and Street as part of the legal team headed by Tom Fitch. Howard may have had some off-stage advice during the Spicer hearings, but it was hard to crowd Tom Fitch away from the spotlight.

In 1882, the Earps were in financial trouble, as Morgan was dead, Virgil wounded in ambush, and Wyatt just about broke. Wyatt mortgaged his home to Howard, who turned over $365 in gold to him, payable within three months. Wyatt had no way to pay back this debt, so he lost the property to Howard.

In his two-year Tombstone stay, he made frequent trips back to the obviously more lucrative Los Angeles practice. By the end of the decade, though, Howard faced a divorce, the death of a daughter, and the deterioration of his health. He died in Los Angeles on September 15, 1890. His reputation was such that Glassell, O'Melveny, and other leading lights of the Los Angeles Bar Association arranged the funeral.[125]

HUME, JAMES B. Hume, one of the more important law-and-order figures of the West, was not a full-time Tombstone resident *per se*, but was important in various ways during the first Tombstone bonanza era. He had been a peace officer in Placerville, sheriff of El Dorado County, then in 1871 joined

106

James Hume, noted Wells, Fargo detective, was a victim of an embarrassing stagecoach robbery enroute to Tombstone. *Sacramento Daily Record-Union*, January 9, 1882.

Wells Fargo as a detective. He would be associated with Wells Fargo until his death in Berkeley in May, 1904.

Hume had been to southern Arizona in the late 1870s on business. In March of 1881, the Kinnear stage was held up on the Benson-Tombstone run near Contention, and two passengers were killed. This was a key event in the "troubled times" of Tombstone. Hume arrived in Tombstone on March 19, 1881, to help in the investigation. He worked closely with U. S. Deputy Marshal Virgil Earp, and Wells Fargo provided funds for the posse, which included such stalwarts as Bob Paul and Wyatt Earp. During his time in Tombstone, Hume was in the company of Sheriff John Behan frequently, and later commented on this lawman with scathing prose.

The following year in San Francisco, when Virgil was recovering from wounds after an assassination attempt, he was presented with a five-star gold star to, "City Marshal, Tombstone, A. T., V. W. Earp, with Compliments of Wells, Fargo." This was obviously the doings of Detective Hume.

The next Tombstone chapter for Hume was embarrassing. In early January 1882, he was investigating the January 6 Bisbee stage robbery, in which a Wells Fargo strong box was robbed when, as a passenger on Sandy Bob's Benson-to-Tombstone stage run, the stage he was on was stopped and robbed by four bandits. Among the loot were two revolvers taken from Hume—the Wells Fargo chief detective. In this same period, February 1882, Hume, from his San Francisco office, realized that the financial statements from Tombstone were fuzzy. It turned out that Marshal Williams, the Tombstone agent for Wells Fargo, was cooking the books. Williams found out about the investigation and hurriedly left town (with some female companionship).

Some accounts claim that Fred Dodge was an undercover agent in town for Wells Fargo, but no evidence has ever surfaced to back these accounts. As the Tombstone mine production lessened, the community was seldom of importance to the Wells Fargo San Francisco office anymore, nor to Detective Hume.[126]

HUNSAKER, WILLIAM J. Hunsaker was born in Contra Costa County, California, in 1855, into a pioneering family. He moved to San Diego, studied law, and practiced there from 1877 through 1880, when he shifted to Tombstone. He was one of many lawyers in town

W. J. HUNSAKER

Tombstone attorney William J. Hunsaker later handled some legal affairs for Wyatt Earp and wife Josie in Los Angeles. Hunsaker was president of the California Bar. *Press Reference*, 1913.

and remained less than two years. He did establish a relationship with the Earps, however, which would come into play in the future.

His father, Nicholas, lived in Tombstone for a time, but eventually established a major cattle ranch in the Swisshelm Mountains. Nicholas died in 1913. William's brother, D. N. Hunsaker, was editor of the *Southwestern Stockman* in Willcox, and also a justice of the peace.

After his stay in Tombstone, William returned to San Diego, became district attorney, then moved to Los Angeles. In the coming decades, Hunsaker developed into one of the most significant attorneys in southern California, especially noteworthy for his knowledge of mining and railroad law. It was not by accident that one of his law partners for years was Ben Goodrich, that talented attorney from Tombstone. In 1904, Hunsaker was head of the Los Angeles Bar Association, and later president of the California Bar Association. He subsequently became a consultant to leading state and local agencies on a variety of topics, and also handled much of the financial and legal work for Josephine, Wyatt Earp's widow. Hunsaker died in Los Angeles on January 13, 1933.[127]

HUNT, ZWING Hunt was one of the cowboys who floated from Texas to New Mexico to southern Arizona in the early 1880s. Early in 1882, Deputy Sheriff Breakenridge heard that some cattle were being "borrowed," so he went with a posse and interrupted the work of Zwing Hunt and Billy Grounds. Quite a gunfight ensued at the Chandler Milk Ranch, Grounds was rubbed out as was posse man John Gillespie, and a few others were wounded. There is also strong evidence that this incident was actually precipitated by the murder of Martin Peel (please see his entry for full details) in Millville on March 25, 1882, by Hunt and Grounds. The two were most likely heading for Mexico, fleeing Wyatt Earp's Vendetta Posse, who were on a rampage and had gunned down fellow Cowboy, Curly Bill Brocius, just the day before.

Hunt, shot in the breast, was taken to Dr. Goodfellow's hospital in Tombstone. There he was apparently near death. Goodfellow believed that Hunt was in such bad shape that he couldn't even be moved. However, within days Hunt's brother Hugh showed up from Texas with a wagon, and in a "quiet" period at the hospital, Zwing was placed in the wagon, and the Hunt brothers hastily vamoosed from town.

On April 29, the *Tombstone Nugget* carried this notice from the Huachuca Mountains:

My regards to County Physician Goodfellow. He is really and truly a goodfellow. Every time he touched my pulse I howled like a bedlamite. The truth is, no ball passed through my left nor any other kind of lung. I am today as sound as a roach. Tell the Sheriff to recall his men. I am over the line.

That's a good, cocky story, but apparently soon after this communication, the Hunt brothers were overtaken by Apaches, and Zwing was killed (a body was found). This was not one of the brighter chapters in the career of Dr. Goodfellow.[128]

HURST, JOSEPH HENRY Hurst, an army officer, an immigrant from England, is usually identified as Lt. J. H. Hurst in the many Tombstone accounts. He figures in reports of 1880, when mules were stolen, the McLaurys were named as "participants," and the Earps were in pursuit. This happened in the environs of Camp Rucker, near the

Chiricahua Mountains, and the Earp brothers inter-faced with Lt. Hurst. There is a heavy literature on this event, and whether or not the McLaurys were guilty of any crime, the Earps seem to have been convinced that the McLaurys were involved.

Hurst later had an interesting, though not dynamic, military career. He was a captain in the Wounded Knee events in Dakota Territory. J.H. Hurst died in retirement in Pennsylvania in 1896.[129]

HUTCHINSON, WILLIAM J. and LOTTIE   Billy and Lottie Hutchinson were entertainers, the key people associated with Tombstone's Bird Cage Theatre on Allen near Sixth Street. Billy was a Texan, a miner, and early on the Tombstone stage. The Sixth Street Opera House burned down in the June 1881 fire, so he built the Bird Cage, which opened on December 24, 1881. The Hutchinsons would run this affair for only two years, long enough to establish a reputation as a place with rowdy, dirty miners, rough cowhands, and in general a crowd prepared to fight, clap, roar, and howl during performances.

Hutchinson's preferences and loyalties were easily gauged in the aftermath of the

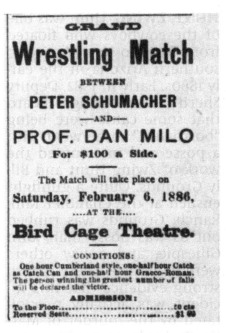

Not only "high culture" was presented in the Bird Cage Theatre. *Tombstone Daily Epitaph*, January 30, 1886.

famous gunfight of October 1881. He was one of the bondsmen for Doc Holliday, siding with the townsfolk against the rural factions.

The Bird Cage had no regular hours; something was going on morning, noon, and night, and many of the "acts" were brought in from San Francisco. This was not a place to bring Mom or Dad or the kids, as the audience could get boisterous, sometimes violent. The Bird Cage deserves its reputation as a venue for the male mining, gambling, and cowboy crowd. The classier acts, to which one could take the fam-

The Bird Cage in 1940, glory days long gone. Library of Congress.

ily, would be held in the Schieffelin Hall, a bit removed from the saloons and gambling area.

In spite of the fact that 1883 was still considered a bonanza year for Tombstone, things were changing, many men were out of work, and attendance fell sharply at the Bird Cage. In August 1883, newspapers in Tombstone, Phoenix, and Tucson reported that Billy Hutchinson considered the dull times semi-permanent, so he sold the place (July 1883) and moved elsewhere. Of note is the fact that during their years in town, William and Lottie were known to be quite charitable, and helped their fellow citizens and town in any way possible. The theater they built was iconic; it still stands and is known the world over to

this day.

The Hutchinsons shifted to Tucson, and for a time in late 1883 and early 1884 may have presented some acts in Tucson at Levin's Park Theater. Apparently, what was a hit in Tombstone was not engaging many folks in Tucson. In June, 1884, the newspapers listed Billy and Lottie Hutchinson with "unclaimed letters" at the local post office.[130]

INGOLDSBY, FRANK S. Ingoldsby, an Ohioan, was in Tombstone as early as 1880. He worked with engineers and surveyors and apparently had considerable artistic talent, along with M. Kelleher and M.R. Peel creating a detailed map of the Tombstone Mining District, along the four borders of which he sketched some of the more prominent mining structures as well as town buildings. The map was printed in San Francisco in December, 1881. Most people who have read about historical Tombstone have probably viewed Ingoldsby's map, one of the more noteworthy of those of Western mining camps.

Ingoldsby remained in Tombstone for a few years, did some mining, went on an Apache posse or two, but by 1885 had shifted interests elsewhere, to Phoenix and Tucson, procuring several major contracts because of his outstanding draftsman skills.

The rest of Ingoldsby's career began with a long stretch in Creede, Colorado, where he designed a new type of wagon for ore. In later years he moved back to the Midwest, and in both Michigan and Ohio held important administrative positions with industrial and railroad manufacturers. Ingoldsby also wrote a book on railroad economics. In failing health, he moved to Pasadena, where he died on November 12, 1919.[131]

ISRAEL, SOL Hamburg-born, by 1880, Israel was in Tucson, Arizona, working for L. Zeckendorf. He early moved to Tombstone, where his steady income was from running the Union News Depot in the Grand Hotel Block, and selling stationery and other office supplies. Israel was also a prospector, mining investor, wanderer, and a practical joker. He sought excitement, and if it were lacking, tried to create it, sometimes planting

The Vizina mining property included part of downtown Tombstone. Ingoldsby, *Map of the Tombstone Mining District*, 1881. Library of Congress.

humorous (sometimes nasty) letters in the local papers, trying to stir things up. For a few years he handled the entertainment arrangements at Schieffelin Hall. To get Israel's slant on things, when Stuart Lake was doing research for his Wyatt Earp project, Israel wrote, "Johnny Behan, he was afraid of his own shadow."

Israel closed shop in 1888 and tried a variety of places and businesses in Arizona, northern California, and even in Seattle for a few years. By 1900, though, he was settled in Los Angeles on West Seventh Street. What he did there varied with the times and the law, selling books and stationery and also "liquids." At least five times between 1905 and 1916, Israel was either warned, fined, or closed down for liquor violations. Of note is the fact that the Earp family were intimately involved in the same (bootlegging, blind pigs, speakeasies) in this time period in nearby Sawtelle, California. By the time of the census of 1920, Israel was listed as "agent, soft drinks." One knew where his heart was. When he died in Los Angeles in late March of 1931, in the death notice his relatives stated, "Tombstone, Arizona papers, please copy."[132]

JACKSON, JOHN HENRY Jackson was born in Ontario, Canada and was mining in Oregon when he learned of the Tombstone silver strike. He arrived in spring of 1879 and for the next few years, living mostly in Tombstone, mined at Contention, the Dragoons, and probably a few other locations. Early in 1882, Jackson was appointed a U. S. deputy marshal by Governor Tritle, to succeed Virgil and Wyatt Earp. He served as a guide and bodyguard for George Hearst and party when they left Tombstone (on January 14, 1882) for the Dragoon Mountains and surrounding areas and back, and again in April of 1882 when they traveled from Tombstone to Deming, New Mexico, to inspect mining/ranching opportunities. During the same period, the Arizona Rangers were formed, mostly of Tombstone personnel, and Jackson became captain of that territorial militia unit. They did some Apache chasing, but not much else.

Soon after, Jackson left Arizona for San Francisco, then traveled up to Oregon. Once again, he was associated with the law, and he served as sheriff of Tillamook County from 1894 to 1898. Around this time, he was attracted to the gold news from the Klondike country, but spent a few fruitless years there. He aimed further south, settled in Escondido near San Diego, and died there on May 16, 1905.[133]

JACOBS, LIONEL M. Lionel Jacobs was born in England in 1840, but the family moved to Baltimore within a few years, then on to California early in the Gold Rush, 1851. They were in merchandising and banking, and Jacobs and brother Barron became pioneers in the banking life of Tucson. They arrived as merchants in 1867 and their Pima County Bank was founded there in 1879.

Soon after the Tombstone silver discovery, Lionel Jacobs invested in the merchant life there, and within a few years had established one of the community's leading financial centers, its first bank, the Agency Pima County Bank, in May of 1880. It was later renamed the Cochise County Bank, after the county name change, in 1882. The bank was housed in the store of, and run by, P. W. Smith with Barron Jacobs (born 1843 – died 1936), and later with Heyman Solomon as cashier. This building, where not only the Earps banked, but also the Clantons, McLaurys, E. B. Gage, and so many famed others involved in Tombstone's 1880s glory years, still stands today as the town's visitor center, on the southwest corner of Fourth and Allen Streets. Until just very recently, one could still read the word "Bank" through the layers of modern-day paint on the building. The original 1880s vault is there to this day, and currently used as a tourist brochure storage area and employee coat closet. Jacobs went into the bank project with major backers, including Pinkney Tully and E. B. Gage. This bank would last through 1889, when the mining downturn and scares in the silver market were too tough to combat.

During these years, Lionel Jacobs was a resident of Tucson, but was in Tombstone many times a month. Like some physicians and attorneys, bankers often kept offices in both communities over a period of many years.

The Jacobs influence in Tucson and Arizona in the following years was major, and can't be overemphasized, as the family controlled the Bank of Arizona, and Lionel was active in many political and social groups and a member of the Pima County Board of Supervisors. He was also a legislator and served a term as the territorial treasurer. A little-known but important point is that the sister of Lionel and Baron was married to prominent frontier merchant Morris Calisher, and therefore they were uncles of Tombstone businessman David Calisher. Although Lionel retired in 1913, he continued to take an interest in family banking matters. He died in San Francisco on February 7, 1922.[134]

JEFFORDS, THOMAS J. One of the most famous Westerners, Jeffords was born in Ohio in 1832 and had important careers on the Great Lakes and in Colorado before arriving in what would become Arizona Territory. For half a century he would be involved in major events mostly in and around Pima County, which would include the new Tombstone mining camp. Over the years, Jeffords was a prospector, a U. S. Army scout, an Indian agent, a mine owner, and so forth. He was also part owner of the Brunckow Mine, from 1875 through the mid-1880s, which figures in the Tombstone saga.

Jeffords was prominent in one of the rare periods of American history when Native Americans and incoming settlers had periods of peace and understanding. The late 1860s/early 1870s relationship of Jeffords with the Apache leader Cochise is the stuff of legend, and has become a staple of literature (the book *Blood Brother*), film (1950s *Broken Arrow.* starring Jimmy Stewart as Jeffords, and *The Lone Ranger*'s Jay Silverheels as Geronimo), and television (in a 1956 series). Their meetings, their arrangements, and the good will with General O. O. Howard, were unusual events in frontier history.

In the 1880s, Jeffords was in and out of Tombstone dozens of times, as he had mining interests in the Huachucas, Dos Cabezas, and in the Chiricahuas. His permanent base was in Tucson, but he still needed Tombstone as his mining base. In the voting register of 1884, he was listed as "mining man, Tombstone."

Although "Apaches" and "Cochise" are the hallmarks of the Jeffords career, he was indeed part of the Tombstone vital life during the bonanza era. His subsequent years saw him involved in prospecting, mining, and ranching, mostly in the Tucson region. He died on his ranch near Tucson on February 19, 1914, and is buried in Evergreen Cemetery, Tucson.[135]

JOHNSON, "TURKEY CREEK" JACK (JOHN WILLIAM BLOUNT) Blount was born in Missouri in 1847, and he and brothers had a nasty reputation there, robbing, shooting up a town, and so forth. They did some mining in Missouri, later around Prescott, but were usually in trouble. Blount seems to have met Wyatt Earp in Tombstone in early 1882, where he was known as Jack Johnson. He leaned on Wyatt to put pressure on territorial officials to pardon his brother, in the pen for murder. He was pardoned, and possibly Wyatt had some influence, as both he and Virgil Earp had been commissioned by Crawley Dake, the U. S. marshal of the territory, and Dake was partial to the Earp family. It is known that Wyatt knew Johnson well in Tombstone, and Wyatt's racehorse there, "Dick Naylor," was the name Johnson had used for a racehorse earlier in Missouri.

After Virgil Earp was ambushed on Allen Street in December 1881, Wyatt was deputized as a U. S. marshal and gathered around him a few tough customers to protect his family and to pursue vengeance. Jack Johnson was one of these tough, experienced frontier types. On March 22, 1882, Johnson was a member of the Earp Vendetta Posse in the Tucson railroad yard where the riddled body of Frank Stilwell was found; and two days later, when Floren-

tino Cruz was killed, it was noted that Johnson was part of the avenging party. Days later, at Iron Springs, when a gun battle led to the disappearance of Curly Bill, "Turkey Creek" Jack was also on hand. These incidents led to inquests that tied the killings to the Wyatt Earp posse, and Johnson was an important part of the killing crew.

After resting at Hooker's Sierra Bonita Ranch, the posse broke up and headed to New Mexico, then on to Colorado, where Johnson had relatives. He seems to have shifted his focus then, as for a few decades, under the name John Blount, he was a farmer or a miner in San Diego, Calico, Yuma (1900), Bisbee, Jerome, and finally Walker, Arizona. According to family sources, he died in Walker, Yavapai County, in 1906, and is buried near Prescott. He had lived and farmed in San Diego County, California (with his wife Kate and three sons, per the 1900 census) for some years. His wife and sons are all buried in Prescott, where they lived after Johnson/Blount's death. It is extremely intriguing to ponder the fact that the surviving Earp family were not far away, in Sawtelle and Los Angeles, California, during some of Blount's later (San Diego) years.[136]

JONES, HARRY B. Exotica could be used to describe this career. The Georgia-born Jones was in Tucson as a notary public in 1874 and practicing law in Phoenix in 1879. This was not your run-of-the-mill lawyer. In May of that year, he was arrested after a brawl with a teamster; Jones had shot the fellow "through the hand." By 1880, Jones was a Tombstone dandy, practicing law and closely associating with the saloon-faro folks.

Jones pushed himself to the front. His law office was on Allen Street, between Fourth and Fifth. He was a power in local Democratic party politics, elected to the city council, and when Tombstone's first fire department organized, Jones was named its first president; Wyatt Earp became secretary.

Jones and Wyatt Earp were involved in one of the West's premier legal events in 1880, in the court of Justice James Reilly. In this complicated mess, an irritated Justice Reilly grabbed attorney Jones by the throat, but Deputy Sheriff Wyatt Earp, nearby, separated them and arrested Justice Reilly. Days later there was more legal action, warrants, and fines, and this time Deputy Earp took Jones to jail in Tucson, where he was re-leased. Deputy Earp was later taken to court, and so on. This is a case study in courtroom decorum.

Other activities in this era brought Jones in frequent contact with the town and rural factions. He and wife Kitty were close with Sheriff Behan, as well as Behan's girlfriend, Sadie Marcus, who would spend her life with Wyatt Earp. It seems likely that it was Jones who introduced Sadie to Wyatt. Jones figured also in the run-up to the famous gunfight. On the morning of October 26, when Wyatt entered the Oriental Saloon, Jones warned him that Ike Clanton, with Winchester and revolver, was on the hunt for him.

By 1883, Jones had departed Tombstone due to a dismal downturn in his fortunes, and ended up in San Francisco in 1884 as a streetcar conductor. The tide turned once again when his mother had died and he inherited some decent money. The Jones couple eventually settled in Colusa County, California where, in addition to practicing law, Jones received the appointment as justice of the peace in the Williams District. "Judge Jones" died there on February 8, 1923.[137]

Cochise County Supervisor Milt Joyce was a saloon operator and rancher and was involved in many of the exciting events of the bonanza era. Ben Traywick Collection.

JOYCE, MILT Joyce was Irish or Irish American, probably born in Massachusetts, and was in California in the 1860s. He was a blacksmith who picked up a lifelong interest in mining environments, spending some time in the Panamint District near Darwin, California. He heard about the Tombstone doings and was one of the early arrivals in 1879. His place was the Oriental Saloon, where he controlled the gambling and restaurant offerings. Every name in Tombstone lore spent some time here; Lou Rickabaugh, the Earps, Buckskin Frank Leslie, Doc Holliday, Bat Masterson, Luke Short, Johnny Tyler—the list would be a local who's who. It was the location of wild card games, drunken rows, occasional shootings, and other non-gentlemanly affairs. Joyce was no milquetoast, getting in a pistol confrontation with Doc Holliday, and once berating Virgil Earp, for which he earned a slap in the face.

He also joined the Arizona Rangers and was captain of a band of these volunteers, who made a few unsuccessful forays after some Apaches who may or may not have been guilty of something. These were not glory-filled romps.

There were other worlds for Joyce at this time. He served on the Cochise County Board of Supervisors, was an early member of the fire department, and a few miles away got control of the Magnolia Ranch, where he spent quite a bit of time. After 1883, when Joyce began his San Francisco period, he had Buckskin Frank Leslie handle most of the ranch affairs, but returned to Tombstone a few times to check into his businesses.

For four years Joyce was one of the key players in the social and political life of Tombstone. If one just followed his activities, many Tombstone slices of life would be explored.

His San Francisco days were off to a quick start when, with former Tombstone associates Vizina and Orndorff, he opened a billiard parlor in Lucky Baldwin's famed Baldwin Hotel. Joyce also got married early in 1889. But the clock had run out on this fellow of forty-two. He had a heart attack and died on November 29, 1889. The Tombstone and later period must have been decent for Joyce, because his estate was worth around $30,000.[138]

KELLEHER, MICHAEL Born in New York State in 1844, Michael Kelleher was an officer in a New York regiment during the Civil War, and in Los Angeles by the early 1870s. He served as city surveyor during 1875-1878. When the Tombstone silver discoveries occurred, Kelleher soon made his way to Tucson. In 1880, he opened offices in Tucson and Tombstone and had much mine surveying work. From 1881 to 1883, he served as the Tombstone city surveyor, sharing office space with attorney Wells Spicer.

Kelleher, an acknowledged authority on mining and engineering and a key figure on the two most important maps of the era, *Map of the Tomb-stone Mining District* (December 1881), and *Map of the City of Tombstone* (July 1881), was also a consultant on the sewer situation. He was a severe critic of the townsite crowd, pointing out that they lacked documentation and were often contradictory in their claims.

By 1884, Kelleher was back in Los Angeles, where he handled huge tracts for real estate development and farming. In the coming years he worked as a civil engineer, surveyor, or mining consultant in San Bernardino and Bakersfield, but was mostly connected with Long Beach. He was retired by 1920 and died in Los Angeles on October 23, 1922.[139]

KELLY, JULIUS A. Famous before, during, and after Tombstone, he was from Indiana, and by the early 1870s was associating with mining mogul Lucky Baldwin. Kelly was superintendent of the Gold Mountain Gold Mine, later clerk at the Ophir in Virginia City, helped established the Baldwin Hotel in San Francisco, and was superintendent of Lucky's Santa Anita Ranch near Los Angeles. By 1879, he was also the deputy collector of the U. S. Internal Revenue Department.

Kelly floated into Tombstone in 1880 well-heeled and

well-liked, and opened the Kelly Wine House on Fremont, one door from Fourth Street. In this adobe building he sold wine, liquor, tobacco, had billiard tables, and even displayed ore samples from the Brunckow Mine, of which he was part owner. Doing so well, he opened a branch saloon at 418 (South) Allen, between Fourth and Fifth Streets, west of the Grand Hotel, selling the Fremont location in September, 1880. Kelly was big in Republican party politics and secretary of the Tombstone contingent. The *Arizona Daily Star* referred to him as "mine host, a jolly, smiling, genial gentleman, did the honors in fine style."

Aside from the elaborate place he operated, Kelly also figured in the events of the famous shootout. On the morning of the street fight, an angry Ike Clanton visited the Kelly Wine House on Allen Street, and in the presence of Kelly, who was tending bar, Clanton complained of the Earp crowd, who along with Doc Holliday had insulted him. Kelly cautioned Clanton about "having any trouble," but Clanton was not to be stopped. These words and attitude would become part of Kelly's testimony in the Wells Spicer hearings.

Kelly's great career in Tombstone fizzled quickly. In early 1882 he was seriously ill, near death; and upon his recovery in March, he sold the main building to Dr. Gilberson, who intended to add a story to the structure. The Kelly residence on Fremont went to Ben Goodrich for $500. In early May of that same year, auctioneer S. C. Bagg sold all of Kelly's household furniture. Julius moved on, back to Los Angeles, where he was again very successful.

He had a variety of investments, was city tax collector, and by the mid-1890s he was a notary public as well as vice-president of the Guaranty Abstract Company. Sounds like a successful life, but in 1897 his wife divorced him. He quickly remarried, but on May 11 of that same year, the *Los Angeles Herald* reported, "Julius A. Kelly Blows Out His Brains." His new wife was wealthy, and Kelly had used her money to open an impressive new saloon, which quickly failed. Our "jovial mine host" had closed the books.[140]

KINNEAR, JOHN D. For a few years during the first Tombstone bonanza era, the Kinnear name was one of the most commonly heard in the district; he operated the main stage line. Kinnear was a native of

Kelly's Wine House on Allen Street was one of the fancier gathering places for sports. Ike Clanton hung out here, making threats against the Earps and Doc Holliday, on the morning of the gunfight. *Arizona Quarterly Illustrated*, April 1881.

Ohio, had farmed and served as a deputy sheriff in Colorado, worked for a time in Silver City, New Mexico, then shifted to Pima County in 1878 with the Tombstone discovery.

Kinnear operated the first stage line between Tucson and Tombstone, going via the Benson route. For these first great Tombstone production years, the Kinnear & Co. coaches were how most people arrived and left the mines and town. There were other attempts at running stage lines, but Kinnear was the leader, in the same way that hauling ore was associated with another famous Western name, Remi Nadeau.

It is hard to exaggerate Kinnear's role in the Tombstone saga. During this era, Tombstone was a vital center, yet there was no railroad service. If you traveled, it was most likely via a Kinnear vehicle. And it was a Kinnear stage, with Bob Paul riding shotgun, that was attacked in March 1881 on the Benson route, when driver Bud Philpot was killed. That attack, and the subsequent posses, were some of the key events of the Earp faction-Cowboy rivalry which culminated in the O.K. Corral Gunfight and subsequent Tombstone historic events.

In the 1890s John married and operated a cattle ranch in the Whetstone Mountains. He later also mined for a time in Pinal County. Tired out, Kinnear opted for the Pioneers' Home in Prescott, where he died in September of 1916.[141]

LAING, JAMES ARTHUR This has got to be the oddest, most exotic personality who ever lived in Tombstone. Laing was born in Scotland in 1843, was in business in London in the 1860s, then in the 1870s in darkest Africa, in Zanzibar; he personally conveyed the body of the renowned explorer Dr. Livingston back to London. He was also involved in another renowned adventure, joining the explorer Stanley on his Niger expedition. Laing was a fellow of the Royal Geographical Society, and by 1880 was in the American West, in the boomtown of Tombstone.

He was to be a Tombstone fixture for six years, referred to and identified as a "clerk," a "searcher of records," particularly interested in land and mining, and he made frequent trips from Tombstone to surrounding venues. On one occasion Laing prepared a detailed report on the mines and mills at Arivaca, Sonora, Mexico, for his Arizona audience.

He was not just a paper-and-pen fellow, as might be expected from his African adventures. In 1885, in a meeting in Tombstone, Laing was hired by A. G. Faye to go to Sonora and superintend the taking down of a stamp mill to be shipped elsewhere. James enjoyed living in Tombstone, but in 1886, when the entire works of the Grand Central Mine were destroyed in a fire, he decided to look elsewhere.

Laing was soon in San Diego where for a decade, on Fifth Street, he operated an office as "searcher of records,"

specializing in taxes and land titles. Things improved considerably for Laing in 1895, as he inherited a half million dollars from an aunt in London. He traveled quite a bit and settled in Hawaii, dying there in February of 1906. His obituary appeared in hundreds of newspapers throughout the world, often with the heading, "Companion of Stanley Dead." His six-year stint in Tombstone was not enough to make the papers.[142]

LE VAN, WILLIAM A. (BILLY ALLEN) These were just a few of the names associated with one of the more interesting fellows of early Tombstone. He was a prominent resident, owned the Le Van House, and was a prospector and investor in local mining claims. Billy was also a Civil War deserter, a crook in Colorado, and a man whose saloon-centered life was associated with Western mining camps, skullduggery, and crime.

Allen, a true Tombstone pioneer, was there by 1879, and soon connected with Wyatt Earp, Doc Holliday, Jim Leavy, and others in some mining claims that led to considerable legal action; these were the Hattie, the Last Decision, and the Intervenor properties. Le Van was not an associate of the Earp crowd, though he did have these mining connections with them.

Billy's real claim to fame came after the gunfight near the O. K. Corral, as he was the star witness for the prosecution. The other main witness was Ike Clanton, an acknowledged blowhard whose testimony lurched toward the absurd. Le Van (whose true credentials were not known at the time) seemed like a level-headed witness, who claimed the McLaury-Clanton fellows were trying to surrender and had their hands on the way up. Regardless of Le Van's fine courtroom presentation, Justice Wells Spicer decided that the faction led by Chief of Police Virgil Earp was acting legally on behalf of the community's citizens.

The subsequent Le Van career resembled his previous years: mining, saloons, and operating boarding houses. He was in New Mexico, Los Angeles, Calico (San Bernardino County), Mariposa, and finally Merced, California, where for the last few years was penniless and senile; he died in the county hospital there on October 20, 1930.[143]

LEAVY, JIM Born in Ireland in 1842, Leavy became one of the most respected and feared gunfighters on the frontier. He first came to notice in Ne-

vada at the mining camp of Pioche. Leavy was a miner and killed a fellow in a noted duel there in 1871, later moving on to mining camps in Montana, Wyoming, and Dakota Territory. By this time, he did little mining, but was mostly a "sporting man," meaning he spent most days and nights in saloons, gambling. It is more than likely that in his Montana and Dakota travels Leavy met with Morgan Earp.

The Leavy career showed little Tombstone time, but it was interesting. When he arrived in 1881 it was, of course, to the world of saloons and gambling tables where Leavy gravitated. There, he became more than closely associated with one of the leading gamblers, Dick Clark, and also spent much time with Wyatt Earp and Doc Holliday.

These friendships extended beyond the saloons. Leavy had several different dealings with Dick Clark regarding mining claims and mineral rights. And with Wyatt Earp and Doc Holliday, he invested in mining claims and water rights in the Huachuca Mountains.

That's pretty much all there is to the Jim Leavy-Tombstone connection. He soon left town and went to Tucson, where he was ambushed on the street by three would-be frontier heroes, and killed, on June 5, 1882. The Leavy name, however, that of a first-class gunfighter, had that important connection to Tombstone in its bonanza phase that included such Western icons as Dick Clark, Doc Holliday, and Wyatt Earp.[144]

LESLIE, BUCKSKIN FRANK
Nashville Franklin Leslie (maybe; we don't know his origins, nor his eventual demise). But the in-between stuff is Western dynamite. His doings in Tombstone alone make the Earp years seem like early childhood play. He was a San Francisco bartender who arrived in 1880, was in the saloon business, a near constant gambler; he killed a rival (over a woman) which led to one of Arizona's longest trials. In November of 1882, facing Billy-the-Kid-Claiborne holding a rifle, Buckskin Frank drilled him. According to diarist George Parsons, Buckskin did this "without losing the ash of his cigar."

The years following his time in and around Tombstone were also filled with drama. He ran the Magnolia Ranch for Milt Joyce from time to time, served as an Army scout in several expeditions into Mexico, killed his woman then tried to blame another fellow, and on and on.

Leslie went on to spend some years in Yuma in the ter-

Buckskin Frank Leslie, Army scout, shootist, saloon operator, braggart, and Territorial Prison alumnus. *Arizona Quarterly Illustrated*, July, 1880.

ritorial prison, but continued to be in the limelight, because that was his need.

The following decades were spent lying and wandering, sometimes as a guide in Mexico, other times seeking a living in San Francisco and elsewhere. In his declining years he stocked grocery shelves, even swamped out a few saloons to make a living. It may be that it was *his* body found near Healdsburg in 1927, which is the point of view of DeMattos and Parsons in *They Called Him Buckskin Frank* (2018). It was all in a continuum, from Tombstone to the end. He was brave, intelligent, a trusted scout, a liar, a prodigious raconteur, nervy, a well-known wife-beater, and a great traveling companion.[145]

LIGHT, HAM Readers interested in Tombstone history have come across this name frequently. Charles Hamilton Light was not only a key witness in the Wells Spicer hearings of 1881, he was also the district's main ore hauler and the leading blacksmith. Ham had worked in mining and freighting in Mohave County, Arizona, and in 1880 moved operations to the Charleston-Tombstone area. The many mines of Tombstone had no mills; those were built at sites along the San Pedro River. Light's huge wagons with sixteen-mule teams controlled most of this traffic for the decade.

During the Earp-Cowboy street fight of October 1881, Light saw some of the action from the window of his home at the corner of Third and Fremont. His testimony not only included details on the number of shots, but also on the position and movements of some of the participants.

After 1890, Light was elsewhere, mining and freighting in Harqua Hala (where he may have run into old Tombstone associates Wyatt Earp and Nellie Cashman), the Quijotoa District, even Globe. He final-

ly settled near Gila Bend, Arizona, did some mining and ranching, and had a respectable fruit ranch. The ranch buildings caught fire in April, 1897, and Light was fatally injured while trying to rescue some papers.[146]

LUCAS FAMILY John Henry Lucas was born in Indiana, headed west, and never looked back. Somewhere along the way he studied law, and in the 1860 census was listed as a lawyer in Iowa. In 1870 he was practicing law in Elko, Nevada, and in the 1880 census he was listed as a lawyer in the San Antonio District of southern Los Angeles. Shortly thereafter, he and several other lawyers had an office in Tucson, with a branch office in Tombstone. That would be the Lucas location for the next decade. In addition to his law business, Lucas was also a probate judge.

The Lucas office was in the Mining Exchange building. On the morning of the famous gunfight, John witnessed some of the action from his office window, and he was later to testify at the Wells Spicer hearings. In particular, Lucas gave details about the whereabouts and position of Billy Clanton during the affray. In the days and months to follow, as a lawyer and judge, Lucas was involved with participants from both Earp and the cowboy factions, regarding suits, arrests, confinements, and so forth.

It is not clear when Lucas left Tombstone, but from 1890 the trail is harder to follow. For most of these years he is listed on many records as a lawyer, practicing in Alameda County, California, where a daughter lived. Yet, at least from 1906 through 1910, Lucas was listed, and very active, as a probate judge in Globe, Arizona. By 1920 he was back in Alameda County, living with his daughter Carrie, and retired. He died there on February 12, 1924.

His daughter Fanny was listed in the 1880 census of Los Angeles as a teacher, age twenty. In January, shortly after the family arrived in Tucson, it was mentioned that Miss Lucas left for Tombstone, hoping to establish a school there. The *Arizona Weekly Citizen* of February 21, 1880, mentioned that Miss Lucas had started her Tombstone school (the first in the community), with a daily attendance of thirty-six.

The lawyer crowd in Tombstone (there were many) were leaders in getting an education system going. Territorial law stipulated that the probate judge in each county was ex-officio superintendent of schools, which meant that in theory, Fanny's boss was her dad, Judge Lucas. The next teacher in this first Tombstone school was Lucy McFarland, sister-in-law of William J. Hunsaker, an attorney in town.

Fanny Lucas was also mentioned in April of 1880 as serving as a post office clerk. Her teaching career, though, was short-lived. By 1883 she was Mrs. Everett J. White, living in Los Angeles. The couple went to Chicago, then to Fremont, Nebraska. A newspaper in 1890 mentioned that White, of Gibson & White, music dealers, was moving to town. He opened a business as a piano tuner. Fanny died in Fremont on March 19, 1891.[147]

MASTERSON, BAT Few frontier figures are better known than Masterson, yet he is seldom connected to Tombstone. He was there for a brief period, but those were exciting times.

The Quebec-born Masterson had been raised in the Midwest, and in the 1870s was in the thick of things with his brothers in the cow towns of Kansas. He was a major player in and around Dodge City, holding several lawman positions, and was an associate of Wyatt Earp. Saloons, gambling,

126

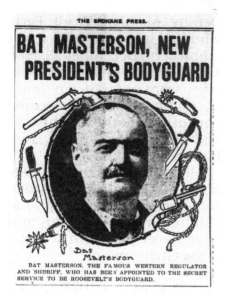

THE SPOKANE PRESS.

BAT MASTERSON, NEW PRESIDENT'S BODYGUARD

Bat Masterson

BAT MASTERSON, THE FAMOUS WESTERN REGULATOR
AND SHERIFF, WHO HAS BEEN APPOINTED TO THE SECRET
SERVICE TO BE ROOSEVELT'S BODYGUARD.

Bat, a close associate of President Roosevelt. This Dodge City friend of Wyatt Earp spent some exciting weeks in Tombstone in 1881. *Spokane Press*, December 16, 1905.

whorehouses, cattle drives; this was the environment of many of the "sporting men" of the day.

The Earps moved on, and in early 1881 Wyatt invited Masterson to come to Tombstone; not necessarily for a friendly visit, but the rural/cowboy crowd was restless, and Wyatt believed that Masterson could be of help.

Masterson arrived at the Oriental Saloon and it was indeed a Dodge City reunion. Soon thereafter occurred an encounter between Dodge's Luke Short and Charlie Storms, on Allen Street on February 25, 1881. Masterson tried to calm the fellows (Storms was a bit tipsy), but revolvers were drawn, and Storms was killed.

The next month was the significant hold-up on the stage, where Bud Philpot was killed; this became a key event in the Earp time in Tombstone. Posses were formed, and Bat Masterson was one of those deputized to track the stage robbers. They were on the trail for more than ten days, without success. The Wells Fargo records indicate that "B. Masterson" received $32 in July 1881 for "pursuit stage robbers." This ended the Masterson stay in Tombstone, as he had learned that his brother Jim Masterson in Dodge City was in dire need of assistance.

The following decades of the Masterson career were as exciting as ever. He served as a lawman in several Western jurisdictions, moved East, and became one of the more prominent sportswriters of New York City. He was a close friend of President Roosevelt, who gave him a federal appointment as deputy U.S. marshal of the Southern District of New York, and from time-to-time Masterson wandered West as a journalist to cover some of the most famous boxing bouts in America. On several of these occasions he had reunions with Wyatt Earp and other frontier types. Masterson died in New York City on October 25, 1921. In 1955, the lead character "Sky Masterson," portrayed by Marlon Brando in the hit movie *Guys and Dolls* (based upon the successful Broadway musical), was patterned after Bat.[148]

MATTHEWS, HENRY M. Dr. Matthews was born in Virginia in 1825 and had years of experience as an army and reservation physician in Arizona before he moved to Tombstone in 1879; he was also the local coroner. In spite of the greater glory of Dr. George Goodfellow, Dr. Matthews in many ways was key to the medical doings of Tombstone in its bonanza years. There were a dozen or so medical men in town, but Matthews and Goodfellow decided most things, and they worked well together. Matthews was not very active in local affairs, although he did participate in some Republican party doings.

Dr. Matthews, sort of an average frontier physician, has earned international recognition related to the O.K. Corral Gunfight. He was the lead physician at the scene, tended the bodies, took inventory, and did the typical coroner's work. In a later incident, Dr. Matthews assisted Dr. Goodfellow as they operated on the arm of U. S. Deputy Marshal Virgil Earp, who had been shot in a street ambush on December 28, 1881. These events meant that obscure frontier physician Henry M. Matthews would become part of the worldwide history and lore related to the Gunfight at the O.K. Corral.

He died in February 1886, and is buried in the Tombstone cemetery. His wife and several children lived in St. Louis and were never part of his Tombstone environment.[149]

McCONE, ALEXANDER J. One of the giants of the Western mining machinery industry, in the 1880s McCone was in Tombstone for a few years, where with James McAllister he began the Tombstone Foundry. McCone left after a few years for the Reno area, operated large machinery works, and was a power in the Nevada legislature. He later shifted to similar industrial activity in San Francisco and Los Angeles.

When James McAllister left Tombstone for Los Angeles, he again connected with McCone to form a large foundry concern there. McCone was also a partner in one of the country's largest retail hardware concerns, Harron, Rickard & McCone, specializing in mining supplies. The McCone story is a broad one across Arizona, Nevada, and California, and always successful.

Alexander McCone died in Los Angeles in early October 1920 and was buried in San Francisco. His son, John A. McCone, became one of the stars of America's twentieth-century life, as chairman of the Atomic Energy Commission and director of the CIA.[150]

McCORMICK, HALE McCormick was a native of Missouri and was mining in Leadville, Colorado, when he decided to join a party headed for the new bonanza at Tombstone. On December 24, 1880, they arrived in a covered wagon. Included in the group were Chris Robertson and his wife Alice, the future parents of Ethel Robertson Macia, who for almost a century was a Tombstone stalwart.

McCormick worked for many mines over the years, either as a foreman or as a trouble shooter. In April 1898, for example, he was hired to work with a crew to open the Black Diamond Mine in the Dragoons. When the Tombstone Consolidated headed the new revival in the early 1900s, Hale was one of the first foremen they hired.

After leaving Tombstone Consolidated, McCormick, although elderly, remained in mining. In February 1905 he took a crew of fifty men to work the Arizona Consolidated claims at Russelville in the Dragoons. McCormick died in Tucson on May 6, 1909, and was returned to Tombstone for burial. His obituary in the *Epitaph* praised his many decades of leadership in local mining.[151]

McLAURY FAMILY Robert Findley ("Frank"), Thomas Clark ("Tom"), and William Roland ("Will") McLaury were born in New York, raised in Iowa, spent time as cowboys in Texas, and as early as 1877 were in the part of Pima County that was later sliced off to become Cochise County. Robert and Tom were cattlemen, working for various ranches around greater Tombstone. There was little significant about their personalities or their activities. They were part of the "cowboy" crowd, which to some Tombstoners meant a combination of thievery and drunkenness. There was no long list of McLaury crimes. They were chummy with the Clanton family, and this resulted in the incident that came to be known the world over.

A series of events related to differences of opinion and

the legality of carrying arms in the city limits led to the confrontation on October 26, 1881, known as the Gunfight at the O.K. Corral, in which the Earp law faction killed Frank and Tom McLaury and Billy Clanton. In the subsequent hearings before Justice Wells Spicer, William McLaury, a Texas attorney and brother of Robert and Tom, was in Tombstone urging justice for his brothers.

Those interested or not yet familiar with the above can feast on thousands of books, magazine and newspaper articles, as well as a mountain of television and movie productions, as this has become one of the world's most familiar events. The words "Tombstone," "Earp," "Doc Holliday," "Clanton," "McLaury," and "O.K. Corral" are known from Moscow to Tokyo to Singapore to Cairo.[152]

McMASTER, SHERMAN This fellow was in Tombstone for a short period of time, but it was quality time. He was a native of Illinois, served in the Texas Rangers for a few years, then was in greater Tombstone early on, mostly among the cowboy crowd. There were some rumors of rustling, and a stage robbery near Globe was connected with him.

It seems likely that McMaster may have met Wyatt and Doc Holliday in Dodge City, and it is certain that McMaster, while in the Texas Rangers, had known Curly Bill (a prisoner at the time). By 1882, McMaster was in Cochise County and had shifted to the Earp faction and was in on several parts of the well-known vendetta carried out by Wyatt Earp. McMaster was on hand in the Campbell & Hatch saloon when Morgan Earp was killed. When the Earp posse eliminated Florentino Cruz for an alleged role in Morgan's death, McMaster was one of the avengers. And, at the Iron Springs episode, where Wyatt most likely killed Curly Bill Brocius, McMaster was present, even sustaining a minor wound in the shooting. He was also part of Wyatt's group when they temporarily rested at Hooker's Sierra Bonita Ranch. From there the Vendetta Posse moved on to New Mexico and Colorado. Beyond these events little is known of McMaster. There were many rumors of his subsequent death, but there is recent credible information that he died in Colorado in 1892.

The McMaster name appears in all of the vendetta literature, so much so that to know the name is to think of riding and shooting. We should remember that these fellows did other things. Morgan Earp was assassinated on the evening of March 18, 1882. Earlier in the evening, McMaster had joined Morgan, Doc Holliday, and Dan Tipton for viewing (and applauding) *Stolen Kisses*, a musical comedy at Schieffelin Hall.[153]

MEAGHER, JOHN G. Wyatt Earp worked closely with John Meagher in Sedgwick County, Kansas, where John was sheriff. John's brother was Mike Meagher, town marshal of Wichita, and Wyatt's boss. Wyatt worked closely with a (different) John Meagher in Tombstone, too. The problem, for the historian and the general reader, is that there were too many on the frontier named John Meagher.

The one that concerns us, John Gregory Meagher, was born in Kingstone, Ontario, in 1845, and very active in the Pacific Northwest by the early 1870s. A sporting man mostly, by 1878 Meagher was in Sierra County, California, where he identified himself as a speculator; this was prime gold mining country. By early 1880, Meagher was in the new boomtown of Tombstone, Arizona Territory.

A saloon man and part of the fast, sporting life of the community, after the fire in June of 1881, Meagher joined Lou Rickabaugh in raising money to rebuild the Oriental Saloon (and give Wyatt Earp faro tables to oversee). In the town-rural alignment, there was no question about John's loyalties. When Big Nose Kate had Doc Holliday arrested in 1881 on a charge of stage robbing, Wyatt Earp and John Meagher were two of the sureties for Holliday.

In the coming years, Meagher also had an interest in the Alhambra Saloon. One public notice appeared in 1886 when he insisted that the *Epitaph* correct its columns, as he was not a member of the Anti-Chinese League. In that same year he and a few others were arrested for "swindling at games of chance." Meagher was a regular at John Doling's racetrack, often handling the purse.

In July 1888, John returned from San Francisco, part of a syndicate to bet on the presidential election. He would bet $10,000 against the $8,000 of Charley Leach, the general manager of the Grand Central. At the end, Meagher backed out of the bet, for which the *Epitaph* laughed at him. This is the type/amount of money often associated with "sporting" men.

Meagher may have hobnobbed with the main figures of town, but not always to his benefit. One legal suit, overseen by Sheriff John Slaughter, was when Dr. Goodfellow in 1889 brought charges of $438 against Meagher; the suit simmered for a few years.

In 1889, as Tombstone's flame dimmed, Meagher headed for Seattle. For a few years the newspapers reported on his doings, which were similar to the Tombstone pattern, for a gambler who had major real estate interests. He was charged in a bogus check scheme in 1891, and in 1895 was the leading man in a "Big Lottery Raid." He was also part owner of the Turf Saloon. By 1900 he was in real estate, living with brother Henry and family. The end for John Meagher was quite complicated. The Seattle man died in Paso Robles, California, on March 5, 1909, then was cremated in Portland, Oregon, and his ashes were buried in Salem, Oregon, the hometown of his wife, next to her grave. His legacy included son Henry G. Meagher, a Hollywood bootlegging baron who was killed in a shootout in 1933.[154]

MEHAN, ANDREW J. Mehan was a Canadian who seems to have been in Tombstone as early as 1880. He was associated with saloon life, law and order,

and mining, which means that over the years he was fairly well-known locally. Mehan was a saloonkeeper who testified at the Wells Spicer hearings after the gunfight of October 1881, saying that Tom McLaury had turned in his pistol prior to the gunfight. In 1885-1886, he was a Tombstone constable, and even during those years was interested in prospecting and mining investments.

For the next few years, Mehan was prospecting in Arizona, New Mexico, and Mexico. At the time of his death in Albuquerque, November 1892, he had been in New Mexico for a few months, trying to interest Easterners in a silver-gold property.

Andrew also figured in one of the West's most important mining cases, that of Martin Costello and the rich copper deposits in the Bisbee-Douglas-Warren region. At one time, apparently, Mehan had been "given the paper" to the Irish Mag claim, one of the rich deposits concerned in this legal wrangle.[155]

MELLGREN (MELGREN), JOSEPH L. Born in Sweden in 1844 and in the West by 1860, he and his wife were Tombstone pioneers. His main interests were saloons and mining. In the rural-town troubles of 1881, Joseph was closely allied with the Earp faction. When Doc Holliday was arrested on a stage robbing charge, Mellgren joined Wyatt and John Meagher as sureties for Holliday. Mellgren owned the Alhambra Saloon between 1880 and 1884 and would also own the Elite Saloon in Tucson, as well as the Oriental Saloon in Tombstone. In 1885, shortly after buying the Oriental, he advertised regularly for assessment work on local mines. Mellgren was city treasurer for a few years in the 1880s, then for some years was the fire chief, as well as chief engineer.

Mellgren decided that Tombstone was his destiny, and over the decades did what he could to make a living. By the turn of the century, he had shifted to mining, and by 1911 was one of the local "chloriders" who worked mostly waste dumps. In 1923, he was one of the Tombstone mining men who closed production. By 1928 he was listed as "hotel man" in the voting register, dying in Tombstone on April 15, 1928. Captain Vallernar G. Mellgren, his son, was in combat in France in World War I, and in the 1920s ran a concentrator on the old Silver Thread Mine in Tombstone.[156]

MITCHELL, ALEXANDER J. Exaggeration is impossible when summarizing this career. Mitchell was born in England in 1867, was a prominent surveyor-engineer in Sydney, Australia, owner of a hotel in Tucson in 1878, and the fellow who surveyed and prepared an excellent map of the mills along the San Pedro River in 1879 for the Tombstone mines. He was then a Tombstone surveyor, assayer, mine owner, close friend of Sheriff Charlie Shibell (who later sued him), was arrested on a perjury charge and taken to Tucson in 1879, and in 1882-1883, was part owner of the Total Wreck Mine. There is too much more to add. By mid-1885 he was looking over prospects in Aspen, Colorado, then in the early 1890s mining, surveying, and doing much more in Yuma County, Arizona.

Mitchell moved to a new world in 1900, to Los Angeles, high finance, and a power in coastal banking and manufacturing; as well as in marine construction, a copper factory, and a dozen other things. Usually referred to as Commodore Mitchell, he owned several award-winning yachts, and earned prizes up and down the Pacific Coast. He was on the board of a dozen major firms, usually as a director, sometimes as an officer.

Tombstone connections? Absolutely. Most of his businesses were in and around the harbor at San Pedro. For years Mitchell was the largest shareholder in the State Bank of San Pedro. The president of the bank was L. W. Blinn, the Tombstone lumber dealer who Mitchell knew very well in the early 1880s. At the time, Blinn was the largest lumber dealer in Southern California. Mitchell retired around 1920 and died in Los Angeles on August 28, 1929.

There is another weird connection here. The first major job for Mitchell in Arizona was in 1879, surveying and mapping the San Pedro River; and the last thirty years of his life would be spent in San Pedro, California.[157]

MITCHELL, JOHN S. This fellow, who became the key hotel man in California, got his start by tacking his career to that of the Bilicke family in Tombstone. John Mitchell was born in Sacramento in 1858, had a good education, did some mining in California and Arizona, then arrived in Tombstone in the early phase of the bonanza. He worked at the Cosmopolitan for the Bilickes, then pretty much followed their lead as they headed to California.

In California, Mitchell was soon plugged into all aspects of hotel life, including management, supply, and insurance. He was the manager of the Hollenbeck Hotel, director of the Alexandria Hotel, head of the Bilicke Rowan Fire Proof Building Company and, aside from A. C. Bilicke, was the leading hotel man in Los Angeles. For years he was the president of the Southern California Hotel Men's Association. After Bilicke's death, Mitchell moved to northern California, where he again was a prominent hotel figure as director of the Cliff House in San Francisco. John Mitchell died in Los Gatos on January 21, 1941, and is buried in Olivet Memorial Park, Colma.[158]

MONTGOMERY, JOHN This native of Ohio was in the California excitement of the 1850s, then tried his luck in a few other Western states and territories. He was in Tombstone as early as 1879, and with Ed Benson opened the O.K. Corral on Allen Street. In addition to the usual livery business, they also handled large supplies of hay and grain. Within a few years, Montgomery was the sole owner.

While not flamboyant,

Montgomery was active in Republican politics and served several terms as a Cochise County supervisor. For Montgomery, Tombstone appeared to be the chosen land, and he died there on May 26, 1909.

The low-key nature of the fellow was not to be his legacy. The O.K. Corral became remembered as the site where the Earp faction faced the Cowboys in the gunfight of October 26, 1881. Throughout the world, the name "O.K. Corral" has become synonymous with "shootout/gunfight/street fight," "Tombstone," "Wyatt Earp," "Doc Holliday," and the "Wild West" (the gunfight actually took place *near* the rear entrance to the corral, not *at* the O.K. Corral itself).[159]

MOSES, THOMAS Moses, who served in a Colorado cavalry outfit in the Civil War, had a long, notable Western career. For most of the 1870s he was in Virginia City, Nevada, at first in mining, then serving a few terms as a justice in the police court.

Shortly after the 1880 census, Moses moved with his family to Tombstone, where for a few years he operated the Capitol Saloon at the corner of Fourth and Fremont. Judge Moses was a man about town, attended various weddings and public functions, was an officer in the Knights of Pythias, and even tried to get elected as town recorder. He also had local mining interests, as well as a gold and copper investment in Sonora.

Moses got some first-hand knowledge of things, as he was a member of the coroner's jury following the O.K. Corral gunfight, dealing with the McLaury and Clanton bodies. They ended up declaring that indeed, the Earp faction had caused the deaths of Billy Clanton and the McLaury brothers. By 1884, however, Thomas left town, trying Colorado, then California, before settling for Seattle. For a time, 1895 to 1896, he was in the Old Soldiers' Home near Los Angeles, but went home to die in Seattle on March 17, 1896.

The Moses angle has an additional intriguing aspect. His daughter Kate married John E. Clancy. The Clancy Brothers controlled most of the gambling action in Seattle and also in Skagway and other Klondike "resorts." When Wyatt Earp used Clancy's facilities to run faro games while escaping the winter at Nome, Catherine, the widow of Thomas Moses, was at home preparing dinner for John Clancy.[160]

MURRAY, WILLIAM B. Murray was from New York State, and in the 1870s out West, investing in Nevada mines with Frederick Tritle. They did quite well, and when the Tombstone silver mines became known, they both headed for southern Arizona. From Tucson, they opened an office of Tritle & Murray in Tombstone in 1880, with Murray pretty much running the show. They were stockbrokers and knew what they were doing.

The role of Murray helps to illustrate how folks were considered in the cowboy-urban situation in Tombstone. On the day of the big gunfight, Virgil Earp was In Hafford's saloon. It was known that trouble was brewing with the Cowboy gang, and Murray looked around the bar and suggested to Earp that he could raise twenty-five men if needed. Earp thanked him, but declined the offer. After the shootout, when things looked bleak for the Earps, Murray was a leader of the Citizens Safety Committee. The fact that he was so closely aligned with Governor Tritle is a further indication of the rural-urban situation in Cochise County.

In June 1882, however, Murray was looking elsewhere, and he moved to some more promising projects near Prescott in Yavapai County. That was apparently not the answer, because in January 1885, Governor Tritle announced that he had learned that his former partner Murray had died of consumption in Hermosillo, Sonora, Mexico, while there investigating mining prospects.[161]

NADEAU, REMI This fellow may be the most well-known hauler or freighter of the West. He made a fortune in the 1870s hauling silver and lead bars from the Cerro Gordo mines of Inyo County, California, down to Los Angeles, where they were shipped to San Francisco for refining. His use of teams, stations, and watering holes were later copied by other freighters. Nadeau's status was such that he built the first four-story hotel in Los Angeles, which had the first elevator. He also had the largest vineyards in the Los Angeles area.

As early as 1879, Nadeau went to Tombstone, talked things over with E. B. Gage of the Grand Central, and made some mining investments. In one transaction in November of 1881, shortly after their famed gunfight, he bought part of the Mountain Maid property from Virgil, James, and Wyatt Earp.

Nadeau did make an arrangement to haul Grand Central ore to the mills on the San Pedro River in 1881. From Los Angeles he had brought over twenty-three wagons and sixty-four horses. And that's the end of the brief Nadeau Tombstone saga. No information has surfaced to explain his departure. He had the experience, the animals and equipment, and in 1880-81 Tombstone was almost in its full bonanza stage. Although he sold his outfit and animals to James Carr and J. E. Durkee in Tombstone, Nadeau made one further freighting move, to the Calico silver mines in San Bernardino, California. His last few years, though, were mostly concerned with his vineyards and fruit projects, as well as the new Nadeau Hotel, which opened in Los Angeles in 1883-84. He died in Los Angeles in mid-November of 1887.[162]

NICHOLS, JOHN MARSHALL ("NAPA NICK") A native of Massachusetts, although his full name was John Marshall Nichols, he was known throughout the West as Napa Nick. As early as the census of 1860, in Napa, California, he was a saloon keeper, and that environment would be his choice until his death in Tucson in 1917.

Gamblers, prostitutes, and hangers-on of saloons are usually difficult to follow, but in his case, he was up front and proud. Pretty much from 1880 through 1900, Napa Nick was a man of Tombstone, familiar with most saloons and having a solid reputation wherever he went. Nick was a white-haired fellow, usually dressed in a decent black suit, and looked so official and proper that he was often called "Judge." Keyed into the folks that mattered in the world of saloons and gambling, it is no wonder that in the aftermath of the gunfight of October 1881, Napa Nick opted to bet a few thousand dollars that Wyatt Earp would not flee Tombstone.

In the early days in Tombstone, Nick was a gambler, but as the 1880s wore on, he often was the owner, or one who leased, famous saloons and places of entertainment. He wanted a forum, and would join others or take a leading role in order to get action.

Napa Nick was a known character, and his trips to Bisbee, Nogales, and Tucson from Tombstone were noted. His family was sometimes with him, but he saw to it that the fortunes of the Tombstone gambling tables would allow them to live a decent life back in Napa. Such decency and fame meant that Nick's career would be followed by many. In 1909 a racing horse named "Napa Nick" was active on the courses from Butte, Montana, to San Francisco.

After 1900, Napa Nick began to consider the saloons and tables of Tucson as his environment, and he spent most of his time there and in other Arizona watering holes until his death in Tucson on October 28, 1917; his body was shipped to Napa for burial.[163]

NEAGLE, DAVID BUTLER Folks interested in frontier mining communities in the West, the world of saloons and gambling halls, and the life of peace officers, will learn much following this fellow's career. He was born in Boston on October 10, 1847, and his family moved to California. A start at Santa Clara College was too boring, and Neagle went to the Nevada mining camps. He was in Pioche, White Pine, then crossed over to the Panamint region of California. Neagle worked as a miner, but not much, ran a saloon for a time, got in some scrapes, including at least two gunfights. He went to Prescott and worked a mining claim for a time, then arrived in Tombstone when things were really getting lively.

Neagle served as a deputy sheriff under John Behan; following the near-fatal ambush of Virgil Earp, he became the Tombstone town marshal in early 1882 and was later elected to the office. In March 1882, Neagle would be part of the Behan contingent which, in Billicke's Cosmopolitan Hotel, attempted to arrest Wyatt Earp and his posse (including the ominous Doc Holliday) after they had just arrived back from their deadly Vendetta Ride. Wyatt and his party boldly brushed right by, snubbing them, and left town, unmolested, for the last time.

The Tombstone of 1882 was a vigorous, bitter series of arguments and electioneering, as Neagle and a few others wanted to be sheriff of Cochise County. As a result of the differences between political parties, as well as internal differences, the candidates were many. The end result was that Jerome Ward won the election.

The Neagle story from here is long, complicated, and sometimes important. He went to Montana for more mining and excitement. It was in California, in August 1889, that he was involved in one of the most spectacular killings in American history. As a deputized bodyguard for Justice Stephen V. Field of the U. S. Supreme Court, Neagle shot and

David Neagle. Who Assaulted James H. Barry, Editor of the "Star," Yesterday.

Western gunfighter Dave Neagle was once Tombstone chief of police. *San Francisco Call*, August 15, 1896.

killed Field's rival, Judge David S. Terry, in a restaurant at a train stop in Lathrop, California. There is an extensive literature on the event, mostly based on the Supreme Court opinion *In re Neagle*, 135 U. S. 1 (1890).

Neagle spent the remainder of his life in the San Francisco-Oakland environs. His name made the papers from time to time, he served as a bodyguard for leading financiers, and was involved in some detective work. Although he was involved in mining, if his name surfaced, it was usually because of his tough guy background. For example, the *San Francisco Call* of August 10, 1896, ran an article about Neagle appearing in police court on a railroad matter. The opening sentence began, "Dave Nea-gle, the Southern Pacific gun man from Arizona..." Neagle died in Oakland on November 28, 1925.[164]

O'GORMAN, MICHAEL M. His career is easy to follow; all that is needed is to locate Richard Gird. Gird, of course, was of the famous trio (along with the Schieffelin brothers) that made the Tombstone saga possible. From the beginning of Tombstone, Boston-born O'Gorman would be linked with Gird and his interests. He invested in a sawmill with Gird, had a piece of the Tombstone Townsite Company, and for the early years of Tombstone was a clerk, running things from the Gird Building; he was Gird's agent.

Wherever Gird went, O'Gorman was not far behind. In the investments in San Bernardino County and in the huge Gird interests in Mexican mining and land, O'Gorman was either a partner or administrator. Because of these connections, O'Gorman was frequently hired by other capitalists to inspect properties in the Southwest as well as in Mexico. When Gird developed the huge railroad, ranching, and sugar beet project in Chino, California, O'Gorman was the project manager.

By the late 1890s, O'Gorman was living in either Los Angeles or Pasadena, and a major stockholder in the Middlemarch Copper Company in Cochise County. He died in Pasadena on February 4, 1910. For thirty years, O'Gorman was never in his own realm, as he was financially and socially linked with Richard Gird. To be closely associated with the founder of Tombstone, one of the Southwest's movers and shakers, is not a bad thing.[165]

O'MELVENY, Henry K. S. Henry O'Melveny started what would become one of the world's legal dynasties. He was born in Kentucky in 1823, spent years in Illinois as a lawyer and friend of Abraham Lincoln, then in 1869 moved to Los Angeles. Within a few years he was head of the city council, became a county judge in 1872, and a superior court judge in 1887.

During the big Tombstone excitement, lawyers by the dozen invaded Tombstone, and not without reason. There were lots of businesses, possibly a hundred mining companies, and the law business thrived. In the midst of this, O'Melveny thought he saw an opening. In 1881 and 1882, in partnership with O. O. Trantum, he opened an office in the Gird Building. Yet, in the sifting and fallout in Tombstone, O'Melveny cashed in, sold his local law library, and headed back to Los Angeles. He died there in November of 1893. His son, Henry William O'Melveny, founded the O'Melveny Law Firm, which became one of the world's largest.[166]

O'NEILL, WILLIAM O. ("BUCKEY") Prescott's celebrated Buckey O'Neill, lawman, mayor, gambler, and famed Rough Rider of the Spanish-American War, has frequently been mentioned as a Tombstone pioneer and a writer for the *Epitaph*; so far, no contemporary source has surfaced to back up such a claim.[167]

O'ROURKE (ROURKE; ROURK), MICHAEL This was "Johnny-behind-the-Deuce" of Wyatt Earp lore. The before and after of his life are unknowns, but in January 1881 in a Charleston saloon, after some type of disagreement, "Johnny" pulled out a revolver and blasted mining engineer Philip Schneider. The "Deuce" was arrested, but fearing a lynch mob he was thrown in a wagon and hastily ushered to Tombstone. At Vogan's Saloon another mob with lynching in mind gathered, but because of the courageous work of U. S. Deputy Marshal Virgil Earp, Marshal Ben Sippy, and Sheriff Johnny Behan, the "Deuce" was safely skirted off to jail in Tucson (from which he escaped).

The name "Johnny-behind-the-Deuce" appears in hundreds of accounts of Tombstone in the bonanza years. Yet, they are all based on the claim that Wyatt Earp stood up to the crowd at Vogan's Saloon and saved the day. There is not the slightest bit of contemporary evidence that Wyatt Earp was at the scene. Decades later, John Clum, Fred Dodge, Allie Earp, George Parsons, and even ex-sheriff and Earp adversary William Breakenridge gave credit to Wyatt for this great deed, but they, too, were not near the action. This great rescue action by Wyatt Earp, known to the four corners of the earth, most likely "did not happen that way." [168]

PALMER, JOSEPH C. A major figure of the California Gold Rush, Joseph Palmer almost figured in the Tombstone saga. He was a partner in Palmer & Cook, which as early as 1849 was involved with Charles Fremont in the quartz mill in Mariposa County, California, the first mill in California. The firm was important (and controversial, and not very successful) in the history of mining and milling in California. In 1880-1882, Palmer was involved with James C. Clark in the questionable manipulations of the Tombstone land dealings, the "Tombstone Townsite Controversy." As late as April of 1882, he was shifting lots to Clark. However, within weeks, Palmer died in California, which ended his play in the Tombstone saga. [169]

PARKER, EMMA Her origins are obscure, but her life in Tombstone from 1881 through 1885 was exciting enough to frequently make the local papers. She was a prostitute, a successful one, a loudmouth, a force to be reckoned with on the streets or wherever else she met or entertained. Emma had a few working girls, owned several pieces of property, and feared no one, certainly not Marshal Virgil Earp, with whom she had a few encounters, nor Mayor John Clum. Prostitutes and their business environs were subject to specific fees, which did not please "Red Emma." When upset, she would fight, and would sometimes do so while drunk.

By 1885 the Tombstone bonanza call could not be heard very far, and Emma Parker left, showing up in San Diego for a time in 1886-87, again running a few girls in a house of ill fame. In 1889 she returned for a time to Cochise County, bought some property, and tried to earn some money from the Benson railroad personnel. This didn't work out, and her last press notices were in 1889-90 in Phoenix. In one incident, after being arrested on various charges, Emma showed up intoxicated before a judge, slurring and pleading her case.[170]

PARKER, WILLIAM CROWNOVER, Jr. A true downward-slope saga here. William Parker's father was a military physician, a California pioneer, and a major stockbroker in San Francisco and Oakland. However, most of his fortune was eaten in the Ralston banking collapse in San Francisco. Yet, in 1880, he had enough to bankroll Junior, who went to Tombstone with Milt Joyce to operate several of the facilities in the Oriental Saloon. Parker is mostly remembered because he was behind the bar in October of 1880 during a shooting affray between Milt Joyce and Doc Holliday, receiving "a stray bullet in the big toe."

A few years later, Parker was in Santa Cruz, California, listed as a merchant in 1888, and soon after that was a clerk working in downtown Los Angeles. He returned to Santa Cruz, where

in the 1910 census he was identified as a hardware store clerk. Soon thereafter, and until his death on August 13, 1931, Parker and his wife Minnie operated a small candy store in Concord, Contra Costa County.[171]

PARSONS, GEORGE W. Anyone interested in the first era of Tombstone in bonanza need only read the *Tombstone Epitaph*, *Tombstone Nugget*, the *Daily Tombstone*, and the detailed diaries of George Parsons, who was there from 1880 to 1887. This native of Washington, DC, left a mediocre banking job in San Francisco for the new camp at Tombstone. There he was a mine laborer, later a mine agent, and had mineral interests as well as in nearby Sonora, Mexico. Parsons was a close associate of Dr. Goodfellow (he kept his books), rode on posses with the Earp brothers, and played cards and met frequently with John Clum, L. W. Blinn, and other Tombstone dignitaries. Fortunately for us, he noted in his diary his insights regarding events in the lives of these fellows and dozens of other men, women, and girls of greater Tombstone. No similar account exists for any other mining camp in the American West; another Tombstone mystique factor.

Parsons moved to Los Angeles, where he was a founder of the Los Angeles Chamber of Commerce and was active in the Los Angeles Mining & Stock Exchange. Like A. C. Bilicke, he was a magnet in Los Angeles for old Tombstoners, such as Wyatt Earp, John Clum, Henry Hooker, and E. B. Gage, for many years. Parsons was a key player in the rivalry between Santa Monica and San Pedro, both vying to become the port for Los Angeles, and was one of the significant figures responsible for preserving the picturesque seaside resort city of Santa Monica, for citizens and tourists alike, to delight in to this day. For years, he led the movement for desert signposts for water for travelers. Parsons served as one of Wyatt Earp's pallbearers upon Earp's death in Los Angeles in January of 1929; he himself died in Los Angeles on January 5, 1933. Parsons was known for many things during these four decades in Los Angeles, although historians and readers of Western history remember him mostly for his significant, unique, and enlightening diaries of the best Tombstone years.[172]

GEORGE WHITWELL PARSONS

Tombstone's George Parsons, an important Western diarist, became a kingpin in the Los Angeles Chamber of Commerce. *Sunset Club*, 1916.

PARSONS, WILLILAM C. William Parsons, from Dorset, England, was in the West by the 1860s and would be an important mining, land, and financial figure from the Pacific Northwest to the swamps of Florida. His career was so diverse and successful that no attempt will be made here to examine it, other than some relevant comments. In general, his base was San Francisco, and secondarily, Prescott, Arizona.

In 1878, when the Schieffelins and Dick Gird were having trouble financing their Tombstone discoveries, Parsons came to the area, and became a major backer for the new mining camp. Soon, with a few others, he incorporated the Western Mining Company, which contained the rich properties of the Contention, Sulphuret, Girard, and a few others of promise. The Schieffelin party was able to do what they intended, and Parsons remained in the camp for a few years, took an administrative role in the efforts, and became very wealthy.

His later decades saw him join with Governor Safford of Arizona in an effort to drain the Everglades, purchase important waterfront property in and around San Francisco, and develop and profit from gold mining operations at McCabe, near Prescott. When he died in 1911, he was a multi-millionaire, and his will included a grant of $50,000 to the Arizona Pioneers' Home in Prescott. Much of the huge success of the Parsons career was related to his backing of the Schieffelins and Gird in the difficult early years of Tombstone.[173]

PASCHOLY, JOSEPH People who do not know this name are not very familiar with Tombstone history. Pascholy was born in Switzerland in 1850, arrived in Tombstone in 1880, and was a major presence in that community for a decade. Pascholy owned things, ran things, was in-volved in public and private dealings, and probably one of the most interconnected men in town. The Arcade, Russ House, and Occidental Hotel are a few of the places he either owned, leased, or managed. Pascholy had major business dealings with Nellie Cashman, Godfrey Tribolet, and Andy Ritter, and was knowledgeable about (and successful with) the hotel, saloon, and undertaking businesses. He also owned a ranch In the Dragoon Mountains.

Pascholy's Tombstone days began to wane in 1889, when for a year or so he managed the hotel at Fort Huachuca. From 1892 through 1902, Pascholy was in Nogales, and was invested in or controlled a bank and several businesses. He then shifted to Los Angeles, where he was an investor or administrator with several manufacturing enterprises. His success was such that in 1903 he took his family to Switzerland for a six-month visit.

Joseph Pascholy, a solid, successful businessman, died in Santa Clara, California, on June 10, 1920. His important career was based on his experiences and partnerships from the Tombstone bonanza years.[174]

PAUL, BOB His career is one of the highlights, in a positive sense, of law and order on the Western frontier. He was a native of Massachusetts and was in Honolulu when he learned of the California gold discovery. From the 1850s through the early 1870s, Paul worked as a miner and as a lawman in several California districts; as constable, deputy sheriff, and sheriff. He was a large man, capable, and respected.

In 1874 he joined Wells Fargo, and in 1878 they assigned him to the new Arizona districts, largely because of the silver discoveries near Tombstone. The Wells Fargo records, for example, detail the salary Bob Paul received for his stage runs to Tombstone from August through October, 1880.

In one of the key events of Tombstone (and Wild West) history, the Kinnear & Co. stage left for Benson on March 15, 1881. Paul was on board, riding shotgun. Shortly after Contention, the stage was attacked, rifles and revolvers spoke, and several men were killed. More damage would have been done, except that Paul's bravery, words, and actions forced the robbers to flee. The stage driver, Bud Philpot, was one of the fatalities.

Paul would later have much to do with the Earp/Holliday faction, as by then he was sheriff of Pima County. Frank Stilwell had been killed in Tucson by the Earp Vendetta Posse, and that group then absconded to Colorado. Paul was pressured by authorities in Colorado and Arizona to have the Earps and Holliday extradited to Arizona, which did not happen.

Bob Paul continued with high service in many callings, including U. S. marshal for Arizona Territory and as a special officer for Southern Pacific Railroad. He died in Tucson on March 28, 1911.[175]

PEABODY, ENDICOTT Peabody was from a prominent merchant family in Salem, Massachusetts, and was educated at Cambridge, England. He then returned home and entered an Episcopal seminary.

After one semester, he was offered and accepted a six-month sojourn at an Arizona mining camp that needed assistance. Peabody went west, arrived in Benson, from there got on a Sandy Bob stage, and arrived in Tombstone on January 29, 1882.

The Peabody stay was brief, but not lacking in excitement or activity. This was only months after the O.K. Corral gunfight and hearings, and the Earps were still around; Morgan would be killed by ambuscade in Hatch's Saloon in March of 1882, during the Peabody sojourn in town. Peabody preached sermons (his first was in the Mining Exchange Building) and was highly effective raising funds from all, including faro players, prostitutes, even cowboys. Peabody was tall, strong, and an outstanding athlete. He formed Tombstone's first baseball team, and was a good boxer, which he demonstrated several times. He was liked, was good press fodder, and

Rev. Endicott Peabody.
Founder and headmaster of Groton School.

Episcopal rector Endicott Peabody, popular Tombstone clergyman, became a prominent national educator and officiated at the wedding of Franklin D. Roosevelt. *American Magazine*, Vol. 59 (1904-1905).

enjoyed his Tombstone stay.

Peabody went back to New England where he became a minister and an outstanding educator. In 1884, he founded the highly touted (to this day) Groton School. His students included four sons of Theodore Roosevelt, as well as future United States president Franklin D. Roosevelt; and years later, he would be the officiating clergyman at Franklin's marriage. Peabody died on November 17, 1944.[176]

PEACOCK, EDWIN (EDWARD) R. Born in Kentucky in 1842, Edwin Peacock moved with his family to California in the 1850s. They became well established in San Bernardino. Edwin was interested in the theatre as well as in art, and for years he identified himself as a painter, later as an artist. How one makes a living as an artist on the frontier is not easily understood, but there are a few examples. In 1867, Edwin was in Visalia as a painter, and in 1874 in Santa Barbara he painted and gilded an omnibus "equal to that of the best carriage painters in the country." He soon left and opened a shop and studio in San Bernardino.

Peacock was very early on the Tombstone scene, checking in at the Cosmopolitan Hotel on November 20, 1879. He worked on various projects for merchants and mining companies, and even invested in some mining property.

But Edwin Peacock was not a laid-back or reclusive artist. He was also a sporting man, which got him in a bit of trouble with Deputy Sheriff Wyatt Earp. In August of 1880, a boozed-up Peacock got in a loud, "violent riotous language" duel outside of a saloon on Allen Street with Charles Calhoun, a wealthy, major, controversial figure in pioneer Tombstone. Sheriff Wyatt and Officer J. W. Bennett arrested them, took them to jail, then to Justice of the Peace James Reilly.

Edwin was in Tombstone for a few more years. One of his commissions was for an engine house of a hose company: "an oil painting of the Tombstone M. & M. Co.'s main works, executed by Mr. Ed. Peacock, is quite a gem of art." This was in April of 1882. Although Tombstone was still in bonanza, it lost its appeal, and by 1884 Peacock was in Pomona, Los Angeles County, and died in Colton in October 1886.[177]

PEEL, BRYANT LARENDO A native of North Carolina, Peel had been a justice of the peace in Los Angeles County before moving to Tombstone in 1880.

He would be the area's first probate judge and in 1882 was named a justice of the peace there. Peel was interested in many things, such as investing in mines and being part owner of a saloon. He also served in the territorial legislature. Because of his many roles, Peel's name appears in thousands of Tombstone documents in the county recorder's office. His name is thus associated with Dunbar, Behan, Goodfellow, Earp, Cashman, Joyce, Rickabaugh, Blinn, Clanton, and on and on.

A distressing incident in Peel's life was the killing of his son Martin (see entry below), a surveyor, who was shot during a robbery of the Tombstone Mill & Mining Company office at Millville on March 25, 1882, the day after Wyatt Earp's "Vendetta Posse" killed Curly Bill Brocius.

By the end of the 1880s, Bryan Peel returned to Los Angeles County where he continued to practice law. He died in Alhambra on September 25, 1897.[178]

PEEL, MARTIN R. Martin R. Peel was born in Texas in 1854, and studied surveying in Los Angeles in the 1870s. He qualified as a civil engineer and became an assistant to city surveyor Michael Kelleher. Both Kelleher and young

Peel moved to Tombstone in 1880 and were well-placed in the mining community. They were the compilers of the famous Ingoldsby *Map of the Mining District of Tombstone,* published in San Francisco in 1881. Peel joined the firm of the Tombstone Mill & Mining Company and was in charge of building a dam near Millville-Charleston on the San Pedro River. He was murdered in a major incident of Tombstone history on March 25, 1882, in the aftermath of the Wyatt Earp-Curly Bill confrontation. Suspected were Cowboys Zwing Hunt and Billy Grounds, in their desperation to finance their swift departure from southern Arizona (fleeing Wyatt's posse and "Vendetta Ride" in the aftermath of Morgan Earp's murder). They were afterward tracked down by a posse led by Deputy Sheriff William Breakenridge, at the Chandler Milk Ranch (where incidentally, the Cowboys had had their last meal before their famous O.K. Corral fight), and in an ensuing gunfight, Grounds was killed and Hunt severely wounded, then jailed in Tombstone. He subsequently "escaped" Behan's jail, and in an inquest after Martin Peel's murder, no definitive conclusion was reached. As a side note to this whole affair, as recently as the late 1920s and beyond, it was to be observed that there was only one still recognizable grave/tombstone in all of Boothill: that of Martin Peel. [179]

PHILLIPS, KIV A New Yorker of Jewish heritage, Phillips was early on the scene in Tombstone. By 1881 he clerked in a local store, was a member of the Rescue Hook and Ladder Company, and from time to time served as a deputy sheriff to Sheriff John Behan. In July, 1882, while working as a constable, Phillips was called to the Capital Saloon, where Filomino Orantes was causing trouble. In the confrontation that followed, Phillips and Orantes fired revolvers, and Phillips was killed. Dr. Goodfellow was able to save the inebriated Orantes for a time, but Orantes subsequently died of his wound in August, and his brother arrived in town the next month from Mexico, "seeking revenge." Kiv Phillip's body was shipped to his family in San Francisco, then placed in the Jewish Hills of Eternity Cemetery at Colma. In the nineteenth-century West, this was one of the few examples of death in the line of duty for a Jewish man of the law.[180]

PLATT, GEORGE H. Born in Michigan in 1832, George Platt became a sergeant in an Ohio cavalry unit during the Civil War. He was in President Lincoln's bodyguard, present at the assassination, and had a bloodied theater program as a souvenir of the event.

By the 1870s Platt was in Pima County, and in the early opening of the Tombstone mines, a carpenter at Contention. He soon developed a ranch outside of Tombstone and for years was a regular supplier of milk to the community. He was active in the local G. A. R. and somewhat involved in local Republican politics, running for justice of the peace in 1892 but losing.

Very soon thereafter, in the doldrums of greater Tombstone, Platt headed for the more active gold mining camp at nearby Pearce, where he again operated a farm near town. He died there in early August, 1900.[181]

PRICE, LYTTLETON Price was a Michigan native, educated in Ypsilanti, then went to San Francisco to study law, and began practicing there in the early 1870s. He next went to Arizona Territory and became a close confidant of Governor John Fremont; Price was also the U. S. attorney. When the new Cochise County was sliced off from Pima County in 1881, Fremont named Price district attorney of the new county. Fremont, not a very talented political leader or administrator, muddied the waters, and named both Republicans and Democrats to new posts in Cochise County, which is why Lyttleton Price and John Behan were among the new leaders.

Price was not important in the history of Tombstone, nor in Cochise County. Yet, as district attorney, he headed the prosecuting team in the Wells Spicer hearings, where charges were brought against the Earp-Holliday faction by the Clanton-McLaury group. The Spicer hearings have been one of the most discussed and written about legal events of the history of the American West. However, in spite of the ink spilled on these hearings, Lyttleton Price has not become a household name. To the average reader or interested party in this Western saga, the two legal names that stand out are Tom Fitch (Wyatt Earp's choice) and William McLaury (brother of the two McLaurys killed in the shootout).

The main Price period in the West was in Idaho. He practiced law for years there, married there, was a district judge, then settled and practiced law in Boise. He died while on a trip to Salt Lake on September 12, 1907.[182]

PRIDHAM, GEORGE The Pridham name is scattered around dozens of events in greater Tombstone during the 1880s. A New Yorker, by 1869 George Pridham was in Los Angeles, running a cigar store and helping to found the first fire department there. In Tombstone by 1880, he opened the Tasker (Joseph) & Pridham general merchant house on the southeast corner of Fifth and Allen. He became a member of the city council, and was appointed the Cochise County public administrator by Governor John C. Fremont. In that capacity, he took charge of the affairs of the McLaury brothers after the fatal encounter of October, 1881.

In the following years Pridham continued to have an active Tombstone presence, even though he was a major cattleman with a ranch in Sulphur Spring Valley. In May, 1890, he invited his friend Dr. Frank Haynes and his brother-in-law, prominent Los Angeles attorney Robert Hardie, for a visit and "vacation" to the area, during which Hardie was murdered in Rucker Canyon by a group of fugitive Apaches led by the infamous Apache Kid. By 1895 Pridham left the area, and for a time was interested in some profitable mining claims in Randsburg, California. His brother William was an important Wells Fargo administrator in California.

Around 1900, Pridham shifted to Long Beach, where for years he operated a large grocery establishment. He died in Los Angeles on January 4, 1914.[183]

PURDY, SAMUEL The Purdy family was from Buffalo, New York, and shifted to California, where Samuel's father was lieutenant governor. Samuel Purdy attended Santa Clara College, and served as an officer during the Civil War. In 1878, he moved to Yuma as a journalist and was soon in the Arizona territorial legislature.

In 1882, Purdy moved to Tombstone and was involved in two major activities, neither one of which brought him any glory. He was named editor of the *Tombstone Epitaph*, and was noted for his vigorous (actually vicious) attacks on the Earp faction, the law-and-order crowd. This was noteworthy because the *Epitaph* had been a strong backer of the Earps, and Purdy, who castigated them right and left, didn't even know them. A strain of Democrats versus Republicans also figured in this taking of sides, which is beyond us here. Purdy also got involved in a famous duel with Patrick Hamilton, editor of a rival Tombstone newspaper, in September of 1882. The duel was famous for a broken bone and inadequate firearms, which in actuality resulted in a non-duel.

Purdy's few Tombstone years, non-glory-filled, ended, and he moved back to Yuma. By the time of his death there in May of 1898, he was working mostly as an attorney specializing in land business.[184]

RANDALL, ALDER The Randalls were natives of New Harmony, Indiana, who as early as the 1860s were in Alameda County, California. Alder was in the Mineral Park, Arizona, area when the news of the Tombstone silver strike came his way. He was one of the pioneers of 1879; a child was born to the Randalls in 1880 in Tombstone.

Everything went his way, but only for a short time. He operated a saloon and a billiard hall on Allen Street, and in 1880 was elected Tombstone's second mayor. Then he got enmeshed in the Tombstone Townsite controversy; in fact, he was a major player, and earned the wrath of his fellow citizens. In the nasty, confus-

ing business, Randall was pretty much forced out of town; lynching was discussed.

Alder headed for Los Angeles County and as early as 1884 listed as a farmer in Downey. This is pretty much what he did until his death there in 1897. His other modest roles were serving as a local election clerk from time to time, and being the Downey road overseer. A check of any ten books about Tombstone will indicate Randall's key role in the Tombstone Townsite controversy, and the bitter feeling created by this lot-selling. Strange, then, that in his obituary in the *Mohave County Miner* of June 12, 1897, that mentioned his recent passing in Downey, he was referred to as "jolly, good-natured."[185]

REILLY, JAMES This County Cavan, Ireland, son arrived in New York in 1848 at the height of the potato famine, then served five years in the Western frontier army. Much of his later time was spent in Arizona, New Mexico, and Texas, and he worked, studied, and wrote in Yuma before trying the doings in Tombstone in 1880.

Reilly, Tombstone, and Cochise County would be synonymous until his death in Long Beach on June 8, 1909.

Justice James Reilly was controversial, liked, and disliked in Tombstone for over three decades. *Portrait and Biographical Record of Arizona*, 1901.

In Tombstone he was more than "known;" he was known too well. An attorney, justice of the peace, district attorney, and member of the territorial legislature, he was also a firebrand almost seeking trial and trouble. In this era in Arizona, no other person sued or was sued more than James Reilly. He was a fantastic friend, a severe enemy, yet could change sides easily. It seems that confrontation was his need.

Justice Reilly not only knew all the players, but often fought with them. He had ugly interactions in his courtroom with Deputy Sheriff Wyatt Earp, frequently met with Nellie Cashman as they planned fund drives for church and hospital (as well as for Irish causes), and became a keen master of much of the law regarding mining. One of the most memorable mining cases in the West was when Justice Reilly, on behalf of Martin Costello and Bisbee Copper, went to the U. S. Supreme Court and won the day in 1899.

Tombstone and Arizona Territory had dozens of famous justices, judges, and attorneys in this era, but none caused more ink to be used than Justice James Reilly. Some of his cases were of fantastic local, regional, even national significance. Yet others were trivial, even petty. For him, it almost didn't matter; the game was to ensure action.

The famous names and events associated with Justice James Reilly were main ingredients in what caused Tombstone and its doings to be so widely known.[186]

RENE, WILLIAM This fellow just as frequently identified himself as George William Von Rene. Born in Germany in 1852, and by the early 1880s a miner in Bisbee, he would be in Cochise County for thirty years, usually in Bisbee, but also in Benson, Douglas, and Tombstone.

He is best known for the role he played in the aftermath of the Bisbee Massacre of 1883. In 1884, when the leader of the robber gang, John Heath, was in jail in Tombstone, around a hundred men, led by some Bisbee miners, took Heath from the jail, and from a telegraph pole on Toughnut Street, lynched him. William Rene was one of the principals in this deed. In a story published nationwide in 1910, "Rene was the man who climbed the telephone pole and flung the rope over the cross-arm, after which he assisted in hoisting the desperado into eternity."

One other of the few entries for Von Rene in the local press was a claim allowed for the board of supervisors in 1901: $5.00 to Von Rene for "watching dead bodies, Douglas." Rene died in Tombstone on January 15, 1910, and was identified as a painter.[187]

REPPY, CHARLES D. This Illinois native had a long association with journalism. He was with several newspapers in Missouri and Mississippi before heading West, keeping in the same game. Reppy was in Harshaw, Arizona, then went to Tombstone and was part of the exciting doings of that mining community. One of the founders of the *Tombstone Epitaph,* associated with the *Tombstone Republican,* then the *Cochise Record,* and all of this happened in the first Tombstone bonanza period of 1880-1887. Reppy was a man of many interests, operating a ranch in the Huachuca Mountains, and in 1894 working for the *Phoenix Herald.* He also worked as a customs officer, then was in the Territorial Assembly.

For some years Reppy was in Florence, where he owned the *Florence Tribune,* and also had real estate interests in Globe and Miami. By this time the newspaper business had ceased to be the important part of his life. Reppy moved to Eagle Rock, California, in Los Angeles County, and for some years was the local right-of-way man for the Southern Pacific Railroad. Reppy died there on August 8, 1918.[188]

RICKABAUGH, LOU Lou Rickabaugh was a sporting man, which in the talk of the day meant someone who loved horse racing, gambling, casinos—the saloon life. He came from a farm family in Ohio that continued to farm in Iowa. He registered for the draft in the Civil War but did not serve. From 1866 into the 1870s, Lou left the life of farm and wagon for the faro tables of Denver. In various directories and news accounts he was identified as a speculator and was described as "portly." By 1880 he was a known figure in the dens of San Francisco.

From 1880 to 1882, Rickabaugh was a key figure in Tombstone's sporting life. He seems to have been in control of the betting arrangements at the Oriental Saloon, and it was Rickabaugh who figured that it would be good to give Wyatt Earp a portion of the action. Wyatt was a known Dodge City lawman, had served as a Pima County Deputy Sheriff, and brother Virgil was Tombstone town marshal. Many things were happening in Tombstone in this era, and Rickabaugh, supposedly the man handling the tables, was involved in three or four scuffles, sometimes with firearms, interesting enough to make the newspapers. When the Earps were arrested after the gunfight, Rickabaugh was one of those who posted bond for Wyatt.

The Rickabaugh life after Tombstone began in Tucson in late 1882. For the next few years, he was running things in a few saloons there, and his new wife, Emma, was playing the piano. Lou got into a well-publicized gunfight in Tucson in 1885, shooting another "sporting man," who had relentless-

ly challenged and threatened him, in the left knee. He moved on to Los Angeles for a few years, with his presence being noticed for sporting affairs, illegal gambling, and similar activities. In the beginning of the 1890s he was mostly in San Francisco, there a part of the horse racing scenes, especially close to Wyatt Earp and Lucky Baldwin.

From that point on, when Rickabaugh's name surfaces, it is usually with horses. He owned several in California, but gradually shifted his racing interests and betting to the Midwest, sometimes winning, at tracks in Detroit, St. Louis, and New Orleans. His horses (and his name) can be followed in the turf publications of the 1890s. Rickabaugh died in New Orleans on January 2, 1899. A few newspapers, even the *Chicago Tribune,* carried notices of the "veteran owner and trainer," stating that he had been known on the Western circuit for decades. By that time, Rickabaugh was known for the racetrack, not the faro or poker tables of Tombstone.[189]

RINGO, JOHN Any cut-and-dried book about Tombstone would carry no entry for John Ringo, although he is highly revered by Hollywood; his time in town was little, and very insignificant in the grand scheme of things. This Indiana-born cowboy spent some time in California, then headed for Texas. He was involved in a few interesting episodes regarding ranching and law-and-order in several Texas counties (the Mason County Hoodoo War, for example), even serving a spell as a constable and some jailtime (in Burnet County for murder). In the early 1880s he entered southeastern Arizona and became close to some of the local Pima and Cochise county rural folks.

He did a little gambling, certainly knew his way around the world of saloons, but no major incident regarding Ringo in and around Tombstone has come to notice. He and Doc Holliday may have frowned at and threatened one another on Allen Street, but they were arrested before any action was possible.

The only well-known incident regarding Ringo is that he was shot and died in the Chiricahua Mountains on July 13, 1882; more than likely he took his own life, although many others have laid claim to that honor through the years, and conspiracy theories abound.

The Ringo "legend" grew, though, as five or six fellows (including Wyatt Earp, Buckskin Frank, Doc Holliday, "Johnny-Behind-the-Deuce," and a few others) were said to have tracked him down and killed him. Also, the Ringo name has a "ring" to it, so with the town of Tombstone involved, the legend and lore cranked along. The "king of the cowboys" was a fellow few knew who was responsible for nothing. A solid work by Jack Burrows, *John Ringo: The Gunfighter who Never Was* (1987) has an accurate title. David Johnson wrote a good book, *John Ringo* (1996; 2008), presenting solid information on his Texas years. Yet, Johnson, too, couldn't figure out how to handle the topic of Tombstone. He devotes pages to the Gunfight at the O.K. Corral, then mentions in an aside that Ringo was in New Mexico at the time. Good research has also been done in this regard by authors Steve Gatto, Michael M. Hickey, Jack Burrows, and a few others.

Ringo is important to the Tombstone mystique only because of the legends and the screwy lore that has evolved. Amateur historians and the general public believe that Ringo "should have done this," or that "he wanted to do that."[190]

RITCHIE (RITCHEY), WILLIAM

William Ritchie had one of the more interesting, varied careers of longtime residents of Tombstone. He was born in Tennessee in 1841 and was in Tombstone, working as a miner, at least by 1880, when Ritchie's Hall went up on Fifth Street. When rebuilt after the fire of 1882, this hall was two stories, had a "theater" for dramas (one even featuring Nellie Boyd), and also room for a few grocers. Ritchie in 1881 put up a bond of $1,000 for Virgil Earp when he became chief of police.

For most of the 1880s William worked as a miner, but spent some time as a foreman for the Grand Central, a leading local silver producer. In later years he was also a prospector, and spent some time in the copper deposits around Nacozari, Sonora.

From around 1890 until his death in 1906, Ritchie is mostly associated with mining and with being the Tombstone jailer. He married in Tombstone in 1892, and was not only around as a jailer during the raucous time of jail-breaking Burt Alvord, but had other, earlier excitement. In 1893, politics in Cochise County were scrambled, and there were two competing boards of supervisors. Because William allied himself with one faction, he paid the penalty. One newspaper heading was "JAILER RITCHIE JAILED." Sheriff Scott White returned from Tucson and smoothed things over for him.

Ritchie died in Tombstone in September of 1906 and was buried in a fine ceremony, with attorney Allen English highlighting some of his Tombstone years.[191]

RITTER, ANDREW J. (A.J.)

World famous? Yes. Undertaker Ritter prepared the bodies of Billy Clanton and the two McLaury brothers after the O.K. Corral gunfight and placed them in coffins. The subsequent photos of the result of his work have probably been seen by more people than have the photos of most, if not all, other corpses. Maybe views of Mussolini hanging upside-down rival Ritter's work for views.

Ritter was an important figure in Tombstone in this decade. For most of the time he was an undertaker, but was also a builder, overseeing the construction of the Cochise County Courthouse, to this day one of the most visited sites in Arizona. He was also on the cemetery committee, and like most Tombstone folks, invested in mining claims.

Ritter became Cochise County treasurer, and that was a mistake, as he cooked the books and was forced to resign in 1887. A. J. remained in town, but kept a much lower profile. For a time, he worked some of the "old ore" of the Sunset Mine. In 1895 he left town, moved to Mammoth, Pinal County, Arizona, busied himself with a project or two, and even worked at mining for a time. The good days were gone, and Ritter died in Mammoth, on April 29, 1899.[192]

ROBERTSON, ALEXANDER M. Mark Twain, Jack London, Robert Louis Stevenson, Frank Norris, Bret Harte—these were close friends, intimate literary associates of Robertson, who for more than fifty years was a major publishing force on the Pacific Coast from his San Francisco book-selling operation. He was part of the upper echelon of things social and literary in San Francisco and one of the early members of the Bohemian Club. On October 30, 1920, a San Francisco conference was held to celebrate his fifty years of work in the literary world. He died in Palo Alto on February 11, 1934.

Tombstone, though, was part of the earlier Robertson life. He left San Francisco late in 1881, and in Tombstone, on Fifth Street between Allen and Fremont, opened a business featuring books, stationery, and periodicals, "2 doors down

from the post office."

Robertson was in town for at least three years, those years which happened to be the most active in the mining, business, and saloon life of Tombstone. He was a keen observer, knew most people in town, and even served a brief stint as a deputy sheriff. Robertson was married in early 1882 and had a son Henry (aka "Harry"), born in Tombstone on December 16, 1882. Harry worked with his father in San Francisco in later years, and inherited the bookstore. Robertson, and the

A. M. Robertson Is Honored by Booksellers

Alexander M. Robertson's fiftieth year of bookselling and publishing in San Francisco is to be celebrated at a dinner given in his honor by the Booksellers' Association of San Francisco Bay Counties Saturday evening, October 30, at 7 p. m. in the palm room of the Hotel Bellevue.

Robertson was publisher for Ambrose Bierce, Joaquin Miller, Louis Alexander Robertson, Peter Robertson, Charles Warren Stoddard, Daniel O'Connell and other writers who were Californians by birth or adoption.

Living authors who may welcome this opportunity to pay tribute to the veteran publisher are George Sterling, David Starr Jordan, Professor Ryder, Clark Ashton Smith, Robert E. Cowan and Edwin Markham.

Robertson is a resident of Redwood City.

The leading book store in San Francisco was operated by Aleck Robertson. Prior to that, he ran a small book store in Tombstone during its first bonanza era. *San Mateo Daily News Leader*, October 15, 1920

Tombstone townsfolk he met, never forgot these days, as the Earp Papers in the Huntington Library make clear. Over the years, Robertson's store in San Francisco was a must-stop when Wyatt Earp, George Parsons, Lewis Blinn, Buckskin Frank Leslie, and other pioneer Tombstoners were in town.[193]

RULE, RICHARD Rule was one of the "big guys," associated with the bonanza years of Tombstone, first arriving there from Tucson in autumn of 1881, and there is no easy way to summarize his significance. He was a newspaperman with experience in Nevada with the *Territorial Enterprise* newspaper, who ended up in Tombstone being associated with both the *Nugget* and the *Epitaph* newspapers. That covers a lot of Western journalism. Add to that the *Tucson Star* and the *El Paso Herald,* and you can concoct an interesting rendition of journalism in the West. You have to add that during Rule's Tombstone years he had a ranch in the Sulphur Spring Valley, was a secretary to the territorial prison commission, and until the end of his life was connected with Western law as well as journalism.

Rule was a customs inspector along the border, for years part-owner of the *El Paso Her-*

ald, and at one period in 1894, a bartender in Pecos, New Mexico. He died in El Paso on September 23, 1908, a true man of the Western frontier.[194]

SAFFORD, ANSON PACELY-KILLEN (P. K.) The Schieffelins and Gird may have discovered the Tombstone silver deposits, but it was the financial backing and political clout of Safford that led to the rapid development of mines and mills. He was born in Vermont in 1828, held important positions in California and Nevada, then in 1869 was appointed governor of Arizona Territory. His frontier career was important and is easy to follow.

He and John Vosburg were quickly convinced of the Tombstone finds of 1878, and the next two years were filled with activity and promotion. They were in and out of the area frequently, and Safford opened a local office there, as well as a second financial institution, the Safford, Hudson & Co. Bank, on July 1, 1880 (shortly after the Agency Pima County Bank, which opened May 10, 1880). He owned several mining companies, parts of others, and in particular pushed the Tombstone Mill & Mining Company. A few examples will indicate the reach of his influence. In August 1879, the Philadelphia newspapers praised Safford's work with the Tombstone Mill & Mining Co., which just declared a dividend. The *Arizona Weekly Citizen* of September 11, 1880, printed an interview with him in which he used words like "unsurpassed" and "remarkable" to describe the Tombstone riches, and predicted that within a year the population might be as high as 20,000. It is seldom that new mine developments get such flattering attention from high government officials.

Having done it all (and gotten very rich), Safford left the Southwest for Tarpon Springs, Florida. He maintained contacts with some Tombstone investors and residents, even still held property there, while becoming a major presence in Tarpon Springs and that section of Florida. A Safford Avenue (there is also one in Tombstone, just north of Fremont) and the Safford House Museum there are indications of that status. Safford died in Tarpon Springs on December 15, 1891.[195]

SCHIEFFELIN BROTHERS Not much is needed here to summarize the careers of Ed and Al Schieffelin. Ed was the major figure of these two Pennsylvania-born prospectors.

Governor A. P. K. Safford of Arizona grubstaked the Schieffelin discovery of the Tombstone silver. Farish, *History of Arizona, VIII*, 1918.

They were early in the West and sampled and prospected terrain in half a dozen western states and territories. What they eventually did was to discover, then arrange to develop, one of the most interesting precious metals areas in the United States. This happened in 1877, in what Ed would refer to as "Tombstone." The details, the events of the discovery and development during 1877 through 1880 have been well told by historians, as well as by accounts of Ed Schieffelin and Richard Gird themselves. An interesting slant on things is that neither the Schieffelins nor Gird would play important parts in the development of the community of Tombstone.

Ed liked what he found, but it was the searching and finding that inspired his travels. The post-Tombstone years included an almost-call to South Africa, serious efforts of prospecting in California, Oregon, and Alaska, and a marriage, but not really settling down. Ed died in a cabin in Oregon sometime in May of 1897. As per his wishes, his body was sent back to Tombstone for burial, where a major monument west of town was erected to this important pioneer. Brother Albert, always sort of a sidekick to Ed, didn't have the pushing need to prospect. He died at age thirty-six of "consumption" at his mother's home in Los Angeles, in October 1885, only a few years after the famous discovery.[196]

SEVENOAKS, JOHN This fellow, one of the most talented prospectors of the American West, was in the Tombstone district off and on during the original bonanza days. It was said that he could practically smell gold and silver. He usually acted on behalf of others, most of the time for George Hearst and James Ben Ali Haggin of San Francisco.

In 1882-83, Sevenoaks was in and out of Tombstone often, mostly getting property for Hearst in the Dragoons,

but also scouting and prospecting in other parts of Cochise County. He usually went where there was tall talk or speculation. In 1882, for example, at the famous non-duel of editors Pat Hamilton (editor of the *Independent*) and Sam Purdy (editor of the *Tombstone Epitaph*), who disagreed on so many things they agreed to a duel in 1882, Sevenoaks and Dr. Goodfellow were seconds for Purdy. Both backed out at the last moment.

In 1888-89, Sevenoaks was mostly involved with the gold rush to Harqua Hala, again on behalf of George Hearst. This Harqua Hala rush could almost be called a Tombstone reunion, as Wyatt Earp, former sheriff of Pima County Charlie Shibell, James Coyle, Nellie Cashman, and other notable Tombstone veterans were on hand.

By 1890 Sevenoaks passed through Yuma, but not quick enough for authorities. He was arrested for being drunk, raising a revolver, and so forth. This was the Sevenoaks pattern. He was a man of extremes, in the forefront of the rush to the great precious metal fields, but frequently drunk and causing trouble. The big-time speculators and horse racing enthusiasts like Hearst, Haggin, and Lloyd Tevis may not have particularly liked Sevenoaks, but they liked what he produced. It was Sevenoaks who convinced George Hearst to invest in the Homestake Mine in South Dakota, the richest gold producer in the history of the United States.

For thirty years, Sevenoaks used as his base Santa Clara and San Jose, California, with frequent forays throughout the Western gold and silver camps. He died in Pueblo, New Mexico, in February of 1897.[197]

SHERMAN, WILLIAM TECUMSEH General Sherman is one of the better-known figures in American history. He is best known for his March to the Sea during the Civil War. In the post-war era most of his service was in the plains and mountain states. His status was such that in 1869 he was named the commanding general of the United States Army by President Ulysses S. Grant.

As part of a tour of Western posts in April of 1882, Sherman and party visited and inspected Fort Huachuca, Tombstone, and Tucson with his old friend and well known Tombstoner, George Parsons. He arrived in Tombstone in the evening of April 7 with two six-horse military ambulances. Tombstone, the mining community in bonanza, a household name in the United States, did not have railroad service. The few days in Tombstone were busy and included a public gathering in front of the Grand Hotel, a meal with local dignitaries (including John Clum) at the Maison Doree, in the Bilicke-owned, Earp-favored Cosmopolitan Hotel, and an evening reception at Schieffelin Hall.

Tombstone's *raison d'etre* was mining, and General Sherman probably had more of that emphasized than he wanted. He was given an underground tour of the Toughnut Mine, followed by the same at the Grand Central, then was lectured on the workings of the Girard Mill. Some Tombstone notables were part of the entourage, and included editor John Clum, mining engineer John Church, and Judge George Berry.

After the party's brief sojourn in Tombstone, they continued on to Tucson, for more public gatherings and receptions. The Tombstone visit was not just that of an army general visiting a mining camp. This was the leading general in the nation who was acknowledging Tombstone's significance.[198]

SHIBELL, CHARLES A. Midwesterner Charles Shibell arrived in Arizona in 1861 during the Civil War with the California Fifth Infantry. He was a farmer, freighter, and miner, and served as sheriff of Pima County between 1876 and 1882. These were important times in the territory as the Tombstone bonanza was in full swing. Tombstone was in Pima County, and Sheriff Shibell appointed Wyatt Earp as one of his local deputies there. In the ensuing period when Cochise County was created, Shibell continued to have frequent contact with Tombstone and the newly named district, as mining and transportation controversies and roving posses were fairly frequent. Folks like Virgil Earp, Wyatt Earp, John Behan, Bob Paul, and a host of lawyers and judges were all part of the mix that included Sheriff Shibell. His subsequent careers included roles as deputy sheriff, county recorder, census marshal, mining at Tombstone, merchant houses in New Mexico, and hotel operations in Tucson.

An interesting Tombstone re-connection occurred in 1889 when gold was discovered at Harqua Hala in Yuma County. For a few weeks, Charlie Shibell, Nellie Cashman, and Wyatt Earp were working practically adjacent claims. Shibell died in Tucson on October 21, 1908, and is buried in Evergreen Cemetery; not far from his former Tombstone sheriff Johnny Behan.[199]

SHORT, LUKE Short is one of the bigger names when discussing the exciting parts of Western frontier life. He was born in Arkansas in 1854 and over the decades saw most of the action towns in the West, such as Dodge City and the other Kansas cow towns, Tombstone, and so forth. He was many things, including gunfighter, cowboy, scout, gambler, and saloon proprietor; and his name was linked with many of the brighter stars known for frontier high living. Later in life he even made several trips to Chicago, where he had horse racing interests. He knew well all the famous Dodge City crew that moved further west, including Bat Masterson and Wyatt Earp.

Short spent only a brief time in Tombstone in 1881, where at the Oriental Saloon he was part of the faro team headed by Lou Rickabaugh and Wyatt Earp. At about one o'clock on the afternoon of February 26, 1881, Short got into yet another argument with gambler Charles S.

Storms over a dispute regarding some faro doings at the Oriental. Apparently, their disagreements had been simmering for a day; and Storms was now determined to kill Short. On the day in question, things erupted, and even Bat Masterson was unable to diffuse the situation. Storms may have been a bit tipsy. On Allen Street, both men drew revolvers, and Storms was fatally wounded, with Luke Short casually walking away.

The shooting was obviously of some interest, as quite a few people commented on the event over the years, including diarist George Parsons, bystander Bat Masterson, and Dr. George Goodfellow, who was interested into what extent the fatal bullet had flattened.

A few days later, Justice A. O. Wallace cleared Luke Short of any charges, indicating that the situation was one of self-defense. Short soon after left Tombstone and until his death in Kansas on September 8, 1893, continued the various activities included in the era's term of "the sporting life."

In 1883 he was a member of the famous "Dodge City Peace Commission," in the midst of the brief Dodge City Saloon War, and posed for one the Wild West's most iconic photos in that regard, with Wyatt

Texas/Kansas gunfighter Luke Short was a participant in one of Tombstone's most famous shooting scrapes. Public Domain

Earp and Bat Masterson and company. On February 8, 1887, Short would be involved in another legendary gunfight, this time with Marshal Jim Courtwright, whom he killed in the dual, in Fort Worth, Texas; further enhancing his notoriety as one of the West's premier and feared gunfighters.[200]

SILLS, H. F. Sills may have been a Canadian. Supposedly he was a railroad man, in Tombstone on a layoff from the Atchison, Topeka, and the Santa Fe. He stayed in a lodging house, and for a week or so had been in the hospital.

Sills appears to have been the most important witness at the hearings conducted by Justice Wells Spicer concerning the Gunfight at the O.K. Corral. He stated that while standing in front of the O.K. Corral, he'd heard threats against the Earps, and learning who Marshal Virgil Earp was, warned him about those threatening his life. Moments later, Sills witnessed the bloody encounter.

The Sills comments at the hearings coincided exactly with the position of the Earp faction. Furthermore, a stranger to Tombstone, Sills had no stake in these events. With such clear statements by an uninterested bystander, the decision in Earp's favor was assured. There were other witnesses, details galore, praise and condemnation, but the beacon of light from Sills meant that Justice Spicer concluded that Marshal Virgil Earp and his deputies had been acting appropriately as men of the law.

That's it for him; his origins, as well as his future days, are a blank, though many researchers have tried to uncover more about this fellow. He remains one of the leading shadowy figures in Western courtroom history.[201]

SIPPY, BEN This Pennsylvania native, a mining man, arrived in Tombstone in 1880 and almost had a dazzling career. Sippy was not there long but was involved in some exciting incidents.

He had some claims in the Mule Mountains, which were not productive, so clung to the Tombstone possibilities. The years 1880-81 were busy, with a few shootings in town, talk of lynching here and there, and in the midst of Tombstone confusion, Ben Sippy became chief of police. He was busy in and out of the saloons, and was on hand at Vogan's when a nasty mob thought of lynching "Johnny-Behind-the-Deuce." If one kept a score card of the law-and-order events that concerned Sippy, one could conclude that he was sort of okay as a policeman.

However, in June 1881, after having held office for only seven months (from his November 12, 1880 election victory over Virgil Earp, through June 6, 1881), Police Chief Ben Sippy was given a two-week leave of absence and disappeared, apparently owing money in town. Australian researcher and Tombstone historian and Wyatt Earp Vendetta Rider/ Posse authority Peter Brand has tracked his career, including his pre- and post-Tombstone treachery.

As a figure in Tombstone history, he was important due to his presence there in the early, active days. And, in the world of Earp concerns, it must be pointed out that there were two elections for chief of police in this period. In the first, the voters of Tombstone selected Ben Sippy rather than Virgil Earp, who didn't contest the second. Wyatt would later claim that Sippy left as he "couldn't handle the town" and was paid ("bought off") by the citizen's safety committee to leave.[202]

SMITH, MARCUS AURELIUS Smith was a Kentuckian, and became a lawyer there before moving West. He arrived in Tombstone in 1880 and was soon practicing law with partner Ben Goodrich. For this decade, Smith knew all the players, as in addition to being a lawyer and interested in mines, he also became district attorney. His name will be found in legal and mining records associated with practically all men of note in greater Tombstone. He was also active in fishing and hunting, which gave him contact and familiarity with much of this part of the territory.

By the 1890s, Smith was on a wider stage, not only in Arizona Territory, but also nationally. For years he was a delegate to the United State Congress, and after statehood, became a United States senator; he was active, very controversial, and on key committees regarding mining, Indian affairs, and water. When he eventually lost an election, Smith managed to get a government appointment which kept him in Washington. Smith died in 1924, a leading legal and political figure in the transition from territory to statehood. Although the last decades of his life were mostly Tucson-based, it was the Tombstone beginnings that had prepared the way for his successful career.[203]

SMITH, O. C. Origen C. Smith, aka Charlie, or, frequently, "Harelip," was not important in a who-was-who of Tombstone, but he was entangled with dozens of the people, in many the incidents, that helped give Tombstone its reputation. From Connecticut and in Tombstone during the 1880s, he had half a dozen occupations including ranching, mining, and farming, and was frequently a lawman.

O.C. Smith was a close friend of Fred Dodge, which means the law-and-order or Earp faction. In his Tombstone years, Smith must have witnessed or participated in several dozen saloon brawls, some including gun play, for which he could show cars; in one year he was shot three times. In March of 1882, Charlie was a member of the Wyatt Earp Vendetta Posse against the cowboy element. From the mid-1880s forward, he was usually a deputy constable to Fred Dodge, and this means dozens of trips to ranches, canyons, abandoned mine shafts, and so forth, in and around Tombstone. A reader can follow Smith's trail in the newspapers, court records, and mining deeds, and find out much of what was happening in Tombstone.

But after a while, not much happened. In the 1890s Smith moved to the Phoenix area, pretty much doing the same things: mining, ranching, and farming. Because of his Tombstone experiences, he also was named as a constable, and was for a time a justice of the peace. Smith died while on a visit to Tucson in late November, 1907.[204]

SMITH, PHILIP W. (P.W.) A Kentuckian who was a Mexican War veteran and settled in the West Philip Smith was variously employed in California and Arizona and was early on the scene in Tombstone. In May of 1880, Smith established a branch of the Pima County Bank (the Agency Pima County Bank, Tombstone's first bank) in his store on the southwest corner of Fourth and Allen (the old J. B. Allen store), which obviously had to change its name to Cochise in 1882 (with the county name change from Pima to Cochise). Smith joined with Heyman Solomon, the Tombstone city treasurer, in some mining ventures around town, as well as in the Winchester Mountains in the northern part of Cochise County. Things didn't work out, and an assignee's suit of 1886 for more than $35,000 gives an idea of costs involved in these mining schemes.

After the mid-1880s, Smith shifted his focus to the Dos Cabezas area of Cochise County, where he would be involved in the merchant life and mining until his death in July 1901. He was active, but at best only moderately successful in his various ventures.[205]

SMITH, WILLIAM JEFFERSON RANDOLPH ("Soapy") This was Soapy Smith, one of the most famous con men in American history. He got his start in Denver in 1879, and for a few decades had spurts of success and fleeing the law in many Western states and territories.

His nickname of "Soapy" was based on wrapping bars of soap with paper currency, then further wrapping the bundle. Stationed on a street corner, he and cronies would talk up whether or not one could select the bar of soap with the money. From time to time an "associate" would howl with delight, which might encourage a bystander to try his luck. In this type of scam, the luck belonged to Soapy.

Why skip Tombstone when that place was in bonanza? In January and February of 1882, Soapy was in town and for some days registered at the Cosmopolitan Hotel. Although he was committing no crime, many of the locals were on to his game, and the *Nugget* wrote of the "fakir" and the "soap racket" that was going on at the corner of Allen and Fourth Streets. Other evidence shows that the community had a few suckers because Soapy returned for a lucrative visit in Tombstone in December of 1883.

His later stops included Denver and Creede, Colorado, and many other places, until he landed at his dream community, Skagway, Alaska, which was the leading depar-

ture point for those going to the Klondike gold fields. Soapy controlled the town for months with a gang of fifty. In June 1898, at the local wharf, with rifle on shoulder, he was threatening a guard, Frank Reid, who shot Soapy twice with a revolver, killing him. Reid, also shot in the exchange, died days later.[206]

SOLOMON, HEYMAN/HYMAN
Here is a fellow to challenge any biographer. He was from Prussia and was naturalized in Nevada County, California, in 1856. Solomon probably worked as a miner for some time, then by the late 1860s was operating a restaurant in San Diego, where he remained for some years. By the late 1870s Solomon was in Florence, Arizona, in business with S. Mund. Yet, by 1879, he was in in San Francisco, associated with the merchant Tobias Oberfelder. Apparently Oberfelder sent him to Tombstone, at least by 1880.

Solomon would be in Tombstone through 1884, most of that time as manager of the Pima County Bank (name changed to Cochise County bank). For a few years he was also the Tombstone city treasurer and had been a Cochise County supervisor. His son Charles was a cashier in the Safford, Hudson Bank, then in the Cochise County Bank.

Solomon was certainly active. He was in business with George Hearst, owning mines in Tombstone and several in the Winchester Mountains. In 1882, when Wyatt Earp began his famous Vendetta Ride, Earp was walking by the Cochise County Bank, and Solomon asked him if he needed anything. Wyatt mentioned that Doc Holliday needed a gun. Solomon went in the bank and returned, handing Wyatt his best Winchester.

By the mid-1880s Solomon was in Los Angeles, and in the various voting registers of that decade was identified either as a miner or a saloon keeper. He ran a restaurant in the Nadeau Hotel in 1892. During that era, his wife, Emma, operated a restaurant and a small L. A. hotel. Solomon died there in late December 1901, and in his obituary, it was stated that while working for Charles Ducommun, the hardware merchant, Solomon was the first in Los Angeles to produce a marketable artificial ice. This all hangs together because for some years he and Ducommun had been in the same Los Angeles Masonic lodge. His daughter Lillie married into the prominent Glassell family.

It seems that all of the above, the various occupations and locations, must concern several different men, but the documentation all along the way (naturalization, names of wife and children) all point to Heyman Solomon as having a very diverse set of careers.[207]

Banker and city treasurer Hyman Solomon was part of the Earp faction. *Arizona Quarterly Illustrated,* July 1880.

SORIN, THOMAS R. and SARAH The Sorin career is one of the most solid in southern Arizona. After Civil War service with a Pennsylvania unit, Thomas Sorin headed West, worked mostly as a printer and journalist, was in Tucson in 1879, and soon headed to Tombstone. There, in 1880, with John Clum and Charles Reppy, he founded the *Tomb-*

stone *Epitaph*, one of the landmark publications of the mining frontier. Sorin gradually drifted, as he was fascinated with prospecting, mining, and speculation, having had several moderate successes, and becoming widely known for his promotion of local mining. He later headed the Arizona mineral show for the Columbian Exposition in Chicago in 1893, and was a delegate, speaker, and officer at many mining and mineral conventions in the West.

In 1898, Sorin married Sarah Herring (the daughter of Tombstone attorney William Herring), who would become a leading attorney in southern Arizona Territory. Born in New York, January 15, 1861, in 1893 she became the first woman to practice before the Arizona Supreme Court, and in 1913 the first (without the assistance of a male), to argue a case before the U. S. Supreme Court. Thomas and Sarah gradually shifted to Tucson, but much of their time was spent at their retreat in the Dragoon Mountains. Thomas died there in March of 1923, and was taken back to Tucson for burial next to Sarah, who had preceded him in death, having died at age fifty-three, on April 30, 1914, of influenza pneumonia, in Globe, Arizona.

The Sorin career was much wider than Tombstone, but his dramatic start there in founding the *Tombstone Epitaph,* and his many decades of association with people like John Clum, Thomas Herring, Dick Gird, C. S. Fly, E. B. Gage, and George Parsons, as well as his marriage to Sarah Herring, assured that practically anything written about Tombstone would include some role for Thomas Sorin.[208]

SOULE, WILLIAM H. Often referred to as Billy, Soule was a Massachusetts native who served as a bugler in the 2d California Cavalry during the Civil War. By 1880 he was in the new settlement of Tombstone, where he was listed as a farmer. In the following four or five years, Soule was a "government man," on the payroll of Sheriff Johnny Behan as a deputy, as well as a jailer (not a very good one), and later a member of the Tombstone police force. Soule gets his name in various Tombstone accounts for his inadequate work as a jailer, and for the fact that he was in the area on the day of the famous 1881 gunfight. He was a witness at the Spicer hearings because he rounded up the horses of the McLaury brothers after the confrontation.

Soule was married in Tombstone in 1883 and seems to have moved to Los Angeles by 1889, operating a saloon there at least through 1891. At that time, he applied for a Civil War pension. When admitted to the Old Soldiers' Home in Sawtelle, Los Angeles County, in 1910, he identified himself as a miner from Bisbee. Soule died in the Old Soldiers' Home on July 1, 1916, and is buried in the adjacent cemetery in Section 30, row A, number 8.[209]

SPANGENBERG, GEORGE F. A native of Albany, New York, George Spangenberg was in Tombstone in 1880. He would become the town's leading gunsmith, one of the better-known in the territory, for several years operating a place on Fourth Street, near the post office. Because of his business, Spangenberg knew most of the leading personalities in town, the mining types, saloon attenders, cowboys, and the law-and-order community. Once, while serving on a grand jury committee, he was particularly harsh regarding the administration (or lack of it) in the sheriff's office headed by John Behan.

Despite his strong Tombstone connection, Spangenberg left in 1882 to try his hand at the Alaska gold excitement. He didn't do so well and returned home from Nome to San Francisco, with "the gold hunting Schieffelin party," led by Tombstone founder Ed Schieffelin, on October 6, 1883. "The party ('Unsuccessful Gold Hunters') left San Francisco a year ago last summer, buoyant with the hope of suddenly acquiring wealth, but it is said they returned $25,000 poorer than when they set forth." He then headed to Phoenix, opening a hardware store. In a newspaper ad of 1890, Spangenberb's friend from Tombstone days, L. W. Blinn, announced that his lumber deals in Phoenix could be facilitated at the Spangenberg Hardware, because of the new telephone connection there.

The Spangenberg career, though, would be in the Northwest, not the Southwest. By 1894 Spangenberg was in Seattle, where he married, and he would be in that city in business for decades. His "operation" on Main Street was a major dealer in cutlery, guns, fishing tackle, and sporting goods of all kinds. Spangenberg kept threatening to go out of business, but as late as 1920 was still pushing cutlery. He died in Seattle on July 15, 1942.[210]

SPENCE, PETE Known also as Peter Spencer, Elliott Larkin Ferguson, and a few other names, this Texan had some Confederate service and also had good reason to flee a robbery charge in 1878. He became part of the Pima County cowboy crowd. Spence had some bartending experience in Bisbee and Tombstone, was accused of robbing a stage (with Frank Stilwell), and his wife asserted that he was a participant in the assassination of Morgan Earp in March of 1882. Pete was conveniently in jail when the Wyatt Earp Vendetta Posse visited his wood camp, but they at least managed to rub out Florentino Cruz, also implicated in the Morgan Earp assassination.

He was smart enough to leave Tombstone, and for a time was a constable and deputy sheriff in New Mexico. Spence was also involved in a saloon brawl over a gambling match in Clifton which resulted in a gunfight with a fellow named Martinez. Both men were shot, but Martinez fatally. Spence subsequently ended up spending time at the Yuma Territorial Prison. He received a governor's pardon, and some years later married the widow of Phin Clanton. Spence (E. L. Ferguson at the time) died near Globe on January 30, 1914, and was described as a "well known character throughout the southwest." [211]

SPICER, WELLS Born in Tioga County, New York in 1831, he became one of the better-known personalities of Western history and had intimate association with two of the Wild West's key incidents: the Mountain Meadows Massacre and the Tombstone gunfight of October 1881. Prior to arriving in Tombstone, Spicer had been an attorney, a government clerk, and a journalist.

In Tombstone he was only one of six or seven justices of the peace. It was in the court of Justice Spicer that the hearings would be held to determine if the killing of Billy Clanton and Tom and Frank McLaury, by the faction led by Marshal Virgil Earp, should be sent to a higher court for final decision. The month-long Spicer hearings, with thirty witnesses, is one of the most well-known legal events in American history. Spicer's role in this, and his entire life saga, has been carefully researched and written in several places by Lynn Bailey.

The following years of his career were mostly spent out of Tombstone. He was a prospector, actually worked some claims, invested in others. There were several properties in Sonora, especially around

171

Ures, that took much of his time. He later concentrated on the Quijotoa Mining District. Several newspapers in April 1887 reported that Judge Spicer was last seen "several months ago" after leaving Quijotoa, supposedly with the thought of committing suicide. That was the end of the active trail for Wells Spicer.[212]

SPRINGER, ALBERT A. Born in Bavaria in 1847, Springer joined the employ of the Zeckendorf firm in Tucson in 1879. Two years later he became partner in a merchandising business in Charleston, hoping that this community would at least rival nearby Tombstone. Things didn't work out, and by 1883 Springer was living in Tombstone.

In 1883-84 in Tombstone there was a banking shake-up. The former Agency Pima County Bank became the Cochise County Bank. Heyman and Charles Solomon, father and son, manager and cashier, had fallen out of favor with Lionel Jacobs of Tucson, the majority owner. The Solomons had become too close to the mine owners in town, and Jacobs didn't like that connection. Springer was hired as the cashier, and for a few years Jacobs spent quite a bit of time in Tombstone. Springer was retained as cashier into the late 1880s.

Springer then went to New York City, where he again became a banker. His career can somewhat be followed in the New York newspapers from 1892 onwards. Springer's daughter, Edna Hackes Springer, "born in Arizona," became a famed singer, dancer, and elocutionist.[213]

STILWELL, FRANK Frank and brother Jack had origins in Iowa and Missouri. By the late 1870s Frank was in and around Charleston, Arizona, doing some saloon work, and working as a freighter on the Tombstone ore run with Ham Light, who operated a stage and freight service. He also had connections, and some work, in Bisbee, Arizona.

From 1877 through 1881 Stilwell was "known" in the area, as there were a few killings and robberies where his name was mentioned. And his name was part of the fabric of two of Tombstone's leading events, the street ambush of Virgil Earp late in December 1881 and the assassination in the Hatch saloon of Morgan Earp in 1882.

All of this deadly, murky stuff was enough to convince the Earp and law-and-order faction that Frank Stilwell was one of the fellows that needed treatment. On March 20, 1882, the Wyatt Earp party was in Tucson at the train station, seeing that the wounded Virgil Earp and deceased Morgan Earp were sent off to Mom and Dad in California. It was learned that Frank Stilwell had been lurking nearby, and possibly intending to finish up the job. Details are contradictory, but there is no question that the body of Frank Stilwell was found on the railroad tracks, riddled with bullets, and the coroner concluded that this was the responsibility of the Earp faction. This rubbing-out of Frank Stilwell in a Tucson railyard was a key incident in the Tombstone Earp saga.[214]

STILWELL, SIMPSON EVERETT "JACK," "COMANCHE JACK" This noted frontiersman had a few days or so in Tombstone, but his presence and personality deserve a mention. Simpson E. Stilwell (1850-1903), raised in Kansas, became a U. S. Army scout, deputy U. S. marshal, police judge, and a U. S. commissioner. He had roles and impact on Indian affairs and settlements in many Western states and territories. Jack was the hero of the legendary "Beecher's Island" (Colorado) standoff against a Cheyenne Indian war party in September 1868, and in great part responsible for saving his fellow troops/scouting party, who were under siege. His reputation was of the highest order.

When he learned that his younger brother Frank Stilwell had been obliterated by the Wyatt Earp Vendetta Posse in a Tucson railroad yard, Jack at once went on to Tucson and Tombstone to unravel and set to rights the murder of his brother. The consensus of historians seems to be that it didn't take him long to realize that brother Frank had been a loser in many ways and was no doubt responsible for the ambush and killing of Morgan Earp by shooting through a saloon window in Tombstone on March 18, 1882. Jack was also perplexed by the term "cowboy," which in Arizona and the far West meant things disreputable and criminal, whereas in the cattle country of Middle America, the word had a more positive connotation. He left Arizona an informed man, no longer interested in avenging his deadbeat brother. [215]

STILWELL, WILLIAM H. Stilwell was a well-educated New York lawyer who was sent west to help establish the law system in Arizona Territory. In 1881 he was named an associate justice of the Territorial Supreme Court.

There were three justices, and each was assigned to a block of counties. Judge Stilwell was assigned to the first judicial district, which contained the counties of Pima, Cochise, Graham, and Pinal. He was not a Tombstone nor a Cochise County judge, yet organized the first district, with Tombstone offices, having a similar role in Tucson, Safford, and Florence.

After the famous gunfight of October 26, 1881, the hearings before Justice Wells Spicer determined that the Earp faction had been justified, so the matter did not proceed to a higher court; any higher court action would have involved Judge Stilwell. However, Stilwell was in Tombstone during part of the Earp vendetta days and was drawn into the legal quagmire by the issuing of warrants for posses and so forth. On one occasion he told Wyatt Earp, regarding warrants: "Next time you'd better leave your prisoners out in the brush"—the term

During the Tombstone bonanza era, Judge William H. Stilwell was an attorney specializing in mining and water rights. Roy B. Young Collection.

"mesquite" is quoted by some authors—"where alibis don't count."

Judge Stilwell also figured in the dramatic assassination in Tucson of Frank Stilwell (a distant relative), by Wyatt Earp and his Vendetta Posse. Wyatt, convinced that Frank

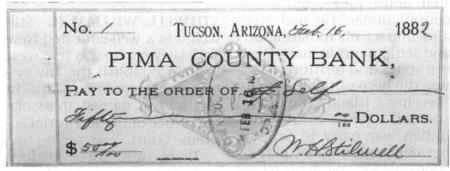

Although Judge Stilwell was responsible for four counties, he spent much of his time in the thriving bonanza town of Tombstone, Cochise County. David D. de Haas, MD Collection.

Stilwell had caused the killing of Morgan Earp a few days earlier in Tombstone, caught up with him in the Tucson railyard and filled him full of lead on March 20, 1882. At this time the grand jury was meeting in Tucson, and they heard testimony from witnesses and presented a true bill to Judge Stilwell, stating that the deed had been committed by Doc Holliday, Wyatt Earp, Warren Earp, Sherman McMaster, and John Johnson.

Tombstone's existence was based on mining, and as district judge, William Stilwell presided over one of the territory's most significant mining/legal issues, the apex question, which concerned surface and underground vein rights. The case, *Tombstone Mill & Mining Company v. Way Up Mining Company*, would be a hallmark of Arizona legislation for years. The case moved up to the Arizona Territorial Supreme Court on appeal, where the decision was affirmed. And who was on this appeal's court? Judge Stilwell, who had been the judge in the lower court decision.

However, local and territorial politics were hard on his career, and he was removed from the bench in the middle of his term in 1882, in a politi-

cally motivated "clean sweep" by Washington, DC (during President Chester A. Arthur's administration), a sweep that at the time also involved (in varying circumstances) John C. Fremont, Frederick A. Tritle, John J. Gosper, U. S. Marshal Crawley Dake, and Colonel Zabriskie; this sweep newspapers referred to as "wholesale stalwartising." Stilwell settled in Tombstone and opened a law office, with cases mostly there and in Tucson. He became an authority on land, mining, and water law, and later served as Cochise County attorney. In 1894 Stilwell moved to Phoenix where he continued his successful law practice.

In 1899-1900 his career took a turn. He became a major in the U. S. Volunteer Army and served as paymaster during the Spanish-American War, most of the time being stationed in San Francisco, which was the center of the forces serving in the Philippines. After the war, Stilwell returned to his Phoenix legal practice. His name in legal circles is particularly associated with a few important water cases, so important in southern Arizona. He died in Phoenix on May 8, 1928.[216]

STREET, WEBSTER This Ohio native was educated in the law when he went west to Arizona Territory, practicing in several places before winding up in Tombstone in the early 1880s. Street was deep in local politics, the local mining and social scene, and served a term as Tombstone city attorney, in on most of the important legal events of Tombstone, including the well-known townsite controversy, which caused much litigation in the early 1880s.

In 1885 and 1886, there were several ways in which Judge Street was involved in this controversial Tombstone townsite question. In 1885, he ruled against "Townsite Clark," who for years had claimed the choice property of Tombstone. That this was of vital interest was made plain when a twelve-pound can of explosives was found under Clark's house. In February 1886, Street again ruled against claimants in the Mountain Maid Mine case, which was related to the townsite issue.

By 1887, though, with the end of the bonanza, Street headed to Phoenix, joining Ben & Briggs Goodrich as partners in a law firm. Street rose to the highest levels possible in Arizona Territory, becoming chief justice and later the U. S. attorney general, another who rode the Tombstone beginnings to the fullest. He died in Los Angeles on September 21, 1908.[217]

TACK, MARY There were not many ways on the frontier for a woman to make a living, but running a boarding house was fairly common. Mary Tack was born in Sweden in the early 1830s and most of her family immigrated to the Midwest. In the 1870s she was in San Francisco, working in a hotel, moving to Tombstone in the early 1880s and opening a rooming or boarding house on Allen Street.

This would be an important merchant house for more than a decade. Tack had a sound reputation, a good location, and was also interested in the community. She invested in mining claims, owned part of the ice works at Fairbank, and was known for her charitable work. Tack had her share of troubles, such as several robberies and thefts, and was not hesitant to take folks to the justice courts in order to collect debts. Her boarding house also served as a minor social location; several weddings and other celebrations were held there.

By the mid-1890s, however, traffic to Tombstone had thinned, and Mary Tack moved to Bisbee, that other local mining center that would thrive for decades. She put up the Belmont Hotel on Subway Alley, which became a solid addition to Bisbee commercial life. Her reputation in Bisbee remained the same—a solid, reliable, respectable business lady. Mary Tack died in Bisbee in late 1915, and was buried in Minnesota, where her brother Andrew lived. Her estate was estimated at more than $40,000.[218]

TASKER, JOSEPH This New Hampshire native lived in San Diego, then in 1880 went to the new community of Tombstone and entered the liquor business. Within a short time, he combined with George Pridham, and the Tasker, Pridham & Co. grocery on Allen and Fifth was a leading business in the town. When Cochise County was created in 1881, Tasker became one of the first members of the new board of supervisors. All of this pointed to a major career in the mining community in bonanza.

It was not to be. Within a few years Tasker moved to the area near Phoenix, where he had a farm, vineyards, even a saloon. He soon returned to Cochise County, though, at Soldiers Hole, operating a successful horse and cattle ranch

for many years. Shortly after 1900, he moved back to San Diego, married there in 1909, and by 1920 was retired. Tasker died in San Diego on July 26, 1921.[219]

TIPTON, DANIEL "TIP" Tipton was one of the members of the Wyatt Earp Vendetta Posse, organized to seek revenge on the cowboys who had attacked his family. Tipton arrived in Tombstone from Virginia City, Nevada, where mining and gambling had interested him, in March of 1881, with gunman/gambler Jim Bruce, and was apparently a friend of gambler Lou Rickabaugh and may also have known Bat Masterson. In December of 1881, Virgil Earp was ambushed and wounded in Tombstone. Tipton was one of the rough crowd that Wyatt recruited as part of his legendary Vendetta Posse.

By February, 1882, tensions had risen, and Tipton and Ben Maynard got into a fistfight in the Alhambra Saloon, and both were arrested and fined. On the evening of March 18, when Morgan Earp was slain while playing pool in the Campbell & Hatch Saloon, Tipton was present. A few days later, when Florentino Cruz was killed by Wyatt Earp's posse, Tipton was a participant and so noted in the coroner's inquest. He was not at the Iron Springs shootout, where Wyatt eliminated Curly Bill Brocius, though. Tipton had other important duties, as he was transporting $1,000 expense money in cash from E. B. Gage. Tipton rejoined the Earp posse at Hooker's Sierra Bonita Ranch, north of Willcox, Arizona.

This was the last phase of the Earp Vendetta Posse, as they made their way to New Mexico, then some went on to Colorado. Tipton's career path is not known in detail from that point onwards, but he was for a time employed by the U. S. customs center in El Paso. He apparently tried to use some inside knowledge and in 1897 was arrested for smuggling Chinese labor certificates. He was convicted and sentenced to twenty months in the federal penitentiary in Ohio, but lasted only four, dying there on February 25, 1898.[220]

O'BRIEN, MARY TOOMEY Quite a saga of frontier grit here. Mary Harrington was born in County Cork, Ireland in 1849, at the height of the potato famine, and the family arrived in the United States in 1863. The Toomeys (or Twomey, etc.) were in the mining camp of Grass Valley, California, where Mary met and married Dennis Twomey. They were in mining for some years in Nevada, then moved to San Bernardino, where Dennis died in 1878.

In 1880, saddled with at least four children, Mary parceled off a few to friends and relatives and took two with her to the new camp of Tombstone. Shortly after her arrival she married Thomas O'Brien, a miner. Mary became one of Tombstone's more successful businesswomen. She is often compared with Nellie Cashman (with whom she had several arrangements).

In her decade in Tombstone, Mary O'Brien was mostly connected with the Bodie House, the Arcade Restaurant, and the Russ House. Some of these, at some times, were also lodging locations. From time to time, she also earned a few dollars by providing meals to the local prisoners.

Mary's children fit in well in the community and were usually on the school honor roll. In 1886 she was praised by the *Epitaph* for firing her Chinese help, as "the Chinese must go." Sadly, this was somewhat typical in Tombstone at this time, as there was a big Anti-Chinese League effort locally, and even Nellie Cashman advertised having "white cooks."

By 1887 the town was declining, and in that year her husband died. Forced to adjust to new situations, Mary opened the Miner's Restaurant in Bisbee in 1890, but was only there a few years. By 1894 she was in Los Angeles, operating a restaurant as well as a boarding house.

It had been a tough grind for Mary, and by 1913 she was in the Boyle Heights area of Los Angeles, an inmate in the Little Sisters of the Poor, which was a home for the aged. These many, final years must have been tough. She died in the home on May 25, 1928.[221]

TRIBOLET FAMILY From five to fifteen members of this Swiss family left marks on Tombstone and southern Arizona and California. Historian Lynn Bailey has been one of the few capable of unraveling these fellows, who are frequently confused with one another. Several had vital Tombstone roles.

Around 1880, Godfrey Tribolet started the Eagle Market in Tombstone and soon launched into the Golden Eagle Brewery, which was also a saloon and restaurant. It burned down on June 22, 1881. He invested in mining, had a seat on the city council and was head of the fire department. Within a few years, Godfrey had large ranching and cattle interests, which fit in well with the family needs, and in later years he tackled many enterprises, even considerable mining attempts near Santa Fe. Godfrey died in Phoenix in December 1902.

Siegfried Tribolet opened the Crystal Palace Saloon on June 18, 1882, and operated it for years, on the same site the old Golden Eagle Brewery had previously occupied in Tombstone: the northwest corner of Fifth and Allen. Cattle interests as well as mining were part of his Tombstone years. In the 1890s, he opened one of the largest markets in Phoenix, specializing in meat and fish, and boasting that the Tribolet Market supplied seventy-five percent of the meat for Phoenix restaurants. A measure of the Tribolet success is his passport dated 1921, which shows meanderings in France, Switzerland, Italy, then on to Egypt and Australia. Siegfried died in Phoenix on August 17, 1932.

To read about Tombstone from 1880 through 1900 is to spot the Tribolet name hundreds of times. They were businessmen, sometimes active in politics, and from time to time involved in borderline activities (illegal booze). And, if a Tribolet were involved in a project, often two or three brothers were part of the mix. This was a large family that tapped into a dozen or so topics and enterprises that were important in southern Arizona.[222]

TRITLE, FREDERICK A. Frederick Tritle was an important Western political and financial figure, who had a brief but interesting connection with Tombstone. Tritle was from Pennsylvania, and in the 1860s was a leading figure in some of Nevada's mining and milling circles, having major investments in Virginia City; in 1866, he became Nevada's first elected state senator.

By the late 1870s Tritle was looking elsewhere, and with a few Easterners invested heavily in mining claims in southern Arizona and in Sonora, Mexico. Soon Tritle was spending much time in Tucson, Tombstone, and Sonora. In January 1881, he was praising the Grand Central South mine of Tombstone, and in March, Tritle and William B. Murray opened a stock investing firm on Allen Street. This was also to be the central point for controlling their Western and Sonora mining properties.

This practically ends his close contact with Tombstone, because in February, 1882, President Chester A. Arthur appointed him governor of Arizona Territory. The Tritle years as governor were filled with problems. There was considerable

Tombstone stock broker Frederick A. Tritle became governor of Arizona Territory. *Portrait and Biographical Record of Arizona*, 1901.

carry-over from the Earp-cowboy troubles, and Apache problems along the border were serious. Ranger units were formed, conditions stabilized somewhat, but the Indian situation was not solved. In February of 1885, Tritle resigned as governor, remaining in Prescott for some years and continuing in government service (as county recorder and supervisor), dying in Phoenix on November 18, 1906.[223]

TYLER, JOHNNY E. One of the more prominent Western gamblers, it was only right that he would find his way to Tombstone in the bonanza era. Johnny Tyler was born in

Missouri in 1839 and by the 1870s had tasted and tested the saloons and tables of Salt Lake City, San Francisco, Pioche, Virginia City, and a few other faro locales. Aside from being a man of faro, he was also one tough customer, and gunplay was common in his career.

His time in Tombstone was 1880-1881, and the accounts of gambling and the world of saloons have some vivid tales of his stay there. Firearms, drunkenness, and hard feelings surfaced on a few occasions, and some of his encounters involved Wyatt Earp, Doc Holliday, and Milt Joyce. Mixing alcohol and firearms led to shots in saloons, which were well documented in the *Tombstone Nugget* and *Tombstone Epitaph*. On one occasion, in June 1881, Wyatt Earp forcibly ejected Tyler from the Oriental Saloon, to the bemusement (and with the assistance) of Doc Holliday, after Tyler had been threatening and trying to intimidate Earp associate Lou Rickabaugh with a gun, at his own faro tables, very shortly after they had first been put into operation.

Tyler was forced out of Tombstone by Wyatt, departing to Tucson, Leadville (where he would again encounter Doc Holliday), Grass Valley, and other Western mining camps. Ty-

ler ended his days on January 21, 1891, after collapsing on the streets of Spokane, Washington, the day after an episode of heavy drinking followed by delirium tremens ("the DT's") that night. The subsequent inquest included the phrase "Delirium Tremens;" newspaper and eyewitness accounts claimed alcoholism, pneumonia, heart attack...[224]

UPTON, ROBERT H. Born near the Michigan-Ohio border in 1834, Robert Upton was in California by 1860, and would put in more than half a century extracting Western riches. He was in Grass Valley by 1870, mining and working as a teamster, soon moving to Mineral Park in Mohave County, Arizona, and by 1879 to the new Tombstone diggings.

Upton, a prospector and miner and a well-known local figure, was named local agent for the Cincinnati Gold & Silver Mining Company in 1880. In late 1881 he located the promising gold deposits in the Winchester District north of Tombstone, soon selling these locations to P. W. Smith, Heyman Solomon, and George Hearst. He also got involved in one of the nastier aspects of Tombstone history. In March 1882, Morgan Earp was assassinated by a shot through the window of the Campbell & Hatch Saloon. Upton was a member of the coroner's jury that determined the dirty deed was done by Frank Stilwell and crowd.

In and out of Tombstone for the rest of the decade, Upton was always prospecting and mining, using Tombstone as his base. By the early 1890s, though, he moved to Kern County, California, where by 1896 he was one of the major figures in the rich gold fields of Randsburg. His success there also had a strong Tombstone flavor, as he was in partnership with Los Angeles attorney Ben Goodrich, whom he had known in Tombstone.

In the following years the Upton successes included mining, real estate, and the new petroleum business. He died in Kern County in early March 1912, and his estate included many houses and lots.[225]

VERMILLION, JOHN OBERLAND ("TEXAS JACK") Born on October 31, 1845, in Culpepper County, Virginia, Vermillion was a Union veteran (Ohio infantry; March 5, 1864 – July 30, 1865) who had seen considerable action (and sustained extensive injury) in the Civil War. After spending time back home with his family and around the Midwest

after completing his duty, he eventually moved out West. On June 8, 1880, Texas Jack was documented in the census as having been living in Silver City, New Mexico for the past year. By early 1881 he was working as a carpenter in Tombstone, and in June was named a special policeman by Virgil Earp to control things after the disastrous fire in the community.

Vermillion got caught up in the Earp-Cowboy feud and was part of the vendetta phase of local events. Wyatt Earp had been commissioned a deputy U. S. marshal after brother Virgil was ambushed, and he gathered a few tough frontiersmen to help guard his family and to seek out certain members of the Cowboy gang he deemed responsible. Vermillion was not part of the team that slaughtered Frank Stilwell in the Tucson railroad yard, but in March 1882 he was named as one of those who had killed Florentino Cruz (aka "Indian Charley"), and a few days later he was at the Iron Springs incident, where the Earp posse eliminated Curly Bill. During that skirmish, Vermillion was not injured, but his horse was shot out from underneath him, collapsing upon Vermillion's leg and pinning him down. He was rescued by Wyatt as the posse withdrew. The accounts in the Tombstone and Tucson newspapers seldom used the name Vermillion; just "Texas Jack."

After the posse broke up at Hooker's Ranch, they headed to New Mexico and Colorado. In June 1883, Texas Jack joined friends Wyatt Earp, Bat Masterson, Luke Short, and several other esteemed gunslingers, in Dodge City, as part of the legendary "Dodge City Peace Commission," although he was one of several left out of the group photo, now designated by many as the most famous of all Wild West photographs. For a time in 1889 (and possibly as early as 1885), Vermillion was in Denver as part of the infamous Soapy Smith fraud squad. He died in the home of his younger brother Oliver, in Sunbury, Ohio, at the age of seventy-six, on November 1, 1921, and is buried in the East Liberty Cemetery, Delaware County, Ohio.[226]

VICKERS, J. V. One of the giants of the Tombstone bonanza years, John Van Vickers was born in Pennsylvania in 1850, had a sound education, and arrived in Tombstone in 1880 as a representative of the New York Life Insurance Company. For the next decade he was prominent in mining, the world of cattle, and the local political scene. For the next twenty years, no matter what the important issue in Tombstone or Cochise County, Vickers was part of the mix. County officer, territorial legislature, land development, ranching: Vickers was a man to be considered. If you omit him in your study of Tombstone, you are working without the essential tools.

Vickers was no dummy, and when Cochise County and Tombstone ceased to be action spots, Vickers turned to Southern California and merely extended his financial and real estate experiences, becoming as important there as he had been in southern Arizona. Soon, Vickers was a kingpin on Santa Rosa Island, a Channel Islands location that would become a center of an important cattle industry. He was part of a southern Arizonan contingent (which included Walter Vail, Henry Hooker, Richard Gird, and John Vosburg) that was very successful, both with California real estate and the cattle industry. Vickers died in Long Beach on December 28, 1912.[227]

VIZINA, JAMES M. For one of the key figures in the founding of Tombstone, Vizina left few traces. He was a major San Francisco caterer, shifted to Tucson, then arrived in Tombstone at the beginning of things. Vizina threw some money around, apparently in the right places. The *Arizona Daily Star* of February 5, 1880, mentioned that he was in town, handling the $35,000 recently received for his Tombstone property. Vizina joined with Benjamin Cook in financing one of the most important buildings in the community, at the northeast corner of Allen and Fifth, known as the Vizina & Cook Block, and which housed the Oriental Saloon. The Vizina name is scattered around Tombstone as well as in Cochise County, attached to mines, buildings, billiard halls, saloons, restaurants, and so forth. He was an alderman for a time, but in general was not as active in the community as his name suggests.

Because of his investing, he made a fortune, but his life would be in San Francisco, not in southern Arizona. By the late 1880s Tombstone had become a pleasant financial memory for him. His subsequent life in San Francisco would also be associated with catering and restaurants related to hotels. Vizina died in San Francisco on April 16, 1907.[228]

VOGAN, JAMES A native of Plattsburg, New York, James Vogan headed west, where he had a saloon-filled life. Vogan had been in business in Tucson, but wasted no time when bonanza hit Tombstone. In 1880, he and Jim Flynn opened a place on Allen Street promising choice liquors "in packages of five gallons or less."

There were many saloons in town, but Vogan's place was the scene of a few of Tombstone's more noteworthy events. The famous "Johnny-behind-the-Deuce" incident happened here in 1881, the stand-off where Deputy U. S. Marshal Virgil Earp and Sheriff John Behan managed to stop a lynching. In the same year, a famous fight took place, a tough saloon brawl

JAMES M. VIZINA—One of the first Councilmen of Tombstone.

Vizina was one of the first to profit from Tombstone silver. *Arizona Quarterly Illustrated*, July, 1880.

where Town Marshal Ben Sippy decided not to arrest the mob, as Tombstone only had one cell. Instead, the wild crew left, and headed to the Alhambra where they continued their business. A reading of justice files and local newspapers will reveal many other drinking, fighting, and shooting affairs in Vogan's place. James Earp worked there for a time.

In June of 1881, Vogan advertised that he had "Renovated and Improved" his saloon at 634 Allen, and renamed it the "Crystal Palace Saloon," across Allen Street and a few blocks east from where *the* legendary Crystal Palace Saloon would subsequently open (at its present-day location) over a year later in July 1882; east of where the Bird Cage Theatre would be built. One must remember, though, that this was right about the time, and near exact zone of, Tombstone's first major fire, on June 22, 1881, so if the business did re-open under that name, it may not have been for long.

After a few years, the Vogan and Flynn team left town. In 1885, Flynn was running the Congress Hall in Tucson, when old buddy Jim Vogan showed up, and had a few drinks "to alleviate his sufferings." Shortly

thereafter Flynn checked the scene, believing that Vogan had dozed off. Vogan was more than dead drunk; he was dead, at only forty-nine years of age, but most of those were spent attending or operating saloons.[229]

VOSBURG, JOHN S. This was one of the most successful mining men of the American West. He was from New York State, opened a successful gun shop in Tucson in 1870, became a member of the Arizona Territorial Legislature and a close friend of Governor Safford, then the adjutant general of the territory. These successes would pale next to the dramatic happenings around what would become Tombstone.

The Schieffelin brothers and Dick Gird found the precious silver, and convinced Safford and Vosburg to back them financially to get the Tombstone complex off and running. Of these five, only Gird and Vosburg would continue to have a role in what would become Tombstone; the Schieffelins would wander elsewhere, and Safford would be a significant promoter before he shifted to Florida.

From 1878 through 1881, Vosburg hit the Tucson-Tombstone-Los Angeles trail dozens of times. He was a major initial developer, not with shovel or hammer; but, as he was rich with mechanical and technical skills, and demonstrated administrative ability, the opening phases of Tombstone development and the roads and mills along the San Pedro River had considerable input from him. There is one aspect of Vosburg's personality that may have hampered his role in greater Tombstone. In the early phase, when overseeing some mill construction along the San Pedro River, he insisted on banning liquor of all types. This may have been a sound position, but was not regarded with enthusiasm by the workers.

Then he took the money and ran, all the way to Los Angeles County, dying there on January 9, 1931. Vosburg seems to have been one of the few people who knew what to do with gains from a mining windfall. He lived in the area surrounding the new development of Pasadena, which was turning into a visitors' paradise with its mountain scenery, fancy hotels, and significant citrus industry. Again, the Vosburg money and administrative skills were at the forefront and he developed huge fruit enter-prises, headed several citrus marketing organizations, and founded the Vosburg Water Company.

For half a century, Vosburg was a major economic presence in southern California, all based on the tremendous success at Tombstone. He was a frequent visitor to Tombstone over the decades, and in downtown Los Angeles would visit with Tombstone diarist George Parsons, who became a leading figure in the chamber of commerce and in Los Angeles port development. The great fifty years for Vosburg in southern California were based on his wise handling of some Tombstone profits.[230]

WALKER, THOMAS E. Born in Utica, New York, and a cousin of Richard Gird, Walker started life in the West at the top and kept at that level through his life. He was with the Schieffelins, Gird, Bidwell, and others in 1878 primitive Tombstone, and had a variety of talents. Acting as assayer, he kept the books and managed a few mines, all in which would become a major Western silver camp. Walker was in the forefront of those who established the Tombstone Mining District.

Walker also helped bring

to life the Grand Central, Contention, and Toughnut, some of the leading local properties. Shortly thereafter, he moved on to California (as did Gird), and found a solid niche in Oxnard, Ventura County, where for decades he served as superintendent of the local water company. Walker died there on June 10, 1930.[231]

WALLACE, ALBERT O. This Ohio native had been early on the scene in San Diego, arriving in 1852; he was a merchant who served for a time as a deputy sheriff and postmaster of North San Diego. He was in Tombstone by 1880 and in his years in the community served as a merchant, city recorder, undersheriff, and justice of the peace.

As a Tombstone justice of the peace, Wallace was involved in many significant events. It was Justice Wallace who had to deal with things when Marshal Virgil Earp bashed in the head of Ike Clanton on the day of the famous shootout. Justice files, newspaper accounts, and county records indicate his years in Tombstone were memorable.

Wallace left Tombstone in 1887 and returned to San Diego, again working as a merchant. He died in that community in May of 1895.[232]

WARD, JEROME The second sheriff of Cochise County, replacing John Behan in 1882, his time in office was unfortunately when the Bisbee Massacre occurred, a bungled robbery where several innocents were killed. The gang was taken to Tombstone, the county seat. There, while Sheriff Ward was "indisposed," ringleader John Heath was lynched. Ward subsequently presided over the (legal) hanging of the remaining five of the crew, one of the largest such public events in Western history. The bad national press spelled the end of his career, and in the

John Heath on Toughnut Street experiencing some local justice (lynching) in 1884 in one of the West's most publicized events. Library of Congress.

187

next election he was replaced as sheriff by Bob Hatch.

Ward moved to Phoenix and returned to his former occupation, freighting. Then in the 1890s he worked as a guard at the territorial prison in Yuma and later in Florence when that became the new prison center. The Wards had previously lived in San Diego, so he retired there in 1912. On September 26, 1913, he died following a truck accident.[233]

WARNEKROS, PAUL BAHN
A German immigrant, Warnekros arrived in California in the 1860s, tried some mining in Pinal County, then shifted to Tombstone in March 1878, a true pioneer. He was a store clerk, going into business in 1887 as the Ranchers

Paul Warnekros, who had a hand in more than a dozen businesses, was Tombstone's largest property owner. *Tombstone in History*, 1903.

and Miners Supply Store, and became the leading merchant in these declining Tombstone years. Warnekros soon owned many properties in Tombstone, including a hotel and part of Schieffelin Hall, and served as mayor of Tombstone in 1895 and 1896.

Warnekros also speculated and worked many mine properties at Pearce, Gleeson, and in the Dragoon Mountains. He closed the Tombstone store in 1895 but lived there until 1908, when the family moved to Los Angeles. He continued to frequently visit his mining properties in and around Tombstone; in July of 1912 he was putting a force to work at a prospect in Gleeson, Cochise County. His brother, Dr. William Victor Ludwig Warnekros, was the dentist in town (often wrongly claimed to be Paul in the literature) who accidently overdosed celebrated Tombstone attorney Howard Herring during a dental procedure on November 1, 1891, leading to a series of seizures and Herring's premature death.

In the era 1885-1905, Warnekros probably controlled more property and mining claims in and around Tombstone than anyone else. He moved to California for good in 1912, dying in Los Angeles on November 4, 1922.[234]

WATERS, TOM Although little is known of his life and his days in Tombstone were few, he is known in many parts of the world today for the role he played in one of the most bizarre incidents of the violent Wild West.

Tom Waters was a miner, a Tombstone pioneer, and for some time shared a cabin with fellow miner Edward L. Bradshaw. One day in late July 1880, Waters bought a new shirt, a black and blue plaid type, and started making the rounds of a few saloons. Several fellows he met made comments about his new shirt, sort of teased him about it. Getting irritated about the attention, he yelled, "I'll knock the first son of a bitch down that says anything about my shirt again." Just at that time, Bradshaw walked into the saloon, saw him, and complimented him on his new shirt. Waters slammed Bradshaw across the face and he fell to the floor.

A short time later, Bradshaw saw Waters drinking at Corrigan's Alhambra Saloon and asked, "Why did you do that?" After a comment or two between them, Bradshaw pulled out his revolver and shot Waters four times. In pioneer, frontier Tombstone, Bradshaw was exonerated.

As the years passed, this gradually became known as the "Tombstone plaid shirt murder," and is often used as an example of senseless frontier violence in an environment of single men, saloons, and firearms.[235]

WATT, GEORGE R. Born in Pennsylvania in 1849, George Watt served in the Civil War, and by the 1870s had gone west. He was a carpenter and in Tombstone by 1882. Watt did all sorts of carpentry, especially the much-needed woodwork on the many mines and mills, extending his skills in a slightly different direction a few years later when he entered the undertaking business in Tombstone with Charles Tarbell. By the mid-1890s, when things were really slow in Tombstone, Watt moved to Nogales.

From his base in Nogales, he undertook considerable carpentry contract work for mines, mills, and smelters in southern Arizona and nearby Mexico. A few of these contacts were at Oro Blanco, others in the Dragoon Mountains, and a few were for the Sonora Copper Company. Watt was awarded a Civil War pension in 1911 and may have retired shortly thereafter. He died in Nogales on February 26, 1925.[236]

WEHRFRITZ, BERNHARDT Usually called Ben, Wehrfritz was a German who was in Tombstone by 1879. He was in several projects with the Tribolet brothers, including the renowned Oriental and Golden Eagle Breweries. Although much action took place at the gaming tables of the Oriental Saloon (which opened on July 21, 1880), Wehrfritz was the fellow mostly responsible for Tombstone entertainment. The Wehrfritz buildings, at the corner of Fifth and Allen, housed the Golden Eagle Brewery; which burned down on June 22, 1881. Subsequently the Crystal Palace replaced it, opening on June 23, 1882, on the same site, directly across Fifth street from the Oriental Saloon, where Wyatt Earp had worked for a time. The Oriental featured a theatre as well as a saloon; a reading room was adjacent. Wehrfritz billed himself as sole proprietor (the gambling, saloon, and concessions were leased by various others such as Milt Joyce, Lou Rickabaugh, Wyatt Earp, and others through the years), and promised entertainment every night. For a few years, this was the liveliest place in town, probably in the entire territory.

Following another disastrous fire in May of 1882, Wehrfritz looked elsewhere.

Ben tried his luck operating a brewery/saloon in Nogales, but by the late 1880s was in the Northwest, listed as a Tacoma bartender in 1889; he then moved to Seattle, operating a saloon there for many years. Wehrfritz died while on a trip to Cananea, Sonora, Mexico, in August of 1904.[237]

WHITE, FRED A New Yorker, who was in the West by the early 1870s, Fred White and his father arrived in Tombstone in 1879. In November he was elected the community's first marshal. Fred White was well-known, did not seem to favor any faction or merchant house, and in general was considered to be doing a satisfactory job.

On October 27, 1880, things fell apart for Marshal White and, some say, for Tombstone. A few cowboys were in town having fun along with some drinking and rowdy behavior. Marshal White approached, gradually convinced the culprits to calm down, and relieved them of their firearms.

One fellow, though, protested: "Curly Bill" Brocius. In trying to wrest the revolver from Brocius, a shot rang out, and Marshal White was fatally wounded. Nearby was Wyatt Earp, a Pima County deputy sheriff. He was unarmed at the time, borrowed a revolver from Fred Dodge, and creased the skull of Curly Bill.

Curly was taken to jail in Tucson; Marshal White died the next day. Before dying, he pretty much exonerated Brocius of murder, feeling that it was partially his own fault for jerking the pistol away from Brocius just as Wyatt Earp grabbed him from behind.

Perhaps in some Western communities similar events played out, but this was an initial action in what evolved into events leading to the Gunfight at the O.K. Corral. Brocius was "steaming" that Wyatt Earp had interfered, and the death of Marshal White led to the appointment of a new town marshal, Cowboy nemesis U. S. Deputy Marshal Virgil Earp.[238]

WHITE, JOSIAH HOWE This Massachusetts-born engineer and surveyor had a Midwestern railroad career, then was active in Sacramento and San Francisco in the 1860s and 1870s. He was early on the scene in Tombstone (by 1880), and a major figure in the initial investing and construction of the mines and mills; he was involved with the Sulphuret and the Contention as well as the Corbin Mill at Charleston.

Although a Tombstoner for years, he was also heavily invested in Phoenix, where he owned the gas works. White suffered an industrial setback in Tombstone in 1892 when the Contention shaft burned, and in 1895 invested in other mining projects in southern Arizona, especially in Pearce. However, as his health deteriorated, he gradually made California his base of operations. He died in Alameda on September 23, 1897.

White had been one of the few early investors in Tombstone mining who continued to have a hand in local operations for years; Schieffelin, Gird, Safford, Vosburg and other pioneers of the field had quickly looked elsewhere for their futures. White had done well with his Tombstone silver projects. His estate was worth more than $300,000, and the San Francisco newspapers referred to him as a "capitalist."[239]

WHITSIDE, SAMUEL M. General Whitside, born in Toronto in 1839, joined the U. S. Cavalry in 1858 and had a distinguished military career until his retirement in 1902. He served in more than twenty frontier posts, with names like Pine Ridge, Wounded Knee, and Santiago de Cuba only a few of the memorable places of his career. Samuel was an officer in the 5th, 6th, 7th, and 10th U. S. Cavalry regiments.

He never lived in Tombstone yet had tremendous influence on the fortunes of that mining community. In 1877, as a captain, Whitside founded Fort Huachuca, which was so important to the Schieffelins during their prospecting. During the evolution and growth of Tombstone, water was of major interest, and it was brought in from sources near and far from town, inconvenient and expensive. Captain Whitside, from his detailed knowledge of the Huachuca Mountains and his familiarity with the lay of the land and elevation changes, suggested that water could be gathered and stored in canyons in the Huachuca Mountains, then piped down slope to Tombstone.

This project of the Huachuca Water Company came into being in 1880-82. This amazing delivery system, more than thirty miles long, not only provided Tombstone with an inexpensive water supply for homes and businesses, but enabled new milling facilities to be built nearer to the mines.

Colonel Whitside had a major role in the Cuban campaigns during the Spanish-American War and ended his service there as a brigadier general in 1902.[240]

WILKES, CHARLES This New Yorker had an eventful mining career at the Comstock and at Bodie before he arrived in Tombstone in 1881. He was bombastic, cantankerous, and easily noticed. In one incident shortly after arriving, he got in an argument with Gus Bilicke of the Cosmopolitan Hotel, which led to some gun play that even included Gus' young son A. C. Bilicke. Justice court action did not lead to a clear decision.

Wilkes would remain in greater Tombstone for three decades, sometimes working as a miner, at other times prospecting and speculating. Even after 1900 he continued this uneven, wandering life. He died in Tombstone in July

Captain Samuel M. Whitside, founder of Fort Huachuca, was also part owner of the Grand Central Mine. Library of Congress.

of 1910. Just before his death, he had been working some property in the Dragoon Mountains.[241]

WILLIAMS, MARSHALL A New Yorker, this Tombstone pioneer arrived from Yuma in 1880 as agent for a stage company, and soon appointed Wells Fargo agent, kept an office in the post office where he also ran a tobacco and stationery business. Well-known in town, a member of the fire department, close to the Earp faction, and liked and respected by such folks as E. B. Gage, J. V. Vickers, and other community leaders, he even participated in several of the posses led by the law-and-order crowd; indeed, he was a solid citizen.

But not quite. In San Francisco, Jim Hume, lead detective for Wells Fargo, believed the books did not read the right way. An investigation into the Tombstone office showed that several thousand dollars were missing.

Somehow, Williams got the word took what he could—including a friendly prostitute—and left town. One newspaper account indicated that he owed more than $8,000. This was one of the more bizarre incidents of Tombstone in the bonanza era.[242]

WINDERS, BOB Robert Jackways Winders was a Pennsylvanian who had a lively career in Texas. After serving in the Texas Rangers, he lived in Fort Worth, operating the Cattle Exchange Saloon; one of his bartenders was Jim Earp. Winders beat the Earp brothers to Tombstone in 1879, and when they arrived, they mixed in all sorts of deals. The Winders name and that of Virgil, Wyatt, and James Earp are on more than twenty pieces of real estate, as well as mining claims. Winders was a sporting man, very active in the saloon and gambling life of Tombstone, where he and Charlie Smith were known for their keno games. After the big gunfight of October 1881, Winders put up part of the bond for the Earps and for Doc Holliday.

In spite of the downturn in Tombstone's fortunes, Winders remained in town for a few years, even though the gambling business was a bit slow. In the voter register of 1886 he was listed as a miner. Winders moved on, though, a bit to the south, and for the next few years invested in some lots and mining claims in Nogales, Mexico and in the Warren District of Bisbee. But the Arizona lure had dimmed, and he returned to Texas, dying in San Antonio on April 24, 1890.[243]

WOODS, HARRY M. An Alabaman, Harry Woods arrived in California with his family in the 1860s. By 1878 he was in Tucson working for the *Star* and *Daily Record* newspapers, then headed to the new settlement of Tombstone. Woods worked on and then later owned the *Tombstone Nugget* and was there for the peak of the bonanza years. His career was unusual and uneven; he served in the Arizona Territorial Legislature and was the one most responsible for naming the new Cochise County. He also served as undersheriff to Johnny Behan.

In 1883, Harry moved to Colorado for more newspaper work, then was back in Cochise County in 1885 to publish the *Southwestern Stockman*. Woods also had a period in Mexico City working on the *Two Republics*. In the early 1890s, Harry shifted from journalism and took a position with the customs service at Nogales. In 1894 Woods was promoted and went to Argentina as a deputy customs inspector, dying in Buenos Aires in February of 1896.[244]

WOODMAN, MAY Gun play and other events of 1883-84 led to May Woodman becoming one of the key figures in Tombstone sagas. She had been living with Bill Kinsman, and a newspaper notice stated that they were to marry. In print, he denied that would ever happen. Embarrassed and pregnant, Woodman found Kinsman in front of the Oriental Saloon and drilled him with a revolver. When told that Kinsman would die, she was ecstatic.

Woodman would cause many a legal and medical drama throughout May of 1883 to great national attention, as she was the first female in Cochise County to be prosecuted for murder, and hanging or imprisonment in the Yuma Territorial Penitentiary were potential outcomes. She was tried, found guilty, thrown in jail, had a miscarriage, and tried suicide several times. The folks involved were Tombstone's noted ones. Dr. Goodfellow was called upon many times, and legal lights such as William Herring and Mark Smith were also involved. Woodman served almost a month in the Yuma Territorial Prison, but public opinion was in her favor. The acting governor granted her a conditional pardon on March 15, 1884. She left Yuma for California, and the trail dimmed.[245]

ZULICK, CONRAD M. A very prominent Arizonan, Conrad Zulick was seldom remembered for any Tombstone tie. He was a Pennsylvanian, practiced law in New Jersey, had a solid career in the Civil War, and a successful political career there.

In the early 1880s, impressed with some ore he had seen from northern Sonora, Zulick and other New Jersey investors decided that Mexican copper was the future. They bought into and controlled several large enterprises, including the Nacozari Mining Company and the New Jersey and Sonora Mining Company. In these ventures, the main Western contacts were Tom and William Farish, who would be associated with Zulick for years.

Zulick and the Farish brothers decided that Tombstone would be the base for these Sonoran operations. And Conrad lived there most of 1883 and 1884, a center of mining activity, with a town filled with knowledgeable lawyers as well as the Tombstone Mining Exchange Building. It became the control and supply point for tools and equipment for these Mexican operations, and newspapers of Los Angeles and San Francisco regularly reported on the Tombstone-Sonora connections. Big money was involved, hundreds of thousands of dollars.

Things didn't work out so well, for a variety of financial and geological reasons. Nevertheless, Zulick and the Farish brothers were now a team, and they threw in their lot with things related to Arizona. In 1885, President Grover Cleveland appointed Zulick governor of Arizona Territory, a post he held through 1889. Conrad rewarded those who had followed his trail. Tom Farish became his personal secretary, and John Behan was named warden of the Yuma Territorial Prison. The Arizona bloom faded, though, and Zulick returned to New Jersey and an active legal and political life, dying there in early March, 1926. [246]

THE SECOND ERA, 1886-1900
Era of the "Chloriders:" Borrasco/Bust

IF A PHRASE COULD BE USED TO DESCRIBE THE TOMBSTONE OF 1886 to 1900, "era of the chloriders" would be appropriate. How and where the term "chloriders" originated is in dispute, but the meaning is not. It refers to miners working waste ground. The "waste" was sometimes poor ore, or rock passed by; but the waste could also actually refer to ore in the mine passed by in earlier days in order to proceed to richer, deeper ore.[247]

The typical situation would be for a man, or a group of three or four miners, approaching mine management, then working out an arrangement for them to work that property. One early arrangement by Tombstone Mill & Mining Company was to allow chloriders on certain property, for a royalty of one-third of any profit. Dozens of Tombstone mining companies made arrangements with a hundred or so "mining teams" over the years. The logic was that some income was better than none. The mining company had no liability; if the chloriders failed, or if they were killed in an accident, such worries were for the chloriders, not the mine owners.

This chloriding became so important that by the 1890s, three to four hundred men could be found working the mines of greater Tombstone, while at the same time only two or three actual mining companies were actively working their ground. In 1892 the Grand Central leased to chloriders for a royalty of twenty per cent. Such operations permitted the community of Tombstone to survive, but just barely.[248]

The standard worldwide interpretation of this mining practice appeared in the textbook by Sir William Le Neve Foster: "a gang of men agree to hand over to the mining company all the ore they raise, on condition that they receive a certain proportion of the value." What many people don't realize, even those familiar with Tombstone history, is how early this chloriding practice began. In 1883, the Defense, the Tombstone Mill & Mining Company, and the Mamie were some of the mines with lease arrangements with miners. In 1884, for example, chloriders on the Bob Ingersoll mine were "taking out fine paying ore." So, there is a tendency among readers to conclude that reports of the Grand Central, the Lucky Cuss, or the Toughnut give the picture of all Tombstone mining, while all around these and other properties, groups of men were digging away on their own on their leasing arrangements.[249]

A few incidents indicate how locals were involved in the chloriding practice. In 1886, John Clum, Richard Rule, and Ed Wilson worked out a "new reduction process," which was being worked on poor ore "with success," and thought they would probably realize a fortune from the process. Clum and Rule were former kingpins with the *Tombstone Epitaph*, but had no knowledge or experience with metallurgy or geology. The "process" was a failure, and Clum went off to grow oranges in San Bernardino County, California.[250]

This was not the case of Lewis Aubury. In 1886 he leased the rights to the Mayflower Mine, adjacent to the Tombstone Consolidated. He worked hard, experimented, read widely, corresponded with people in the East and in England, and devised a way to use cyanide on the tough ores. He was soon shipping his mineral to El Paso for a decent profit. This was the kind of news that encouraged other chloriders. An important angle of this tale is that the Mayflower was one of those Tombstone mines that had been abandoned because of the water trouble.[251]

Other events helped the Tombstone economy go into tailspin. On May 26, 1886, a massive fire that started in the boiler room of the Grand Central Mine soon engulfed the entire property. The twenty-five men working underground were able to leave through air vents, or via the connection to the Contention Mine. The hoisting works and outbuildings all were lost. The phrases used indicate the extent of loss were: "razed to the ground," "charred timbers," and "heap of ashes." The *Daily Tombstone* referred to this as "the most disastrous fire that ever visited the camp."

The Grand Central was not just a Tombstone mine; it was the centerpiece of what remained of the producing companies. Aside from the hundred-plus men thrown out of work, many dozens of wood choppers, teamsters, and mill men no longer had an income, and it is obvious what impact this had on the merchant and entertainment life of Tombstone. The scar of the Grand Central was a dismal addition to the problems of water in the mines and the labor troubles of 1884. After the fire, the *Epitaph* was already reporting that some men were leaving the camp "to permanently reside and invest in some more favored place."[252]

The totality of the demise of all the San Pedro River milling facilities can be understood with the example of the Corbin Mill, in the Millville-Charleston part of the river. The chief engineer of the Tombstone Mill & Mining Company, W. F. Staunton, not only closed the mill in May, 1886; he had his men physically transfer the entire workings of the Corbin Mill to the Girard milling works as an adjunct. This was in Tombstone near the Toughnut, Head Center, and Sulphuret mines. Eighty men were also shifted from the San Pedro River location to new jobs in Tombstone.[253]

And in yet another ominous harbinger of their waning town, in 1887, the town passed "Ordinance No 60." One would wish this was in the hope of preserving their image (as pioneers of historic preservation), but far more likely just striving to maintain and it, and not wanting to see their community dismantled and transferred elsewhere. Introduced by council member S. C. Bagg, and signed into law by city attorney James Reilly and Mayor C.N. Thomas, the ordinance aimed "to secure the protection of property within the limits of the City of Tombstone, forbidding under penalty of imprisonment and/or fine, the removal of any structure (building, dwelling, cabin, or other...) without first obtaining a permit from the Mayor or the City Council."[254]

A situation in the first part of 1890 further indicates the dismal prospects of the community. The Blinn Act was pushed by many locals, dealing with getting new authority, reincorporating, changing water rights, tax structure, reducing excessive municipal fees, and so forth. As part of the act, a new town name was proposed, "Richmond," and the world knew why. The *San Antonio Daily Light* of May 13 suggested that it was time for Tombstone to move on from the graveyard connotation. Some residents apparently believed a new name would shape a different, better future, and attract investment once again from East Coast capitalists, as the Tombstone name was associated with "deviltry and border ruffians," as one miner put it.

The Blinn Act generated much discussion and newspaper ink, but in the end, fortunately, with wonderful foresight, the locals stayed with what they knew: "Tombstone," and for the town's long-term viability, it's a good thing they did.[255]

A great national issue of the 1890ss—bimetallism—the rivalries of paper currency, gold, and silver; the severe Depression of 1893; and the great political struggle which almost put William Jennings Bryan in the White House as he championed the silver of the West against Eastern financiers who preferred a gold standard, were several factors of importance in the final decade of the nineteenth century, as was the Sherman Silver Purchase Act of 1890, which was a major shift in government policy. Largely pushed by Western mining states, the act raised the price of silver, and the government promised to buy huge amounts. This did happen, so much so that the act was repealed in 1893, as the government was saddled with too much silver. This was part of the nation's troubles which caused the major Depression of 1893.

It may seem counterintuitive, but these important questions had little impact on Tombstone, or on Arizona. Times had changed, and Tombstone's role in the metals market was barely noticeable. The huge silver producers were Colorado, Montana, Utah, and Idaho, with Arizona a distant fifth in production. This status, and these ratings, did not budge from 1888 into the mid-1890s. Tombstone, the big silver bonanza camp of 1880, was a bit player by then, a mere bystander. The situation was so bad that at the beginning of the Sherman Silver Purchase Act, the *Tombstone Prospector* of December 10, 1890, wondered how the new government silver pricing system would affect places producing low-grade silver (i.e., places like Tombstone).[256]

At the end of the nineteenth century, the place called Tombstone was seemingly living up to its name. Denver's *Mining Reporter*, after summarizing the great success of Tombstone, then listed some of the disasters, such as the horrible water problem and the huge fire at the Grand Central in the 1880s, and concluded: "The camp has probably been the deadest that could be found in the west."[257]

Water in the mines, serious labor troubles, destructive fires, and a deterioration of the silver content of the ore were factors that led to many inhabitants leaving town for greener pastures, and to a rapidly declining population in the late 1880s. Chloriding, which began a few years earlier, would develop into the norm for this era in Tombstone history. Most silver production would be from individuals and groups working on lease arrangements. The few surviving mining companies in these years received the bulk of their income from these "chloriders."

THE "SECOND ERA" FOLKS FROM TOMBSTONE

ALVORD, BURT The Alvord family put in a good decade in Tombstone, starting in 1880. Head of the family was Charles E. Alvord, who was one of the four or five justices of the peace. Justice Alvord had a son, Albert Wright Alvord, who was thirteen when he arrived in Tombstone. In his glory days (and later in his criminal days), he was known as Burt Alvord. He was a stocky, strong young man and grew up among Tombstone's miners, lawmen, and gamblers; and frequently could be found hanging around the O.K. Corral doing odd jobs. When John Slaughter became Cochise County sheriff in 1886, he appointed young Alvord a deputy sheriff.

Alvord knew all the local ins-and-outs, was handy with firearms, was a practical joker, and got to know the entire county from his Tombstone headquarters. In the following years he became a lawman in the gold mining town of Pearce, later in the cattle center of Willcox. He then became known as one of the more famous peace officers who turned to crime. He planned several well-known train robberies, was arrested, escaped several times, and put in a spell at the Yuma Territorial Prison, being released in 1905. The weird saga of Burt Alvord, lawman/crook, son of a justice of the peace, has been told in books, newspa-

THE ODYSSEY OF
BURT ALVORD
LAWMAN, TRAIN ROBBER, FUGITIVE

By Don Chaput

Mining Camp Chronicles — Volume Five

Alvord, a lawman and train robber, was the son of a local justice of the peace. Chaput, *Odyssey of Burt Alvord*, 1996.

pers, and magazines.

He fled the area, and the trails were many and confusing. There is some evidence that he worked on the Panama Canal dock projects, and spent some time working on a railroad project in Brazil, under the name Tom Wright. The most solid evidence comes from a 1938 visit by several Alvord relatives to the Arizona Historical Society. Apparently, Burt had contracted malaria or some other serious disease and was sent to British Barbados to recover. The American Consul verified he died in Barbados in November 1909, and several Arizona newspapers carried this news in 1910.[258]

AUBURY, LEWIS E. One of the most prominent mining men on the West Coast made his reputation by experimenting with the "junk ore" of Tombstone's Mayflower Mine. Aubury, a native of Placer County, California, was trained and educated as an assayer and metallurgist, and worked on properties in California, New Mexico, and Arizona. He was in Tombstone, at the Mayflower, as early as the beginning of the second era, in 1886. Like most Tombstone mines at the time, the Mayflower quit work. Aubury leased the property, and for a few years

the ore was decent enough to justify shipping it to El Paso for reduction.

As the quality further diminished, Aubury searched for some way to get the silver and gold from his ore dumps. He would be the man who made the cyanide process a reality in Arizona and the West. He tinkered, corresponded, experimented, trying all sorts of methods to work the sulphides which contained some silver and gold. Cyanide methods were already being used in South Africa, but his efforts were ignored or scorned by Tombstone locals. By the early 1890s, Aubury had demonstrated that although there were only minor amounts of silver

Tombstone mining innovator (first use of cyanide) Lewis Aubury later became the California State Mineralogist. Puter, *Looters of the Public Domain*, 1907.

and gold in some ore, proper treatment with cyanide could lead to a profit. This was the MacArthur-Forest process, which thanks to Aubury would soon be used in the West for dozens of low-grade deposits, or with discarded dumps of passed-over material.

By the late 1890s, Aubury was in the high echelons, even involved in major projects with Senator John P. Jones of Nevada, one of the country's wealthiest mining moguls and a founder of Santa Monica, California. In 1901 Aubury was named state mineralogist of California, a position he held through 1911, working under four governors. He lived in San Mateo County, and continued to do consulting work with mines and mills until his death there in early May, 1933. The path to his rapid rise in status was based on his initiative with impoverished Tombstone ore.[259]

BAGG, STANLEY C. (S.C.) A Detroit newspaperman who wandered to the West, he once wrote: "I arrived in that camp (Tombstone) the morning after the Earps and McLowry had their famous battle." Bagg operated a few businesses, then in 1887 launched the *Tombstone Prospector* and soon bought out the *Epitaph*.

In 1893, from his Tombstone home, Bagg began peddling real estate in the desirable and upcoming community of Santa Monica, California. This would end up later having a vast peripheral impact on the surviving Earp family, as in the first decade of the twentieth century, they all would gather one last time in the nearby neighborhood of Sawtelle, California, and its recently formed Old Soldiers' Home. Bagg ran the *Prospector* through 1895 and had his fingers in many aspects of Tombstone life, even serving as a court clerk for a time. He was associated with Dr. Goodfellow in a few Arizona and Sonoran mining projects, and also served on the board of the territorial prison. He was the first cousin of infamous frontier gambler/conman Charles "Doc" Baggs (part of the Soapy Smith gang), who Virgil Earp had been briefly associated with in Omaha, Nebraska and Council Bluffs, Iowa in 1875.

Bagg sensed the declining future of Tombstone, selling his *Prospector* and *Epitaph* newspapers (to William Hattich in April 1895), and leaving town in July of 1895. He was involved in a few mining projects in California and Arizona, which were less than mediocre. Finally, in Mohave County near El Dorado Canyon, Bagg "hit the big one," then selling out to a Chicago syndicate in 1916 and investing heavily in some gold properties near Randsburg, California.

Stanley Bagg and his wife retired to her hometown of Santa Barbara, where he died in October of 1931. Although Bagg found riches in Mohave County and in the Randsburg District, his obituaries tended to emphasize the years in Tombstone, which had been more than three decades earlier.[260]

Publisher Stanley C. Bagg arrived in Tombstone the day after the famous street shootout. Lee Silva Collection.

BIGNON, JOE This Montreal-born entertainer got his start in the mid-level towns of Michigan and Wisconsin, and in 1879 had a brief period in Tombstone, then in Tucson.

He worked for a few years in San Francisco, touring with several groups of players and musicians. In 1885, Bignon returned to Tombstone, and in mid-January 1886 leased (from San Francisco entrepreneurs who had purchased it in July 1883 from the Hutchinsons) and remodeled the Bird Cage Theatre, which he renamed the Elite Theatre. He closed the theatre on February 22, 1890, due to "dull times," and in July of 1890 took over the Crystal Palace. In these and subsequent years, Bignon also sponsored entertainment in Tucson and Phoenix, as well as in Kingston, New Mexico. His new wife, Maulda (or Minnie, etc.), was a bulky performer/entertainer, and they were quite a local pair through 1894.

By this time, Bignon had tinkered with some mining claims, and in subsequent years would mostly be associated with local gold mining. His last three decades were in and around Pearce, Cochise County, which had a few good years of gold production. Minnie having passed on, Bignon married again, and operated a saloon in Pearce and invested in some minor claims nearby. Bignon died in Pearce in December of 1925; not in Tombstone, but not too many miles distant.[261]

For a time the Bird Cage Theatre was operated by Joe Bignon. Ben Traywick Collection.

BURNETT, JAMES C. James Burnett was a New Yorker who was at Charleston, Arizona as early as 1879, and that would be his base. He was a rancher, farmer, justice of the peace, and one of the most disliked persons in the district. Burnett argued, fought, and fined. Many of his justice court fines were based on "intuition," or what the fellow could pay. By the mid-1890s he also had the big beef contract for Fort Huachuca. His ranch was on the San Pedro River, a bit south of that of William Greene.

Apparently, Burnett wanted more water flowing his way and seems to have arranged for the dam to be exploded. The next day, two of Greene's daughters and a girlfriend went for a swim, unaware that the water level was higher. Ella Greene and Katie Corcoran drowned.

What followed were major events in Tombstone history. Convinced that Burnett had caused this tragedy, Greene spotted him on Allen Street on July 1, 1897, and drilled him with three revolver shots. In the subsequent jailing, legal quagmire, and trial, Greene was found not guilty of the brutal murder, a decision which, sadly, surprised nobody in Cochise County. [262]

CHINA MARY Her name and career are riddled with myths and contradictions. She was in Tombstone from the 1880s until her death in 1906 and involved in most of the hidden economy and social life of the place, including gambling, brothels, and opium dens, as well as legitimate activities such as loam-making, running an employment agency, and operating laundries and restaurants. China Mary was one of those connected with the Can Can Restaurant for years. Few sources exist for her off-the-radar world and she has received more attention from historians than her countryman, Ah Lum, who was really plugged into the more formal, public life of Tombstone.

In March 1906, China Mary and Ah Lum were in front of Judge Frank Goodbody for an "Oriental Wedding," which was well publicized. The union was indeed brief, as China Mary died on December 16 of the same year. She was carried in a procession through town to the old cemetery (Boothill), and the newspapers of Tombstone and Bisbee noted that "the usual Chinese custom was observed." [263]

CRABLE, LAURA (LAURA BERNARD) Born in 1878, Laura Crable was the stepdaughter of William Harwood, Tombstone's first mayor, and she had much to do with the development of the community. She attended school in Tombstone, and over the years her stepfather was variously identified as a mine owner, investor, and so forth. Laura frequently assisted him in his affairs. In 1898, when the Tombstone postmaster resigned, Laura Crable received the appointment as his replacement.

She took that position at the most dismal time in Tombstone's history, yet within a few years, when the mining revival took place, Tombstone again became a bustling mining center, and Crable thrived with the new situation. Yet, in the middle of the revival, she had other interests. In 1908, in Chicago, she had a "secret marriage" with G. A. Bernard, and they moved to Los Angeles. [264]

DOAN, FLETCHER M. Doan was an Ohio native, studied at the Albany Law School in New York, and arrived in Arizona in 1888. In 1897 he was named an associate justice of the Arizona Territorial Supreme Court, and judge of the 2nd judicial district. For most of that time, until statehood in 1912, Doan made his home in Tombstone.

These were indeed busy years for the judge. International law, mining cases, murder trials, gambling charges—these and many other situations were covered in the courtroom presided over by Doan. Chinese deportation cases as well as mining cases that made their way to the U. S. Supreme Court were handled by Judge Doan. He heard petty cases of illegal faro in Tombstone, and in another instance oversaw the court dealing with Ricardo Flores Magon, which involved international conspiracy as well as the role of the Arizona Rangers.

Judge Doan's court was also the scene of dozens of outbursts, complaints, ridicule, and rude behavior during the era 1900-1903, when the Alvord-Stiles gang of rain robbers held the nation's attention. A strange legal circumstance happened at this time as, while the judge was in charge of the court, his son, Frank Doan, was an attorney for train robber/jail escapee Bill Stiles.

With the coming of statehood, the judging days for Doan ended, and he moved to Douglas where for years he practiced law with son Frank. This was also at the time when mining lagged in Tombstone, and the action shifted to the Bisbee/Lowell/Douglas area. Judge Doan died in Tucson on October 24, 1924.[265]

DOYLE, MICHAEL Doyle was from New York state, and his early career included some years in the army in the frontier West, some work as a cowboy, much time in saloons at faro and, from time to time, work as a teamster and a miner. He was in Tombstone off and on in the 1880s, and in the 1890s was police chief there on several occasions, and also worked as a constable.

These were not the "shoot-em-up" days, and much of Chief Doyle's time in Tombstone was spent overseeing chain gangs working on roads and fences. By 1900, however, Doyle was well established in Bisbee, where he also worked as a constable, for a time was a deputy U. S. marshal, and operated a hotel.

Doyle, usually in the press referred to as Biddy Doyle, was a character, a known practical joker, and had close ties with Burt Alvord, Billy Stiles, and other locals who spent much time in jail cells. His days on the streets of Tombstone and Bisbee, as well as in the saloons and at the faro tables, are mentioned in many accounts of Cochise County doings. Doyle would remain in Bisbee until his death there in December of 1926.[266]

DUNCAN, JAMES F. One of the most important men in the history of Bisbee and Tombstone, James Duncan was a Pennsylvanian with Civil War service who had worked in the oil fields and been trained as a blacksmith. He arrived in 1879 in Tombstone and within a few months went some miles to the south, becoming a pioneer of Bisbee and their first justice of the peace, and was appointed to the Arizona Territorial Legislature; then in 1890, he shifted back to Tombstone.

Duncan served as a public official for decades, receiving city, county, and federal appointments. He was a Tombstone justice of the peace, with offices on Fremont Street; a member and clerk of the Tombstone Common Council; city treasurer; clerk of the Cochise County Board of Supervisors; and a U. S. commissioner. Duncan continued to be very active in government affairs through the mining revival (the third era). After 1910, he published many accounts of the founding of Tombstone and Bisbee in newspapers in Arizona and California, and they are known for their fascinating details and accuracy. By 1920 Duncan was retired, and he died in Douglas on February 1, 1926, with burial in Tombstone.[267]

FITTS, GEORGE H. A Massachusetts native who arrived in Tombstone in the early 1880s, George Fitts operated a store which handled groceries and a wide assortment of other products, and gradually improved his lot. He expanded by 1890, served a term as mayor of Tombstone, and by the mid-1890s was keenly interested in mining. In 1895, a few miles near the gold strike of Pearce, Fitts hit a decent patch of the

yellow stuff. For about a year, most Tombstoners were vitally interested in the new communities of Pearce and "Fittsburgh," but the Fittsburgh deposit quickly gave out. His business also declined, and he spent much of his time prospecting, as well as attending political meetings in Phoenix and Tucson. The trail dims after 1900.

An interesting item appeared in the *Tombstone Epitaph* of July 10, 1898. Apparently the "genial and 300 lb. ex-Mayor of Tombstone" went to Bisbee on business, where he spotted old friend, Tombstoner police chief Fatty Ryan; their "heavyweight" image, as they stood beside one another, stopped all the traffic on Main Street.

Recent evidence has surfaced that shows that Fitts went home. In fact, in 1899 he married in Massachusetts, identifying himself as of Tombstone, Arizona. In the census of 1910, he was a resident of Essex County, living with wife Addie, and working as a salesman of "specialties," a far cry from owning a gold mine in Cochise County. A George H. Fitts died in 1924 in Everett, near Boston, and that appears to be the last stop for one of Tombstone's mayors.[268]

Frank "Fatty" Ryan among other things was a constable, fire chief, police chief, health officer, and tax collector. Ben Traywick Collection.

GAGE, DANIEL W. Gage, born around 1830, was in Tombstone by 1882 and for some years held law enforcement positions as watchman and deputy sheriff. While working for the Grand Central Mining Company in 1889, he was elected police chief of Tombstone.

By this time Tombstone was a mining camp in rapid decline, and there were few deeds of honor or of significance. Chief Gage, himself, was not always under control; he was once arrested regarding concealed weapons, and from time to time his faro debts were on the high side.

The faro tables did him in.

In late evening of May 11, 1890, Chief Gage believed the end had come. Owing a creditor $100, but having only $80, he was told he could forget the difference, but Gage insisted that he clear his debt, returning to the faro tables, where he lost in the saloon of Mc-Donough and Noble on Allen Street. Chief Gage walked to the rear of the building and blew his brains out (a favorite newspaper phrase of the era). This is a classic case of bad gambling—throwing good money after bad.

The Gage suicide is a prime example of how and why Tombstone became widely known in the country. The saga of a chief of police, corrupted by the gambling tables, in a saloon, then taking his own life, was covered by newspapers in such widely dispersed areas as Boston, San Francisco, Kansas City, and Chicago. The unhappy event would sadly be repeated: In May of 1904, in Los Angeles, his son Charles Gage also committed suicide by using his own revolver.[269]

GANZHORN, JACK Ganzhorn was born at Ft. Thomas, Arizona Territory, in 1881, and by the mid-1880s his father William was in Tombstone, tending bar at a few of the watering holes. Young Jack spent around a decade in Tombstone, so obviously had some feeling and knowledge of the place.

However, Ganzhorn is included here as a warning. Later in life he concocted all sorts of tales of Tombstone cowboys and lawmen and was particularly an advocate of the Mc-Laurys and the rural folks of Cochise County. He later had several government positions in New Mexico and California, did quite a bit of hanging out in Hollywood, and advised on a few of the early Westerns. Ganzhorn died in Los Angeles on September 19, 1956.

The trouble about him is his book, *I've Killed Men: An Epic of Early Arizona* (New York: Devin-Adair, 1959). Although parts are interesting, when he discusses the goings-on of Tombstone in the 1880s, one must remember that he was born in 1881. His "history" and "facts" were apparently rumblings and gossip that he heard over the years from the tipsy friends of his father.[270]

GEE, HENRY M. and MARY
This is the couple associated with the origins of the Rose Tree Inn. He was a mining engineer from England, she was from Scotland, and they had a daughter, Cathy. Henry first arrived in Tombstone with a group of investors from En-

gland in the summer of 1893 and bought up the old Guard Mine near the Lucky Cuss. On June 17, 1894, he moved there with his new wife, Mary. Sometime thereafter (not 1885, as historical markers and books classically state, as they had not even arrived in this country from England yet), she received some cuttings from a relative in Scotland of the Lady Banksia rose variety which, with the help of widow Mrs. Amelia Adamson, the owner of the Cochise House Hotel, she planted at the boarding house near the grounds of the Vizina Mining Company, on the corner of Fourth and Toughnut Streets. The rose certainly thrived over the years.

Henry Gee was involved in mining for a few decades, even though local production was less than modest. He was part owner of the Old Guard Mine, regretting it when facing court action in 1894. Gee passed some of his days as a local volunteer weatherman, publishing the rain results in the *Epitaph* and *Prospector*, and Mary Gee was well-known as a leading local pianist.

Mary died on November 13, 1905, and was buried in Tombstone. The next year there was a flurry of legal activity, as Henry was sued for diverting part of the estate for personal use and was removed as executor. This was enough for him to leave town. The last notice of Henry M. Gee was in 1907 when he was associated with the Sunset Telephone Company in Tucson.

The Macia family took over the Rose Tree Inn in 1930, and by then the bush had not only attained tree status; its reputation led to its inclusion in the *Guinness Book of Records*, as well as to much publicity in *Ripley's Believe it or Not*. In the twentieth century, under the Macia-Devere descendants, the inn became the Rose Tree Museum, an important botanical and cultural part of modern-day Tombstone.[271]

GREENE, WILLIAM C. This Wisconsin native had a long, exciting career as a mining magnate connected to the rich copper deposits around Cananea, Sonora, Mexico. He had a modest career in Cochise County as a farmer, rancher, and prospector. Although not living in Tombstone proper, that community was his supply base, and he was there frequently.

His main Tombstone connection (leading to infamy) were the events of the summer of 1897. Greene's daughter and a young friend had drowned in a swimming hole, and his conclusion was that the swimming hole had deepened because Justice of

Copper King Greene was often featured in the nation's press. *Harper's Weekly*, November 15, 1902.

the Peace Jim Burnett, his rival, had arranged for the dam above the swimming hole to be destroyed. He encountered Burnett by chance in Tombstone on Allen Street, near the O.K. Corral, and assassinated him with three revolver shots.

That event and the subsequent wild trial are among the most dramatic in Arizona history. Needless to say, public support and jury opinion were largely in Greene's favor. This whole regrettable business had a tremendous influence on Tombstone's economic fu-

The hanging of the Halderman brothers for murder in 1900 was one of the more publicized frontier events. *Los Angeles Herald*, November 17, 1900.

ture. In the coming years, when Greene became one of North America's copper kings and controlled a massive financial empire, he never forgot those many Tombstoners who had come to his aid. The mining camps of Sonora, Mexico, and the businesses and banks of Tombstone, Bisbee, and Douglas were filled with the men (he repaid) who had stood by him during that personal tragedy.

The major Greene copper empire collapsed with his death on August 5, 1911, in Cananea, when he was fatally injured after his horse bolted, overturning his carriage.[272]

HALDERMAN BROTHERS William and Thomas Halderman were Texans who, in the late 1890s, did some ranching and freighting in Cochise County. They were suspected of rustling, and Constable C. L. Ainsworth deputized Ted Moore to help him look into the matter. On April 6, 1899, an encounter occurred with rifle and pistols; Ainsworth was killed, Moore wounded, but managed to escape and sound the alarm, then died of his stomach wounds.. Posses from Arizona and New Mexico captured the Haldermans near the border.

The arrest, trial, and execution of the brothers seemed

to be sort of a routine event in frontier history, but the Halderman case went national. Petitions were signed, parades were held, "Free the Haldermans" was shouted far and wide. The national press picked up the strange saga, and there were several attempts to get a presidential pardon for the brothers. For a few weeks, across the nation the words "Haldermans" and "Tombstone" were leading topics of conversation.

A strange event, part of the Alvord-Stiles criminal saga, came into play. When Alvord and Stiles broke jail in Tombstone, the Haldermans and other prisoners "did good" and remained in jail, hoping for some type of legal consideration.

This did not happen, and the Haldermans were hanged on November 16, 1900, in one of the West's most publicized executions, accompanied by a public "Invitation to a Hanging," free beer, and crowds galore in Tombstone. Sheriff Scott White coordinated and presided over the spectacle. The brothers are buried in Boothill.[273]

HENNINGER, JOHN John Henninger, of German origin, arrived in Tombstone in 1886, and from time to time a few of his brothers were in his wake. He was two things in Tombstone: its most prominent butcher, and the operator of the Can Can Restaurant. For around twenty years, Henninger not only provided the best food in town, but pretty much had the contract sewed up for feeding the prisoners in the city and county jails. His everlasting fame probably came in 1900, when supplying "extra meals" for the Halderman Brothers, who were awaiting their hanging. Henninger's Can Can interior was also one of the features in the magnificent Tombstone pamphlet published by the *Prospector* in 1903.

An indication of Henninger's status and material prosperity comes through in a board of equalization "raise" in July, 1901. His block improvements were raised to $1,000; merchandise to $500; saloon fixtures to $250; three hogs were listed at $9; restaurant furniture and fixtures, $35; household furniture, $35; and sewing machine, $10. This helps us envision what went on in the world of Can Can.

After 1910, the Henninger sightings were many, as he was noted in the Tombstone press as being a butcher, or working in a restaurant in San Bernardino County, Gila, Winkelman, Holbrook, Globe, and Casa Grande. By the early 1930s, Henninger was in Prescott, where prior to 1940 he entered the Pioneers Home; of note is that Big Nose Kate was also a resident there during these same years. He died there on April 20, 1944.[274]

HERRERA, FRED Herrera had one of those unusual backgrounds that made it easy for him to blend in and do well in southeastern Arizona. He was from San Francisco, of Peruvian and French ancestry, and arrived in Tombstone in the early stages of the good times. He had a ranch near Charleston (according to the 1880 census), spent most of his time in Tombstone, was literate, thoroughly bilingual, and an excellent bookkeeper. He did a variety of jobs for many companies and agencies in Tombstone, often "experting" the books for the board of supervisors. Herrera was also an organizer. In 1886, one of the more active local groups was the Tombstone Stockgrowers Association; Fred Herrera was their secretary. As another example, at the large farewell party for Dr. Goodfellow in 1889, he oversaw entertainment and all other arrangements.

Herrera expanded his ranching interests, then in the early 1890s he moved a bit to the south and west of Tombstone. In 1895 he became mayor of Nogales. Herrera was cashier of the local bank in 1896 when Three-Fingered Jack and crew tried to rob the place. He whipped out his revolver and ended the attempt. When the new County of Santa Cruz was created in 1899, Herrera became the first treasurer. He was later appointed to the governor's staff with the title of major. Herrera subsequently expanded his cattle and mining interests, especially into northern Sonora. He died on December 1, 1909, while on a business trip to Los Angeles.[275]

KING, BILLY (WILLIAM AURELIUS) Louisiana-born and one of the greatest blowhards of all time, Billy King is a "source" to beware regarding Western history. He was in Cochise County by 1883, ranching at San Simon, then in the Huachuca Mountains. King operated a hotel in Benson, and was a Tombstone resident by the late 1880s, where for Sheriff John Slaughter and later sheriffs he served as a deputy. Unsuccessful in the race for Tombstone constable in 1892, in the 1890s and later he would be associated with the O. K. Saloon on Allen Street, as well as with saloons and liquor sales in Lowell and other local spots. He moved around in Cochise County, and in the 1910 census was listed as a liquor merchant in Lowell, Arizona; by 1914, he was a resident of Los Angeles.

In 1894, Billy King married Louisa Clark, the widow of Dick Clark, who died the year before. They would be together until her death in 1932. This was an important union for understanding contorted history. Dick Clark had been a major frontier sporting man. He had been a partner with Wyatt Earp and Lou Rickabaugh in running the faro games at the Oriental Saloon. Clark later owned the Alhambra and other saloons, and operated the Snake Ranch near the San Pedro River. Clark's wife, Louisa, had been a faro dealer at the Oriental.

This means that Billy King and Louisa Clark between them knew all the major players in Tombstone from 1880 to 1900. Johnny Behan, Buckskin Frank, Dr. Goodfellow, Virgil Earp, Ike Clanton, John Clum, John Ringo, Dave Neagle, John Slaughter—the list is long. With such credentials, King should have been a major source on the history of Tombstone. He met Professor C. L. Sonnichsen in El Paso, and the result was *Billy King's Tombstone: The Private Life of an Arizona Boom Town* (Tucson: University of Arizona Press, 1972).

Almost every event, every person in this book bears little resemblance to what in reality happened. The motives are wrong or distorted, most dates are King's imagination only, and he confuses famous people and the wrong communities. Anyone familiar with the death of Johnny Ringo or the doings of Buckskin Frank Leslie will read Billy's version and wonder what planet he was describing. To use Billy King as a source for the history of Tombstone would be like consulting the *Wizard of Oz* for understanding the story of Kansas. King died in El Paso on June 1, 1945, lionized to the end as a leading figure of Tombstone's past, in those "gun totin' days."[276]

LAND, EDWARD W. Edward Land was born in in 1870 in Elko County, Nevada, where his father was in mining. He arrived in Tombstone in 1890, a young, eager attorney. Even in decline, Tombstone had more attorneys than needed, and from 1896 through 1897 Land opened an office in Bisbee, where he was also a notary.

By 1899, though, Land was back in the Tombstone county seat, serving as district attorney, holding the position for a few years. Some of his work was interesting and exciting, but that doesn't mean he was enjoying it. He was involved in the nasty business of finding and then extraditing the Halderman brothers from New Mexico; they hanged in Tombstone in 1899 for murdering two lawmen. In 1900-1901, Land, as district attorney, permitted Billy Stiles to visit Burt Alvord in Jail; they both escaped, in one of Arizona's weirder escapades.

Maybe these events altered Land's thinking. By 1904 he moved to nearby Benson, where for the next few decades he was an attorney and a notary public, and handled quite a few land cases. Land fell ill in August of 1938, went to Douglas for treatment, and died there on August 30.[277]

LEWIS, ADELBERT V. Utah-born, Del Lewis was well-established in Bisbee in the mid-1890s, having a lodging house as well as a livery business; he also served as a Bisbee constable. From 1899 through 1903, Lewis served two terms as sheriff of Cochise County, and he moved to Tombstone at this time and lived on Toughnut Street. Del also did some farming near St. David and worked a few mining claims near Tombstone.

Sheriff Del Lewis was a well-known, popular fellow in Cochise County, but was often accused of being too nice a fellow; he did not, apparently, "carry a big stick." Lewis was sheriff during the chaos in Tombstone in 1900-1903, caused by the train robbers Alvord and Stiles. They were captured, housed in the Tombstone jail, escaped two times, and had criminal trials lasting for months, making Tombstone the laughingstock of the law enforcement world. During these chaotic times, Sheriff Lewis was not the sole authority; the Tombstone police force was also involved, as were federal officers (robbing the U. S. mails was one of the charges against Alvord). Nevertheless, he was one of the lawmen tarnished by the Alvord-Stiles era. Lewis died on December 30, 1910.[278]

McCLURE, ERNEST O. Born on an Ohio farm in 1856, when McClure died in California in 1913, he was again identified as a farmer. But to say that McClure was a farmer is like stating that Mozart wrote a few tunes. Ernest McClure arrived in Pima County in 1880 as a deputy customs collector at Charleston, and within a year was head of that office. He was the nephew of John Wasson, former surveyor general of Arizona and a prominent political figure.

In Charleston, in addition to his customs job, McClure teamed up with Fred Herrera, a general merchant. Soon they had land, cattle, and a thriving business. In 1886 they moved into Tombstone at the corner of Allen and Fifth. They were general merchants, handling everything from groceries to hay. Not only did this business thrive; so did their ranching operations. By the end of 1887 they sold their Tombstone business to E. Sydow & Co. They remained in Tombstone, but concentrated on ranch development. In that year, when the board of supervisors raised assessments, Herrera & McClure were near the top of the list for valuable holdings.

They were enormously successful. Herrera, the more outgoing of the duo, was a leading Tombstone figure, active in entertainment circles, and an officer in the stockgrowers association with Dr. Goodfellow, J. V. Vickers, and other local notables. Soon, Herrera and McClure were traveling frequently, to California and to Kansas, where they kept pasturage for their thousands of cattle. They also attended cattlemen's conventions from Minneapolis to Dallas and had the choice contacts and contracts, including supplying the hay needs of Fort Huachuca. They had other contacts as well, such as when they were sued in Justice Alvord's court in 1895 by C. L. Cummings.

Times were changing for both, as Herrera moved to Nogales, becoming a leading financier and politician, and in 1899, the year he married, McClure moved to Los Angeles, there again noted as "farmer." The *Los Angeles Herald* on February 6, 1906, pointed out that McClure had just sold forty-six acres, not far from downtown Los Angeles, for $66,000.

McClure then shifted to the Modesto area, developing a major dairy operation. He died there on March 26, 1913. All his financial success was based on his work as a Tombstone hay dealer.[279]

MEADE, WILLIAM K. Although Meade lived in Tombstone, held office, and mined there, he had many Arizona connections. A Virginian who arrived in Tombstone in 1879, for a time he was in management at the Red Top and Merrimac properties and in business in Charleston. William held a variety of local, county, and statewide offices, and was a member of the legislature from Pinal County; he was U. S. marshal of Arizona from 1885 to 1889, later undersheriff of

Cochise County, and also superintendent of the Territorial Prison at Yuma. Researchers into law and order, Democratic politics, the Wham Payroll Robbery, mining, and international politics have a lot of ground to cover with Meade. Once during a semi-legal foray into Sonora, he was arrested and held by Mexican authorities.

After serving as marshal of Arizona, Meade moved back to Tombstone in 1890, putting in a lot of time and money at the Uncle Sam Mine. He also later joined many another Arizonan in the Klondike stampede of 1898-99. Meade had been married in Tombstone in 1887, later lived with his wife in Los Angeles for some years, and frequently visited with George Parsons while in Los Angeles. He made many Los Angeles-Tombstone trips, and died in Tombstone on March 14, 1918.[280]

William K. Meade, merchant and mining man of Charleston and Tombstone, later served as U. S. Marshal of Arizona Territory. *Arizona Quarterly Illustrated*, October 1880.

MILLER, JACOB Miller, a native of Missouri, was in Tombstone by the mid-1880s as a merchant involved in the bakery and restaurant business. For a time, he ran the bakery associated with the Maison Doree Restaurant, which had been in the Billicke's Cosmopolitan Hotel until May 1882, when that building burned down (in Tombstone's second catastrophic fire); then in 1892, Miller took ownership of the restaurant, which by that time was back at its previous location at 409 Allen Street, after having moved to Fifth Street in 1883-1884.

Miller was also very active in local politics and government, was named city treasurer, then, in the mid-1890s, was a Tombstone councilman. This period was a low point in Tombstone economic life, and by 1896, Jacob moved to Bisbee, there opening a bakery on Brewery Avenue, and by 1900, business was so good, he started using a delivery wagon. His final fate is unknown, but the *Epitaph* in 1917 mentioned that a Jacob Miller, who had been to Phoenix and Bisbee, "returned to Tombstone yesterday." [281]

MORGAN, WILEY Morgan was a cowboy and foreman at a ranch near Hookers Hot Springs near Willcox. In 1899 he, his brother, and party suspected that a calf on the John Duncan ranch was theirs. They went to the ranch, confronted Duncan, argued, and Duncan fled, with Morgan in hot pursuit. When the party reached them, Morgan was standing over a dead John Duncan.

This was not properly a Tombstone saga, but it became one. Tombstone was the county seat, where the jail was, where the trial was held, where the attorneys gathered: a major territorial case. All the big guns were on hand, the best attorneys money (or cattle associations) could buy, including Judge Barnes (for the prosecution). This was a trial where witnesses were afraid to testify, where the judge insisted the jury come up with a guilty verdict, and so forth.

Morgan was found guilty and sentenced to Yuma for twenty years, but only served sixteen months. There were further trials, bail, appeals, and the end result was that Morgan went on to a fine cattleman's career. The circus-like court actions drew attention to Tombstone, as did the antics of attorney Allen English, who may have been tipsy during one of his pleas for Morgan. In all, this legal action, which took place between 1899-1903, was one more instance of Tombstone getting the regional and national spotlight for court shenanigans. This was precisely at the time of the wild Alvord-Stiles train robbers, Tombstone jail breaks, and lengthy, disruptive trial antics. For a few years, Tombstone seemed a center of little law and much disorder.[282]

PAGE, SIDNEY M. Sid Page was involved in a shooting incident in Pearce in October 1899 that had tremendous impact on Tombstone at the time and even to this day. The gold mining town of Pearce was truly connected—many of the buildings were erected from disassembled Tombstone structures.

Page, only twenty-two at the time and a deputy constable, was chastened by Chris Robertson for not paying his debts for a stable rental. Pagewas young and cocky, probably had his job because his father, Jasper Page, was a well-connected cattle inspector of Willcox. The argument between Page and Robertson led to many shots being fired, and Robertson died. Whether or not they each had a firearm was in dispute, even though there were many witnesses.

The trial was held in Tombstone in December, with all the "big guns" on hand. District attorneys Edward Land and Marcus Smith led the prosecution, while Page was defended by Charles Bowman and Allen English. A hung jury was the result, and retrial the next year. The judge officiating was George R. Davis, a member of the Arizona Territorial Supreme Court (working from the Tucson judicial district). One of the witnesses was Ethel Robertson (the future Ethel Macia), daughter of the deceased Chris Robertson. In a verdict reached in December of 1900, Page was found guilty of murder in the second degree and sentenced to many a year in the Yuma Territorial Prison.

Page was pardoned in 1906, and joined his father in the Willcox cattle business, in the coming years working as a butcher in Phoenix, where he died on December 18, 1950.

This entire non-Tombstone killing was played out in the courts of Tombstone, and most of the principals had strong Tombstone connections. The murdered man, Chris Robertson, was often referred to as "beloved," or "a most friendly fellow." Robertson's saddened daughter, Ethel, in the coming century would become a symbol of greater Tombstone, and the murder of her father was just one aspect of her unusual life in this community. Ethel and her daughter Jeanne (the future Mrs. Burton Macia Devere) would be prominent in things historical in Arizona into the twenty-first century.[283]

PEARCE, JOHN Cornishman John James Pearce had considerable mining experience in the West before he appeared in Tombstone in the early 1880s. Having worked for some years as a miner, he and a few sons tried cattle raising in the Sulphur Spring Valley. The family also prospected and tried mining in Colorado, but returned to look around Tombstone again.

Good times happened for the family in 1895 as only a few miles from their ranch and some miles from Tombstone, they found ledges of silver. Their six claims were named the Commonwealth, and one of Arizona's better booms was underway. The property produced gold as well as silver. The location, named Pearce, is some thirty-five miles northeast of Tombstone and directly east of the Cochise Stronghold.

The establishment of the town was not just an incident

related to Tombstone. This was a major event, and soon dozens of the leading mining and merchant families of Tombstone flocked to Pearce. Even as late as 1920 there were still more than 1,500 residents, and the operation of a large stamp mill. Among the folks drawn in was Deputy Sheriff Burt Alvord, who became the Pearce constable and later evolved into a well-known lawman/crook.

To get some concept of the magnitude of the doings, the Penrose and Brockman financiers bought out the Pearce interests for almost $300,000, and for some years the Commonwealth Mine was a strong producer of silver. The Pearce family also sold their extensive ranching property and moved to Tucson. Over the years they established homes and other interests in Oakland, California. John James Pearce died in Oakland on September 16, 1910.

The saga is unusual in that knowledgeable mining people prospected, discovered, then sold when the property was "hot," and lived a life of comfort based on their planning and decisions. The Tombstone influence in Pearce was such that many of the family names and businesses matched those left behind in Tombstone.[284]

PLASTER, WILLIAM M. This fellow may or may not have lived in Tombstone. What is known is that he was in Tombstone a hundred or so times, doing business, visiting, and telling stories. This is "Uncle Billy" Plaster, who many are convinced was "The Old Cattleman" in the influential *Wolfville Tales* by Alfred Henry Lewis. He was a Texan, a cowboy, and a veteran of the Mexican War; he was from the El Paso area before he shifted to various Arizona locales.

In the censuses, voting registers, and other documents, Plaster was listed as residing at Naco, at Hereford, at Ochoaville, on the San Pedro River, and so forth. He was frequently mentioned in the Tombstone press, as he told interesting tales, supposedly in a humorous dialect.

The Plaster of reality was a bit different, as he frequently was involved in prospecting and mining, not only in and around Tombstone, but also in Sonora, Mexico, where for a few years he kept a ranch near Cananea.

The standard rendition of Plaster's personality occurred around 1900, when he was part of a grand jury in Tombstone, where a young boy (a Texan) was accused of being a thief. Uncle Billy supposedly yelled, "Turn the son of a gun loose."

Plaster died near El Paso in the summer of 1918 and his obituary appeared in hundreds of the nation's newspapers, largely because of the *Wolfville Tales* connection. According to this point of view "Uncle Billy" Plaster was "The Old Cattleman," and Wolfville was Tombstone.[285]

RAFFERTY, MINNIE Born in San Francisco in 1868 to John P. Rafferty, Minnie Rafferty was in Tombstone by 1880, where her father opened a saloon and became active in community affairs. Minnie became one of the most well-known and popular young women of the place, very active in the Catholic church and frequently praised for her work there as a musician. She and sister Nettie attended the leading balls at the Schieffelin Hall, as well as other community affairs.

From 1885, and for a few years, Minnie operated a millinery business on Fifth Street, which she took over from Mrs. Baker. She advertised frequently for hats, bonnets, and other female attire, and was a leader in organizing sales and benefits for various Tombstone causes. In 1889 she married William Kieke and moved to Albuquerque, where for de-

cades they operated The Maze General Merchandise on South Street, and he was active in local political circles.

Her career as a very young, successful businesswoman in a frontier mining community was most unusual and has received some notice over the years. Minnie Rafferty died in Albuquerque in January of 1942.[286]

SLAUGHTER, "TEXAS JOHN" This Texas-raised cattleman moved into southern Arizona in the late 1870s and would develop the large San Bernardino Ranch in the southern part of Cochise County. As his success and reputation grew, he was pressed into service by his fellow citizens.

Slaughter became sheriff of Cochise County in 1887 (first elected at the end of 1886), and as a result moved his family into Tombstone. He was re-elected for another term (serving from 1887 to 1891), and probably could have served even longer. The Sheriff Slaughter years brought reasonable calm to Cochise County, as he was a no-nonsense lawman and had an effective undersheriff (Enoch Shattuck) and deputies (including Burt Alvord, an efficient sort who later went off the rails).

His Tombstone days pretty much matched his years as sheriff. He returned to ranching and also to his extensive land interests around Douglas (moving there in the early 1900s) and Bisbee. Slaughter was also one of the organizers of the Bank of Douglas. He reluctantly agreed to serve a term in the Arizona Territorial Legislature in 1906, but again returned to ranching. He died in Douglas on February 15, 1922.[287]

SWAIN (SLAUGHTER), JOHN This ex-slave was often referred to as John Swain Slaughter because of his long association with "Texas John" Slaughter and family. Swain was born in Texas in 1845 and when his mother died, he was taken in and raised by John Slaughter. Along with the other ranch hands, he moved with the Slaughters to southern Arizona in 1879 and then into Tombstone in the mid-1880s, when Texas John became sheriff of Cochise County. He worked as a rancher, had a small farm, and was frequently deputized by Sheriff Slaughter, especially for posse rides.

In later years he did some prospecting and mining, and also had a productive garden. He lived for decades in a home behind the courthouse. Because of his varied activities and long association with Sheriff Slaughter, Swain was a well-known personality, not only in Tombstone but throughout the county. He died in Douglas on February 8, 1945, age 99 described as "Tombstone's Oldest Citizen," and "the only continuous colored resident of the town for the past 35 years." Permission was granted for him to be buried in Boothill near his longtime friend, the merchant Quong Kee. These were among the last of the Boothill burials. His funeral and memorial activities were handled by officers of Fort Huachuca, which from 1913 through 1933 was the home of the 10th cavalry of the "Buffalo Soldiers," and the fort's military band performed, an unusual event for a Boothill burial.[288]

STILES, BILLY Topping the Stiles career is difficult. From the Casa Grande district, where he did some ranching and mining, Stiles headed for the new mining bonanza of Pearce, northeast of Tombston, in the late 1890'se. There he became associated with (and a lackey of) Constable Burt Alvord. When Alvord took his lawman authority to Willcox, Stiles and a few other Alvord cronies followed.

Alvord, Stiles and crew, officers of the law, started to rob trains but were only partially successful. From 1899 through 1904, the names Alvord and Stiles were featured in the press, not only in the West, but nationally. Their train robbing, shootouts, and complicated jail breaks from Tombstone made a mockery of law and order. Once, out on some sort of parole, Stiles got in the jail and freed Alvord. In another instance, when Alvord was "running wild" near the Mexican border, Stiles was made a "special agent" of the Arizona Rangers to help bring him in.

Their many absurd sagas occurred in Arizona Territory and Sonora, Mexico, but the various jail breaks and the legal shenanigans took place in Tombstone. Needless to say, in these years Tombstone was not regarded as a community with a solid legal foundation.

After a dozen or so escapades, Stiles absconded to Humboldt County, Nevada where, using the name William Larkin, he was appointed a deputy sheriff. There, on December 5, 1908, he was shot and killed over a disagreement regarding a court summons.

The above may seem confusing and distorted, but to read more about the career of Billy Stiles merely compounds the confusion. A two-time train robber, a two-time jail breaker, then promoted to the status of an Arizona Ranger—his experience was the experience of the Western frontier.[289]

WHITE, SCOTT This Texan was one of the giants in the history of southern Arizona, arriving in the early 1880s and working for the Cochise Mining & Milling Company near Bowie. He shifted to doing assay work, was then with a mine near Dos Cabezas, and in 1886 began serving a few terms in the Arizona Territorial Legislature. Although by this time White had financial interests also in cattle, Tombstone would be his base for decades.

Pretty much the man in the town and county, White served as sheriff, then clerk of the district court, and again was elected sheriff. During his terms several major events occurred, such as William Greene's shooting of Justice Burnett on the streets of Tombstone, as well as the hanging in Tombstone of the Halderman brothers.

The relationship that emerged between Greene and White would end up having tremendous economic impact on greater Tombstone. Greene became one of North America's copper kings, with his massive empire in nearby Sonora, Mexico. White became Greene's main consultant for years, which led to hundreds of people from Tombstone, Bisbee, and Douglas getting on the Greene payrolls.

The Scott White influence in the Southwest was significant, even after the empire of Colonel Greene collapsed. He was a major rancher, became warden of the state prison in Florence, and then Arizona secretary of state. White retired to the Pioneers Home in Prescott, where he died in early March, 1935.[290]

WILLIS, GEORGE C. Dr. Willis, a physician educated in England, was practicing in Tombstone by 1882. Because of the presence of Dr. Matthews and Dr. Goodfellow, other physicians did not have a steady stream of clients. Gradually Willis found a niche. He was on the school board, active in cultural affairs, and after 1885 replaced Dr. Goodfellow as the county physician.

He was the physician who cared for cowboy Billy Claiborne ("Arizona's Billy the Kid"), after he was shot by "Buckskin Frank" Leslie in their infamous gunfight outside the Oriental Saloon on November 14, 1882. Claiborne was brought to Willis' office by his friends, "in a condition of shock, bordering on collapse," immediately after the incident. After examining him, Willis noted an entrance wound in his left side (upper abdomen) and an exit wound in his back, near his spinal cord. There was blood noted in his urine. Claiborne was given "stimulants," the wounds dressed, and he was referred to the hospital. Dr. Willis surmised that the bullet had passed through the spleen and left kidney and injured the "spinal column," giving the opinion that it was in all probability a "fatal wound," but the wounded man was still alive when he left the doctor's office. Claiborne stated he was shot in the back by Leslie, whom he called "a murdering son of a bitch" for backshooting him. Willis argued that his examination showed otherwise, and that Claiborne was shot in the front as the eyewitnesses had claimed.

Willis also became fascinated with local mining, did some speculating, and helped an English firm get control of the Old Guard Mine. They named Dr. Willis as superintendent, but this was a pretty minor property. After a time, the mine employees were let go, and the only employee left was Dan Shankland, the watchman. Such nothingness caused the English investors to pull the plug. Without any ore, who needs employees? On January 2, 1891, Dr. Willis went to the Old Guard location and told Shankland the news: no mining, no men needed, the game is over. Shankland, furious, and believing he had a lifetime job as a watchman, whipped out his revolver and shot and severely wounded Dr. Willis. Dr. Goodfellow was quickly on the scene, but it was too late to help Willis. The interesting medical and mining life for Dr. Willis ended at age thirty-nine.[291]

WISER, JOHN CHARLES A Pennsylvanian who served in a Kansas regiment during the Civil War, he was in Tombstone by 1882 and over the years identified as a miner and prospector. By 1890, Wiser had become the Tombstone tax collector, and by the mid-1890s began many years of service as a Tombstone constable.

His constable period ran from 1896 through 1906, and for periods of time he was also acting police chief of Tombstone. These were not quiet times for Officer Wiser. Two of the violent landmark events happened during this time. In 1897 there was the vicious street shooting when William Greene rubbed out Justice Jim

Burnett. The time between 1900 and 1903 was the absurd reign of the Alvord-Stiles gang, which included several Tombstone jailbreaks, paroles, and drawn-out controversial trials, all of which made Tombstone a laughingstock in the world of law and order.

The last local notice of Wiser occurred in 1906, when the position of constable was declared vacant, as he had been away without cause for more than three months. Apparently, what was unknown in Tombstone was that Civil War veteran Wiser had gone to California, enrolled in the Old Soldiers' Home near Sawtelle on November 14, 1905, and died there on October 6, 1908. He is buried in section 15, row D, number 20 of the adjacent Los Angeles National Cemetery.[292]

WISTER, OWEN Born in Pennsylvania in 1860, Wister became an important figure in American literature, and one of the giants in writing about the Western frontier. Wister began his writing career in 1882, and often traveled to locations to get the proper feel and perspective.

In 1894, Wister considered the Earp-Clanton confrontation for several articles in *Harper's*, and visited southern Arizona in June, spending three days in Tombstone, but for a variety of reasons, dropped the project. He was not impressed with the place, calling it, "the most depressing town I have ever seen." This was, of course, not only at the low point of the Tombstone mining saga, but it was also shortly after the Depression of 1893.

Wister went on to other projects and considerable fame, most remembered for his novel *The Virginian* (1902). In this book, Wister created possibly the most significant person in Western fiction, a hero, a strong figure of high standards, a man of few (but important) words. This fellow ("the Virginian," or "Jeff") became copied thousands of times in short stories, novels, movies, and television productions. One his more famous phrases was, "When you call me that, smile." Wister's *The Virginian* was dedicated to his longtime friend, Theodore Roosevelt. Wister was also closely associated in a personal and professional way with the artist Frederic Remington.

Wister died in Rhode Island on July 21, 1938. It is tempting to consider how close the entire Tombstone spectacle came to becoming the main thread of Western sagas as early as the late 1800s. Such immense, enduring fame did end up coming Tombstone's way, but nearly half a century after Wister had first considered the place for his Western heroes.[293]

THE THIRD ERA, 1901-1910
The First Revival: Second Bonanza

THE NEXT PHASE OF TOMBSTONE AS A MINING CENTER WAS ITS "first revival" (third era), which we date from 1901 to 1910. This was pretty much the fulfillment of the earlier, first era's, most important Tombstone mining figure, E. B. Gage. During the Tombstone decline (the second era), Gage shifted to Yavapai County, where in the early 1890s he took control of the Congress Mine, a decent gold producer. Along with him was William Staunton, who had also been a key figure in Tombstone's original bonanza era. During the 1890s, Gage, doing well with his Yavapai project, began to slowly and quietly buy up and consolidate dozens of the claims, mines, and prospects around Tombstone. Included were the Grand Central, Head Centre, Tombstone Mill & Mining Companies, and many other of the well-known properties. This was done by the Development Company of America, and its subsidiary, the Tombstone Consolidated Mines Company, became the public face for the impressive new project.[294]

When E. B. Gage and colleague William Staunton were wandering the Tombstone hills and buying up defunct mining properties in the 1890s, they were not overly concerned with the struggle between silver and gold. To them, rich silver deposits remained to be tapped. Only the freak situation of water at depth had ruined the Tombstone economy. New situations and modern technology would create the next Tombstone bonanza.

From 1895 onward, Staunton took charge, which meant clearing all titles, dewatering the mines, putting in new shafts, working out a milling process, and making arrangements with smelters, mostly in El Paso, for final treatment of the mineral. The amount of money needed, and the extent of the work, can be understood by a few statistics. They had drained the lower levels in sixty-eight mines in the Tombstone district. The milling would come a little later, as at the end of 1902 there were only two stamp-mill systems available; a twenty-stamp mill on the site of the old Toughnut Mine, and another a mile west of Charleston. [295]

So, the dreams of E.B. Gage, Frank Murphy, and William Staunton, and capital from their highly successful Yavapai Congress Mines (sold in the spring of 1900), led to the purchase, accumulation, and consolidation of claims about town and to the Tombstone Consolidated Mine Company (May 1900) and its holding company, the Development Company of America (November 23, 1901). With their guidance, capital, and new and improved mining techniques (such as much more powerful pumps to pull the water out of the submerged mines shafts), Tombstone made a gradual, measured comeback to its former greatness, and its future looked bright.

By 1902, praises were widespread as the new pumps were working efficiently, even a hundred feet below the water table. Judge Ben Goodrich was back in Tombstone and received a franchise for a new waterworks for Tombstone, using, of course, the vast amount of water being pumped from the properties of the Tombstone Consolidated Mines Company.[296]

One of the great handicaps of Tombstone in the first bonanza era was lack of a railroad. This was solved on March 24, 1903, when finally, the train arrived from Fairbank, part of the El Paso & Southwestern Railroad. The depot was at Fifth and Toughnut. In 1903, for the first time since Ed Schieffelin discovered silver in 1877, Tombstone would have adequate transportation for its ore, freight, equipment, and passengers. All these developments led to local jubilation, and William Hettich's *Tombstone Prospector* published a detailed, illustrated booklet, praising the mining revival, the new railroad, the leading personalities, and the great future for Tombstone.[297]

What happened in the next few years was pretty good for Tombstone. Many men were rehired and at work, and outside recruiting even became necessary. Some of the merchants expanded, and a few new merchants and professionals came to town. A leading professional journal, *Mines and Minerals*, devoted a four-page spread to the new operations, entitled "Tombstone, Arizona, Restored."[298] The old mine names such as Grand Central, Lucky Cuss, or Toughnut were transformed ("consolidated"), and most information about mining, milling, and ore transportation were now under the umbrella term of the Tombstone Consolidated Company. In mid-1907, the *Tombstone Epitaph* ran an article headed "Bright Tombstone Prospects." The mines had passed the 1,000-foot level, good ore was reached, and "never was the prospects more brighter [sic] for Tombstone."[299]

Another part of the revival effort was to re-work the thousands of tons of waste or reject material from the mills along the San Pedro River. The Contention and Grand Central mills had mountains of the remains from two decades of milling and processing. The Tombstone Consolidated contracted with Slimes Tailings Company of Los Angeles in 1905. Within a few years they were near Fairbank, working 200 tons a day with a cyanide process. The cost was about .57 cents to work a ton, so if work continued, it was obvious that there was still payable silver left from the old milling processes.[300]

The future of Tombstone, though, began to look less promising very soon, and in 1908 and 1909, mixed with news of good ore and prospects came word of that old nemesis, water. In mid-1909 the *Los Angeles Times* wrote, "Pumps Clear Flooded Mine," pointing out that not only was the Tombstone Consolidated flooded, but work in the mills, too, came to a halt, as they had no product to mill.[301] Production was resumed, and there were periodic positive statements, such as the high-grade ore, the mill running steadily, with regular shipments to the El Paso smelters. Yet, by September 1910, the water news and news of other mining issues, were enough to alarm anyone. The mines were pumping six and a half million gallons of water daily, and at the old Contention, it was "favorable for opening a large ore body." The work below the water level looked "encouraging." These are not the type of statements that impress investors, nor merchants, nor miners and their families.[302]

This was more than handwriting on the wall; this was water dashing hopes on the Tombstone revival. In 1910, both E. B. Gage and William Staunton eased away from the Tombstone scene. The *Epitaph* printed a chart of the leading mining companies in Cochise County, and the Tombstone Consolidated was placed fifth; other producers were mostly working copper properties.[303]

The leading professional journal, the *Mining & Scientific Press*, announced early in 1911 that the Tombstone Consolidated had shut down because of the enormous expense of pumping water. They also remarked that "the ores are not high grade."[304] Now that Gage and Staunton had departed, Frank Murphy was president of Tombstone Consolidated; he suggested the mines would be dewatered, and when that happened "bonanza ore will undoubtedly be struck." This sounds more like someone selling stock than a realistic observer.[305]

The cause of the collapse of the Tombstone revival was water in the mines, which was the main cause of the collapse in the 1880s of the original Tombstone bonanza. There may have been rich ore at depth, below the water level, but the inability to handle the excess water in the 1880s and again in the period 1901 to 1910 meant that stockholders would refuse to keep paying for inadequate dewatering systems.[306]

It must be emphasized that the talk and reality of water in the Tombstone mines was beyond what was typical for a mine in the West. Tombstone was indeed unique, in such a negative way, that the *Mining & Scientific Press* of February 20, 1909, had this to report:

> In sinking the main shaft of the Tombstone Consolidated Mines Co., there was struck what is probably one of the largest continual flows of water ever dealt with in the history of shaft sinking.

The dismal future for Tombstone mining again turned to the past; back to the chloriders, those individuals and small teams of miners who worked for themselves. As early as August of 1910, the State of Maine mine was leased to a few men, and the next February, the Tombstone Consolidated leased the Toughnut dump to a few chloriders, who intended to send their product to El Paso. In March of 1911, the show was obviously over, as the Tombstone Consolidated announced that it had leased property to twenty-six different parties of chloriders, even including equipment, for a royalty of twenty percent.[307]

Despite periodic statements and publicity releases of great optimism for the Tombstone mines, the collapse was total. In 1914, the Tombstone Consolidated was in receivership, and at the receiver's sale there was only one bid, for half a million dollars. This was from Walter Douglas representing the Phelps Dodge copper empire. The dozens of Tombstone mines that over thirty years had produced more than $25 million in silver would now be considered for their unknown deposits of copper.[308]

THE "THIRD ERA" FOLKS FROM TOMBSTONE

ABELL, FRANCES J. Her husband, Wilbur Abell, was a successful hardware merchant in Mesa, Arizona, who in 1900 moved to land six miles south of Benson. He put in an excellent well and developed fine vegetable and fruit gardens, mostly for the Bisbee market. William died shortly thereafter, and although his widow Frances retained the farm, she began spending most of her time in Tombstone, soon becoming one of the more important public women of the area. Frances Abell was a notary public, took testimony and provided other dictation at various functions, and then became secretary/treasurer of the Gibson Abstract Company. She also had many professional arrangements with T. R. Brandt of the First National Bank of Tombstone. Frances Abell's decision to enter this aspect of professional life came exactly at the time of the Tombstone mining revival, so the years from 1902 to 1910 were busy for her, with the rise in local population and the increase in land sales. Frances remained in the area following the mining decline. When her son Norman registered for the draft in World War I, he was serving as the deputy recorder of Cochise County, later becoming a member of the Arizona State Legislature. Mrs. Abell died in Phoenix in November, 1925, while en route to Tombstone, where she was later buried. The death certificate described her as "housewife," a very inadequate word that ignored her many active occupations.[309]

AXFORD, JOSEPH M. (MACK, MAX) Mack Axford, one of the best-known cowboys of southern Arizona, arrived from Michigan in the mid-1890s as a fourteen-year-old. For years he would be associated with stock raising, working for Colonel Greene in and around Hereford. For fifteen years, he claimed Tombstone as his address on official documents, as that was the center of his world. Axford also had mining interests in the Swisshelms and other parts of Cochise County. By 1907, while

233

Colonel Greene was making millions from his Cananea copper, his superintendent of the Greene Cattle Company was Mack Axford. Axford also served as a justice of the peace in Hereford.

The era when Axford was in and out of Tombstone hundreds of times, between 1900 and 1905, were exciting years. This was when the Alvord-Stiles gang dominated the news by breaking jail twice and tying up the courts for three years; it was also the "hanging party" time for the Halderman brothers. These events, plus mining

William Phipps Blake, international authority on metal mining, wrote the key geological studies of the Tombstone Mining District. *National Cyclopaedia of American Biography*, X, 1900.

and stock-raising, would give Axford rich material for his well-received book, *Around Western Campfires*.

By 1915, however, the Tombstone days had crashed. Colonel Greene was dead, as was the Tombstone mining revival. Axford shifted geography and moved to Oregon, where for some years he was superintendent of a stock-raising outfit in Wasco County, and afterwards manager of a truck system for an oil distributing company. In his later years, Axford renewed Tombstone ties and seldom missed a Helldorado gathering, where he was parade marshal for a few years. His book was published in 1969, and he died in Mesa on June 26, 1970, with burial in Tombstone.[310]

BLAKE, WILLIAM PHIPPS Not a regular Tombstoner, this scientist may have had more to do with the production and history of Tombstone than any other person. A New Yorker who was educated at Yale, as early as the 1850s he was well-known in geological, surveying, and mining circles. His geographical range was great, from Georgia and the Carolinas to the Empire of Japan for consulting work. He was a professor at mining schools in the Dakotas as well as Arizona, and a consultant and administrator at mining and milling properties in a dozen Western states. In his last few decades, William was mostly concerned with Arizona projects and education.

Blake was in and out of Tombstone dozens of times over the years, and on several occasions served as an expert witness regarding the Way Up, Contention, and other local mines. As early as 1882, he wrote on the mining and geology of the Tombstone District for the leading publications, the *Mining & Scientific Press* of San Francisco and New York's *Engineering & Mining Journal*. When the Tombstone District began its first revival (the second bonanza, between 1901 and 1910), Blake authored the leading study of the project, *Tombstone and Its Mines,* 1902. His last years were mostly connected with the University of Arizona. He died in Berkeley, California, on May 22, 1910.[311]

BRANDT, THOMAS R. Brandt operated a store and was postmaster at San Simon in Cochise County in the late 1890s, moving into Tombstone and becoming a major figure during the mining revival. The First National Bank opened in 1902, and Thomas was named cashier.

This was the beginning of the mining revival, and for the next decade the bank, and Brandt, did well. He became one of the better-known bankers in southern Arizona Territory during these years.

In spite of the rapid decline in mining after 1910, Brandt remained in the community. However, being a good banker and protecting the interests of his customers cost him his life. In early November of 1917, a lone gunman entered the bank demanding money, and Brandt reached for a revolver. The would-be robber, Fred Koch, fired, and Brandt fell to the floor. Koch fled but was soon apprehended. Brandt, seemingly recovering after several operations, had a setback and was taken to a hospital in El Paso, dying there on December 10, 1917. He was returned to Tombstone for burial.[312]

BRAVIN, GEORGE From England, George Bravin was a miner in Tombstone in the mid-1880s, and adjusted well to local life. From time to time he worked in Pearce or other local mining areas, but Tombstone was his center.

For around three decades, Bravin would be the most well-known, and longest serving, lawman in greater Tombstone. He was a constable, tax collector, deputy sheriff, jail-

235

er, and Tombstone chief of police, having been first elected to that position in 1903, and serving in that capacity until his death. By 1916, the job of police chief of Tombstone had certainly changed. Instead of stage robbers or shootouts on Allen Street, Chief Bravin was concerned with filling potholes, cracking down on illegal fireworks, and giving tickets to speeding motorists.

Bravin died in Tombstone in October of 1918. He had been a key figure in the Alvord-Stiles business of the early 1900s, which led to several jail breaks and lengthy trials. His reputation was such that in a 1900 jailbreak by Alvord, in which Bravin had been wounded and around fifty inmates had been offered freedom and firearms by Alvord, Bravin was able to convince them to remain in jail.[313]

FLANNIGAN, THOMAS E. His time in Tombstone was only a few years but covered exciting events. He had been district attorney in Maricopa County in 1899, then shifted his practice to Tombstone.

There, from 1900 through 1904, Flannigan was caught up in the wild, absurd criminal career of ex-lawman Burt Alvord. He was Alvord's attorney during most of this time, which meant practically daily newspaper coverage. The Alvord-Stiles gang was in jail in Tombstone; that is, except for the two times they escaped. At one time, when Alvord was "over the line" in Sonora, attorney Flannigan had secret meetings with him as well as with Mexican officials. Flannigan was often over-confident about what he could do for his client. Alvord did eventually receive a term in Yuma Territorial Prison, but Flannigan arranged for it to be for interfering with the U. S. mails, rather than for more serious charges.

Flannigan went on to a successful law career in southern Arizona, for years maintaining offices in Bisbee, Tombstone, Nogales, and Globe. After his wife died in the 1930s, he moved to the Pioneers' Home in Prescott, dying there in January of 1936.[314]

GIBSON, O. His name varies even on official documents; it was either Ostoria or Ostora Gibson, and such a name explains why in his career he was known as O. Gibson. Born in Missouri, raised in Kansas, and in the 1890s located near Flagstaff, he was a cowboy and for a few years studied law.

Gibson moved to Tombstone in 1900 to open a legal

practice. By this time, it was no secret that things were going to happen there. For some years E. B. Gage had been buying up dozens of mines in greater Tombstone, and deep-pocket investors were frequently around. Gibson ran a typical lawyer's office, but also began to specialize in mining and land law, for a time advertising as Gibson Abstracts, a title/escrow company.

Attorney Gibson did not only ride the mining revival wave in Tombstone, he liked the area so well he stayed even after the severe decline set in. Being one of the few lawyers around, he had plenty enough clients. In the early 1920s he became mayor of Tombstone, probably not a very important position in a near-ghost town. Gibson died in Tombstone in December of 1925.[315]

GOLL, OSKAR K. Goll, who became a giant in world publishing, arrived in Tombstone in 1904 as an inexperienced twenty-year-old from Brooklyn. Goll was taken in hand by Billy Hattich and was soon writing for the *Prospector* and the *Epitaph*. Within a year or so, he became the city editor of the *Prospector* and known throughout the area. He was appointed to the board of commissioners of the Territorial Fair Association. In Tombstone, Goll had become an accomplished journalist, but the downturn there after 1910 became obvious. He moved to Douglas in 1913, working at the *Dispatch,* and in 1921 was named editor of the *Santa Cruz Patagonian.*

All of the proceeding was preparation, and Goll returned east, worked for the *New York Times* and the *New York World,* was a foreign correspondent for the Associated Press, and for years was chief editor for *Encyclopedia Britannica.* He remained tied into an active writing and publishing life until his death on October 11, 1955. Goll's meteoric rise in the world of New York publishing was based on his successful early years with the Tombstone newspapers.[316]

GROW, ARTEMUS L. Grow was a native of Michigan, served several years as a naval engineer during the Civil War, and by 1871 was in Arizona Territory. He moved to Tombstone as early as 1879 and had a dozen or so major roles over the decades. He worked as a civil engineer, as a mining engineer, as a customs agent, and for a time was superintendent of the Tranquility Mine. He was very active in political affairs as well as in the veteran's organizations, and also served as a Tombstone school trustee.

When the Tombstone mining revival finally collapsed in 1911, Grow was placed in charge as trustee of the drastic steps needed in the sad affair. It seemed that Grow was a Tombstoner forever, but poor health in 1916 led to his departure for California. He moved to Sawtelle, adjacent to the Old Soldiers' Home, where he could take advantage of medical care. He died at his home in Sawtelle on September 19, 1918.[317]

IJAMS, EDWARD T. Ijams, one of the Arizona telephone pioneers, spent almost a decade in Tombstone, which for him was one stop among many. He was from a prominent family in Safford, Graham County, Arizona, and in 1901 applied to the city council for the Tombstone telephone franchise, which he received. This was significant not only to his plans, but because this was at the beginning of the Tombstone mining revival. By 1905, there were telephones throughout the mines, mills, stores, and professional offices in town, and the Tombstone Telephone Company was a leading communications outfit in the territory. Sons Shel-

don and Clyde would join the firm, as they began extending their geographical coverage.

After 1910, Ijams began concentrating on his Tucson interests, which were extensive. He sold the Tucson telephone system to the Mountain States Company in 1912, and his son Sheldon joined that firm. Ijams died in Southern California in December of 1917.[318]

KELLY, JAMES E. James wanted to have been born in Tombstone, but just didn't quite make it. His parents, starting from Texas in 1880, had to stop along the way, where James was born; they finally arrived in Tombstone in 1881. James was a product of the Tombstone schools and by the early 1900s was active in Democratic politics. In 1904, he became a Tombstone constable and held that post for six years, during the height of the mining revival.

Kelly was the right-hand man of Chief George Bravin, and because of the increase in Tombstone's population, they were busy. A few examples shed light on Tombstone in that era. In December of 1906, while placing a fellow in jail, Kelly removed a massive razor which the man had hidden up his sleeve. In February of 1908, while walking Allen Street at night, Kelly spotted, and was able to stop, an arsonist in the midst of his work. These and similar incidents received high praise in the Tombstone and Bisbee newspapers.

In June of 1908, Chief Bravin and Constable Kelly were called to the dwelling of Consuella Yecaza, where a would-be Romeo, Marcello Mendez, was causing trouble. This was at night, led to many revolver shots, a wounded woman, and an escaped Mendez. After a thorough search, Kelly used a flashlight and found him hiding under the bed. Mendez opened fire, the officers responded, and as many as fifteen shots were heard. Mendez did not survive, and reports stated that "blood stains mark the spot of the pitched battle."

By 1910, Kelly had moved to the Hereford area and the West Huachucas, and for the following decades would be a major rancher and mine operator in Miller and Ash Canyon. He had several tungsten and manganese properties, working them intermittently, and on his frequent visits to Tombstone was listed as a cattleman and mine operator.

These long, successful post-Tombstone decades did not end well. In late 1940, at the mouth of Ash Canyon, Kelly got in a vicious argument with prospector William King regarding the documentation of a used car. Kelly yelled at King and drew his revolver, but King, cradling a rifle, fired first. This was the last chapter in the life of the ex-Tombstone constable.[319]

MACIA, JAMES HERBERT From Massachusetts, James Macia (also known as Bert) came to Tombstone at the beginning of the third era mining revival. In 1904 he married Ethel Robertson, who had been born in Tombstone in 1881, the daughter of Chris and Alice Robertson; her father was murdered before her eyes in Pearce, Arizona, in 1898. In the twentieth century and beyond, the Macia family had much to do with the preservation of the legacy of Tombstone.

Bert Macia for most of the revival was either foreman or superintendent of the Tombstone Consolidated Company. When the company folded in 1910-1911, the family remained in the area. Macia would continue to be associated with Tombstone-area mining for the next thirty years, as an owner, prospector, or laborer. His death certificate in 1951 stated that he was in mining (copper).

Ethel, from the 1920s onward, was part of the Tombstone social, political, and cultural environment, being an officer or "sparkplug" in dozens of activities, including the Helldorado Days events. The Macia family owned the property of the old Vizina buildings in Tombstone, which became the well-known Rose Tree Inn. Their daughter, Jeanne Macia, married Burton Devere; Jeanne and Burton's son, Burton Devere Jr., and his family, still operate the museum there to this day (as of 2023). Ethel Roberston Macia died in August, 1964.[320]

MAGON, RICARDO FLORES In 1909, this Mexican anarchist/revolutionary caused international attention to be focused on Tombstone for a time. He and many like-minded Mexicans for years had plotted against the Diaz government, without much success. The group decided their chances would improve if they did their planning in the border regions. So in 1907-08, in the environs of Douglas, Cochise County, they plotted to buy weapons and to invade, cripple and destroy the Greene copper empire at Cananea, Sonora, which was a bastion of American capitalism. This was to be the spark to start a successful revolution.

Unfortunately for them, the Arizona Rangers intervened, captured Magon and many others of his ensemble, and placed them in jail in Tombstone. There, in May of 1909, in Tombstone's well-used courthouse, the proceedings were followed by much of the nation's press. Magon and several of his co-leaders were found guilty of violating U. S. neutrality laws, conspiracy to foment a revolution against Mexico on United States soil. The sentence handed down by Judge Doan was eighteen months in the Yuma Territorial Prison; they were soon shifted to the new prison in Florence. This was a mere blip for Magon, as he and crew were released in 1910 and headed to Los Angeles to continue their political mischief. For Tombstone this was one in a long line, a string of events, or court goings-on, that kept the name of the community in front of the public. The Magon trial added some international intrigue to the Tombstone legacy.[321]

McDONALD, J. PORTER Porter McDonald was a Texan who arrived in Cochise County in the 1890s as a cattleman and worked at San Simon, Sulphur Spring Valley, as well as near Soldiers' Hole. By 1900 McDonald had moved to Tombstone, where for the rest of his life he would be involved with law and order as well as with running some cattle. He was a jailer and deputy sheriff during the weird Alvord-Stiles stay in the Tombstone jail. In 1905 Porter left to serve a two-year stint with the Arizona Rangers; he also served as a livestock inspector, a reasonable conclusion based on his cattle and law and order background.

Wells, Fargo guard Jeff Milton, with one arm shortened after he thwarted a train robbery near Tombstone. Hornaday, *Camp-fires on Desert and Lava*, 1908.

During the 1920s, McDonald was the Tombstone Chief of Police, and the McDonald family lived on Allen Street. He was usually also named a deputy sheriff. McDonald died in Tombstone on February 20, 1934, after three solid decades as a respected lawman.[322]

MILTON, JEFF Jefferson Davis Milton was born in Florida in 1861, where his father John was governor, but his own career would be to the West. In the pantheon of Western lawman heroes such as Elfego Baca, Wild Bill Hickok, Bob Paul, Ben Thompson, Wyatt Earp, Seth Bullock, James Hume and the like, Jeff Milton would find a place.

He was a Texas Ranger for some years, an inspector for the New Mexico Stock Association, deputy sheriff in Socorro, chief of police in El Paso, and in the mid-1890s was hired as a messenger and security guard by Wells Fargo, mostly in their southern Arizona operations.

Milton was the key figure in one of the most fantastic, botched train robberies in history. In February of 1900, the Alvord-Stiles gang decided to rob the train and station at Fairbank, Arizona, which was Tombstone's contact with the world. They learned that Jeff Milton would not be working on a specific day. Unfortunately for them, the schedule had been changed, and he *was* on duty. In a serious exchange of revolver, rifle, and shotgun fire, a wounded Jeff Milton was able to ward them off in a shootout. This would become a renowned border classic of Western encounters. Milton then went to San Francisco, where Dr. George Goodfellow was able to patch up his (shortened) arm.

For the next few decades, Milton was mostly in and around Tombstone, had a home on Third Street, and was employed by the department of commerce as an immigrant inspector, often identified as a "Chinese Inspector." The Tombstone/Fairbank/Nogales region was his normal zone, the *Epitaph* of November 4, 1917 reporting that Milton was again in town on business, "in his Ford Roadster." The frontier and the role of a lawman, though, was not always smooth. The previous April, while in a buggy in the Gunsight Mountains near Ajo, his pistol fell from the buggy, discharged, and slammed Milton in the groin, which led to hospitalization in Tucson.

By this time, Milton was shifting his interests to the Ajo region in Pima County, where he worked several mining claims. In the 1920s and 1930s, he gradually shifted from Tombstone to Tucson, dying there on May 7, 1947.

The Milton career includ-ed routine law enforcement, border and stock inspections, and stints with Wells Fargo and other entities. For almost half a century he was a prominent figure of authority and respect, and several decades of this time were spent in the Tombstone area.[323]

MURPHY, FRANK M. Born in Maine in 1855, Frank Murphy would be part of a dynamic Arizona family in business, transportation, and government. He was the brother of the governor, Nathan Oakes Murphy. Frank had dozens of interests in Arizona banking, railroads, and mines; he headed the Prescott National Bank as well as the Santa Fe, Prescott, & Phoenix Railroad.

The Tombstone connection came in the early 1890s, when E. B. Gage shifted from Tombstone to Yavapai County. There, in partnership with Murphy, the Congress Mine was reorganized and became a major Western gold producer. This enabled Gage to buy up and consolidate the many silver properties in and around Tombstone. When the revival was in full swing after 1903, Murphy became part of the team, and he and Gage were part of an important silver producer until 1910. After that period, when Gage moved on,

Frank took over as head of Tombstone Consolidated, but it was on its way to bankruptcy

After 1910, Murphy spent most of his time back in Prescott, and died there on June 23, 1917.[324]

STAUNTON, WILLIAM F. If you believe that Tombstone was an important Western mining development, follow this fellow's career. An Ohio native, Staunton was educated at the Columbia School of Mines in New York and very efficient in his Arizona work. He arrived in Tombstone in 1883, was an assayer, then superintendent at the Tombstone Mining Company. This was *the* fellow. If you wanted to know the quality of the ore, the shipping system of the bullion, the geology of the place, or the future of the district, you listened to what Staunton had to say.

However, as rich ore dwindled Staunton, like other folks, began looking elsewhere. For him, as with E. B. Gage, this meant Yavapai County and the Congress Mine. In the first decade of the twentieth century, Staunton would again coordinate with E. B. Gage, this time in the rejuvenation of the various Tombstone properties. By 1910, though, this was again a dead end for serious Tombstone mining. Staunton would still have a solid mining and financial career, but that was mostly post-Tombstone. After Yavapai County, he had further success with the copper mines of Jerome. Having had a sound mineral career with the silver and copper of Arizona, Staunton died in Los Angeles on February 12, 1947.[325]

Following his Tombstone success, Staunton became a leading figure in Western mining. *Los Angeles Herald*, September 12, 1912.

WARDWELL, DAVID K. A native of the District of Columbia, David Wardwell served in both the Mexican War and the Civil War and had a noteworthy record. He spent time in Mexico before arriving in southern Arizona in 1880. For some years, General Wardwell was postmaster at Fort Huachuca, and later served two terms in the Arizona Territorial Legislature, by the turn of the century, living in

Tombstone, where he was a justice of the peace.

He decided in 1906 to move with his wife to the Old Soldiers' Home in Sawtelle, Los Angeles County, California. The next two years of his life can be followed in the nation's newspapers. It was determined that his wife had leprosy and was therefore sent back to Cochise County, expelled from there, then taken to a hospital in California, from which Wardwell

Gen. Wardwell Escorted His Wife to the Station Pistol in Hand to Prevent Capture by the Health Authorities.

General David Wardwell, a Tombstone justice of the peace, later figured in a nationwide leprosy case. *San Francisco Examiner*, September 6, 1908.

abducted her. A series of horrors followed, as he died in Arizona in mid-1908, and his wife was left alone, and found walking the streets of Los Angeles; then chained to a bed in the county hospital, where she died in December of 1908. These were the retirement years of General Wardwell.[326]

WENTWORTH, ARIOCH Born in Maine in 1850, his railroading interests took Wentworth to Fairbank, Arizona, in 1885, the nearest rail station to Tombstone. Wentworth was the local Wells Fargo agent.

He moved to Tombstone in 1892, operating a billiard parlor. His main interests were politics and administration, serving several terms as county recorder, then as county treasurer, and over the decades, a few terms as a justice of the peace.

In 1903 through 1910, Wentworth was mayor of Tombstone. These were the precise years of the "Tombstone Revival," so he had an interesting role in Western history, as few mining camps had a successful second life. Years later, still boosting Tombstone, in 1919 he opened a tourist bureau on Allen Street. Wentworth died in Tombstone on March 2, 1921. [327]

WILCOX, GEORGE B and PHILO

The Wilcox brothers from New York had careers in Tombstone during the mining revival, all based on the unusual activities of brother George. He was in the West by 1885, was in the Indian wars, assisted in the capture of Geronimo, and was an officer in the Rough Riders in their famous campaign in Cuba.

As is well known, following the Spanish American War, Theodore Roosevelt took care of the Rough Riders; many of them received key appointments, especially in the Western states and territories. George Wilcox was named clerk of the district court in Tombstone in 1902, and shortly after this, brother Philo was named deputy clerk of the same court.

It just so happened that the appointment came exactly at the start of the Tombstone mining revival, so the Wilcox brothers would participate in the vibrant life of a community in second bonanza. As population increased, new businesses and entertainment were part of the Tombstone atmosphere. Philo left in 1909, for Los Angeles, where he would be in real estate for several decades; he died there on April 29, 1940.

George Wilcox left Tombstone in 1910, which was pretty much the end of the good years of the first mining revival. He would remain in Arizona, though, and over the decades owned pharmacies in Phoenix, Warren, and Bisbee. As a Rough Rider, he was in frequent demand as a speaker, and when World War I erupted, he was recalled to active duty as a major in the U. S. Army, as part of the training of recruits. In retirement Wilcox favored the Bisbee area, and died there on July 2, 1949.[328]

THE FOURTH ERA, 1914-1923
Manganese and World War I:
The Second Revival/ Third Bonanza

WE COMMENCE THE FOURTH ERA WITH THE PURCHASE OF THE assets of the once-dominating Tombstone Consolidated Mining Company, and Development Corporation of America, out of their bankruptcy court proceedings; proceedings that led to the end of the third era, by Dodge Phelps, in 1914, followed by the beginning of World War I. The war stimulated the need for precious metals and mining throughout the country.

In 1914-1918, with much ballyhoo, Phelps Dodge appointed Dr. Emil Grebe to reinvigorate the Tombstone Consolidated, especially the Bunker Hill area. Within a year he had four hundred men at work, copper was right around the corner, and the *Mining & Scientific Press* declared, "Tombstone has come back."[329]

The population uptick during World War I deserves some notice here also. After war erupted in 1914, and before the United States entered the conflict, world metal markets went askew. Armaments and munitions manufacture increased dramatically, and the United States, not a belligerent, was well positioned to feed these markets. There was a particular demand for manganese, important as a flux in steel manufacture, but with many other industrial uses too. Practically from the beginning of the conflict, Phelps Dodge, owner of most Tombstone property, took advantage and built new facilities and hired more men, especially at the Bunker Hill and Old Guard properties. The many Phelps Dodge annual reports indicate this, with the number of employees at Tombstone increasing from 297 in 1915 to 403 in 1916.[330]

After the United States entered the war, more than three dozen locations in Arizona provided shipments of manganese, with Tombstone and Bisbee being the leaders; by the end of the war, Bisbee was the largest shipper of manganese. The difficulty in providing specifics of employment is that around Tombstone, much of the production was not from Phelps Dodge, but from chloriders, groups of men working on their own, scattered across the landscape, who were not closely accounted for. They were looking for silver as well as manganese. It would be reasonable to estimate that wartime needs for manganese increased the mining population of greater Tombstone by about 400 to 600 men. To better emphasize the impact on all of Cochise County, which was involved in this mini-boom, one can look at its population figures during this time period: these show an increase from 35,500 in 1910 to 60,000 in 1918.[331] By 1918, however, the good news turned bad. One interesting headline provided confusion: "Bunker Hill Mining Co.'s famous Silver Mine, at Tombstone Closes Down." This meant 400 men out of work. The article played up the low silver content of the ore, but concluded that mine output "for the past six months or more has been confined chiefly to manganese."[332]

And, as peace followed in the armistice of November 1918, the several-year Tombstone surge was abruptly ended. Folks, and companies, were lining up for relief, as many war claims were filed for those firms that had rallied to the government's urging for an increase in metals production. These few good years at Tombstone had been artificial, caused by government interest and pressure, not by the laws of supply and demand.[333]

In 1918, Judge Frank Baxter of Yuma published a pamphlet regarding the mining code of Arizona, listing and printing the laws over the years, how liens and ownership should be addressed, who could own or file claims, relationships between chloriders and mine owners, and so forth. These practices and laws had their origins in the humble Tombstone chloriding beginnings of the early 1880s. It was comforting to have this all spelled out, but by this time it was of little help to Tombstoners.[334]

The era of serious mining in and around Tombstone was over. The mining news from that district for the next twenty years was usually a list of names of chloriders, where they were working, and whether or not they had a small strike or were hurt in an accident.

All the above comments about bonanza, chloriders, mining revival, and collapse can be seen in the following population figures: [335]

Tombstone	1880	973
	1882	6,000
	1884	4,000
	1889	3,000
	1890	2,000
	1891	1,800
	1900	646
	1910	1,582
	1915	1,800 (estimate)
	1920	1,178
	1930	850
	1940	800
	1950	900
	1960	1,200
	1970	1,200
	1980	1,600
	1990	1,200
	2000	1,500
	2010	1,400
	2021	1,300

By 1919, the Phelps-Dodge comeback was so dismal that their Dr. Emil Grebe was sent to a mid-level Mexican mine in Coahuila, and at Tombstone a second-stringer took over to wind down the efforts.

The period 1918 to 1923 saw Tombstoners almost get optimistic once again. The Pittman Act was passed through the efforts of Senator Key Pittman of Nevada. This was to peg the price of silver at $1.00 an ounce for a time, so that the U. S. mint was assured of a supply, and that mining firms with silver and ore in process would not face hardship. The program was to end in a few years.

This did lead to increased employment in Tombstone, but the enthusiasm was limited and short-lived. The leading silver states were Montana, Utah, and Nevada; and even in Arizona, much of the silver production was an offshoot of production in the copper mines. The Lucky Cuss, Bunker Hill, and Silver Thread mines increased local production, but much of the increased silver production at this time was from leases, the old "chlorider" system. Most of the ore was handled at smelters in Douglas and El Paso, Texas. By early 1923, the program was over, and at Tombstone, "where many small leases are being worked, every effort is being made to have all ore in sight cleaned out as soon as possible." The brief period of al-most-recovery (the fourth era) was over.[336]

A major legal and industrial incident that played out in Tombstone in this era was the well-known "Bisbee Deporta-tion," which was caused by activities elsewhere, but kept the town in the limelight and helped provide financial support. In 1917, labor troubles in several Arizona copper mining cen-ters received wide publicity, as the government feared that in wartime, crucial copper production would cease. In a highly publicized move in July of 1917, the Cochise County sheriff, working with deputies and "posses," rounded up more than a thousand miners in and around Bisbee, put them in cattle cars, and shipped them off to New Mexico.

In 1920, the Superior Court in Tombstone was the focus for one of the largest trials ever held in the United States; in one day, more than three hundred defendants were arraigned, including lawmen, bankers, businessmen, and many "regular citizens." This circus-like legal affair lasted most of January through April of 1920, with hundreds of news stories carrying the saga of the trials, which were held in the county seat, Tomb-stone. A big day was on March 30, when Sheriff Harry Wheeler took the stand. The newspaper account featured his image as Captain Harry Wheeler, back from the war in Europe. In spite of the tremendous publicity and awareness of the Tombstone court doings, the main word was "acquit," and those who had planned and executed the Bisbee Deportation had nothing to fear.[337]

The above court cases, and the shifting of the county seat from Tombstone to Bisbee in 1929, touch on even more reasons for Tombstone's fame or notoriety. From 1879 until 1929, Tombstone was indeed immersed in the law. There were dozens of justices of the peace, judges by the score, as Tomb-stone was the location of federal, territorial, state, district, and county courts. Every year in Tombstone, there were hundreds, sometimes thousands, of legal decisions handed down; many of a petty or trivial nature, others dealing with important is-sues, some even related to international concerns.

Aside from the many local cases, such as a shooting, bankruptcy, tax problems, wife beating, and so forth, Tombstone was the center of much legal action because it was the county seat. A fracas in Benson, a fence argument near Willcox, or a forgery situation in Bisbee would frequently lead to court action in (and national attention to) Tombstone.

Crowded court calendars in other parts of Arizona also meant some action was shifted to Tombstone. One example was in early 1904, when Ira Harper of Clifton was charged with illegally cutting, using, and selling timber from the Black Mesa Forest Reserve. This was an important case as Harper, a supervisor of Graham County, was a major livestock rancher, performed well-digging and other construction work for local mining companies, and had financial interests in three counties. The case was tried in the federal court in Tombstone, with a judgment against Harper for $1,300 for hacking away at $1.5 million of timber. This was not even a footnote to the Harper career. At the time of his death in May of 1918, he owned the important Harper sawmill north of St. Johns.

The point here is that the charge involved action more than a hundred miles north of Tombstone; yet due to the vagaries of legal life, the case, and thus its associated notoriety, was linked to Tombstone. There were many other such Arizona cases concerning events and individuals very distant from Tombstone, but it was often the Tombstone name that was associated with the court action and gained the publicity.[338]

THE FOURTH ERA FOLKS FROM TOMBSTONE

COSTELLO FAMILY Martin Costello was born in Donegal, Ireland, in 1867, and it didn't take him long to advance quickly in the new community of Tombstone. By the mid-1880s, he owned the St. Louis Beer Hall, had the Anhauser Beer franchise for the area, and for many years wore legitimately the title of Tombstone's Beer King.

Yet, even in these Tombstone years, it was Bisbee and copper (rather than silver) that made Costello a millionaire as well as one of the better-known mining personalities of the Southwest. Through mining investments, acquiring obscure mining claims, and smart real estate deals in and around Bisbee, he came to own or control some of the West's richest copper properties; these became the highly successful Calumet & Arizona Mining Company. Fellow Irishman James Reilly, the territory's most feisty legal figure, joined Costello in some terrific court battles that reached the U. S. Supreme Court, and were decided in their favor. The paper trail is indeed thick and easy to follow.

Costello, with his wife Mary and their large family, would gradually make Los Angeles their base, but they never forgot their Tombstone, Bisbee, and Cochise County connections. The good years gradually dimmed for Costello, though, as a series of health problems led him to suicide in Los Angeles on September 15, 1911.

Mary Costello proved to be a competent manager of the family fortune, investing wisely and assuring solid educations for their children. From around 1915 through the mid-1920s, she was either a board member or president of the First National Bank of Tombstone, seemingly the only female bank president in Arizona. A few of her children were also employed in the bank. These situations indicate what the Tombstone connection meant to the family, as by this time they had been residents of Los Angeles for many years, Mary dying there on December 12, 1941.[339]

CUMMINGS, CHARLES L. This native of Oxford, New York arrived in Tombstone in 1880 and probably had the longest connection of anyone with that community. There were few occupations or investments unknown to Cummings, as he was a butcher in both Tombstone and Bisbee, had major stores in Tombstone, served as its mayor (1921-1922), for years owned the Bird Cage Theatre (which he purchased on December 14, 1906, then using it to display his Old West collection), owned the impressive Box Canyon Ranch in the Chiricahua Mountains, ran the Tombstone Pharmacy, and owned a grape operation in Fresno, California.

His financial, business, and political connections seemed to touch all aspects of life in greater Tombstone. He was a county supervisor, member of the Arizona Territorial Legislature, and president of the National Bank of Tombstone. Even law and order were part of his life, as earlier, under Sheriff C. S. Fly, he had served as a deputy sheriff (1894-1896).

In one of the more unusual cases brought to the Arizona Supreme Court, in 1919 Cummings had to do "time" for buying metal and junk from Miguel Galvez, who was under sixteen years of age. Businessman Cummings claimed that he frequently needed wire, and from time to time purchased items from Galvez and others. These "products" included a faucet, a piece of rubber tube, and similar items. A jury of the Tombstone local court found him guilty, and even though practically every resident signed a petition in his favor, the higher court affirmed the sentence he was handed (fifty days, and a fine of $205). This weird incident had no impact on the long Cummings business career in Tombstone.

He died at age seventy-six on November 30, 1930, fifty years after he had arrived in Tombstone. In the early 2000s, a fascinating newsreel filmed

ARIZONAN EXPIRES AT 75

Charles L. Cummings Was Heyday Mayor of Tombstone.

TOMBSTONE, Ariz., December 1 (*P*). —Charles L. Cummings, 75, former mayor of Tombstone and owner of the Bird Cage Theater, famous during the heyday of this city's swashbuckling past, died yesterday.

Cummings was important enough to receive a death notice in the nation's capital. *Evening Star* (Washington, D.C.), December 1, 1930.

on December 22, 1925, was resurfaced by Earp/Tombstone town historians. Filmed by Jerry McFarland and entitled "Fox News Man Shoots Tombstone," it depicts various scenes about town including men and newsboys in front of the *Epitaph* newspaper office on Fremont Street. In front of his Bird Cage Theatre appears C. L. Cummings smoking his pipe, spitting, and smiling for the cameras. After his death, Cummings' widow would continue helping to promote the town of Tombstone to tourists. She sold the Bird Cage Theatre to the Ohm Family in July of 1944.[340]

GIRAGI FAMILY Frank and Sarah Giragi, from southern Italy, were in Tombstone by the early 1890s, and their family would be in the center of community life for decades. Frank was a miner, and for a time worked in the Pearce gold mines. His children Carmel (born in Tombstone on September 12, 1894), Columbus, Mary, Louis, and George were good students of the Tombstone schools, and Mary would become a clerk in a local store. Carmel and Columbus were hired by Billy Hattich to work in the print shop of the *Tombstone Prospector.* In 1913, the family bought out Hattich and took control of the *Prospector.* This was mainly Carmel and Columbus, although father Frank was part of the publishing group. The management, and the paper, was usually referred to as "the Giragi Brothers."

For more than a decade, the Giragi family controlled the Tombstone news. They had experienced the Tombstone mining revival, lived through and reported on the many ups and downs in the following years, and when things were dull in the mines, they informed their readers of local news and of Tombstone's role as the county seat, where major trials, such as that of the Bisbee Deportation, took place. The family enjoyed a good life in Tombstone. In 1923, Mrs. Giragi took son Louis and went to visit her hometown in Sicily.

The father, Frank, was also quite active, and not the sort of a fellow to just stand around doing nothing. Several times he was documented on jury duty, and as noted in the *Tombstone Weekly Epitaph*, on June 8, 1902, was granted citizenship. In the early 1900s he had several mining claims around Tombstone, and in 1908 was listed as a livestock owner with his mark shown in that year's *Brands and Marks* publication.

Although life in Tombstone was interesting, the Giragis were not impressed with the town's future, and instead chose other parts of Arizona. In early 1925, they took control of the *Winslow Mail*, hoping to publish both in Tombstone and Winslow, but soon said farewell to Tombstone. In the next decade the family operated the leading newspapers in Winslow, Holbrook, and Flagstaff, and carried considerable influence in several parts of the Arizona business and publishing worlds. They also owned the Hotel Chief in Winslow, where they installed their father Frank as the manager. The Giragis had taken their education and experiences from Tombstone and used them to good effect in other Arizona locales. Sadly, Carmel, publisher of the *Winslow Mail* newspaper at the time, died in a plane crash near Winslow, Arizona, April 17, 1933. Father Frank died on November 1, 1935. Commendably, the Arizona Newspapers Association Hall of Fame includes entries in 1958 for Carmel Giragi, *Holbrook News*, *Tribune* & *Winslow Mail*; and in 1978 for Columbus Giragi, *Coconino Sun*, Flagstaff.[341]

HUGHES, EDWIN A. A Californian who headed for Tombstone at the beginning of the first mining revival, by 1904, Edwin Hughes was identified as a clerk, and by 1910 as a bookkeeper, in the county recorder's office in Tombstone.

Hughes would soon be assessor of Cochise County, a position he held for a decade. His work in the recorder and assessor offices gave him intimate contact with all parts of Cochise County, and he was intricately connected with state officials in various departments. By 1922, while still living in Tombstone, Hughes became a part of the state tax commission, a position he would hold for decades. He died in Phoenix on October 25, 1941, and was listed as cashier, sales tax commission.[342]

THE FIFTH ERA, 1927-2023
Living on the Legend: The Final Revival/Bonanza

THE 1920S, A DOWNWARD SLOPE FOR TOMBSTONE, WAS partially salvaged by the evolution of the nation's highway system. By 1917, work had begun on the Borderland Route, a New Mexico-California road that passed through Tombstone. By this time, A. H. Gardner of the Huachuca Water Company was vitally interested in local traffic, was secretary of the Cochise County Highway Commission, active in Arizona Good Roads, and a very influential member of Old Spanish Trails association. By the mid-1920s, increased auto ownership and traffic made highways a major consideration, and Gardner and Tombstone were in the forefront, with Gardner making certain that publicity and funds would come Tombstone's way. There were races held on portions of the road, some of these contests passing through Allen Street in Tombstone.

Tombstone, thought by many to be on the brink of oblivion, pushed mightily to deny such thinking. As an example of the situation, Harry Locke of Los Angeles made several trips to Arizona specifically to visit with Gardner. In this era, Locke was the "map king" of the West and carried considerable influence on transportation.

On the national scene, U. S. Highway 80 was named, and routes selected in 1926-1927, and this included the small town of Tombstone. In these same years, the road from Nogales to Tombstone, State Route 82, was completed. The almost-ghost town was now at a highway crossroads, with national and state recognition. This amazing, fortuitous occurrence was further enhanced in 1927 (hence the beginning of the fifth era), with the publication of Walter Noble Burns' *Tombstone: An Iliad of the Southwest.* The highways, the publicity generated by Gardner and others, and the important book by Burns would be major underpinnings for what would become a leading Western tourist destination.[343]

Even more so than the other "eras" we have already discussed, the beginning of the fifth era could be considered by

257

many to be somewhat arbitrary and up for further debate. After much discussion, we chose 1927 as our starting point for "the final bonanza," knowing full well that Tombstone was not technically back in "bonanza" just yet by any means; but this was the year Burns' influential Tombstone book was released,[344] followed shortly thereafter by ex-Deputy Sheriff William Breakenridge's *Helldorado*. At this same time, national highway development was working to Tombstone's distinct advantage. A few years later, in 1929, the town's first

By 1929 it was obvious how Tombstone intended to interpret its past. Original 1929 Helldorado program, David D. de Haas, MD Collection.

"Helldorado" celebration was held, and in 1931, Stuart Lake's seminal book, *Wyatt Earp: Frontier Marshal* was released.

Things now started to rapidly change in the psyche of the town. Instead of a sanitarium, or returning once again to mining (for a fourth time), for the first time, Tombstone now began to focus on the possibility of using its unique fame/legend/mystique to propel it forward into the twentieth century. We all know how that worked out. If it weren't for this shrewd move, and a group of talented young entrepreneurs with a vision, Tombstone's future more than likely was as a ghost town, it would not be flourishing to this day, flaunting its thriving and unique tourist trade.

One could argue that we just as easily could have picked 1919, when Frederick Bechdolt's *Saturday Evening Post* articles came out, or 1922, when his book arrived. He definitely made significant contributions about town, most meaningfully in 1923, insisting, officially for the first time, on the renaming and reclaiming of the dilapidated town cemetery as "Boothill." Or how about 1930 as the beginning of this era, when another series of *Saturday Evening Post* articles appeared, these by Stuart Lake? Or 1932, when the flood of Earp/Tombstone movies commenced on the big screens across the country and throughout the world? Or 1955, when the Wyatt Earp television show first aired? The early 1960s, when Harold Love's consortium came to town and really began to shake things up, igniting the tourist trade even further?

We end our eras with a sample of the folks who bridged that gap, and many of whom are still around town to this day. All have made significant contributions to keep their chosen city alive. Most of the "modern day" Tombstonians we have selected for in this group are major contributors who have supported their town for 30 or more years. We considered, and could have picked a few others, but feel this group is a good representation of those who have been active about, promoted, and supported their town sometime during its last 95+ years, Tombstone's Fifth Era.

THE FIFTH ERA FOLKS FROM TOMBSTONE

ANDERSON, GORDON Born on September 9, 1965, Gordon Anderson moved with his parents from Minnesota (at age fourteen) to Mesa, Arizona, and then one year later to Tombstone, in September of 1980. His father, who worked as a corporate manager, was searching for business and investment opportunities and always loved the history of the Old West and Tombstone in particular. When Anderson, Sr. found Tombstone's Larian Motel for sale, he jumped at the opportunity and moved his young family southwest. This motel was built in 1952 on Fremont Street, on the site of the old Samuel L. Hart gunsmith shop; next to historic Schieffelin Hall, it was named for the original owners, Larry and Ann). For a teenager, Gordon handled the transition well, and spent four years at Tombstone High School, where he was active in sports, graduating in 1984. He has four older sisters, two of whom relocated with the family to Tombstone, and still live in nearby Sierra Vista to this day.

When his father died in 1983, Gordon at age eighteen began to assist his mother in managing the Larian, and eight years later, when she retired in 1991, he assumed full responsibility, at age twenty-six. She passed in 2007, at which time he assumed ownership. Anderson has worked hard to keep the facility up to date, even adding several rooms; currently there are thirteen in total. He even built a saloon out back to entertain his close friends, but sold that off a few years back. In 2012, Anderson bought a home in nearby Sierra Vista as an investment, and to spend some of his leisure time away from work when not supervising at the Larian. His long-term assistant manager, Linda, alternates with him to allow hard-earned days off.

Anderson has dedicated his life to his adopted hometown and has done everything in his power to make certain it prospers, working tirelessly to that end, many times at risk to his own health. Such an example is when he conceived of, worked nonstop toward, and then brought to reality as the "producer" the enormously popular and successful Tombstone Movie 25th Anniversary Reunion in July of 2018. This was a two-year-plus process for him, as well as for his cherished California friends Bob and Julie Ann Ream, who are Hollywood event producers/promoters and Valley Relic Museum curators. Anderson did the same once again for the 30th reunion event in June of 2023. Many of the film's stars (Michael Biehn as Johnny Ringo; Dana Wheeler-Nicholson as Mattie Earp; Peter Sherayko as Texas Jack; Billy Zane as Mr. Fabian; actor Wyatt Earp as Billy Claibourne; John Philbin as Tom McLaury; Robert Burke as Frank McLaury; Lisa Collins as Louisa Earp, Joanna Pacula as Big Nose Kate, Chris Mitchum as Hooker's Ranch Foreman; Frank Stallone as Ed Bailey), plus production designer Catherine Hardwicke, and many others, visited Tombstone for the four-day weekend events, staying at the Larian and other local facilities about town, to greet the huge crowds of their fans, pose for photos and sign autographs. In 2014, Gordon started Tombstone Forward, a charity whose stated mission is to "enhance the visitor experience," and which encourages groups to stage events in town. He also serves as the towns "assistant director of international tourism." In his role on the Arizona Film Commission, Gordon represents Tombstone and Cochise County. He is himself a part-time actor and has appeared in several documentaries. Gordon's contributions to Tombstone and its mystique tirelessly continue to this day; he's genuinely "a man of many parts."[345]

COLE, WALTER H. An Ohio printer-journalist born in 1877 who was still there practicing his trades at the time of the 1920 census, he and wife Edith went West and in May of 1930, at the age of fifty-three, just six months after the town had lost its prestigious county seat status, Cole purchased the *Epitaph* from William Kelly. Cole worked hard, promoted the community, pushed for dams along the San Pedro River, and did his best to boost Helldorado Days and other local events. He undoubtedly coined the catchphrase, "the Town (That's) Too Tough to Die" for Tombstone, which first appeared on the front page of the *Epitaph* on February 26, 1931. However, he himself was not tough enough to last. He sold the *Epitaph* in 1938 and shifted for a few years to Los Angeles. He and Edith eventually settled in Kingman, Arizona, where for years he was again associated with printing and newspaper work. He died there on July 23, 1963. Cole was an experienced journalist and businessman, but his years in Tombstone came at a dismal time. The nation was suffering the Great Depression, the local mines were mere shadows of their past glory, and Tombstone's lucrative county seat status was sadly no more. [346]

DEVERE, ROBERT and DEVERE, BURTON Jr. This pioneer family traces its Tombstone roots right back to the town's very foundation, and still own the Rose Tree Museum and most of the east side of Fourth Street from Toughnut up to the corner at Allen.

Robert was born October 19, 1966, in Torrance, California, where his father was working at the time. He has one brother and a sister, and is the son of John and Marcia Devere. His father, John Devere, is the brother of Burton Devere, Jr. These are the sons of Jeanne Macia (1914 – 1977) and Burton Devere. Jeanne Macia (Robert's grandmother) was the daughter of Ethel Robertson Macia (born August 16, 1881, in Tombstone; died August 3, 1964) and James Herbert Macia (born 1872; died in April, 1951). Ethel was the daughter of Alice Robertson (born in 1864; died in 1895) and S. C. "Chris" Robertson (born in 1854; died in 1899), whose cruel murder, you may remember, was tragically witnessed by young daughter Ethel. Chris and Alice Robertson wed on October 19, 1880, and first arrived in Tombstone on

Christmas Eve of 1880. They were acquaintances of Wyatt Earp and his brothers.

Robert and his wife Chrystie have three children. After living in the town on and off as a young child, he came back home to Tombstone to stay in 1989, and opened the popular Territorial Book Trader bookstore on the corner of Fourth and Allen Streets in 1990. It was known as a meeting spot for aficionados from around the globe to debate all things Tombstone when in town, until he sold it in October 1998.

Robert began teaching math at the local Tombstone High School in 2000, while also coaching the varsity softball and basketball teams there, and often serving as the public announcer for school football games. He worked his way up the ranks, becoming dean of students and athletic director. In 2006 he became principal, and subsequently superintendent in 2015. This is a position he holds to this day. The Rose Tree Museum is currently run by his cousin Jeff, son of his Uncle Burton Devere, Jr. (author of the book *Bonanzas to Borrascas: The Mines of Tombstone, Arizona*), who has now retired. This is another important Tombstone pioneer family who traces their roots to the camp's very beginnings and are still a force there to this very day.[347]

ELLIOTT, STEPHEN and MARJORIE After having first met in 1989 in Burbank, California, in an acting class, Steve from Wisconsin and "Marge" from northern California married in Tombstone on December 17, 1990, because Steve had always loved the town. They officially made it their home on the Fourth of July, 1991.They opened The Silver Lady Antique Shop a month later, and in January of 2001, opened the popular Tombstone Western Heritage Museum on the southwest corner of Sixth and Fremont Streets, right next to their antique shop and in front of their home, which at one time was the office of prominent Earp attorney William Herring. From the moment they first came to town, the Elliotts were active promoters of the history of their chosen home, and involved in town affairs. A special area of interest was town fire safety, but Steve and Marge also were fervent supporters of the preservation and promotion of the city's artifacts. They often led group campouts/tours to historical sites relating to Tombstone history. Steve sadly passed away in early August of 2014 and since that time, their museum has been open only on sporadic weekends for special guests/friends. Marge has remained active in the local Cameo Ladies Social Group.[348]

ESCAPULE, DUSTIN "DUSTY" Born in Tucson (as his mother didn't trust the small Tombstone Hospital at the time) on June 4, 1948, Dusty's family dates all the way back to the town's very beginnings. His great-grandfather, John Escapule (please see his full biography here under the first era) was a reporter for the *San Francisco Chronicle* and first arrived at Fort Huachuca in 1877, while researching a story on the capture of Geronimo.

John Escapule met his wife Emma Teresa Trappman (died, 1907), whose family were also Tombstone pioneers, at their nearby Monument Ranch. They had five children together, one of whom, Ernest Bernard Escapule (born at the State of Maine mine May 29, 1896; died, December 24, 1980), is Dusty's grandfather. John and Emma's only daughter, Emma Escapule Main, would come to own the O.K. Corral. She hired Sid Wilson to restore it to its original state in 1958, then sold it to Harold Love's Historic Tombstone Adven-

tures (HTA) in 1963. (Harold's son Bob still owns and operates it, and the *Tombstone Epitaph* newspaper, to this day).

Ernest Bernard Escapule and his wife Mildred went on to have five children, including Ernest Henry Escapule (born at the Lucky Hills ranch on May 9, 1923; died in 2009) who, along with his wife, Bernice (born-1929; died-1977; quite active on the Tombstone Helldorado committee), were the parents of Dusty, as well as two other sons and two daughters.

Dusty was educated in the local Tombstone and Sierra Vista schools and came to serve as deputy sheriff of Cochise County from 1969 to 1978; he then returned to his family business of mining and ranching around town.

Fourth generation Tombstoner Dusty Escapule has served several terms as mayor. *Herald Review*, July 2020.

From 1979 to 1986, Dusty owned and operated the last major silver producing mine in Tombstone. The mine generated as much silver and gold as the original mines had in the 1880s. He had 260 employees, including geologists, chemists, equipment operators, and numerous laborers. This mining operation was an open-pit mine known as Tombstone Exploration Inc. (TEI), which was one of the largest open-pit silver mines in the United States at that time. It was forced out of business in January of 1985, after a 1983 cyanide spill required mine closure with loss of production at a time of diminishing silver prices, and cleanup expenses proved overwhelming. In 1986, with plans to reopen the mine, Dusty helped form Cochise Silver Mine, Inc. and became its vice president and general manager, but new bureaucratic regulations regarding cyanide/pollution monitoring, along with ever-increasing wages and costs before mining could even begin, led to the closure of the mine in 1990.

For the past twenty-nine years, Dusty and his wife have owned and operated Old Tombstone Tours, stagecoach tours throughout the historic district of Tombstone. In 1998, Dusty was elected city councilman for two years. Since the year 2000, he has on and off been elected to and served as the mayor of Tombstone, a position which he currently holds for his eighth two-year term, having been reelected in August of 2022. In 2020, Mayor Escapule was chosen to be the "Helldorado Grand Marshal."

Dusty and Cheri, his wife of forty-seven years (married in 1976), have six children (four boys and two girls), several of whom are still active in town; their son also runs a stagecoach line, and their daughter, the photography studio. Another daughter is a schoolteacher in nearby Benson, Arizona. The Escapules have eighteen grandchildren and twelve great-grandchildren.

Dusty and Cheri currently live across the street from the city cemetery (which is on land donated by his great grandfather, John), their family ranch and extensive land holdings having long since been sold. He has known Tombstone's Ben Traywick since approximately 1969, and Bill Hunley since 1958 when (as a teenager) Bill came out to visit his grandparents, the Ohms, who owned the Bird Cage Theatre; and Dusty states he "cannot even remember a time" in his life when he didn't know the entire Macia/Devere family. All "Tombstone Royalty," without any doubt.[349]

FOSTER, WALLY C. Walter C. Foster was born in Wisconsin in 1914 and raised in Madison. He was in the U. S. Army during World War II as an aviation academic instructor, and later was chairman of the Madison district of Disabled American Veterans. In 1947 Wally and a friend headed to Tombstone "for his health," and opened a curio/gift shop, Wally Y Jack Tienda.

His background and personality pushed him forward in many spheres. By 1948 he headed the American Legion post, and in 1949 was secretary, then president of the chamber of commerce. In November of 1950, as a Democrat, he was elected as mayor of Tombstone, and would serve as Tombstone's mayor through 1961.

These were significant years, as Tombstone was thrust into the nation's consciousness as a major tourist destination; the decade when the Tomb-stone Restoration Commission was created, when Hollywood movie manager D'Estell Iszard and others laid the groundwork for buildings, streets, and historical markers to show off the interesting aspects of its past.

Throughout the decade, Foster was the public face of this Tombstone vitality. In 1950, for example, he did the casting for Helldorado Days, picking certain Tombstoners for the roles of Buckskin Frank Leslie, Johnny Ringo, Luke Short, and others. For some years Foster also sponsored "fast draw contests" and other frontier events. The *Arizona Republic* of June 4, 1959, published a photo of Mayor

This 1931 gathering included Harry Carr of the *Los Angeles Times*, author Woodworth Clum (son of John Clum), Dr. C. G. Toland, a USC professor, and Mayor R. B. Krebs of Tombstone. UCLA Special Collections.

Foster, waving goodbye to a stagecoach (on a railroad car), en route to a Lions Convention in New York City. In March of 1961, in a Boothill event, Tombstone officials had a "necktie ceremony" for a visitor, the mayor of Nigata, Japan; placing the necktie was Mayor Wally Foster and a "band of vigilantes."

Mayor Foster's most memorable moments were part of his running feud with President Harry S. Truman. In a campaign speech in 1952, President Truman mentioned a Tombstone Boothill marker: "Here lies Jack Williams. He done his damnedest." Mayor Foster wrote to the President denying any such marker and any such individual. Truman was forced to comment about this nationally on several occasions. Hundreds of newspapers across the land ran long articles about the Tombstone mayor-President Truman feud. As late as January 15, 1956, the *Corpus Christi Caller Times* published a detailed article on the fracas, headlined "Tombstone Controversy May Revive with Truman's Visit."

An interesting aspect of this controversy was the public stance Tombstone took to indicate that, unlike most Western Boot Hills, Tombstone was aiming for authen-ticity when recalling those bygone days. An even more unusual circumstance was that the Mayor Foster-President Truman controversy became part of the presidential papers, not a common circumstance for small-town mayors.

Foster's last term as mayor ended in December of 1961, and by then Tombstone was on the trajectory of becoming a major Western historical venue. He moved to nearby Sierra Vista, and for many years was the contractor and manager of the municipal airport. Foster died there on December 8, 1983, and is buried in the Tombstone cemetery. [350]

GARDNER, ARLINGTON HAMILTON Born in Dubuque, Iowa in 1867 and arriving in Tombstone in 1905 from Natchez, Mississippi, where he had been in business, he was associated with the Huachuca Water Company and would be the manager of that facility into the 1930s.

"Arlie" Gardner became well known in Arizona, not only as a booster of Tombstone and business, but also for the Good Roads movement, and held local and statewide positions in that organization for years. To Gardner, these elements were necessarily combined: progress, an efficient water system, business, tourism, and good roads. He was an extremely active Tombstoner, helping to organize, and becoming secretary of, Tombstone's first chamber of commerce, the Tombstone Commercial Club, on November 1, 1917, and therefore serving as guide/host to influential author Frederick Bechdolt when he first visited the town in August of 1919, and promoting "The Broadway of America," until ill health slowed him down in 1937. He died in Douglas on October 21, 1942. By this time, Gardner had accumulated considerable business and residential property in Tombstone.[351]

GIACOMA, ANTON and JOHN
Three Giacoma brothers from northern Italy arrived in the Southwest shortly after 1900, intending to mine in northern Mexico. Within a few years, Anton and John Giacoma would be solidly entrenched in Tombstone, remaining for more than half a century.

Public men, in the forefront of business, mining, and political life, they had interests in silver and manganese property around Tombstone, in Baja California, and in the Dragoon Mountains. Anton headed Tombstone entertainment venues, being in charge of the Crystal Theatre for years (after purchasing it in June 1915). The brothers also headed a local auto agency (Ford and Studebakers), as well as a wholesale oil business.

These fellows were indeed "active." In 1922 Joe Tholio, an ex-Bisbee miner, came to town intending to end the "earthly existence" of Anton. Tholio ended in a doctor's office, then the local jail, "nursing two black eyes, several bruised ribs, a badly cut head, and minus several teeth." This happened because he threated Giacoma with a pistol.

In 1929, when Mayor Krebs was pushing the Helldorado Days concept, he arranged for Anton Giacoma, the theater man, to be on several committees. This circumstance was practically repeated in 1949 when the Tombstone Restoration Commission was incorporated. The kingpins in this move were Mrs. Ethel Macia, Anton Giacoma, and his brother John, then serving as Tombstone's mayor.

The brothers were Tombstoners to the end. John died there on February 5, 1955, and Anton in Tucson on April 26, 1958; both are buried in Tombstone.[352]

GOLDSTEIN, STEVE Born in the Bronx, New York City on February 15, 1942, Steve Goldstein first came to Tombstone in 1961, as he had entered the army to support his mother and family after his father died, and was stationed at Fort Huachuca. While there, he was intimately involved in the United States activities during the Cuban Missile Crisis, and was selected to lead an elite group on a secret "suicide" mission into Cuba if need be.

He met his wife Gloria at a Tombstone High School (where she was a student) football game, and they were married in 1964. When the opportunity presented itself in 1974, Goldstein purchased (on IOUs, as he had no money) both the Bucket of Blood Restaurant/Tombstone Hotel, complex, renaming it the Longhorn Restaurant, and the Allen Street Bar, renaming it Big Nose Kate's Saloon. Unable to make the payments/payrolls on his new restaurants while cooking and bartending there, Goldstsein commuted back and forth to New York two to three times a week for eleven years, working multiple jobs there, while Gloria and his young family remained home in Tombstone, living with her mother.

In 1976, he moved his mother and sister (Arlene Klein; owner of several shops in Tombstone since and to this day) to Tombstone. Goldstein returned to Tombstone full time in approximately 1985, as his businesses started to succeed and he tired of the commute.

In approximately 2010, the opportunity arose to purchase the famous Russ House, built in December 1880 and then taken over by the renowned Nellie Cashman (and her partner Joseph Pascholy) in 1881, and Goldstein opened Café Margarita there. After COVID hit in 2020, for lack of chefs and other restaurant employees, Goldstein was forced to convert it to its current, period-correct "Russ House Bed and Breakfast. Steve has two daughters, one of whom (Susan) still lives in town and is currently the president of the Tombstone Chamber of Commerce, which she has been active with for over ten years, and is also on the Tombstone Restoration Commission, along with Mayor Dusty Escapule. The whole family is still extremely active in the community. Steve started the town's little league and introduced Fourth of July fireworks to town in approximately 2000, the first few years picking them up in Tucson and driving them to town himself. He also started the highly popular Wyatt Earp Days, celebrated over a weekend each May, and is still a member of Tombstone's first gunfighter group, the "Vigilantes" having played Johnny Behan for more than twenty-five years, beginning in the 1960s. He also is a member of the Buffalo Soldiers and many other local organizations, and along with Gloria actively fundraises for the Shriners Children's Hospital.[353]

HUNLEY JR., WILLIAM M. From Sullivan, Indiana (born there on January 7, 1941), William Hunley, aka "Mr. Tombstone," spent much of his childhood in Tombstone with his grandparents, and purchased the Bird Cage Theatre in approximately 1960 at the age of 19, from his grandmother Mrs. Minnie Ohm (his mother was Mrs. William Hunley of Dugger, Indiana, daughter of Mr. H. F. and Mrs. Minnie Ohm, who had purchased it from Mrs. C. L. Cummings in July 1944). From that time forward, and through to his recent sudden death (RIP; November 12, 2021), Bill was a passionate promoter of everything Tombstone, as were his wonderful wife Paula Jean, and his extended family,

including son Billy Hunley, daughter Nancy, and granddaughters Felicia Valdez, Arabella Martinez, and Rebecca Elliott). He was chosen grand marshal of Tombstone's 2018 Helldorado, having endorsed the unique history of his beloved town and advocating for it in every way possible. He even gave nighttime "ghost tours" of the haunted Bird Cage Theatre, which brought in yet another genre of Tombstone enthusiasts and led to numerous related and eagerly scrutinized otherworldly television shows and documentaries, further adding to the "Tombstone Mystique." His charismatic, enthusiastic, and energetic wife Paula Jean, whom he met in Tombstone and married in 1989, ran the Boothill Graveyard gift shop on the outskirts (west) of town from 1993 through 2005, and currently runs the extremely popular Fallen Angel Sweet Sin Parlor, an ice cream and fudge shop just west of the Bird Cage. Shortly after his recent death, in a tribute, the *Tombstone Epitaph Monthly Journal* proclaimed, "He left a major hole when he died... Bill was involved in practically any and every Tombstone organization and event...he made such a great difference [in his adopted town/second home]." His legion of dear friends he left behind will readily attest to that.[354]

ISZARD, D'ESTELL This fellow was the ideal consultant for what became Tombstone's "Wild West" personality. He was born in the mining camp of Cripple Creek, Colorado, in 1896, raised there and in Nevada, and spent his teens in Santa Monica, California, having arrived there in 1914 from Reno with his family. Iszard joined the National Guard in June of 1916 and served along the Mexican border through October of 1916, spending time in Nogales, Fort Huachuca, and Tombstone, making his first contact there in this period.

He followed this all with a stint as a sergeant in World War I (1917 – 1919), in a machine gun company involved in several major battles in France. Between 1919 and 1923, he spent much of his time in Tonopah, Nevada (as the Earps had, less than two decades earlier), and married in nearby Goldfield. Afterwards, Iszard was in clerking, then accounting, in Santa

Monica, and was soon working at MGM Studios. When World War II erupted, Iszard joined the army (in 1942) as a lieutenant. For a time in 1945-46, he was stationed at Fort Huachuca, Arizona, and became fascinated by Tombstone's history, becoming heavily involved in the town's doings from approximately 1945 to 1960.

In the late 1940s, although Iszard was located in Hollywood, he spent so much time in Tombstone he was considered a resident. Iszard was the driving force in the creation of the Tombstone Restoration Commission (with its office in Schieffelin Hall) in November 1949, whose stated goal was to return the town ("The West-

THE TOWN TOO TOUGH TO DIE has clung desperately to life from more than 25 years and residents are trying to breathe some of the oldtime fire into old Tombstone. Pictured at a banquet starting off plans for a restoration program are from left to right Joe Grill, restoration secretary, D'Estelle Iszard, restoration director, and Mort Palmer, head of the restoration committee.

D'Estell Iszard, center, the Tombstone Restoration director, in the late 1950s was also the consultant for the successful television production, Tombstone Territory. *Tucson Daily Citizen*, January 30, 1950.

ern Show Place of America") to its early 1880s appearance. He served as their "Director of Operations," and for some years as historian, research consultant, and head promotor, even producing a film back home in Hollywood documenting these efforts. Iszard was largely responsible for pushing the Wild West aspect of Tombstone, and focused on the buildings and events that would most interest tourists and other visitors. He was joined in his efforts by several other prominent townsmen, including Tombstone *Epitaph* publisher Clayton A. Smith, who was appointed assistant director of restoration, and C.M. Palmer, who was named president of the board of directors.

Heading back home to Hollywood, Iszard had several roles in movie and television production, including work on a Jack the Ripper effort. When *Tombstone Territory* was produced for television in 1957-1960, Iszard was the lead consultant for all episodes. His frontier upbringing, service in two world wars, and familiarity with all aspects of show business were major factors in creating the Tombstone that people today now recognize primarily as a Western tourist attraction. Iszard died in Los Angeles on November 28, 1964, and is buried in Westwood Memorial Park.[355]

KELLY, WILLIAM H. (W. H.) Born in Bisbee in 1902, his few years in Tombstone would certainly be memorable. He had the proper background; his father, W. B. Kelly (born December 7, 1875), had been with newspapers in various Arizona places, then published the *Bisbee Daily Review* and subsequently the *Arizona Daily Star* (of Tucson) for some years. His grandfather, George Henderson (G. H.) Kelly (born February 8, 1854), published numerous different newspapers, including the *Douglas International*, and became the first president of the Arizona Newspaper Publishers Association. On January 1, 1923, granddad G. H. Kelly was appointed Arizona state historian by then-Governor G. W. Hunt; and in 1928, G. H. published a book, the *Legislative History: Arizona*, and subsequently launched a quarterly magazine, the *Arizona Historical Review*. G. H. Kelly died on November 10, 1929, in Phoenix, from an illness he incurred two weeks earlier while attending Tombstone's first Helldorado celebration in October.

With that type of pedigree,

young William Kelly took control of the *Tombstone Epitaph*, which was purchased by the family printing company, Kelly Printing and Publishing Company in 1926. By early 1929, the Tombstone future was bleak, and Kelly, Mayor Krebs, and Ethel Macia decided to do a Tombstone makeover. Taking advantage of the publicity generated by former deputy sheriff William Breakenridge's recent book, *Helldorado*, they chose that as the title for what would become "Helldorado Days," a very significant multi-day event which would focus on the exotic aspects of Tombstone's past. They corralled Breakenridge, ex-mayor/*Epitaph* publisher John Clum, and other Western notables to come to Tombstone for four days in October to liven things up, emphasizing the glory days of the Western frontier. The role of William Kelly in all of this, as head of the publicity in Arizona and California, was a key part of the success of Helldorado Days.

That was pretty much the story of Kelly and Tombstone. In May of 1930 he sold the *Epitaph* to Walter H. Cole, and by June, had returned to Tucson and the *Arizona Daily Star* newspaper. Early in the 1930s, he become fascinated with anthropology and ethnology, obtained a Ph.D., and studied many aspects of Pima, Cocopah, and Papago culture and history. By World War II, Kelly was a research associate at Harvard, working primarily in the Peabody Museum, where he was an acknowledged authority on Southwestern ethnology. Kelly died in Tucson on February 9, 1980.[356]

KREBS, RAY B. Born in Ohio in 1882, by 1910, Ray Krebs was in Bisbee, working for the YMCA. In 1912 he received the appointment as deputy clerk of the superior court and moved to Tombstone. For the next half century, Raymond Burton Krebs would be a key business and political figure in the area, always connected to goings-on in both Bisbee and Tombstone. During World War I, he was clerk of the local draft board, and later served in the Arizona House of Representatives, often connected with large events and projects. Even when operating a Nash automobile dealership in Bisbee in later years, Krebs continued to live in Tombstone.

In 1929, while serving as Tombstone mayor, Krebs pushed the concept of making the community a histor-

Ray B. Krebs, a mayor in the 1920s, was a strong advocate of Helldorado Days. Helldorado Program, 1929.

ical tourist destination. He convinced the city council and threw in a substantial sum to sponsor create and sponsor Helldorado Days; it was Krebs, taking advantage of the recent Breakenridge book, who actually came up with the name for the four-day occasion. This was not only important locally, but over the years became a model for other Western communities interested in promoting their past.

Into the 1940s, Krebs continued in the auto sales business, at times having operations in Tombstone, Bisbee, and Douglas. He died in Tombstone on January 4, 1955.[357]

LANDIN, EDNA L. Thure (Ted) and Edna Landin were from Cincinnati, where he had a successful textile business. Seeking "clean Western air," they moved to Tombstone in 1950, but Ted soon died. Edna, however, from the beginning had been captivated by Tombstone's history. For the next fifteen years she would be a local whirlwind, convinced not only to stem any decay, but to push for major revitalization of the community.

A listing of her activities and roles would take considerable space. She was on the city council, president of the chamber of commerce, and served several terms as head of the Tombstone Restoration Commission in the 1950s, the real start of what became Tombstone as the public would see and know it to this day.

Her most noteworthy accomplishment was to have the courthouse in Tombstone become part of the Arizona state parks system. This structure, without purpose when the county seat moved to Bisbee in 1929, served as a mediocre hotel, storage facility, and a place for occasional gatherings. Today the Tombstone Courthouse Museum is one of the most visited historic buildings in the West.

The 1950s and early 1960s

were when the major efforts to create a "new, old" Tombstone took place. People like the Macias/Devere and Escapule families assured a major continuity with the town's past, and others, like D'Estell Iszard, brought in the Hollywood showbusiness angles. Landin, however, was the administrator, the lobbyist, the letter-writer, the organizer, who made these various Tombstone organizations effective and successful. In 1956 she was named Woman of the Year in Tombstone.

Edna Landin died on December 18, 1967, her work and connection to her adopted community acknowledged by the creation of the Landin City Park in Tombstone.[358]

LOMBARDI, WALTER Walter was born in Tombstone in 1893. His father, Louis, from Switzerland, was a Tombstone miner by as early as 1888. Louis also had mining claims, some livestock, and ran a dairy in Tombstone; he died in a mine cave-in near the State of Maine property in 1913 while working as a chlorider.

Walter Lombardi was educated in Tombstone, on the baseball team, became a mechanic, and was working in Columbus, New Mexico when he registered for the draft during World War I. Lombardi had other interests and served time in the New Mexico State Penitentiary in 1918 for peddling booze too close to a military base. He then returned to Tombstone, where he would remain for nearly half a century.

In Tombstone, Lombardi was always in business and never shy about promoting his doings. He owned a pool room, purchased the Crystal Palace in 1930, and in various documents over the years usually identified himself as a tavern owner. This also had its dark side. In 1938, the Crystal Palace was robbed and considerable damage done, as the safe was blown. In that same year, Walter contracted the Tombstone disease—prospecting. He and a partner received wide publicity as they filed sixty-one claims near Tombstone, claims purportedly containing the country's largest deposit of cobalt ore. This was just another of the false alarms associated with mining camps.

Lombardi was very active in the Tombstone Restoration Commission until his death there in September of 1956.[359]

LOVE, HAROLD O. In September of 1963, a group of four, led by Harold Love (born in 1909) of Detroit, Michigan, formed an organization entitled Historic Tombstone Adventures, to (hopefully) profit on the preservation, development, and maintenance of Tombstone's historic landmarks—an Arizona Disneyland of sorts. In 1964, the group purchased the *Tombstone Epitaph* newspaper, the O.K. Corral, the Crystal Palace, and Schieffelin Hall. In June of 1974, the "National Edition" of the *Tombstone Epitaph* was introduced and published on a monthly basis. Subscriptions increased significantly, and the paper finally became profitable. On February 2, 1975, owing to decreasing circulation, the local *Weekly Epitaph* newspaper was switched to a biweekly, and turned over to the University of Arizona for their journalism students to produce/publish.

In 1977, Love and his wife Sara Elizabeth ("Betty;" born November 5, 1914, in Detroit) moved to Tucson, and continued to work to restore and promote Tombstone. Upon Love's death on March 21, 1986, Wallace Clayton succeeded him as the publisher of the "National Edition" of the *Tombstone Epitaph*. Son Robert E. "Bob" Love maintained control of the O.K. Corral. When Betty died on November 23, 2011, she was buried together with Harold in the Tombstone City Cemetery, with an impressively huge and unique monument/mausoleum marking their gravesites.[360]

MACIA, EDITH ALICE ROBERTSON The younger sister of the well-known Ethel Macia was born in Leadville, Colorado, in 1884, and would spend half a century in Tombstone. In 1917, Edith married miner Harry Macia, who was the brother of Ethel's husband James, and through time held several positions in greater Tombstone. For some years she was involved with tax collection projects for Tombstone and for Cochise County. In 1926, Edith was appointed postmistress of Tombstone, and served efficiently through 1935.

However, it was the subsequent post-Tombstone years that threw her into the national spotlight. The family moved to Los Angeles. There in the politically chaotic postwar years, she was approached by the FBI. They convinced her to join the Communist Party and serve as an undercover agent. Edith did this, attended countless meetings, was in a "cell," had a false "spy name," and for more than three years was seen as a dedicated, reliable member of the Communist Party. In the 1950s, Edith Macia "came out" and appeared before several congressional committees. She was able to present extensive details on party aims, finances, and so forth.

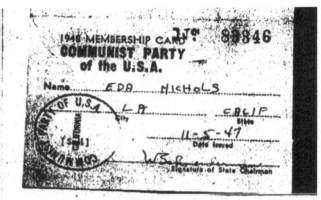

The national press gave considerable coverage to her role, mentioning her many years in Tombstone as well. Some of

Ex-post mistress of Tombstone, Edith Macia, later worked in California as an FBI undercover agent. *Los Angeles Times*, March 29, 1953.

the typical newspaper headlines were "Arizona Woman Names 146 Reds" and "Legion to Honor Grandma Spy." She eventually settled in Prescott, dying there on July 17, 1974.[361]

MACIA, ETHEL Born in Tombstone in 1881 to Chris and Alice Robertson, recent arrivals from the mining camp of Leadville, Ethel Macia was raised and schooled in Tombstone, and the family moved to Pearce in 1898, though her mother had died a few years earlier. Her father, operator of a saloon and a livery business, was killed by a debtor lawman in 1899 in a messy murder over some unpaid livery bills the officer owed. The remaining Robertsons moved back to Tombstone with Ethel as head of the family after the murder.

Her siblings were Edith (who died in 1974), Olive (who died in 1970), Ralph (who died in 1945), and Curtice (who died in 1950).

Ethel Robertson worked at a clerical job in the local tax office, attended the University of Arizona for a year, then in February of 1904 married James Macia, a newly-arrived mining man. Macia would be a major Tombstone personality for decades as a mining foreman, superintendent, and consultant with many silver and copper properties. In 1919, the couple bought the Arcade Hotel (formerly the Cochise Hotel) on the grounds of the old Vizina Mining Company land, one of the leading mines of the first Tombstone bonanza era, on the northeast corner of 4th and Toughnut

Streets. They operated this as a hotel and boarding unit and in 1936 changed its name to the Rose Tree Inn, which became well-known throughout southern Arizona. Over the years Ethel became active, and in many cases was a leader, in social and cultural causes. She was a force in local conservation and preservation, an officer in the Cochise and Arizona historical agencies, a founder of the Arizona Children's Home, a key member of the local hospital boards, and a favorite of many Helldorado campaigns.

Her husband James died in April of 1951, and Ethel died in Tombstone on August 3, 1964. Their daughter Jeanne married Burton Devere, and they continued to operate the Rose Tree Inn, which became the Rose Tree Museum. The Robertsons, Macias, and Deveres represent a unique Tombstone continuum, from the bonanza year of 1880 into the twenty-first century, involved in the various Rose Tree establishments. To this day, the museum is famed for its rose tree, planted in the 1890s after gifted from Scotland (to Mary Gee). It is now known as the world's largest (listed in *Ripley's Believe It or Not!* and the *Guinness World Records*), and is a favorite attraction for tourists, who visit from all over the world to take in its magnificence.[362]

MEDIGOVICH, SAM and THEDA The Medigovich family seems to have been one of the largest contingents of Serbians in the nineteenth-century West. They were in the mining camps of Nevada, California, and Arizona by the 1870s. Bisbee was their Arizona center, and they were connected with the mines, smelter, and business houses there. An earlier (different) Sam Medigovich was issued citizenship papers in Tombstone in 1890.

Our Sam was born in Petrovac, Serbia, in 1908, and arrived in this country with his family in 1910. He was educated and worked in Bisbee, became a plumber, and along with his wife, Theda (they married in 1938), operated his successful plumbing company at least through 1940.

The couple moved to Tombstone sometime in the mid-1940s, and for more than three decades were active in dozens of business and civic activities. They operated the Wagon Wheel Restaurant as well as the Silver Nugget Museum, and both served as officers of the Tombstone Restoration Commission in 1949 and 1950. "Active" to them meant using their money, and huge amounts of time. As one example, in 1977, Theda joined with a few other locals and made a trip to Germany to spread the word about Tombstone's role in the West. To accentuate their objective, they dressed in Western garb.

There were many ways in which Sam and Theda contributed to pushing the Tombstone legacy, but the most important was seeing that their Tombstone collection found the proper home in the Arizona Historical Society. There, in some twenty boxes, are thousands of insights into the legal, medical, business, educational, religious, and civic life of Tombstone's past. Theda died in Tombstone on November 13, 1984, Sam on August 15, 1987; both are buried in the Tombstone City Cemetery[363]

NUNNELLEY, LELA B. and EMMETT CROOK Emmett and Lela Nunnelley were Easterners who moved to Tucson in the 1930s. He was in the construction business, had a side interest in mining, and a passion for Old West history; so, they moved to Tombstone in 1945. Emmett arranged with the city of Tombstone to "clean up" and restore/organize the graves and grounds of Boothill Cemetery in ex-change for the right to open a giftshop on the site, but died in his office there on November 6, 1946, before completing the project. Per his wishes/their request, the family received permission for his unusual modern-day burial in Boothill more than sixty years after the graveyard had officially closed.

This was the beginning of Lela Nunnelley's sixteen-year association with Tombstone's Boothill Cemetery. She was appointed the historian, caretaker, and custodian of the place and also operated the souvenir shop at the site. Taking over where her husband left off and determined (as her husband was before her) to clear up the many mysteries about the graveyard, such as the number of burials, names of the deceased, and causes of death, she launched into a decade-long project of poring over vital records, reading all of the Tombstone and Tucson newspapers, interviewing the surviving local old-timers, and corresponding with descendants, friends, and neighbors of the deceased.

The useful result of these labors was her 1952 pamphlet, "Boothill Grave Yard: A Descriptive List *of the More Than 250 Graves in Boothill.*"

The information in this (now updated) pamphlet is still distributed at Boothill to this day. In subsequent years, Ben Traywick and wife Red Marie carried on with the research and published their own book (several editions) on Boothill, presenting new data and acknowledging the pioneer work of Lela and Emmett.

One incident in the 1950s indicates the widespread knowledge of Tombstone's Boothill and the role of Lela Nunnelley. In a few campaign speeches, President Harry Truman falsely referred to an alleged burial in Tombstone which had this nonexistent marker text: "Jack Williams. He done his damnedest." Mayor Wally Foster and Lela Nunnelley were drawn by the media into this controversy, as their intention was to try to keep Tombstone's Boothill authentic.

Lela carried on as the Tombstone Boothill custodian until 1961, when she retired to Tucson, dying there on January 24, 1983. Cremation followed, so there was no Boothill or other cemetery finale for her.[364]

SMITH, CLAYTON A. Born in a small town in North Dakota in 1913, Clayton Smith arrived in Tombstone in 1936, a year that was a true nadir in the town's history. He purchased the *Tombstone Epitaph* from Walter H. Cole on October 6, 1938, and wrote, edited, and published that newspaper until his death in 1964.

More than anyone else, Smith was responsible for turning a potential Western ghost town into practically a cash-cow community. Building on the Helldorado Days concept of 1929, Clayton "shifted" the local history. Rather than an important frontier silver mining community, Tombstone was soon regarded as a major Wild West shoot-em-up place, a shift helped tremendously by the Stuart Lake biography of Wyatt Earp in 1931 and by the Tombstone movie and television presentations which began in the 1930s, all kick-started by Smith and the *Epitaph*.

The *Epitaph*, and Smith, were in the forefront of local, regional, and state legislation and policies that encouraged tourism, and pushed for community boards and organizations that promoted Tombstone as a tourist destination. He was a sparkplug urging historic preservation and zoning. His energy seemed endless, as he was on the school board, was a scout leader, a volunteer fireman, and served as a justice of the peace.

His adventuring attitude led to a premature death. In January of 1964, as the pilot of a small plane, he crashed near the Whetstone Mountains, killing himself and his two passengers.[365]

TAYLOR, DON Raised in Houston, Don Taylor moved to Tombstone from Phoenix in 2002 after frequent visits there beginning in 1994. Owing to his passion for the history of the place, Taylor obtained a position as the assistant manager of the Tombstone Courthouse State Historic Park. After five years working there, he left to become the manager of the O. K. Corral in 2007, and remained there for four more years.

In 2010, at the invitation/urging of Ben Traywick, the "Official Tombstone Town Historian," who was retiring, Don agreed to assume his position, and was then voted in by Mayor Dusty Escapule and the city council, retaining that position to this day, having been voted back in every two years since.

Between 2007 and 2011, Taylor served as the president of the Tombstone Chamber of Commerce. Under his watch, between 2007 and 2010, vis-itors to the town increased from 500,000 to 1.25 million annually. He was elected to the city council and served from 2012 until 2014.

Don has written two books and edited two others. He is the author of *Tombstone: The First Fifty Years*, and *An Arizona Vendetta: The Truth About Wyatt Earp*; and was the editor of *Wyatt Earp*, by John Flood, Jr., and *She Married Wyatt Earp*, by Josephine Marcus Earp. He is also the author/editor of numerous newspaper and magazine articles, and has appeared more than thirty times on television and radio promoting his beloved adopted home, Tombstone.[366]

TRAYWICK, BEN T. (aka "Evil Ben") Born August 3, 1927, in Watertown, Tennessee, Traywick served in the U.S. Navy, enlisting at age fifteen and working two separate, three-year stints, both during and after WW II. The first was on a destroyer in the South Pacific at the same time his father was in the army deployed in Europe. By the time Traywick turned eighteen, he had earned ten Battle Stars and a Presidential Citation. In 1953, after his service, he achieved his B. S. degree in chemistry, and then spent the next thirty years working in the field of explosives in Oak Ridge, Tennessee (atomic), Sacramento, California (missiles), and finally the Apache Powder Company outside of Tombstone. Traywick moved his young family from northern California to Tombstone, Arizona in 1968 after first falling in love with the town following a brief visit while traveling from Tennessee en route to California. Soon thereafter he began working as a safety engineer/general manager for the Apache Powder Company (1969–1982) just west of town. Traywick became chief of "The Vigilantes" troupe, but subsequently left and formed his own troupe, the Wild Bunch Gunfighter group, a nonprofit with all proceeds going to the city of Tombstone, in January 1971. This group staged reenactments of the O. K. Corral gunfight, and he himself played Wyatt Earp for twenty years, with his son Billy then taking over for the next twenty-two years when, in Traywick's own words, he became "too old and fat" to play Wyatt himself. They put on reenactments around town with his then-wife, "Red Marie," and her company they had also cofounded, the Hells Belles. Based in the O. K. Corral with shows every weekend, this became the longest-running act in Tombstone. They

are noted for their huge advertising billboards seen on the major highways from the moment one first enters the state, with son Billy prominently featured portraying Wyatt Earp.

In 1972, Ben began the Rendezvous of the Gunfighters, an annual event that took place every Labor Day weekend (the first weekend in September), and which brought a remarkable amount of publicity to the town, as it was covered by the press worldwide. The event was changed to The Annual Showdown in Tombstone in 2014 after forty-two years.

In 1982, Traywick opened the Red Marie Bookstore in the first floor of the home he himself built for his family, on the east side of Fifth street, between Fremont and Allen. His years of research have led to the thirty-seven books, forty pamphlets, and more than seventeen hundred magazine and newspaper articles written on Wyatt, Doc Holliday, the O. K. Corral, and Tombstone in general. Traywick was appointed by the mayor and city council as "Tombstone's [first] Official Town Historian" in 1969, a role he faithfully fulfilled for more than forty years, until he retired in 2010 (at which time the city council unanimously designated him "Historian Emeritus"). During his tenure, he brought in crews to the city that produced more than 279 films and TV shows. Traywick can frequently be seen in documentaries on the History Channel, National Geographic, the Discovery Channel, and many others as a "talking head," interviewed more than 270 times, supporting his cherished town. His gunfighter troupe has donated more than $328,000 (the admission fees from their performances) to the city.

Traywick met Bird Cage Theatre owner Bill Hunley when he Traywick first arrived in town in 1968, sparking a deep, enduring friendship for the duo who would become the two best-known and influential personalities in Tombstone for the next fifty-three years. When his time comes, Ben has made plans to be buried in the Tombstone City Cemetery next to his first wife, Red Marie ("Red" for her hair). She died in 1997 after fifty-five years of marriage. He already has his plot and monument in place at her side.

TRAYWICK, MARY DELORES Mary, Ben Traywick's current and second wife (they married on October 3, 2002), was born in Flagstaff, Arizona on March 20, 1949, but moved to Tombstone at the age of three in 1952, and has spent more than sixty-four years there. Her family first arrived when her father, a World War II air force medic and subsequent military civil servant, was transferred to Fort Huachuca. She has two sisters and one brother who were all born in the Tombstone hospital, which today serves as the visitor's center, and in the first era served as the Agency Pima County Bank (where the Earps and Cowboys kept their money), on the southwest corner of Fourth and Allen Streets. Mary attended Tombstone High School, where she was homecoming queen in 1967, and where she subsequently worked for many years. She divorced her first husband, Pete Vasquez (who was born in Tombstone in 1943) and met Ben in 1998 while working in the town bookstore (Robert Devere's Territorial Book Trader). Mary has four children with her first husband.

Ben and Mary moved in February of 2021 from their long-term and well-known home and bookstore on a lot that had been a Wells Fargo store and museum in the past. It was a must-visit for Tombstone tourists and historians for the past forty years, and a gathering place for all authors, western actors, and Tombstone researchers in the know who ventured into town. The office was a renowned site for intense (but fun) Tombstone/Earp related discussions/debates; and viewings of Ben's comprehensive research files. They have downsized due to advancing age, and currently reside on the northwest side of town. To this day, Mary still volunteers at the Sacred Heart Catholic Church thrift shop, and serves as a church usher every Sunday. She has also herself penned a popular book, *Fiery Foods of Tombstone*, and coauthored *Men and Mysteries in Mexico* with husband Ben, and is an amazing chef. [367]

VALENZUELA, DENAY TURNER and AL E. TURNER Alfred Eugene Turner was a noted Tombstone/Earp scholar, researcher, historian, and author, having written/edited such significant works as *The Earps Talk in 1980* and *The O. K. Corral Inquest* in 1981. The limited-edition, leather-bound numbered versions of these books are quite collectible to this day. Another notable contribution to Tombstone history and Earpiana is his September, 1971 interview (along with Bill Oster) of Hildreth Halliwell, the grandniece of Allie Earp, Virgil Earp's wife, at her home in Valley Center,

California, shortly before her death. Alfred Turner was born in 1912 in Kansas, but his family moved to Peoria, Arizona when he was seven years old. He received his B. A. degree at Arizona State University in 1939, and his M. A. in 1950. He served as a teacher (English, machine shop) and school bus driver in Benson, Arizona early in his career and then subsequently in southern California, for many years. Al and his second wife, Marge Ruth Turner, moved to Tombstone in 1974 to enable him to continue his in-depth research on the town and the Earps. At the time of his death on April 8, 1987, his massive Wyatt Earp manuscript was nearly completed, but sadly never made its way to publication. Margie was quite a bit younger and lived until April 6, 2009.

Al and Margie both had children from their previous marriages, and in 1965, in Torrance, California, they had their only child together, a daughter, Denay. After the family's move to Tombstone, when Denay was eight, she was brought up and attended the local schools there. Denay has been married to Thomas Valenzuela, who was born in the Tombstone Hospital on Allen Street (present-day visitor's center), for more than thirty-six years. They have five children and eleven grand-children, who all still live in the area.

Denay has lived in Tomb-stone for nearly fifty years now and during that time has served her city in many capac-ities, including as a volunteer EMT on local ambulances (her favorite job) for eight years, in the post office for eight years, as a dispatcher for the marshal's office next to the city hall on Fremont Street, and has worked in many of the local businesses in the historic district around town, including the Wagon Wheel Restaurant and The Shady La-dy's Closet (owned by Gloria and Steve Goldstein). She also worked at the Top of the Hill restaurant for many years.

One of her passions is his-tory and reading the lore of her hometown. As a very young girl, Denay met many of her father's associates and well-known historians/authors in the field, including John Gilchriese, Ben Traywick, Wayne Winters, Nino Cochise, Harry Stewart, Don Shumar, Jack Henderson, Sid Wilson, William Hunley, and Glenn Boyer, spending many hours listening to their prolonged conversations on everything Tombstone and Earp. She also frequently visited John Gilchriese's Wyatt Earp Mu-seum with her dad, and of course, having been raised in Tombstone, has befriend-ed pioneer family members such as current mayor Dusty Escapule and Burton and Rob-ert Devere, as well as Steve and Gloria Goldstein, and Mary Traywick (her daughter's god-mother). Denay most recently has worked in the historic dis-trict, with Cheryl Leavere Honey-cutt, another long-term Tomb-stone stalwart/resident and passionate town promoter.[368]

TOMBSTONE'S EXTRAORDINARY MYSTIQUE FACTORS
Closing Arguments / We Rest Our Case

ALTHOUGH THERE WERE A HUNDRED OR SO MINING CAMPS and towns in the West, Tombstone had a variety of events, situations, and exceptional folks that set her apart from all the others. For fifty years (and still to this day), Tombstone and its townsfolk were frequently in the regional, national, and worldwide news, which was not the case for any other mining community.

The strange route and doings that led Ed Schieffelin to locate, then name, Tombstone, and the tremendous outburst of enthusiasm for this silver find, was not a typical bit of frontier news. From the start, big guns were at work. The distinguished moneybags in this instance, ex-governor Anson Safford of Arizona, was more than a talker and sponsor. He was part owner of the best silver properties, and with the backing of Arizona and California investors, Safford went East, corralled financers in Philadelphia, Boston, and New York, and more money began to flow. Mills, new equipment—the purses were wide open, and leading capitalists backed dozens of the Tombstone mines and the mills along the San Pedro River. [369]

The nation's press followed the Tombstone news, attracted by the weird name, but also influenced by the financial giants behind the ventures. The *Chicago Inter-Ocean*, from the town's humble very beginnings, mentioned that Tombstone was "growing wonderfully," and Safford trips to Eastern markets were also followed and covered.[370] The West Coast papers also played up the Tombstone name and its riches. The *Los Angeles Herald* of October 29, 1879, mentioned the continuous stream of silver bricks from the Tombstone mill, and the "great excitement not only in 'Frisco but in the Eastern states."

Some of this publicity in newspapers might be considered fluff, or boosterism, but the message was even stronger in the professional publications. The "bible" of Western mining was the *Mining & Scientific Press* of San Francisco, and their assessments in late 1879 contained the highest praise. They mentioned the current production, stated that there would be a "large, permanent and prosperous place," and that there was something new every day at the Toughnut, Lucky Cuss, and Contention. By December, the town had fifty permanent residents, more than forty houses were under construction, as were many mines and mills. Things were so advanced that the place even had keno games and two hurdy-gurdy dance houses "nightly filled."

The enthusiastic endorsement of the goings-on in Tombstone in 1879 by the leading authorities on Western mining was the prelude to the big bonanza:

> *No country on top of the earth, of equal extent, that contains as many valuable mines and as much precious metal as can be found within a circle of 100 miles in diameter with Tombstone for the center.* [371]

These, then, were some of the things that made Tombstone unique from the very start. For its founder it had Ed Schieffelin, the tall, handsome, bearded prospector with rifle on shoulder, the type who would make Hollywood casting directors drool. And, for its biggest backer/promoter, it had Arizona's former governor, Anson Safford, plugged into all sorts of political and business connections, and himself a founder of a leading financial institution. With personalities like this, and mountains of silver to dig, early Tombstone was off to an enviable, newsworthy start.

Although it had a startling, successful bonanza era, between 1877 and 1885, that aspect of the community's past was more or less in keeping with other bonanza places in the West. The obtaining of great fortunes from silver and gold deposits seldom extends beyond two to four years. The notable exception, of course, is the Homestake/Deadwood area, which churned out gold for more than a century (the 1870s until 2002). More typical are Sutter Creek, the Klondike, Nome, Pioche, Comstock, Creede, Cripple Creek, Goldfield, and Bodie. Huge fortunes were made, vibrant communities erupted, but the good stuff seldom lasts.

Truly successful mining over the long term is with the base metals, especially copper and lead. The Calumet & Hecla of Michigan's Lake Superior provided copper for a century. The Anaconda of Montana, Bisbee's Copper Queen, Alaska's Kennecott, and a half dozen lead mines in Missouri were productive for decades. The precious metal mines don't have that kind of longevity. The metals are precious because they are rare. Tombstone, as a precious metal camp, was pretty much destined for the short term.

Therefore, the mining revival also certainly set it apart from other Western mining camps. Although we bracket Tombstone's first revival from 1901 to 1910, it really had its foundations in the late 1890s, when E. B. Gage returned and quietly, slowly began acquiring the defunct silver properties. And it wasn't until 1903, with the arrival of its first railroad and the working of new pumps, that serious silver production broke out, which would be sustained at least through 1910. The most unusual aspect of the Tombstone mining revival was that it was headed by a giant from its earlier, first-era bonanza days, E. B. Gage. Twenty years after he profited from the great doings of the Grand Central mine, Gage was once again profiting, now from the Tombstone Consolidated, which included the Grand Central. Such incidents are not commonplace in Western mining history.

The phrase "mining revival" has meaning when Tombstone is considered. However, in most Western mining history and in the newspapers and professional journals, the phrase was one of hope, not necessarily reality. One journal in 1896 suggested that Placer County "expects a needed mining revival;" in Spokane in 1900, a piece claimed that a planned exposition "will trigger a mining revival;" while a Denver publication in 1914 predicted a "revival is promised" in Goldfield; but none of that ever happened. In general, when recoveries were discussed, the meaning was that one *could* happen.[372] The *Mining Investor* of Denver on June 2, 1913, stated that, "We are on the eve of a big mining revival." These many general, district-wide revival comments had nothing in common with Tombstone, which in the years 1901 to 1910 actually had a successful revival, with some of the same personnel and on exactly the same mining ground as previously. That is a real mining resurgence.

Another unique feature of the Tombstone story was the development of the town-rural conflict, the rise of the rivalry between the Earp faction and the Cowboy Gang, and the eventual shootout in October of 1881, known throughout the world as the Gunfight at the O. K. Corral. Because these troubles transpired in the middle of the mining bonanza, they attracted more regional and national attention.

The entire bonanza concept would play out in many Western mining camps; new towns meant a search of factions for power as new legal entities were created. Important positions like sheriff, boards of supervisors, and mayor were up for grabs, and in all, a jockeying for positions meant upheaval—political and social. It did not help the Tombstone situation that the territorial governor was John C. Fremont, pretty much a cipher in the life of Arizona. That a hack like John Behan was able to convince authorities to appoint him as sheriff of the new County of Cochise suggests that the struggle for local power was going to be tough and political.

The town-rural rivalry did come to a boil, the famous shootout did occur, and the subsequent ambushes of Marshal Virgil Earp and his brother Morgan, the wipeout of Frank Stilwell in the Tucson railyard in retaliation, and the vendetta by the Wyatt Earp posses were part of subsequent chapters. Only in 1882-83, with a new territorial governor and changes in positions of county sheriff and chief of police, were conditions somewhat moderated in greater Tombstone, as well as along the border between Arizona, New Mexico, and Mexico.[373]

The unusual nature of the above events, for a variety of reasons, attracted the interest of many parts of the world, which led to the evolution of histories, sagas, exaggerations, and elaborations that exist to this day. To many people around the world, the names Wyatt Earp, Doc Holliday, Johnny Ringo, Ike Clanton, Curly Bill, and John Behan are better known than the name of their local governor or favorite television personality. The names "Wyatt Earp," "O. K. Corral," and "Tombstone" have become synonymous and so prevalent, so iconic, that they have pushed to the side, to the background, most events that took place in other Western mining camps.[374]

Murder, robbery, lynching, and a major hanging took place in Cochise County in 1883-84, which combine many of the elements that made Tombstone so unusual. This was the Bisbee Massacre. Bisbee, a major copper-producing town south of Tombstone, experienced an attack at the Goldwater & Castenada Store on December 8, 1883. It was a botched job, and several innocent people were killed, including a woman bystander. The pistol-wielding robbers fled, and in the subsequent days, in places as distant as the Chiricahua Mountains, were all captured.

From this point on, the attention shifted from Bisbee, as the big actions would take place in Tombstone, the county seat. Five men and alleged leader, John Heath, were housed in the county jail in Tombstone. On February 22, 1884, a large group of miners gathered at the jail, selected some Bisbee residents to "take the lead," and soon John Heath was lynched, swinging from a telegraph pole on Toughnut Street, to great applause. Supposedly the county coroner, Dr. Goodfellow, pronounced the cause of death: "emphysema of the lungs which might have been, and probably was, caused by strangulation, self-inflicted or otherwise, as in accordance with the medical evidence." The iconic photograph of the telegraph pole dangling the body of John Heath is one of the staples of mining camp history, and still featured in souvenir shops about Tombstone, and in books and articles the world round, to this day.

The rest of the story concluded after the trials of the five other robber-murderers. They were legally hanged on March 28, 1884, in Tombstone, in a public ceremony with more than a thousand in attendance, one of the largest assemblages for a group of condemned in American history.

Although the lynching and the hangings were most unusual even in a wild frontier environment, historians have not grasped the various threads of what was going on in Tombstone at the time. This was truly a watershed, and water in the mines was involved, as was men being laid off, some fired, and the union beginning to organize the hundreds of discontented miners. These many factors coalesced. Certain it was that John Heath was in jail, but it was also certain that Tombstone was on edge. The *Arizona Weekly Star* of February 28, 1884, pointed out that a group of more than a hundred miners, mostly from the Grand Central and the Contention, were just hanging around, time on their hands, and they were the ones who instigated the rush on the jail. They were hanging around because they were unemployed, and unemployed because of the water in the mines. [375]

The fact that there were many Irishmen in Tombstone was not unusual in Western mining camps; there were more than a thousand in Butte, and most of the gunfights in Bodie seemed to involve the Irish. In Tombstone, more than five hundred residents were Irish, by far the largest ethnic majority. Names like John Behan, Martin Costello, Nellie Cashman, Dave Neagle, James Reilly, and Milt Joyce come to mind. However, an Irish "tangle" in 1884 gave Tombstone an unusual slant on community life. The first priest of the new parish, Father Patrick J. Gallagher, had a huge resentment against Justice James Reilly, which resulted in a highly conspicuous fistfight in the streets. Violent confrontations on the street between a justice of the peace and a knife-wielding Catholic priest were not commonplace, which is why this is part of the Tombstone lore/mystique.[376]

The "Apache Threat" was also part of the Tombstone mystique, even though that absurd phrase contained a contradiction. Although the concern for Apache troubles in the countryside was legitimate in the 1880s, it was inconceivable that the Apaches would be foolhardy enough to bother a good-sized town. A well-publicized random incident on May 25, 1890, offers one more illustration of exaggeration of the Apache-Tombstone threat. Canadian born, Los Angeles-based attorney Robert Hardie and his brother-in-law, Dr. Francis L. "Frank" Haynes, were vacationing (for two weeks, "for their health") in Rucker Canyon in the Chiricahua Mountains, Arizona. Out for their daily ride, they were ambushed by the infamous Apache Kid and a few other renegade Apache Indian companions, who were on the run after their highly publicized escape from custody on November 2, 1889. They had murdered Gila County sheriff Glenn Reynolds and his deputy, William "Hunkydory" Holmes, who were transporting them to Yuma Territorial Prison after the Kid was convicted of shooting celebrated chief of scouts Al Sieber. Hardie was killed, but Haynes, horse shot out from under him, managed to escape. A regional, national, and international (encouraged by Hardie's Canadian family) brouhaha erupted. Hardie's body, on its way to his hometown of Los Angeles for burial, was first transported to Tombstone, where many prominent local characters were involved. The vacation invitation had been from merchant George Pridham, the ranch they were staying on belonged to Mike Gray, former justice of the peace, the autopsy in Tombstone, arranged by Judge William. H. Stilwell (a close friend of Hardie's), was performed by gunfighter surgeon Dr. George Goodfellow, and *Tombstone Prospector* publisher S. C. Bagg was on the coroner's inquest jury. Prompted by the United States secretary of war, the army was called in to investigate, headed by frontier-wise General Nelson Miles. These were some pretty big names about Tombstone, and the entire country, and attracted extraordinary attention.

The Mining Exchange is to the left in a 1937 view by eminent photographer Dorothea Lange. Library of Congress.

The ensuing huge press coverage (national as well as international) was partly related to Hardie's background; he had been a well-known legal figure in eastern Canada, too. An article in the *Hamilton Weekly Spectator* of October 16, 1890, was entitled, "A Canadian's Death at Tombstone, Arizona." This is the type of information that helped link "Tombstone" and "Apaches," and intensified the town's mystique. Rucker Canyon, in eastern Cochise County, is around fifty miles from Tombstone, not exactly next door.[377]

Women of the mining frontier is another category where Tombstone was unusual. Nellie Cashman was in Tombstone for the bonanza years. She had been in mining camps in British Colombia and Nevada, involved in both mining and running restaurants and boarding houses. Her doings in Tombstone were extraordinary. Not only did she make a living by running a restaurant and hotel, she invested in mining claims and prospects and was the sparkplug in the local Irish organizations and the lead fundraiser for the hospital as well as the Catholic church.

Her reputation was such that in 1883 she was the leader of a gold prospecting expedition that went to Baja California, in tough desert country. They never found much, but the fact that Milt Joyce and other experienced Tombstoners put themselves under her guidance says much about reputation. There were other notable women in the mining camps, but they were mostly folks like Big Nose Kate, Calamity Jane, Baby Doe Tabor, Madame Moustache, or Poker Alice. Nellie Cashman took her talents to other mining camps of the West until her death in 1925.[378]

"Chloriders," in the era 1885-1920, was another term or concept that came to be mostly associated with Tombstone, although it was also used throughout Arizona and, to a lesser extent, in California. As mentioned, the word referred to a few men who made separate arrangements with mine owners to work their property in exchange for a portion of the earnings. Tombstone was a big camp and had half a hundred mines, dead mines, prospects, and claims, and often there were hundreds of chloriders at work in all directions of Tombstone when not a single mining company was in operation.

In the copper mining areas of the Midwest, and in places like Australia and South Africa, the word was "tributers," and the men worked the gold, silver, and copper mines "on tribute." What this meant was that the word "chlorider" in the mining news and other publicity came to indicate Tombstone more than any other location, just another factor in adding up to the Tombstone individuality.[379] On the other hand, the word "lease" was used in so many different circumstances that it is seldom that either "chlorider" or "tributer" was intended. In greater Tombstone, the locals and the newspapers most frequently used the words "chloriders" or "chloriding." When formal arrangements were made between miners and companies, the word "lease" was preferred.

The topic of railroads is another area where Tombstone displayed a certain uniqueness. Ed Schieffelin discovered the silver of Tombstone in 1877, but it would be twenty-six years before a railroad entered the town. Consider that strange situation. A leading silver-mining district, with some production for twenty-five years, and not an ounce of silver or silver ore ever left Tombstone in other than a wagon, stage, or in someone's pocket. Every chunk of ore had to be placed in wagons for the haul to the mills to the west on the San Pedro River, around ten miles away at Fairbank. This was the closest rail point to Tombstone until 1903.

Compare the Tombstone railroad situation with Virginia City, for example. In 1879 (a year after the Tombstone District was recorded), the Virginia & Truckee Railroad made daily runs to San Francisco (sleeping cars and so forth). At the important gold-mining town of Bodie, the Bodie & Benton Railroad in 1881 connected to the Mono mills, some thirty-two miles to the south. In the Homestake-Deadwood area, the Deadwood Central operated for years, until it was sold to the Burlington & Missouri line in 1893. [380]

To shoot and kill a man on the streets of a mining town was not unusual in the American West. But the shooting of unarmed Justice Jim Burnett by wealthy rancher William Greene in Tombstone on July 1, 1897, put Tombstone in the nation's headlines once again. The community, including lawmen such as Sheriff Scott White, were most sympathetic to Greene, and in general had sharp disrespect for Justice Burnett. The sub-head of the *San Francisco Examiner* was, "Deliberate Murder Committed on Tombstone Streets in Broad Daylight." This was way beyond local interest; a wealthy rancher, a justice of the peace, one unarmed, two dead young girls, a killing on Allen Street in Tombstone? Lock him up. But this did not happen. Until he was declared not guilty in December, there were thousands of news stories throughout the United States and Canada, considering every aspect of this tragic affair. The leading newspapers in San Francisco, Chicago, New York, Boston and even in Ottawa, Canada, had column-long articles on Tombstone, the guilt (or not) of Greene, what was society coming to, and on and on. [381]

This impossible-to-concoct melodrama did indeed happen, and for almost a year had the nation's citizens reading about what constituted frontier justice, with Tombstone as the point of reference. As impressive as this event was in raising the country's awareness of Tombstone, this incident would lead to even more significant economic impacts, and worldwide attention, a few years later.

During the subsequent jail time and trial, Greene became close friends with the sheriff, Scott White. By 1900, the Greene world had indeed changed. He prospected, investigated, and had gained control of the Cobra Grande and other extensive copper properties around Cananea, Sonora, not far south of the Arizona-Mexico border. Within a few years, the Greene Consolidated Copper Company was one of the wealthiest and most productive in the world, and Colonel Wm. C. Greene was acknowledged as a "copper king," and one of the wealthiest men in North America. For a decade, Greene would hold such status, until shortly before his death in August of 1911.

The Tombstone angle here is one of really high finance, and of friendship born in tragedy. Greene never forgot the understanding and humane treatment he received from Sheriff Scott White while he was in jail awaiting trial in Tombstone. As Greene's world copper empire grew, so did the role of ex-sheriff Scott White and the others who were sympathetic to Greene. Soon, White was the leading consultant to Greene, his deputy, often in charge of decisions regarding rail lines, hiring, equipment, and marketing.

Greene had lived some years in Cochise County, and was well known in Tombstone, but Scott White was the one with Tombstone mining and business connections. White served as a recruiter for Greene, and thereby some of the most talented foremen, shift bosses, and miners from greater Tombstone were placed in prominent positions in Cananea, Sonora. Not only that; through White, the banks in Bisbee and Tombstone were soon handling much of the financial traffic of the Greene copper empire. Of such importance was the Tombstone connection.

As an example of these working relationships, the *Tombstone Prospector* of March 23, 1901, stated that Colonel Greene and Scott White were at the border town of Naco, planning efficient rail improvements to Cananea. And in 1903, when Tombstone finally had railroad service, one of the first trains to arrive in town brought the private railroad car of Colonel Greene. All of these good things for Tombstone and Cochise County have their origin in that horrific 1897 murder on Allen Street which, in the end, also served to enhance its third-era recovery, influence, and aura.

The extraordinary public hanging of the Halderman brothers (William and Thomas) in November of 1900 was another unusual Western saga that played out in Tombstone (and indeed nationally), only because it was the county seat. [382]

The Burt Alvord years in Tombstone in 1900-1903 included some of the nastiest, most brutal, incomprehensible, shocking deeds in the history of the West. Alvord was a constable/train robber who broke out of the Tombstone jail twice, whose crooked buddy Billy Stiles was given a lawman's badge to bring him in, but instead helped him escape. The Alvord gang were in court in a series of trials that mocked the law, perplexed the authorities, and in many ways made Tombstone once again the national symbol of things gone wrong. In one of their jail escapes, for example, the jailer was out for lunch, and several dozen prisoners scampered. All of this, of course, was associated with the name "Tombstone." [383]

Yuma Territorial Prison has the reputation of being the nastiest, hottest prison on the Western frontier, "the Hell Hole," though many statements regarding its history are exaggeration. Nevertheless, the prison, like the name Tombstone, creates certain vibes and exotic thoughts for many citizens. What they should know is that though they were miles apart, Tombstone and the Yuma Territorial Prison shared many close bonds throughout the prison's existence, 1876 through 1909.

Other counties also had many contacts with the prison, but Cochise County (Tombstone) usually received more publicity. Of the prison's inmates, none was better-known than "Buckskin Frank" Leslie, lady-killer and conman who started the prison pharmacy, fell in love there (with a pen pal), and was interviewed and photographed by a San Francisco newspaper while serving time. Other notable inmates included Jerry Barton, a former Tombstone resident who may have wiped out twelve fellow citizens; May Woodman, who killed her lover on the streets of Tombstone; and of course, Burt Alvord.

It was a common thing for county sheriffs to take convicted prisoners to Yuma, but it seemed there was a constant parade from Tombstone annually, when Sheriff Fly, Sheriff Slaughter, or Sheriff White would personally escort the convicts to their new home.

Even more notable, it seemed that Tombstoners received more of the plum jobs at the prison. Ex-Sheriff John Behan served as prison warden from 1888 through 1890, and former U. S. marshal William K. Meade, ex-Tombstone miner, was appointed superintendent in 1893. Even some of the next-level positions at the prison were filled by Tombstoners. Bob Hatch, former sheriff of Cochise County and close friend of the Earps, who was playing pool in his saloon with Morgan Earp at the time of his murder, was appointed captain of the guards at Yuma in 1890 and served for years in that and other law enforcement jobs. Former Tombstone chief of police James Coyle served as assistant warden at the prison in 1895-1896. S. C.

Bagg, owner of the *Tombstone Prospector* newspaper, and first cousin of the infamous frontier conman Charles "Doc Baggs," became chairman of the territorial prison commission in 1893; and Dick Rule, associated with the Tombstone *Nugget* and the *Epitaph* newspapers, in 1887 was appointed secretary of that commission. Both "Tombstone" and "Yuma Territorial Prison" have certain iconic frontier associations and interpretations, and as the above examples illustrate, they reinforced one another other in the mind of the public.[384]

The vicious, bizarre, sometimes unexplainable violence that took place in Tombstone sets it apart from other Western mining camps. Certainly Bodie, California, had some tough days and considerable gunplay, but only for a few years. Things happened in Tombstone over decades. Tom Waters got killed on Allen Street in 1880 because someone didn't like his plaid shirt; Luke Short had a celebrated duel with Charlie Storms in 1881; the O. K. Corral gunfight happened in 1881; in 1882, Buckskin Frank showed Billy-the-Kid Claiborne that his revolver was better than the Kid's rifle; the Bisbee Massacre of 1883 left some dead there, one fellow lynched and undulating from a pole in Tombstone, and another five done in with a public hanging; in 1897, William Greene killed an unarmed justice of the peace, to public acclaim; the Halderman brothers were hanged in Tombstone in 1900; and lawman/train robber Burt Alvord broke jail twice in Tombstone in the early 1900s, and kept posse's busy for three years.

The summary of the Tombstone saga and its historical impact can be seen in the evolution of the Tombstone Sanitarium. Yes indeed, the two words don't seem to go together very well, but the local powers tried hard. This was the era when health and mountain resorts were being promoted, especially in New Mexico, Colorado, Arizona, and California. The locales enjoyed a great climate, fresh air, and were a boon to health and to the local economy. Tombstone created a sanitarium overnight. In January of 1892, Dr. Isaac Hamilton, regarding the existing county hospital, "concluded to make this institution the sanitarium of Arizona." The pure mountain water, excellent Tombstone drainage, furnishings "all made in Chicago," and the consulting of Dr. George Goodfellow, assured success of the project. The next year businessman Fred Herrera was scampering about the West, and a small fortune was to be spent promoting the haven "for asthma sufferers."[385]

Such falderol would go on for decades, as forces in Tombstone tried to convince the world of local health advantages. Companies were formed, dinners held, pamphlets published, all extolling the benefits of living in greater Tombstone. As late as 1920, the *Epitaph* was hoping for a sanitarium and expounding Tombstone's "wonderful prospects of such an institution."[386]

This information and attitude should be viewed in the light of a Cochise County grand jury report on the county hospital in 1904. The soup was watery, there were worms in the oatmeal, the bedding was very filthy, and some of the patients had maggots. There were enough bedbugs "to carry off the institution."[387]

The sanitarium and "healthy Tombstone" angles lost out, and in the 1920s, the ghoulish name provided by Ed Schieffelin, and the bullets provided by the Earp faction at the Gunfight at the O.K. Corral, won the day. It was time for the "Helldorado" legacy to kick in. After all, the name "Tombstone" doesn't really fit well with hospitals and health resorts, but it finds a proper niche with street shootings in a Western mining camp.

The thousands of Hollywood Western movies and television presentations about the West featuring cowboys, Apache Indians, gambling, saloons, hangings, the Yuma Territorial Prison, lynchings, rustling, gunfights, and stage robberies were frequently built on sagas, true or imagined, of events that transpired in Tombstone. There is no other Western settlement, or worldwide, for that matter, that contributed more raw material through so many years to the world's journalism, literature, and show business, than Tombstone.

The concept of a "Boothill" is another fabled Western topic where Tombstone stands out from the rest. The general public knows of Boothill as a graveyard of tough types who died with their boots on. The phrase has been around for more than 150 years, and these days when using it, one usually means the most notorious of these, in Dodge City or Tombstone. As a point of interest or as a tourist destination, however, Boothill cemeteries only became venerated in the 1920s and 1930s.

Recent scholarship has shown that the term was actually first used in Hays, Kansas, in 1872, years before Dodge City was even founded, and where in the 1860s Wild Bill Hickok, Gener-

The earliest indication of what
would become Boothill cemetery
is on this map of July 1881 by M.
Kelleher, City Surveyor. Arizona
State Archives.

al George Armstrong Custer, and other frontier types put in some time. In 1878, Dodge City's "Boot Hill," the graves of a few cowboys, became the site of the new Boot Hill School. After the school was demolished and a brand-new (larger) school went up on the same site in the 1890s, the phrase "Boot Hill School" was still usually the name favored. The school closed in 1925 and was then revamped as a tourist attraction cowboy statue in 1929, and subsequently, the Boot Hill Museum was added.

In this same era, Deadwood did not have a so-called "Boot Hill." Their original graveyard, the mid-1870s Ingleside Cemetery (sometimes referred to as "a Boot Hill"), was moved further up the hill in 1878, to the Mount Moriah Cemetery as the local burial site (and currently a residential area). Exhumations from Ingleside and reburials at Mount Moriah were completed including the body of the legendary James Butler "Wild Bill" Hickok. For Dodge City, Tombstone, or any other Western town before the twentieth century, a "Boothill" was a thought, a concept, certainly not a place to visit nor a tourist attraction. Arizona historian Sharlot Hall pointed out in 1910 that many Western towns had a Boothill, and the *Tombstone Epitaph* itself in 1917 mentions (for the first time in print, other than in the fictional Wolfville book series) their forlorn, abandoned, generic "Boothill" west of their town.[388]

The first Tombstone Mining District burials were in 1878, near the Grand Central/Contention Mines southeast of modern-day Tombstone. A second location just east of the current Boothill, and closer to town, currently bordered by Safford, Bruce, Sumner, and First Streets, was used in 1879; and subsequently a third, the current Boothill Cemetery just northwest of town, was opened in approximately mid-1881, with its last official burial there in mid-1884. It was "closed" on May 31, 1884. This became the "Old Cemetery" (and then through the years "the Dump," after the town began depositing its trash there) when the Tombstone City Cemetery was opened with its first burial on June 30, 1884. This, the "New Cemetery," on southwest Allen Street, was on land donated by the pioneer Escapule family.[389]

Until the 1920s, there was little to see in these frontier cemeteries. Then, spurred on by new interests in history, both Tombstone and Dodge City began to organize, plan, and promote enhancements that would attract tourism. Author Fred-

When Wyatt Earp's gravestone was stolen (owing to the popularity of the hit TV show) from a northern California cemetery in 1957, Tombstone Epitaph Editor Clayton Smith assured the public that, although accused, his community had nothing to do with the crime. David D. de Haas, MD Collection.

erick Bechdolt and others in this decade did much to spread the interest. While Dodge City at this time was a thriving Kansas community, Tombstone was desperate and rapidly spiraling downward towards extinction and ghost town status if something drastic wasn't done fast.

For two decades the communities struggled between myth and reality. The tilt was often towards the myth, as tourists were mainly interested in bad guys, prostitutes, gamblers, and the gunslingers. Although there has been some criticism of a number of the Tombstone grave markers (John Heath, "Three Fingered" Jack Dunlap, and several others), in general their strategic approach was towards reality. By the late 1930s, pioneer residents like Ethel Macia had stressed that Boothill was a community cemetery, the resting place for folks in all walks of life.[390]

One final but very important point needs to be emphasized about the renaming of many frontier cemeteries (such as in Dodge City) to "Boot Hill." There are seldom fascinating people of historical interest buried in these. Tombstone's Boothill is the one exception, with a variety of legendary outlaws, lawmen, prostitutes, victims of murder (including Town Marshal Fred White), train robbers (Three-Fingered Jack Dunlap), fatalities of the Old West's most famous gunfight (the O. K. Corral; Billy Clanton and the McLaury brothers), Apache Indian battle casualties, (legal) hanging victims (the five condemned in the Bisbee Massacre), a variety of cowboys, miners, gamblers, drunks, miscellaneous suicides, overdoses (opiate, alcohol, and otherwise), influential town Chinese personalities such as Quong Kee and China Mary, the infant son of "gunfighter surgeon" Dr. George Goodfellow, and the wife of Mayor John Clum. Also of note in this regard: although Boothill claims to be the final resting place of the victim of an infamous, highly publicized lynching, John Heath, for his involvement in the Bisbee Massacre, recent research has uncovered the fact that Heath's body was actually brought back home to his "noble mother" in Terrell, Texas, and interred there, where his parents would also subsequently be buried beside him, and not in Tombstone. Unfortunately, there are other such controversial problematic markers.[391]

That the fantastic goings-on in Tombstone were of some worldwide interest can be seen in an article in Australia's *Melbourne Advocate* of April 6, 1939. They were intrigued that a newspaper in a town named Tombstone was called the *Epitaph*. They worked in the phrase "The Town Too Tough to Die," then discussed an event in Tombstone back in 1889 when Deputy Sheriff Alvord and a few buddies were "having a good time" near the O. K. Corral; a brawl ensued, and a man was killed. This all happened three doors east of the residence of Sheriff Slaughter. This was almost too much for the Australian editors: "Tombstone" as a town name, with a newspaper called "the *Epitaph*," a drunken deputy sheriff, and a sheriff named "Slaughter." Western towns in Montana, Texas, or Utah didn't have this type of flair or international intrigue.

On the broader world stage, Tombstone still more than holds its own for recognition and awareness. Most famous mining locales have a regional recognition. The California Gold Rush was one of the great movements of people, yet there is no one renowned locale; there are instead hundreds of them. The most well-known, San Francisco, lacks gold. The well-known Polish salt mines are in several different locations. No region has a more important mining background than Cornwall, England, yet the copper and tin deposits there are in dozens of locations. The important precious metals workings in Potosi, Bolivia and San Luis Potosi, Mexico, were developed under the strict rule of the crown.

Other mining sites in the world are known for their peculiarities, such as Bingham Canyon, Utah being the deepest, or the Homestake in South Dakota being the richest. Some mines are known for their long, productive histories, such as the Rio Tinto in Spain, the Mansfeld in Germany, or the world's oldest corporation, the Falun copper mines in Sweden. A few of the mines in Australia were spectacular successes, such as those at Bendigo, Ballarat, and Broken Hill, but unlike Tombstone, the exciting string of events associated with these places were usually only in the initial years.

THE TOMBSTONE FOLKS: EVEN MORE MYSTIQUE FACTORS

One gauge of the staying power of a mining town's legacy is the number, type, and reputations of people associated with its past. With the precious-metal towns, the number of noteworthy people is usually miniscule. Practically by definition, precious-metal mines themselves have short lives. Nome is a typical instance, as Wyatt Earp headed there for the good times in 1899 and by 1901 was back in San Francisco. To name a famous person of Nome after 1903 is a tough task. Bodie, California, had as many as seven thousand people in its environs, but after a few good years, the place experienced a steep, never-ending decline. This is the norm for gold and silver mining towns. If a person of reputation was there, or if someone gained a type of notoriety, it all happened within a few years.

There were many famous people in these Western communities, but most of them were seldom associated with one place. For example, Poker Alice and Madame Moustache probably played faro and poker in thirty Western communities, all of which claim them as their own. And Rosa May, the kind-hearted prostitute of Bodie, apparently plied her trade in a dozen Western mining camps. Soapy Smith, con man and scoundrel par excellence, scammed people in at least eight Western states and territories.[392]

With some places, only a few names come to mind. For Virginia City, Nevada, the name Mark Twain would be remembered, and perhaps the "Irish Big Four" of Mackay, Fair, Flood, and O'Brien, who profited from the Comstock riches; how about future Earp "O. K. Corral" defense attorney Thomas Fitch? But this was a massive mining, milling, and processing center, with thousands of inhabitants, most of whose names are long forgotten. The Comstock Lode had a longer life than most silver enterprises, partly because it took years to figure out how

Gambling, saloons, gunplay, and words like "wicked" were often highlighted in publicity about Tombstone. *San Francisco Call*, September 11, 1898.

to process the metal. Historians and specialists, but not many others, will recall the name of Philip Deidesheimer, who developed the square-set timbering system for mining there.

Deadwood, Dakota Territory, next to the fabulous Homestake Mine, has some interesting characters associated with its past. On the other hand, the discoverers, Fred and Moses Manuel, are practically unknown outside of the region.

Some of the main owners are widely known, such as Senator George Hearst, Lloyd Tevis, and James Ben Ali Haggin of San Francisco. Of the folks in the community, a few are still remembered. The tale of Wild Bill Hickok getting shot in the back by Jack McCall is one of the staples of Western history. So, too, are the careers of some of his friends, such as "Colorado Charlie" Utter (who buried him), and Calamity Jane, who found girls for various brothels. Even Al Swearengen gets some attention, as he was a leading pimp and operator of a major Deadwood saloon. And Deadwood was not without a well-known man of the law, as Seth Bullock was the area's first sheriff and in 1905 was appointed U. S. marshal of South Dakota, thanks to his friendship in the West with President Theodore Roosevelt.

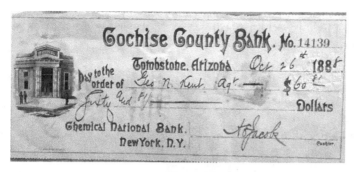

Cochise County Bank. No. 14139

Tombstone, Arizona Oct 26th 1885

Pay to the order of Geo. N. Kent, Agt.— $60 00

Sixty and 00/100 ———— Dollars

Chemical National Bank. H. Jacob
New York, N.Y.   Cashier.

The vignette on the left is of one of the few original buildings remaining, now serving as the town visitors center. The word "BANK" was still visible until just recently when the city painted over it. David D. de Haas, MD Collection.

What separates Tombstone from these other Western mining communities is that unusual events or major figures received considerable attention for more than forty years. Books, articles, movies, television dramas, and internet presentations have been created about some Tombstone topics that took place decades after the bonanza era. The number, diversity, and popularity of these Tombstone-related topics will not be found when investigating the history of Nome, Butte, Bodie, Virginia City, or Cripple Creek.

A few of the legendary personalities with a Tombstone background who are known and made a mark, in many cases internationally, cover the entire gamut of four decades, not just mining camp doings, but when and where they settled later and carried the Tombstone mystique or influence with them to their new destinations. It's an impossible presentation to consistently make for any other Western mining camp.

It would be extremely difficult for any other mining camp to even begin to lay claim to similar international fame of some of the world-renowned personalities who at one time or another, in Tombstone's history, graced her streets. Try matching up with "the Gunfighter's Surgeon" Doc Goodfellow; with Lewis Aubury (one of the first to use the cyanide process in mining in the West) or the camp "Angel" Nellie Cashman; with "silver tongued" orator and Earp O. K. Corral attorney Tom Fitch. Certainly there is no match for gunfighters Wyatt, Virgil, and Morgan Earp; Doc Holliday; Bat Masterson; Luke Short; Johnny Ringo; "Buckskin Frank" Leslie; Jeff Milton; Burt Alvord; Billy Stiles; "Texas John" Slaughter; "Comanche Jack" Stilwell; "Curly Bill" Brocius; Jim Leavy; Charlie Storms; Dave Neagle; "Three Fingered" Jack Dunlap; Billy Claiborne; "Texas Jack" Ver-

million; "Tur-
key Creek"
Jack Johnson;
Dan Tipton;
Sherman Mc-
Master; Billy
Breakenridge;
the Clantons
and the Mc-
Laurys. Others
include Thom-
as Gardiner,
who cofound-
ed the *Los An-*

The tired looking Crystal Palace in 1937. Among other things in its past, it had been a saloon, a gambling center, and a movie theatre. Library of Congress.

geles Times newspaper; Cochise's "blood brother" Tom Jeffords; Owen Wister, the famed author of the classic novel *The Virginian*; Robert Eccleston, the "Finder of Yosemite;" Charles Goodale, great-grandson-in-law of President John Quincy Adams; James Arthur Laing, who was intimate friends with celebrated explorers Stanley and Livingston in Africa Henry O'Melveny, friend of Abraham Lincoln, who started one of the world's largest legal dynasties; George Platt, who was one of President Lincoln's body guards, and present at his assassination; Alexander J. Mc-Cone, the father of John A. McCone, who became chairman of the Atomic Energy Commission and the director of the CIA; millionaire miner, politician, and businessman George Hearst; Oskar Gall, who became editor of *Encyclopedia Britannica*; China Mary; or almost any other of the "Tombstone folks" profiled in the preceding pages.

A good number of other Tombstone Folks are known to those familiar with the history of the West and beyond, though. For those not certain, it should be pointed out that in many circles outside that of casual readers of history, their names, deeds, and misdeeds had major public awareness during their prime. For example, , the *Successful American* magazine of New York was an important publication in the investment community and the world of business and high finance. In the September, 1902 issue, a portrait of William C. Greene was accompanied with a biography and a spread on his empire at Cananea, Sonora. E. B. Gage was similarly featured in the issue of March of 1903, with portrait and biography, pointing out that he was not just a big part of the Tombstone's first bonanza era but also ramrodded its third era, head of the Congress Mine near Prescott and president of the Phoenix National Bank.[393]

A host of factors transformed Tombstone into a magical place of special lore in the world's mining communities. One could be nearly certain that most people around the globe know not a single thing about San Luis Potosi, Rio Tinto, or Broken Hill, but because of its past, and how that has been interpreted, Tombstone, Arizona has a mythical connotation throughout the world. The distinctive moniker "Tombstone" has now come to wonderful advantage with regard to the town's longevity and perception—its mystique.

EPILOGUE

ONE OF THE WEIRDEST CIRCUMSTANCES OF THE TOMBSTONE mystique is that it had its most momentous beginnings in the midst of a second bonanza/major revival, the era from 1901 to 1910. While the town of Bodie was dying, Virginia City dormant, Deadwood forgotten, and Nome concentrating on dog races, Tombstone was re-hiring miners, and another bonanza was in full swing.

The kick-start towards frontier legend and new awareness came from the writings of Alfred Henry Lewis (1855-1914). Lewis was a journalist/editor/author working out of Kansas City and Chicago who made a few trips to the Southwest, and with encouragement began to pump out articles and books on people and places. The never-stated but obvious locale was Tombstone, and he portrayed ranchers, miners, prostitutes, and lawmen, many of them based on well-known folks. The cowboy Billy Plaster was one of his models, as was Tombstone's "gunfighter surgeon," Dr. George Goodfellow.

The Lewis works were neither history nor biography, but his series *The Wolfville Tales,* begun in 1897, less than twenty years after Tombstone's heyday, was a big seller throughout the country. His local-color approach can be seen in the presentation of "Doc Peets," his rendering of Dr. Goodfellow, having Peets declare, "I desires to avoid all reference to recent events of a harrowin' nacher, concernin' the late Tacoma Tom an' a Mexican person we don't lynch...." This absurd dialogue was attributed to Dr. Goodfellow, a nationally-known surgeon and lecturer, who gave talks in New York City and practiced for years in San Francisco. Such corn-pone approaches were a constant feature of the Lewis publications.

Was this important? The Lewis success cannot be exaggerated. He had Theodore Roosevelt, who would soon be elected president, do some of the editing, and most of the art was by world-renowned artist Frederic Remington. These big sellers of Wolfville (Tombstone) were peddling a Tombstone past (1880-1900) that was already being overtaken by modern mining and community expansion. In other words, the nation was learning about the colorful Tombstone past during its first bonanza while a revitalized Tombstone was once again booming and now in its bonanza once again.[394]

Another major figure in re-introducing Tombstone to the general public was Frederick R. Bechdolt (1874-1950). Minnesota-born, he became a leading Western personality who for half a century lived in Carmel-by-the-Sea, California. Usually identified as a poet and author, Bechdolt delved into the folks and places of the Southwest. He spent weeks, sometimes months, in Texas, New Mexico, and Arizona. He was a close friend of John Slaughter and Harry Wheeler, both of whom served as Cochise County sheriffs.[395]

Bechdolt was a serious researcher but seems to have listened too long to the rural-cowboy portion of the Tombstone saga. He wrote a series of articles about historic events and people in Cochise County for the ubiquitous *Saturday Evening Post*, which appeared in the midst of Tombstone's third bonanza. The Tombstone article appeared in the December 13, 1919, issue, and subsequently became part of his 1922 book, *When the West Was Young*. This and following volumes made Bechdolt a leading interpreter of Tombstone history, yet his approaches and conclusions were confused and contradictory. He could write about Jesse James and Wyatt Earp in the same paragraph, implying that they had much in common. As the *San Francisco Chronicle* would point out, when Bechdolt wrote that Tombstone was in possession of "bad men," he was referring to the Earps.[396]

As in the case of Alfred Henry Lewis, the impact Bechdolt had on the depiction of Tombstone's past was significant. He was more than a writer; he was part of the Hollywood "show biz" crowd; even part of the elite party in 1920 when Hollywood motion picture idols Mary Pickford and Douglas Fairbanks married. We should know, however, that while Bechdolt was being praised for his books of life in the West, he referred to himself in the censuses of 1910 and 1920 as "author, fiction."[397] Tombstone itself, however, as late as the early 1920s, still saw its own future as a sanitarium and health mecca, so in March of 1921, when a local film crew was in town proposing to produce "real(istic) western pictures...using the famous old historical town of Tombstone," who in their wildest imagination could have ever guessed just what was happening and about to happen next?[398]

Bechdolt should also receive recognition and credit as the one who, in 1923, was the first to aggressively kickstart the process for the town to officially rename the dilapidated Old Cemetery and call it "Boothill Cemetery," and to have it cleaned out, restored, and preserved as a tourist attraction. At the time, only one marker, Martin Peel's, was identifiable. The city gradually yielded, cleaning out the trash and attempting to locate, identify, and mark the former gravesites with the help of some of the town's old pioneers and young entrepreneurs; an arduous process which was not fully completed for more than three decades, and would involve many other fifth-era Tombstone stalwarts to bring it to fruition—Gardiner, Macia, Ohm, Traywick, the Nunnelleys. In fact, even as late as March 5, 1925, the *Arizona Silver Belt* newspaper reported that the town was still awaiting the legislature's approval of a bill to appropriate the funds to remove "the piles of rubbish," and on March 8, 1928, just over one and a half years before Tombstone's first big Helldorado celebration, the *El Paso Herald* reported, "A.H. Gardiner and others were still planning to apply whitewash...liberally" to the "long-abandoned dump heap." Even two months after the Helldorado celebration, on December 19, 1929, the *Comstock News* in Nebraska reported, "today but one of the many graves there bears a marker..." Even when the Nunnelleys first arrived in 1945, although many metal markers had recently been placed courtesy of the Ohms, the place was still in disarray. Suffice it to say that without Bechdolt's creative inspiration and encouragement, one of Tombstone's most revered and frequently-visited tourist attractions to this day, one hundred years later, would more than likely have been lost to history and referred to as "the Old Cemetery/dump." One could go even further and say that Bechdolt, with his salvation of Boothill and other town contributions, ought to be credited as the father of the fifth-era bonanza, and that his 1923 vision should be credited as the date of its commencement. The only problem with this is the fact that Tombstone was still in borrasca status (at the tail end of its fourth-era bonanza) at this time, and wouldn't be back in a real bonanza for many years to come. [399]

View looking west on Allen Street in 1937. Historic American Buildings Survey, Library of Congress.

Before the end of the 1920s, additional publications and events also had considerable influence on how Tombstone was portrayed to the public. Walter Noble Burns, who wrote the popular *Saga of Billy the Kid* in 1926, followed that with *Tombstone: An Iliad of the Southwest*, in 1927. William Breakenridge, who had been a deputy sheriff in Cochise County during the original Tombstone bonanza era, in 1928 published *Helldorado: Bringing Law to the Mesquite*. These were important efforts at publicizing what had happened in the Tombstone past. There is quite a literature about these books because of the interest in Wyatt Earp. Both authors deceived and ill-used Earp, which is a partial reason for their historical interest. For our own concern in tracing the evolution of the growth of the Tombstone image and mystique, the books passed on this lore and awareness to the next generation, just as the last was rapidly dying off.[400]

Another work of the decade was Lorenzo D. Walters' *Tombstone's Yesterday*, also published in 1928. This well-intentioned book by an apparently qualified writer received much more attention than it was worth. The exaggerations, wrong dates and places, and woefully confusing attempts at motivations point to this as a source to avoid.[401]

In the third week of October of 1929, the first celebration of the town's 50th anniversary, what came to be known as "Helldorado Days" took place. Promoted by the chamber of commerce (Arlington H. Gardner), *Epitaph*'s William H. Kelly (son of W. B. Kelly), and Mayor Ray B. Krebs, the event was named

"Helldorado" after a term first coined by author William Ma-
cLeod Raines, and subsequently used as the title of former deputy sheriff William Breakenridge's autobiography. Well-known
pioneer personalities John Clum as "honorary Helldorado May-
or" and Breakenridge (as "honorary Sheriff") rode at the head
of the opening parade down Allen Street; Anton Mazzanovich
and Jeff Milton were also on hand. Over a few days the Bird
Cage Theatre, Crystal Palace, Oriental Saloon, O. K. Corral (with
an "Earp-Clanton Fight reenactment"), Schieffelin Monument
and Hall, Boothill, and other legendary-locales-in-the-making
were highlighted. There were recreations of an Indian attack
on a covered wagon and old Modoc stagecoach, street holdups,
saloon girls, rowdy, trick shooting cowboys, and the "life of an
early miner."[402]

The success of this first Helldorado celebration must
be measured against reality. Only days after the event, citizens
went to the polls and decided that Bisbee, not Tombstone,
should be the seat of Cochise County. In an article that would
afterward (on November 20, 1929) appear in a Washington, DC
newspaper, Tombstone was somewhat derided for its now even
more inevitable anticipated fate:

> "Tombstone Loses Its Last Glory as County Seat: Ghost
> Mining Town Skips Still Further into Forgotten Past"—
> *Tombstone, roaring mining center of a nearly forgotten past,*
> *slipped another notch towards the limbo of ghost towns to-*
> *day as tabulation of ballets in a special election deprived it*
> *of its principal remaining glory – its position as the seat of*
> *historic Cochise County.*[403]

In a subsequent article which appeared two years later (in 1931) and called Tombstone "a deserted village," it was
also claimed that Tombstone, "the most famous mining camp
of the old Southwest" and "once the largest town in Arizona
is dying a slow death," as the "silver mines have flooded" and
the town lost its status of "being the seat of Cochise County."
"Tombstone is destined to be one of those ghost towns…hav-
ing found no reason for its own existence…Such is the tragic
fate of mining towns…"[404]

Regardless of this devastating loss as the county seat,
Tombstone would continue onward and begin to reflect upon

The Dorothea Lange photo of Fremont Street (looking east) in 1937 highlights the evident decline; on the right is Schieffelin Hall. Library of Congress.

its unusual past. And as we all know today, the *Washington Evening Star* spoke much too soon, as did so many other would-be prognosticators, and couldn't have been more wrong. The folks from Tombstone, and the Tombstone mystique, ensured that its future was bright, and no plunge into ghost-town status inevitable.[405]

A major shift in the Tombstone historical epic occurred in 1931 with the publication of *Wyatt Earp: Frontier Marshal*, by Stuart N. Lake. This was not a work about Tombstone, as Lake gave attention to Kansas, Texas, California, Alaska, and other locations associated with the Wyatt Earp saga. Yet as the years passed, the short time that Wyatt spent in Tombstone would come to dominate not only what people learned about the town, but the combination of Earp and Tombstone would grow to become one of the world's best-known and most appealing conceptions of the entire legendary American Wild West itself. What transpired next in the 1930s, 40s, and 50s[406] led to seemingly endless related movies and television shows expounding upon the Tombstone (and Earp) legend. This was due to the impassioned support of local townsfolk led by Mayor Ray Krebs, pioneer Tombstonian Ethel Macia, Walter and Edith Cole, Arlington Gardner, Clayton Smith, Anton and John Giacoma; "outsiders" such as Hollywood's D'Estell Iszard and Detroit's Harold Love; and attention garnered by a plethora of books and magazine articles. This all was eagerly scrutinized and devoured by the entire country and indeed the world over. By the 1960s, Tombstone's tourist trade was now in full bloom. Many talented young new entrepreneurs (Mayor Dustin Escapule, William and Paula Jean Hunley, Ben and Mary Traywick, Steve Goldstein, Gordon Anderson to name a few) began to take over and help restore, develop, and shape Tombstone into what it has become today.

This surviving Tombstone legacy, its mystique, comes at a cost, though, its mining, milling, political, social events and personalities are pushed to the side. There is not much conversation in modern Tombstone about Ed Schieffelin, Dick Gird, E. B. Gage, William Staunton, Nellie Cashman, John Slaughter, Dr. George Goodfellow, Lewis Aubury, or Burt Alvord, who were major figures in developing the Tombstone aura. Decisions made in the last one hundred years determined that the O. K. Corral, the Earps, Clantons, and McLaurys

FRED R. BECHDOLT

Bechdolt, in newspapers, magazines, and books, was one of the earliest writers to focus on Tombstone's heritage. He is the one who named "Boothill" in 1923 and advocated for its restoration and use as a tourist attraction. *San Francisco Call,* June 27, 1910.

would become the "true" historical Tombstone, regardless of the many other fascinating mining, law-and-order, and political events that shaped the community's past.

A recent study by historians Kevin Britz and Roger Nichols is entitled *Tombstone, Deadwood, and Dodge City: Re-Creating the Frontier West.*[407] These are, indeed, three Western locations well-known, even internationally. All three concentrate on the violent frontier aspects that took place in a short period of time: Tombstone's gunfight at the O. K. Corral, the drilling of Wild Bill Hickok in Deadwood, and the drunken rowdy cowboys of Dodge City. There is a bit of truth in such memories and presentations, but Tombstone's past encompassed so much more, a wide variety of major events with leading personalities over a 146-plus year period, and still going strong now. For such reasons, the Tombstone Mystique sets it apart from other Western frontier communities.

On any given day, and especially weekends, the boardwalks are crowded and bustling much like they were in Tombstone's halcyon days of the early 1880s. Lines form at the various attractions (O. K. Corral, Bird Cage Theatre, Boothill Graveyard, Courthouse, Epitaph Newspaper), the saloons (Crystal Palace, Oriental, Johnny Ringo's, Four Deuces), the restaurants (Longhorn, O. K. Café, Big Nose Kate's, Vogans, Depot, Puny John's), bookstores and souvenir shops, trading/jewelry companies (Arlene's), photo studios, western clothiers (The Shady Lady), and ice cream/fudge shops (Fallen Angel) about the town; enough so, at times, to even make Disneyland somewhat envious. Annual events such as the Rendezvous of the Gunfighters and its current (as of 2014) iteration, Helldorado, Tombstone Vigilante Days, the Tombstone Rose Festival, and Wyatt Earp Days, continue to pull in thousands of tourists from the world round, as does the Bird Cage Theatre's nightly haunted ghost tours. Anniversaries of the O. K. Corral Gunfight and Tombstone movie bring in even visitors, often with worldwide television news coverage. Tombstone's fifth era, aka its "fourth bonanza," the tourist trade, is most-definitely, and astonishingly, even more significant than all the other four eras combined that preceded it. And it is still in full swing to this day. The legend continues to grow, with no sign of ever letting up, COVID-19 be damned, something which has never before occurred in the history of the world's celebrated mining camps. All this is further evidence that the unique folks from Tombstone all contributed to averting "ghost town" humiliation for this once proud mining camp, and generated the Tombstone Mystique that has now forever created an enigmatic "Town Too Tough to Die."

APPENDIX I

(Tombstone Boom-Bust-Boom Timeline)[408]

June 8, 1854 – Gadsden purchase of present-day southern Arizona and southwestern New Mexico by the United States from Mexico approved/takes effect. Charles D. Poston would subsequently be hired by mining syndicate to lead group of prospectors into southern Arizona via Sonora, Mexico. Would hire German geologist, engineer, and assayer Frederick Brunckow in 1856.

1857 – Frederick Brunckow first to discover/mine silver near the San Pedro River, approximately eight miles southwest of present-day Tombstone, in what would, about twenty years later, become known as the "Tombstone Mining District"; murdered at his mine on July 23, 1860, by his laborers.

1865 – Future Tombstone pioneer/developer Dick Gird produces first official map of Arizona Territory.

August 8, 1874 – John P. Clum (future Tombstone mayor) becomes Apache Indian agent at the San Carlos Reservation.

May 17, 1876 – Wyatt Earp becomes Dodge City (Kansas) deputy marshal.

October 30, 1876 – Chiricahua Indian Reservation abolished, and land restored to public domain (notice posted December 1876), opening southeast Arizona Territory to prospectors, ranchers, settlers, and development.

1877 – 1885 – Tombstone's First Bonanza Era.

Early 1877 – Thomas Jeffords and two partners lay claim to abandoned Brunckow mine.

January 1, 1877 – Charles A. Shibell takes over (elected November of 1876) as Pima County sheriff from William Sanders Oury. Would hold office until April 25, 1881.

January, 1877 – Ed Schieffelin leaves San Bernardino, California to prospect in northern Arizona.

March 3, 1877 - Permanent new military site, Camp Huachuca (future Fort Huachuca) established in southeast Arizona; founded by Captain Samuel

Marmaduke Whitside who served as commander of the post until 1881. On this same day, the federal Desert Land Act was enacted. It allowed any settler, for a small per acre price, to claim a portion of U. S. government land (up to 640 acres) as his own, as long as he irrigated it within three years.

March, 1877 – Emboldened by the above events of late 1876 and early 1877, Edward Lawrence Schieffelin accompanies U. S Army Sixth Cavalry troops from Fort Whipple, Yavapai County (along with Hualapai Indian scouts) to help fortify new Camp Huachuca. Schieffelin arrives there on April 1, 1877, and uses the camp as the base for his prospecting.

April 21, 1877 – San Carlos Indian agent John Clum, Mickey Free, and their Apache Indian police surprise and capture (the only ones to ever do so) Geronimo and Victorio and more than four hundred of Geronimo's followers at Ojo Caliente (Warm Springs), New Mexico, and force them back to the San Carlos, Arizona reservation.

May 1877 – several members of the U. S. Army Company E, Sixth Cavalry, searching for Apache Indians at the south end of the Mule Mountains north of the Mexican border in southeast Arizona, find silver and claim the site as the "Rucker Mine." George Warren is hired to work it for them while they attend to their military duties. The site would ultimately become one of the United States' largest copper strikes and the town of Bisbee would develop next to it in mid-1880.

May 29, 1877 – Ed Schieffelin and Sixth Cavalry Indian Scouts arrive at Camp Huachuca.

July 1, 1877 – John Clum resigns as Apache Indian agent at San Carlos reservation.

August 1, 1877 – Using the Brunckow mine as his home base, Ed Schieffelin makes his first silver strike, in the San Pedro Valley east of the San Pedro River; would name it the "Tombstone" mining claim.

September 3, 1877 – Schieffelin files his first mining claim in Tucson (Pima County), and names it the "Tombstone." He would later follow that with numerous other claims including the "Lucky Cuss," "Tough Nut," "Good Enough," "Contention," and "Graveyard" (No. 1 and 2)."

September 30, 1877 – Bridge across the Colorado River between California and Arizona at Yuma, Arizona completed by the Southern Pacific Railroad; part of a transcontinental railroad eastward from San Francisco through Los Angeles, California, to El Paso, Texas, further opening up the trail and supply lines to southeast Arizona and Tombstone in the coming years.

November 29, 1877 – Mormon settlers found town of St. David south of present town of Benson and north of what one year later would become Tombstone, Arizona.

Late 1877 – Tom and Frank McLaury arrive in southeast Arizona Territory.

February 25, 1878 – The Schieffelin brothers and Dick Gird arrive in what would become known as "the Tombstone Hills" in southeast Arizona Territory. Set up prospecting camp/homebase at the Brunckow mine/cabin east of the San Pedro River, and approximately eight miles southwest of where the town of Tombstone soon arises.

April 9, 1878 – The "Tombstone Mining District" officially recorded in Tucson, Arizona Territory (Pima County) by Ed and Al Schieffelin, Dick Gird, Thomas Walker (Gird's cousin), and Oliver Boyer; thereafter obtaining financial aid

from former territorial governor Anson P. K. Safford and John Vosburg.

May 12, 1878 - Wyatt Earp becomes Dodge City (Kansas) assistant city marshal.

August/September, 1878 – Thomas J. Bidwell becomes the Tombstone Mining District's first justice of the peace.

October, 1878 - Stage transportation begins between Tucson and Tombstone Mining District, John D. Kinnear.

October 26, 1878 - The Schieffelin brothers, Dick Gird, Elbert A. Corbin, Governor Anson Safford, and John S. Vosburg create the Tombstone Gold and Silver Mill and Mining Company, and incorporate, issuing stock.

December, 1878 – Tombstone townsite located and surveyed by Salon M. Allis and town plotted out.

December 2, 1878 – Richard Gird named first postmaster of the Tombstone Mining District; names Thomas J. Bidwell assistant postmaster.

1878 – Newman Haynes Clanton family moves into San Pedro Valley, and establishes cattle ranch/dairy farm, not far from mill sites. Become affiliated with cattle thieves/

the "Cowboy gang." Sons Joseph Isaac "Ike," William H. "Billy," and Phin would figure prominently in the mystique of Tombstone in coming years.

March, 1879 – Tombstone Townsite Company formed by land speculators James Clark, Mike Gray, Alder Randall, Thomas Bidwell, A.P.K. Safford, and Joseph Palmer.

March 5, 1879 – After several failed townsite iterations ("Gird Camp/Old Tombstone;" "Richmond," south of the Lucky Cuss Mine; "Emory Gulch;" "Watervale," near the current Schieffelin Monument; "Stagtown," near Brown's Boarding House, the first building in what would become "New Tombstone;" and "Hog-em"), Tombstone Townsite Company (Joseph C. Palmer, James S. Clark, Thomas J. Bidwell, Anson Safford, and Samuel Calhoun) draw up "New Tombstone" townsite at "Goose Flats" mesa; final/current site of town, land-claim and file it in mid-April. All previous iterations failed for various reasons, including lack of water, flat buildable space, proximity/access to mines, roads, and prohibition of alcoholic beverages. It has been asserted that John "Pie" Allen was the one who originally picked the Goose Flats mesa as the best location for Tombstone's permanent townsite, but Allen himself would claim it was Gird's friend Thomas Bidwell who first proposed the idea and then began to push him to move his store over from Old Town to the new site.

March 21, 1879 – It is estimated that 1,500 to 2,000 individuals reside in the Tombstone Mining District.

April, 1879 – Map *Tombstone Mining District* published, showing claims and Richmond townsite.

April, 1879 – First house built in "New Tombstone." Charles Brown opens first hotel (Mohave Hotel) in New Tombstone, in a tent on the northeast corner of Fourth and Allen Streets, just west of where the Cosmopolitan will soon be built. In the summer of 1880, the Mojave was rebuilt as a two-story adobe and renamed "Brown's Hotel." Colonel Roderick F. Hafford will shortly thereafter move his saloon into the first floor of the building. The Earp party would congregate here in October 1881 on the way to their legendary gunfight.

Spring/Summer, 1879 – New Tombstone townsite begins to grow rapidly with business district centered on Allen Street as opposed to (the wider) Fremont Street, as was originally planned. New Tombstone awarded the post office; Richard Gird appointed postmaster (in June). By the end of 1879, "New Tombstone" would become known as "Tombstone."

May/September 1879 –Tombstone's first town jail (single jail cell) built near the northwest corner of 6th and Toughnut Streets, where the Bird Cage Theatre would be built in 1881. Curly Bill Brocius was held here after he killed Fred White in October, 1880. In late 1880, some prisoners were also said to be held at the San Jose House at 437 Fremont Street, on the northwest corner of Fremont and Fifth Streets.

June, 1879 – Tom Corrigan opens the Alhambra Saloon at 433 Allen Street.

June 16, 1879 – Nearly two years after Schieffelin's discovery, Gird ships by wagon first Tombstone Mining District bullion (eight bars valued at $18,744) from mill (Millville) to Tucson's Safford, Hudson & Company's bank, to great fanfare there. This is accompanied by Ed Schieffelin, Thomas Bidwell, and Thomas Walker; from there it would be transported via Wells Fargo to Gov-

ernor Safford in Philadelphia, Pennsylvania. Within one year, Schieffelin would leave the region, Gird within two.[409]

July, 1879 – Carl Gustave Bilicke and young son Albert open the Cosmopolitan Hotel in a tent on the North side of Allen Street near the corner of Fourth. Would become the first two-story building in Tombstone and the future headquarters of the Earps and their affiliates.

July 6, 1879 – Probable first recorded gunfight death occurs in Old Tombstone when Lucky Cuss Mine superintendent Jeremiah "Jerry" McCormick kills John Hicks (a brother of Milt Hicks) and seriously wounds his brother Boyce (blinding him for life) in front of Danner and Owen's Saloon. Said to be the first burial/grave in Boothill.[410]

July 7, 1879 – Michael Gray becomes New Tombstone's first justice of the peace (Tombstone Mining District's second).

September 1879 – Religion first comes to Tombstone. Reverend G. H. Adams, Methodist, preaches first sermon in town, performs first baptism.

September 8, 1879 – Wyatt Earp leaves Dodge City police force to head to new mining town of Tombstone.

October, 1879 – Census taken by Sheriff Charles Shibell, at request of the county board of supervisors, estimates Tombstone District population now at approximately 1,500 citizens; four months earlier, there were only around 100.

October 2, 1879 – Cowboy/Behan ally Artemus Emmett Fay starts the town's first newspaper, the *Tombstone Weekly Nugget*, at 326 Fremont Street. Printing press was the very first in Arizona, and same used in 1859 to print Arizona's first newspaper (*Weekly Arizonian*).

October 26, 1879 – First child born in Tombstone, Inez Fuller, to parents Laura and Henry A. Fuller, blacksmith.

November 1, 1879 – New Tombstone incorporated as a "village;" municipal officers to be elected in January. William Arthur Harwood (first arrived in area in 1878), associate of Dick Gird/Thomas Bidwell, elected interim first mayor in meantime, serving only until January 1880; Fred White interim town marshal. [411]

November 9, 1879 – Frank Stilwell, Pete Spence, Frank Patterson, and three others brutally club to death J. Van Houten at the Brunckow mine just east of the San Pedro River. They are indicted but acquitted for lack of evidence.

November 27, 1879 – Virgil Earp commissioned deputy U. S. marshal (in Yavapai County, Arizona; updated/revised to Pima County, in Tucson, when Earp party first en route to Tombstone) by U. S. Marshal Crawley P. Dake of Arizona Territory.

November 29, 1879 – Earp party arrives in Tombstone from Dodge City, Kansas (via Prescott).

December 1879 – Golden Eagle Brewery (on the northwest corner of Fifth and Allen) opens.

December 1879 – John Montgomery and Edward Benson's O. K. Corral under construction in "New Tombstone" (311 Allen Street). Moved from its prior location in "Old Tombstone" (established there in February, 1879).

December, 1879 – Camillus Sidney Fly and wife Molly (Mary E.) arrive in area and set up photo studio in Charleston just outside of Tombstone, then move into Tombstone and build boarding house at 312 Fremont Street, two lots east of former mayor William A. Harwood's home. The empty lot between would become the actual site of the oft mis-named/misplaced Gunfight at the O. K. Corral.

December 7, 1879 – Fred Dodge arrives by stage in Tombstone.

December 13, 1879 – Map of Lucky Cuss Mine group in *Mining & Scientific Press.*

1879 (approximately; late that year) – Branch of California firm M. Calisher & Company opens in Tombstone on the north side of Allen Street between Fifth and Sixth Streets. Managed by young son David Calisher.

1880/ 1881 – Tombstone ore transportation dominated by Remi Nadeau, the West's leading freighter.

January, 1880 – Wyatt Earp becomes deputy sheriff of Pima County. William Breakenridge arrives in Tombstone from Maricopa County, Arizona. First piano arrives in Tombstone (for Louisa Bilicke).

January 5, 1880 – Seventy-five-mile trip by stagecoach southeasterly from Tucson to Tombstone said to now be made in about eleven hours.[412]

January 6, 1880 – Fred White officially becomes town mar-shal; Tombstone Townsite Company ally Alder M. Randall, Tombstone's second mayor.

January 8, 1880 – Fifteen stage-coaches per week arrive and depart Tombstone Mining District, communicating with Southern Pacific Railroad terminus in Tucson (in June would become Benson, twenty-five miles north). All Tombstone stages stop at Bilicke's Cosmopolitan Hotel.[413]

February, 1880 – Tombstone's first school opens behind P. W. Smith store. Population of Tombstone now increased to 2,000. Tucson's population is approximately 7,000.

February 17, 1880 – Tombstone diarist and Earp ally George Parsons, age twenty-nine, arrives in Tombstone from San Francisco with friend Milton Clapp.

March, 1880 – Saloon owner John Doling lays down race-track on Contention Road.

March 13, 1880 – Ed and Al Schieffelin reluctantly sell their 250,000 shares in the Tombstone Mill and Mining Company to a Philadelphia consortium for $600,000. Richard Gird retains his shares. The three apparently had a secret deal to split all profits.

March 18, 1880 – Per the *Tombstone Weekly Nugget*, there are 480 places of business and homes in new Tombstone, and 21 more currently under construction.

March 20, 1880 – Southern Pacific Railroad (southeast from San Francisco, Los Angeles, and Yuma) arrives in Tucson. Tombstoners hope for a sidetrack extension into their town. To mark the occasion, Dick Gird fashions an engraved solid silver railroad spike from "the first bullion produced by the Toughnut Mine," which he presented in gratitude to railroad president Charles Crocker.

March 30, 1880 (approximately) – Marshall Williams appointed Tombstone's Wells Fargo agent. [414]

April 2, 1880 – Wells Fargo & Co. Express service to Tombstone from Tucson begins. Company office adjoining the post office at 330 Fremont Street (the south side, a few lots east of the O. K. Corral). A few months later it moves to its second location at 427 Allen Street (the north side, a few lots west of the Golden Eagle Brewery/current Crystal Palace Saloon).

May 1, 1880 – first issue of *Tombstone Epitaph* published by John Phillip Clum and partners Thomas R. Sorin and Charles D. Reppy. (This is Tombstone's second newspaper; name changed from *Clarion*.). Office shortly thereafter moved to north Fremont Street between Third and Fourth Streets and directly across the street from the *Nugget* newspaper and post office.

May 10, 1880 – Tombstone's first bank, the Agency Pima County Bank, a branch office of Lionel and Barron Jacob's Pima County Bank in Tucson, officially opens after a slow start-up in December, 1879, in the store of manager P. W. Smith (the old John B. "Pie" Allen store on the Southwest corner of Fourth and Allen. Heyman Solomon is cashier). Name changed on May 1, 1882, to Cochise County Bank.

May 12, 1880 – James Reilly arrives in Tombstone, would become judge upon death of Judge Bidwell in July.

June, 1880 – John Clum becomes postmaster of Tombstone. Population approximately 3,000.

June 21, 1880 – Southern Pacific Railroad reaches (what would become) Benson, Arizona from Tucson, twenty-five miles north of Tombstone. Town of Benson forms with lot sale held on that day and train service arriving from the west the next day. This becomes Tombstone's closest railhead.

June 22, 1880 – "Buckskin" Frank Leslie and friend George Perrine kill Mike Killeen, husband of May Killeen, who had witnessed them cavorting at the Cosmopolitan Hotel.

July 1880 – Galeyville forms approximately ninety-five miles east of Tombstone, becoming one of the Cowboys (rustler) hangouts. Morgan Earp arrives in Tombstone.

July 1, 1880 – Tombstone's second bank, Safford, Hudson, & Company, opens on Fifth Street (in the Vizina & Cook building on the corner of Fifth and Allen Streets, just behind/north of Oriental Saloon). Project is backed by Anson Safford, John Vosburg, and Charles Hudson. Milton Clapp is cashier.[415]

July 8, 1880 – Thomas J. Bidwell, long-time friend and associate of Dick Gird, dies somewhat suddenly after surgery in San Francisco, leaving behind two young children who would subsequently sue Gird for half his Tombstone profits.

July 15, 1880 – Water first piped into Tombstone by the Sycamore Water Company from the Dragoon Mountains.

July 21, 1880 – Oriental Saloon, run by Milt Joyce, opens on the first floor in Vizina & Cook building on the northeast corner of Allen and Fifth Streets. Gaming rooms upstairs run by Earp ally Lou Rickabaugh.

July 21, 1880 – Six government mules stolen from Camp Rucker in the Chiricahua Mountains. Lieutenant Joseph H. Hurst requests assistance from Deputy Marshal Virgil Earp, who enlists help from his brothers Wyatt and Morgan, and Wells Fargo agent Marshall Williams. Tracked to McLaury ranch in Babocomari Valley west of Tombstone, where brands were being altered. First conflict between the Earps and McLaurys/Cowboys.

July 22, 1880 – Occidental Saloon opens on the southeast corner of Allen and Fourth Streets. Ike Clanton and Doc Holliday would have a confrontation here the night before the 1881 gunfight.

July 22, 1880 – Edward Lyter Bradshaw kills fellow miner and roommate Tom J. Waters at Corrigan's Alhambra Saloon on north Allen Street, a few lots west of the Golden Eagle Brewery, after Waters punched him over a playful comment made about a flashy shirt he was wearing.

July 27, 1880 – County Sheriff Charles A. Shibell hires Wyatt Earp as one of his deputies in Tombstone.

August 5, 1880 – After being exonerated of her husband's murder, May Killeen marries Buckskin Frank Leslie at the Cosmopolitan Hotel, with many prominent Tombstoners in attendance. Frank McLaury publicly refutes (in newspaper) Lieutenant Hurst's July 30 accusations that he and brother Tom stole his government mules.

August 12, 1880 – Ordinance No. 9 passed by Tombstone Common Council to regulate carrying of concealed firearms in town.

August 1880 (late) – City Councilman Harry B. Jones, lawyer for George Perrine (who had also been implicated in the murder of Mike Killeen), gets in courtroom brawl with Judge Reilly, forcing deputy Sheriff Wyatt Earp to place both men under arrest.

September, 1880 – Camillus S. Fly builds photography studio behind his boarding house on south Fremont.

September, 1880 – Tombstone's first volunteer fire department created. Wyatt and Virgil Earp are members. Wyatt Earp serves as secretary.

September 9, 1880 – The Grand Hotel opens on south Allen Street across from the Cosmopolitan. Will become known as the "Cowboys Headquarters."

September 14, 1880 – John Harris Behan arrives in Tombstone, relocating from Tip Top, Arizona, with visiting nine-year-old son Albert (the Behans were divorced). Josephine "Sadie" Marcus ("Behan"), aka prostitute Sadie Mansfield and future wife of Wyatt Earp, would soon join Behan there as his "wife" and "stepmother" to Albert.[416]

September 20, 1880 – Dr. George Emory Goodfellow arrives in Tombstone.

September 22, 1880 – Federal government issues Tombstone townsite patent to James S. Clark (Clark, Gray, & Company) with Mayor Alder Randall deeding the entire surface of the townsite to the company on November 8, 1880.

September 22, 1880 – Southern Pacific Railroad reaches Arizona/New Mexico border.

September 23, 1880 – John Henry "Doc" Holliday arrives in Tombstone from Prescott (for a time sharing living quarters there with future Arizona state acting governor John J. Gosper), where he had remained behind to gamble, after first arriving there with the Earp party in November of 1879. Checks into Grand Hotel. Doc's paramour, "Big Nose" Kate Elder, is not with him at this time as they had quarreled.

October 5, 1880 – P.W. Smith, B. Solomon, and J. B. Fried petition city for permission to supply "Village of Tombstone" with gas (manufactured in Tombstone) to supply the gaslights used on the streets and most homes in Tombstone.[417]

October 10, 1880 – Doc Holliday, after first fighting in the Oriental saloon with gambler/gunfighter/tough Johnny Tyler, refuses proprietor Milt Joyce's demand to leave (after Tyler does obey), and is then forcibly thrown out by Joyce. Obtains a gun and returns to have another violent clash with Joyce. After shots are fired by both parties, Joyce is struck in the hand, and William Parker in the foot. Confrontation finally broken up by city marshal Fred White after Doc bloodied by Joyce. Doc charged with assault.

October 27, 1880 – Town Marshal Fred White shot (dies the morning of October 30) by Curly Bill Brocius ("the San Simon cow-boy"). Wyatt Earp pistol-whips Brocius and takes him into custody. Deputy U.S. Marshal Virgil Earp assumes White's role until special election can be held.[418]

November 2, 1880 – Deputy U.S. Marshal Robert H. Paul (supported by Wyatt Earp, who was working under Shibell at the time) faces incumbent Charles A. Shibell (running for his third term, having first been elected in 1876) for Pima County sheriff. Shibell initially declared winner after close vote count, subsequently overturned due to voter fraud in San Simon, Arizona, relating to Ike Clanton and Cowboy gang.

November 11, 1880 – Thinking Shibell had won election, Wyatt Earp (who had supported his opponent Bob Paul) resigns as deputy sheriff. Shibell replaces him with John Harris Behan.

November 12, 1880 – Ben Sippy defeats Virgil Earp in special election to replace Fred White as town marshal.

December, 1880 – Wyatt Earp's horse Dick Naylor stolen in Tombstone and later found by him in the possession of Billy Clanton in Charleston. Taken back by Wyatt after a verbal confrontation and Clanton backs down.

December 18, 1880 – John Clum's wife Mary dies shortly after childbirth leaving behind young daughter and son.

1880 (late) – Future Arizona territorial governor Frederick A. Tritle (appointed by President Arthur, February of 1882) arrives in town from Virginia City with family. Opens mining/stock brokerage firm on Allen Street.

January 1881 – John H. Behan receives appointment as deputy sheriff of Pima County, replacing Wyatt Earp. William Hattich, later-day editor and publisher of the *Tombstone Epitaph* and *Prospector* newspapers, first arrives in town at age eight to join his father.

January 4, 1881 – *Epitaph* editor John Clum elected Tombstone's third mayor. Ben Sippy wins official city election for town marshal.

January 14, 1881 – Gambler Michael P. O'Rourke (aka "Johnny Behind the Deuce") shoots and kills popular mining superintendent W. P. Schneider in Charleston, Arizona, just outside of Tombstone. Lynch mob rapidly forms and after Rourke's arrest, a chase ensues back to Tombstone, where the mob is held off in front of Vogan's Saloon (on Allen Street)

by authorities, including town marshal Ben Sippy, U. S. marshal Virgil Earp, and Deputy Sheriff John Behan.

February 1, 1881 – "Cachise [Cochise] County" created (from southeastern Pima County) and Tombstone named as county seat. John Behan appointed new county's first sheriff by Governor John Fremont.

February 21, 1881 – Arizona Territorial Legislature grants Tombstone a "city" charter.

February 25, 1881 – Renowned gunfighter/gambler and Earp ally Luke Short kills gambler Charlie Storms in a gunfight just outside the Oriental Saloon. Bisbee stage robbed outside of Tombstone.

Spring 1881 – Wehrfritz and Tribolet add second story to their building (Golden Eagle Brewery) on the northwest corner of Allen and Fifth. Dr. George Goodfellow, Virgil Earp, and county coroner Henry M. Matthews open offices there. Across Fifth Street, Vizina and Cook do the same, providing a gambling room above the Oriental Saloon for Earp ally Lou Rickabaugh.

March 1881 – Richard Gird sells out his stock in the Tombstone Mill and Mining Company.

Splits profits with the Schieffelin brothers. Buys ranch in Southern California.

March 1881 - Schieffelin Hall built (construction started December 1880), first event held.

March 15, 1881 - Kinnear stage on its way to Benson accosted just outside of Tombstone; driver Bud Philpot and passenger Peter Roerig killed. Wells Fargo security guard Bob Paul takes reins (holding "for no one") and guides coach to safety. Sheriff John Behan, the Earp brothers (Virgil, Wyatt, and Morgan), Bob Paul, and Bat Masterson lead a posse tracking the perpetrators, eventually capturing Luther King, who shortly thereafter "escapes" from John Behan's jail, setting in motion another series of events which culminate in the legendary Gunfight at the O. K. Corral.

March 20, 1881 - First water documented/publicized in Tombstone (Sulphuret) mines.[419]

April, 1881 - Undersheriff Harry M. Woods purchases Tombstone *Nugget* newspaper from Artemus Fay who shortly thereafter leaves town. Richard Rule also to take part in the publication. E. B. Gage oversees telephone line installation between Tombstone and Contention to connect the Grand Central and Contention mines with one another and with their Tombstone company offices. Billy Breakenridge becomes Sheriff Johnny Behan's chief deputy.[420]

April 1881 - Now incorporated, city of Tombstone population reaches 5,000. "Johnny Behind the Deuce" escapes Tucson jail.

April 19, 1881 - Ordinance No. 9 (drafted by city attorney Marcus Hayne and approved by Mayor John P. Clum) prohibiting deadly weapons in Tombstone town first adopted. Would end up having a profound effect on the history and mystique of Tombstone as it was the main factor which precipitated the Gunfight at the O. K. Corral.

May 11, 1881 - Experienced journalist and Associated Press agent Thomas Gardiner starts new newspaper in town but rapidly gives up and moves on to southern California where, on December 4, 1881, he becomes cofounder of the *Los Angeles Times*, still in print to this day.

May 26, 1881 - Southern Pacific Railroad reaches southeast to El Paso, Texas, from San Francisco.

June 6, 1881 – Chief of police Ben Sippy requests and is granted a two-week leave of absence, but never returns. Virgil Earp, still retaining his U. S. marshal credentials, appointed to replace him; appointment becomes permanent on June 28.

June, 1881 – Haslett brothers Ike and Bill ambush and kill (after they had been warned of their advance) Cowboys Bill Leonard and Harry Head, two of those wanted for the Benson stage robberies, who coveted and were attempting to take over the Haslett's Animas Valley ranch in New Mexico, a prime location to further their gang's cattle-rustling aspirations. Shortly thereafter, San Simon Cowboys retaliate and murder the Haslett brothers. This all foils a plan Wyatt Earp had hatched with Cowboys Ike Clanton, Frank McLaury, and Joe Hill, to lure Leonard and Head in so Wyatt could arrest them; another in the series of events leading to the O. K. Corral Gunfight.

June 22, 1881 – First Tombstone major fire erupts in Arcade Saloon on Allen Street, a few doors east of the Oriental Saloon. Destroys east side (between Fifth, Fremont, Toughnut, and Seventh Streets) of town.

July 1881 – *Map of the City of Tombstone* by M. Kelleher, city surveyor, published.

July 5, 1881 – Sherrif John Behan arrests Doc Holliday on allegations by his intoxicated girlfriend, "Big Nose" Kate Elder (after a quarrel and at the urging of Behan), (who afterwards refused to testify against him), that he was also an accomplice in the March Benson stage holdup. Later that day, Kate is arrested for drunk and disorderly conduct and then rearrested for making threats. Now charged with the murder of driver Bud Philpot and attempted robbery of U. S. mail, Doc is bailed out by Wyatt Earp. All charges were found by the district attorney to be baseless ("not the slightest evidence") and dismissed.

August, 1881 – Tombstone's first fire department opens on Toughnut Street behind the future Bird Cage Theatre. Wyatt Earp appointed secretary of Tombstone Engine Co. No. 1.

August, 1881 – Mining Exchange Building opens in the Gird Block on north Fremont Street between Third and Fourth Streets (just east of the *Epitaph* newspaper office). City and county officials located on top floor; courtroom on first floor. District court (the first) now open in Tombstone; Judge William H. Stilwell presiding. This is where Judge Spicer would hold his hearings after the O. K. Corral gunfight, one of the many reasons some scholars call this perhaps "the most important building in Tombstone and the American West."[421]

August 12, 1881 – Newman Haynes "Old Man" Clanton and fellow Cowboys Jim Crane (the third culprit sought for the Benson stage holdup), Billy Byers, William Lang, Richard "Dixie Lee" Gray (youngest son of Tombstone justice of the peace Mike Gray), Harry Ernshaw and Charles Snow, cattle rustling in Guadalupe Canyon on the border of Arizona, New Mexico, and Mexico, ambushed by Mexican troupe (probable authorities in retaliation for recent Cowboy raids into Mexico). Only Byers and Earnshaw survive.

September 8, 1881 – Tombstone-to-Bisbee stage robbed. Pete Spence (Elliott Larkin Ferguson) and Frank Stilwell tracked down and arrested. Wyatt and Morgan Earp part of the posse capturing them, leading to even more animosity between the brothers and the Cowboy gang, another factor culminating in the O.K. Corral Gunfight a month and a half later.

October 1, 1881 – Cowboy William Claiborne kills James Hickey in gunfight in Charleston Saloon, just southwest of Tombstone.

October 5, 1881 – Apache Indian breakout from the San Carlos Agency and subsequent stolen cattle from local ranches, including the McLaurys, creates fear in Tombstone. Marshal Virgil Earp, Sherriff John Behan, Mayor John Clum, and many others take up chase and rendezvous at McLaury ranch.

October 15, 1881 – John C. Fremont resigns as territorial governor of Arizona; John J. Gosper appointed acting governor while awaiting his replacement.

October 25, 1881 –Tom McLaury and Ike Clanton ride into Tombstone from the Chandler milk ranch. In the Alhambra Saloon on Allen Street, Clanton and Doc Holliday nearly come to blows over words spoken regarding the Benson stage robbery. Morgan Earp (at the urging of Wyatt eating nearby) separates the two, and Ike backs down claiming he is not armed, but soon would be.

October 25, 1881 (evening) – Ike participates in an all-night poker game with John Behan, Virgil Earp, and Tom Mc-Laury in Occidental Saloon. Afterwards Ike confronts and threatens Virgil and proclaims that he will soon make a fight with Doc.

October 26, 1881– Ike retrieves his guns and parades around town making threats against the Earps and Holliday. While walking up Fourth Street from the Capital Saloon on the southwest corner of Fremont to the P. W. Smith Store/Pima County Bank on the southwest corner of Allen, Ike is found and disarmed by Virgil and Morgan Earp who, in the struggle, strike him on his head ("buffalo") and knock him down when he resists and reaches for his gun. Ike, now in custody, forcibly taken to Judge Wallace's court on Fourth Street, south of Allen. There he once again threatens Wyatt and Morgan Earp. Wyatt stomps out of the courtroom, after Virgil appeases the situation, and bumps into Tom McLaury, who has arrived to assist Ike. Tom insults and threatens Wyatt, who then slaps his face and pistol whips him to the ground.

October 26, 1881 (around 2:00 PM) - Frank McLaury and Billy Clanton arrive in town and become infuriated at the news of their brother's abuse by the Earps. They head to Spangen-berg's gun shop, on east Fourth Street just north of the backside of Brown's Hotel, where Wyatt finds them purchasing cartridges and forcibly removes Frank's horse from the sidewalk.

October 26, 1881 – At 2:45 PM, the Wild West's most famous shootout, the Gunfight at the O.K. Corral, breaks out. After confrontation, dead bodies of Billy Clanton and the two McLaury brothers brought over to city undertakers Andrew J. Ritter and William H. Ream on Sixth Street, photographed, and placed on display.

October 27, 1881 – large funeral procession down Allen Street for the gunfight casualties.

October 31, 1881 – Case of *Territory of Arizona vs. Morgan Earp, et al, Defendants* opens in court of Justice of the Peace Wells Spicer.

November 3, 1881 – Older half-brother of Tom and Frank, and indignant Fort Worth, Texas attorney, William R. McLaury, arrives in town and stays at the Grand Hotel. Joins the prosecution in the Earp/Holliday trials and from his subsequent letters back home and to friends, makes it quite obvious he is dead bent on exacting revenge, one way or another, against the Earp party.

November 29, 1881 – After hearings which last one month, much to the chagrin of "the Cowboy element," Justice Wells Spicer declares Doc Holliday and brothers Virgil, Wyatt, and Morgan Earp justified in their actions as peace officers carrying out their official duty during the O. K. Corral Gunfight, after a clever defense led by their brilliant attorney, "the silver-tongued orator," Thomas Fitch.

December 1881 – *Map of the Tombstone Mining District,* by M. Kelleher, M. R. Peel, and F. S. Ingoldsby, issued.

December 14, 1881 – The Benson stage, carrying Mayor Clum who is heading east, home for the holidays, is attacked at night, in an assault considered (but never absolutely proven) to be perpetrated by the Cowboys (with the backing of Will McLaury) to target the staunch Earp proponent. Clum hastily escapes into the darkness in the surrounding confusion.

December 24, 1881 – Bird Cage Theatre officially opens. William James Hutchinson owner.

December 28, 1881 (late night) – Virgil Earp shot by three "concealed assassins," and seriously maimed in ambush by shotgun blasts, at the corner of Fifth and Allen, as he leaves the Oriental Saloon on way back home to Cosmopolitan Hotel. After subsequent surgery/bone and bullet extraction by "the gunfighter's surgeon," Dr. Goodfellow, who fortunately just happened to be one of the first on the scene, Virgil survives, but forever loses use of his left arm. Attorney Will McLaury, who abruptly left town for Fort Worth the day before, once again suspected as one of those behind the atrocity.

December 29, 1881 – Wyatt Earp telegraphs U. S. Marshal Crawley Dake in Prescott, appraising him of last night's events and Virgil's condition; requests appointment as U. S. Deputy Marshal "with power to appoint deputies," which is promptly granted.

January 3, 1882 – John Carr elected mayor; Dave Neagle, chief of police.

January 11, 1882 – The New Mexico & Arizona Railroad runs a branch line south from Benson to Contention City, which would become the closest railroad to Tombstone (eight miles northwest) until 1903. Formally opened on March 10, 1882.

January 17, 1882 – Doc Holliday and John Ringo confront one another on Allen Street.

January 24, 1882 – Backed by warrants issued by Judge William H. Stilwell (no relation to Frank) and certified by Mayor Carr, Wyatt and posse (including Doc Holliday), scour the country for those suspected of Virgil's assault. Fearing retribution by the posse, Ike and Phin Clanton voluntarily surrender to Sheriff Behan and go to jail on January 30.

February 1, 1882 – Wyatt and Virgil Earp submit their letter of resignation (as deputy U. S. marshals) to Marshal Crawley Dake, who refuses to accept them as he is satisfied with the Earps' brave performance against the Cowboy gang.

February 4, 1882 – Railroad extension between Benson and Contention City, Arizona, completed.

February 5, 1882 – Endicott Peabody arrives from Boston and first preaches in town. Remains for a total of five months, with his last service on June 25, 1882.

February 9, 1882 – Camp Huachuca upgraded to Fort Huachuca.

March, 1882 – Grand Central mine strikes water. Superintendent E. B. Gage orders pumps.

March 18, 1882 (early evening) – Morgan Earp, attorney Briggs Goodrich, Doc Holliday, and Dan Tipton attend Saturday night's opening performance of the play *Stolen Kisses* at Schieffelin Hall. Afterward, Holliday heads back home, Morgan and Tipton walk over to Campbell and Hatch's Saloon/Billiard Parlor.

March 18, 1882 (at approximately 11 PM) – Morgan Earp murdered in ambush by Frank Stilwell and others of the Cowboy gang (Pete Spence, Indian Charley) while playing pool in Campbell and Hatch's on Allen Street. Second shot just misses Wyatt. A stray bullet strikes bystander George A. B. Berry in the leg. Funeral services held next day at Bilicke's Cosmopolitan Hotel.

March 19, 1882 – The body of Morgan Earp brought from Tombstone to the depot at Contention City, and transported northwest by train to Benson, Tucson, and then on to his parents in Colton, California.

March 20, 1882 – Virgil and Allie Earp leave for new Benson train connection at Contention City, and from there, to his parents' home in Colton, California. Escorted to Tucson by well-armed party led by Wyatt and Warren Earp, Doc Holliday, Sherman McMaster, and "Turkey Creek Jack" Johnson.

March 21, 1882 (early morning) – Earp party kills Frank Stilwell ("worst shot-up man that I ever saw") at Tucson train station; bloody (and national news-worthy) "Vendetta Ride" begins.

March 21, 1882 (late afternoon) – Earp party arrives back in Tombstone and, as they make their final departure from their headquarters at the Cosmopolitan Hotel that night, are confronted by Sheriff Behan and his group of officers, including Dave Neagle, who attempt to serve warrants for their arrest. The Earp posse boldly brushes by and refuses to be arrested by them, Wyatt telling Behan. "You have seen me once too often…"

March 22, 1882 – Earp Vendetta Posse tracks down and kills Florentino "Indian Charlie" Cruz at Pete Spence's wood camp near South Pass in the Dragoon Mountains. Spence himself hides from the Earp party and seeks sanctuary in Behan's Tombstone jail.

March 24, 1882 – Wyatt Earp kills Curly Bill in gun battle between the Vendetta Posse and the Cowboys at Iron Springs.

March 27, 1882 – Earp Vendetta Posse seeks sanctuary at Henry Hooker's Sierra Bonita Ranch north of Willcox, Arizona. John Behan arrives the next morning with his posse and is rebuffed by Earp partisan Hooker and his ranch foreman, who refuse to provide Behan information or assistance. The Earp party brazenly camp on the hill next to Hooker's Ranch, awaiting/taunting Behan, who wisely chooses not to follow them there, and retreats back to Tombstone.

April 7, 1882 – Famed Civil War general William Tecumseh Sherman arrives in Tombstone with his entourage. Participates in parade in his honor and has dinner in town with local dignitaries (including John Clum, Milt Joyce, Ben Goodrich, R. F. Hafford, and Joseph Tasker) at the Cosmopolitan Hotel's Maison Doree. Tours the local mines the next day, evaluates the current situation in Tombstone, and visits Fort Huachuca with old friend George Parsons.

April, 1882 – Frank Stilwell's brother, the renowned military scout "Comanche Jack" Stilwell, checks into Tombstone's Grand Hotel to investigate the circumstances surrounding his brother's murder and settle his affairs.

Apparently satisfied that his brother did murder Morgan Earp, and Wyatt's retaliation was justified, takes no further action and leaves town for good shortly thereafter.

April 19, 1882 – Renegade Apache Indians up from Mexico (under Chato, Nachez) on a raid about Arizona, attack San Carlos Indian reservation, forcing large group of Apaches living there peacefully (including Chief Loco) to flee with them, causing mass hysteria all over Arizona and nationally and Ranger groups to form. One in Tombstone proposed to be led by flamboyant "scout" Buckskin Frank Leslie.

May 1, 1882 – The *Tombstone Epitaph* newspaper sold by John Clum (who then leaves town) to a democratic consortium led by Milt Joyce, with Samuel Purdy brought in as editor. Its leanings now change from Republican (Earp-backing) to Democratic (Cowboy).

May 1, 1882 – The Agency Pima County Bank becomes the Cochise County Bank (in light of the county name change).

May 16, 1882 – Doc Holliday arrested in Denver, Colorado for murder of Frank Stilwell.

May 25, 1882 (at approximately 3 PM) – Second, larger major fire in Tombstone (starting at the Tivoli Saloon, next to the Cosmopolitan Hotel) destroys most of town business district, resulting in ubiquitous Tombstone "O.K. Corral Fire Aftermath" photo. The Bilicke's Cosmopolitan Hotel (former Earp/Holliday headquarters) burned down and not rebuilt.[422]

May 29, 1882 – Colorado governor Frederick W. Pitkin refuses to repatriate Doc Holliday back to Arizona to stand trial.

Summer, 1882 - Huachuca Water Company completes reservoir and laying of pipes for Tombstone's water supply; water first piped in from the Huachuca Mountains.

June 18, 1882 - First proceedings at still-unfinished St. Paul's Episcopal Church, built by Endicott Peabody on northwest side of Third Street, near Safford.

July, 1882 – Tombstone population approximately 5,300.[423]

July 14, 1882 – Dead body of Johnny Ringo found in Turkey Creek Canyon south of Willcox, Arizona.

July 21 (approximately), 1882 – Ben Wehrfritz opens *the* Crystal Palace Saloon, which replaces Golden Eagle Brewery, burned down in the June

23, 1881, fire. Of note is fact that James Vogan may have opened a different Crystal Palace Saloon, east of and across Allen Street in late May, 1881, at 634 Allen, although that was the time and exact area of the first big Tombstone fire in June of 1881.[424]

August (approximately), 1882 – John Behan's "wife," prostitute Sadie Mansfield (aka Josephine "Sadie" Marcus), leaves Tombstone for her hometown of San Francisco.[425]

November 7, 1882 – First Cochise County general elections held, with Sheriff John Behan knowing better than to run for reelection, in light of all his improprieties and poor handling of the Earp-Cowboy disputes. His deputy, Dave Neagle, loses out to Jerome L. Ward.

November 14, 1882 – Buckskin Frank Leslie kills Cowboy Billy Claiborne in gunfight in front of Oriental Saloon.

Late 1882- early 1883 – Josephine Sadie Marcus (prostitute "Sadie Mansfield," briefly the companion of John Behan) begins full-time relationship with Wyatt Earp in San Francisco, and thereafter becomes "Sadie Earp." [426]

1883 – First serious effort of Tombstone chloriders on silver ore.

January, 1883 – Newly built (cornerstone first placed August 11, 1882, structure thus dated) Tombstone Courthouse on south Toughnut Street, just west of Third, first ready for occupancy.

January 1883 – Construction of Tombstone City Hall on Fremont Street completed. Designed by Frank Walker, who also designed the courthouse. Of note, some wrongly claim the building, which still stands to this day, was actually completed in very late December of 1882.

1883-1885 – The "beginning of the end;" mines begin working below water table, water pumps installed and begin to have difficulty keeping up.

1883- 1884 – The decline accelerates; miners form a union demanding higher wages.

April 7, 1883 – Two-story Occidental Hotel (Joseph Pascholy and Godfrey Tribolet) opens on southeast corner of Allen and Fourth Streets.

May/June 1883 – Tombstone gets a swimming pool ("bath") at the north end of Fifth Street. It undergoes various iterations through the years but is the Tombstone Municipal Swimming Pool, still in use to this day.[427]

June 5, 1883 – Charles Reppy, one of the original *Epitaph* newspaper founders, takes over management once more.

July 2, 1883 – Due to considerably dwindling attendance with mines in decline, William Hutchinson sells Bird Cage Theatre, an ominous sign.

November 24, 1883 – First water pump in Tombstone now functional and begins pumping water out of the Contention mine; next up to be the Grand Central mine.

December 8, 1883 – Joseph Goldwater's store in Bisbee robbed by five thieves who kill three men and a woman in what would become known as the Bisbee Massacre. Would have enormous repercussions for Tombstone (and its mystique) in coming months.

Late 1883 – Milton Joyce departs Tombstone for San Francisco.

February/March, 1884 – In Bisbee Massacre aftermath, John Heath taken by Bisbee mob from Sheriff Ward's custody at the Tombstone County Courthouse jail and lynched from telegraph pole (immortalized in infamous photo seen the world round and to

this day) at Toughnut and Second Streets, February 22, 1884; the five others subsequently legally hanged March 28 in the courthouse courtyard.

1884 – Tombstone bonanza era ending. People begin leaving. Population decreases from approximately 6,000 in 1882 to 4,000 in 1884. Population halves in seven years.

April 29, 1884 – Mineworkers form the Tombstone Miners' Union, in light of impending wage cuts.

April 30, 1884 – In defiance of union, Grand Central and other major mines close down.

May 1, 1884 - Mine owners decrease daily wages from $4 to $3 considering diminishing production/profitability.

May – August, 1884 – Union mobs gather and strike. Water levels in mines rise as they are closed down and pumps turned off for four months.

May 10, 1884 – In another ominous sign, Safford & Hudson bank in Tombstone fails/closes; cashier Milton Clapp hastily "skips out" of town.

August 14-16, 1884 - Company C, 1st Infantry, from Ft. Huachuca, with Captain Wm. Tisdall and twenty-three troops, arrive at Contention Hill, report for duty to Sheriff Jerome Ward during the labor troubles. Their services were not needed. This was the only, limited, role of the U. S. Army in Tombstone's past.

August 24, 1884 – Tombstone Miners' Union, having been broken by the mine owners, formally disbands.

October 13, 1885 – Al Schieffelin dies of consumption (tuberculosis) at family home in east Los Angeles.

1886 - 1900 – Tombstone "Second Era of the Chloriders" (waste ground mines/independent miners).

January, 1886 – Joe Bignon leases/manages the Bird Cage Theatre and renames it the "Elite Theatre."

May 26, 1886 – Grand Central mine (only remaining mine still functioning, until this time, on the San Pedro River) hoist and pump destroyed by fire. Just months later the price of silver slides and miners around the country are laid off. Devastates Tombstone; many more miners/merchants give up and leave town.

1886 (late) – Contention mine closes down. Grand Central mine now the only major company left producing ore. They will shut down a year later.

1887 – Tombstone diarist George Parsons moves to Los Angeles.

March 7, 1887 - Editor S.C. Bagg's *Tombstone Daily Prospector* newspaper begins publication (conceived with assistance from Joseph Pascholy, A. J. Ritter, and James Reilly). William Hattich takes over as owner/editor in 1895. Merges with the *Tombstone Epitaph* in 1924.

May 3, 1887 – Devastating earthquake hits just below the border in Sonora, Mexico. Rattles Tombstone, causing much damage about town.

November 8, 1887 – John Henry "Doc" Holliday dies of consumption at a sanitarium in Glenwood Springs, Colorado.

July 3, 1888 – Celia Ann "Mattie" Blaylock, former common-law wife of Wyatt, dies of overdose of alcohol and opiates (laudanum) in Pinal, Arizona.

September 14, 1888 – Pascholy/Tribolet's Occidental Hotel (Tombstone's largest), on the corner of Allen and Fourth Streets, burns down. Local entrepreneur Pascholy leaves town.

February 1, 1889 – First train (Arizona and Southeastern Railroad) from Bisbee to Fairbank, Arizona, comes through, putting many Tombstone freighters out of business; and as just another slap in the face, due to low silver prices, bypasses the town completely.

July 10, 1889 – In a jealous rage, Buckskin ("Nashville") Frank Leslie kills Mollie Williams, the former girlfriend of E. L. Bradshaw, who was living on Leslie's ranch. To conceal the crime, also shoots and leaves for dead a ranch hand witness who surprisingly lives to report the transgression. Frank sentenced to life in Yuma prison but pardoned for good behavior after six years.

November 29, 1889 – Milt Joyce dies in San Francisco.

1890 – Sherman Silver Purchase Act enacted; government promises to purchase large amount of silver. Raises silver prices.

February 22, 1890 – Due to "dull times" Joe Bignon closes his Elite Theatre (formerly known as the Bird Cage).[428]

March, 1890 – the Blinn Act, proposed by lumber dealer Lewis Blinn, in part suggests name of Tombstone be changed to the more congenial "Richmond," the area's first camp. It seems the name "Tombstone" carried with it a negative connotation (evidence of the persuasiveness of the "Tombstone Mystique" already present at this early time) making it difficult for the towns businessmen to inspire investment from east coast capitalists.

March 1890 – Bob Paul appointed U. S. marshal for Arizona Territory.

May 25, 1890 – Robert Hardie, Canadian-born prominent attorney practicing in Los Angeles, is murdered in Rucker Canyon, Arizona (in the Chiricahua Mountains) by renegade former Apache Scout the "Apache Kid," while visiting on vacation ("for his health") with his brother-in-law, Doctor Francis L. "Frank" Haynes, who was able to evade capture/injury after his horse was shot out from under him.[429]

1891 (approximately) – Lewis Aubury first uses cyanide in Arizona (probable first use in the West and possibly the entire U. S.) on Tombstone waste dumps. Would have big impact on local economy.

December 26, 1891 – Contention Mine's hoist destroyed in catastrophic conflagration. Plans to make yet another attempt to drain the water from the mining district now ceased.

November, 1892 – Tombstone's Sarah Herring first woman in Arizona Territory admitted to the bar.

1893 – Sherman Act repealed as government has too much silver; silver prices tank.

1893 – Major national depression hits. Property values in Tombstone plummet.

1893 - 1895 – E. B. Gage, Tombstone mining mogul, shifts to Prescott, Arizona (Yavapai County), taking over Congress gold mine and taking much of Tombstone's mining population with him.

December 1893 – Bank of Tombstone (old Agency Pima/Cochise County bank building on Fourth and Allen) closes.

June 1894 – Author Owen Wister spends time in Tombstone researching town for potential setting in magazine article/book.

1895 (early) – Miner John James Pearce and family, long-term Tombstone residents, discover gold near their ranch at the base of Dragoon Mountains. Will become the Commonwealth Mine. Mass exodus of townsfolk (especially miners) from Tombstone to new mining camp of Pearce.

January 3, 1895 - C. L. Cummings named undersheriff by Sheriff C. L. Fly.

April 1895 – Stanley C. Bagg sells *Tombstone Prospector* and *Epitaph* newspapers to twenty-two-year-old Billy Hattich. Departs for California.

1895 (late) – Tombstone Mill & Mining Company halts the last of its meager mining operations.

1897 – Only sixteen businesses left in Tombstone.

May 12, 1897 – Ed Schieffelin dies at age forty-nine in Oregon. Per his request, body returned to Tombstone and buried with pick and canteen just west of present-day Tombstone, near his first campsite.

July 1, 1897 – Unarmed justice of the peace James C. Burnett shot dead on Allen Street by wealthy and influential rancher William C. Greene, putting Tombstone in the national spotlight once again.

1898 – 1901 - E. B. Gage with partner Frank Murphy uses funds from his Yavapai Congress Mines (sold to a New York investor in spring of 1900) to slowly buy up claims/mines around Tombstone. Forms Tombstone Consolidated Mine Company (May 1900) to consolidate claims, and its holding company, Development Company of America (November 23, 1901). [430]

July 21, 1898 - Marriage of Sarah Herring, attorney, and Thomas R. Sorin, a founder of the *Tombstone Epitaph*.

1900 - Tombstone population 646, lowest point in all census compilations.

1900 – 1902 - Jail breaks, trial of Burt Alvord, lawman/train robber.

May 1900 – The Tombstone mining interests recently purchased by E. B. Gage, W. F. Staunton, and Frank M. Murphy merged_under the name of the Tombstone Consolidated Mine Company.

July 6, 1900 – Baxter Warren Earp, youngest brother of Virgil and Wyatt, killed by John Boyett in "gunfight" in the Headquarters Saloon in Willcox, Arizona.

October 1900 – E. B. Gage, William F. Staunton, and Frank M. Murphy in town together apparently planning Tombstone's revival, "Bonanza number two." Strategies are contemplated and things slowly/discretely begin to happen about town.

November 16, 1900 – Highly publicized picnic party-like

hanging of the Halderman brothers.

1901 – 1910 – Third Era; Tombstone's mining revival/second bonanza.

March 26, 1901 – Former Pima County sheriff Robert "Bob" Havlin Paul dies in Tucson, Arizona.

April 11, 1901 – In a major presentation, E. B. Gage announces plans for the Tombstone mining revival.

Oct 12, 1901 - death in Bisbee of C. S. Fly, prominent Western photographer, sheriff of Cochise County (1895 – 1896).

November 23, 1901 - Development Company of America, holding company for Tombstone Consolidated Mine Company, formed by Frank M. Murphy. E. B. Gage and W. F. Staunton, who sit on the board of directors.

1901 (late) – James Earp moves to Sawtelle, California.

1902 – Buildings begin to be painted/repaired about Tombstone; new businesses open.

June 1902 – Earp family patriarch Nicholas Earp admitted to the Old Soldiers' Home in Sawtelle, California, just east of Santa Monica, and west of Los Angeles.

July 19, 1902 – Telephone connections between Tombstone and Bisbee made. By end of year, connections made throughout town.

October 1902 – The National Bank of Tombstone opens.

October 1902 – Newton Earp also admitted to Old Soldiers' Home in Sawtelle, California.

October 1902-April 1903 – Virgil Earp in Sawtelle, California.

1902 (late) – The Russ House reopens as guest house; shortage of lodging now present about town as revival begins.

1903 – After many years of service in various capacities as a lawman-about-town, George Bravin first elected Tombstone chief of police, an office he would hold until his death in October, 1918, making him the town's longest-serving police department officer.

January 14, 1903 – First automobile driven into Tombstone (from Tucson). Within two years there would be many others (owned by Tombstoners).

March 24, 1903 – In a tangible sign of Tombstone's imminent mining revival/second bonanza, the first train finally arrives in Tombstone from Fairbank (El Paso & South-western Railroad) to great fanfare. Station between Third and Fourth on south Toughnut Streets. For the first time, Tombstone now has adequate transportation for ore, freight, equipment, and passengers; and a rail connection with its supply center (and Bisbee). Old depot is now the modern-day library. [431]

February 4, 1904 – James Herbert ("Bert") Macia (who had first arrived in Tombstone at age nineteen in 1901) marries Ethel Robertson (daughter of Tombstone Pioneer Chris Robertson).

October 19, 1905 – Virgil Walter Earp dies of pneumonia in Goldfield, Nevada.

August 1906 – Although approved on June 7, 1902, and slowly available about town since that time (in the mines since January, 1902), most businesses now also wired for electricity.

November 1906 – Silver prices increasing.

November 1, 1906 – In light of optimistic prospects on all fronts (performance of water pumps, favorable silver prices), the Tombstone Consolidated Mining Company (T. C. M. C.), to the great amazement and delight of the town's miners/townsfolk, voluntarily increases wages throughout its vast holdings; President E. B. Gage and General Manager William Staunton lauded in celebrations about town.

December 14, 1906 – C. L. Cummings purchases Bird Cage Theatre, which had been closed since February of 1890 (was named the Elite Theatre at that time) by its former proprietor Joe Bignon. Cummings uses it as a storage room for his collection.

February 12, 1907 – Earp family patriarch Nicholas Earp dies in (and is buried at) the Old Soldiers' Home in Sawtelle, California.

1908 – Tombstone mines produce an admirable 51,000-plus tons of ore.

October 21, 1908 – Former Pima County sheriff Charles A. Shibell dies.

1908-1909 – Beginning of the second end; water problem returns to the mines.

January, 1909 – James Herbert ("Bert") Macia, foreman of the Tombstone Consolidated Mining Company, assumes position of superintendent.

1909 – International-tinged trial of Flores Magon held in Tombstone.

June 8, 1909 – James Reilly dies in Long Beach, California.

November 12, 1909 – Citing his ill health, but to great dismay of the town, E. B. Gage resigns as president of the Tombstone Consolidated Mining Company. A series of disasters (pump malfunctions/damages with flooding of the mines), requiring additional burdensome financial expenditures (installation of new pumps) at a time its holding company (D. C. A.) was struggling financially, likely was also partially responsible.

1910 – Six and a half million gallons of water pumped from the mines daily.

May 29, 1910 - Death in Los Angeles of Richard Gird, co-founder of the Tombstone Mining District.

June 20, 1910 – William Staunton resigns from the Tombstone Consolidated Mining Company and moves to Los Angeles, another ominous sign.

January 18, 1911 – Water pumps failing, the Tombstone Consolidated Mining Company shuts down due to the enormous expense of pumping water. Miners fired. Soon thereafter the Development Company of America (D. C. A.), still reeling from its missteps during the stock market crash, national depression, and consequent economic slump of 1907, defaults on debts and declares bankruptcy; creditors furious and clamoring for the company's assets/properties.

1911-1913 – E. B. Gage banking in Phoenix; dies in San Francisco in May of 1913.

1912 – Mollie (Mrs. C. S.) Fly moves to Los Angeles, California, where she had bought land in July 1911. Maintains ownership of her buildings (lodging house and photograph gallery) in Tombstone. Uninsured, would lose everything in a devastating July, 1915 fire. She dies in Santa Ana, California in 1922.

February 14, 1912 – Arizona becomes 48th state; statehood bill signed by President William Howard Taft.

June 7, 1912 – Former Cochise County sheriff and Earp nemesis John H. Behan dies in Tucson, Arizona.

July 10, 1912 – Attorney William Herring dies in Tucson; buried there in Evergreen Memorial Park.

August 2, 1913 – After twenty years as owner/manager, William "Billy" Hattich sells *Tomb-stone Prospector* and *Epitaph* newspapers to his printer's brothers, Carmel and Columbus Giragi, who would run the papers until 1926.

1914-1923 – Tombstone's Fourth Era - Manganese and World War I (the second revival/third bonanza).

July 6, 1914 – Walter Douglas, general manager/head) of Phelps-Dodge (Bisbee's Copper Queen), has winning bid of $500,000 for the Tombstone Consolidated Mining Company's assets ratified . World copper giant Douglas' bid was the only one at the Tombstone courthouse bankruptcy proceedings on June 23, 1914.). Company nearly immediately goes to work about town, making significant investments to get the mines cleared/cleaned and up and running once more.[432]

July 28, 1914 – World War I erupts, leads to great demand for manganese and significant increases in the price of silver, all to the great benefit of the reinvigorated Tombstone.

November 3, 1914 – Prohibition amendment to the Constitution of the State of Arizona voted upon and wins; to be enacted on January 1, 1915.[433]

1915 – Tombstone begins producing manganese; stimulates local economy once more.

February 26, 1915 – Mary Costello's Crystal Palace refurbished; in light of recently enacted Arizona prohibition amendment, reopens as Crystal Theatre, playing movies instead of peddling liquor. Tony and James Giacoma purchase lease.

March 1915 – J. B. Montana purchases Russ House and remodels as hotel.

May 7, 1915 – Former Tombstone Cosmopolitan Hotel co-owner/Earp ally Albert Clay "Chris" Bilicke, dies aboard the ship *Lusitania* after it was sunk by a German torpedo. One in a chain of events which draws the U. S. into World War I.

July 2, 1915 – Former C. S. Fly photo gallery and boardinghouse on Fremont Street burns down, taking with it Mollie Fly's cadre of irreplaceable historic Fly photos. O. K. Corral also threatened but saved. At the time was occupied by "Old French Doctor" Grator who was burned in making his escape from the historic Tombstone landmark. Sadly, Fly's building and its contents declared "a total loss" (approximate estimated worth, $1,880; uninsured). [434]

October 8, 1915 – Schieffelin Hall sold by ex-mayor Paul Warnekros to Arlington Gardner. Building renovated.

1916 – 1918 – Population spurt generated by need for manganese by U. S. military relating to World War I.

February, 1916 – Four hundred men work the Tombstone mining district.

1917 - Six hundred men work the Tombstone mining district.

November 1, 1917 – Chamber of commerce (the "Tombstone Commercial Club") organized by local merchants to promote businesses in and around Tombstone. W. A. McSparron elected president, C. L. Giragi vice president, and Arlington H. Gardner secretary.

April, 1918 – Pittman Act passed. Removes restrictions on exports of silver. Government agrees to purchase entire silver production of all mines throughout the United States.

November 11, 1918 – World War I ends; demand for magnesium plummets, but price of silver skyrockets owing to the Pittman Act and the great demand for silver to support currencies of post-war European and Asian markets. Tombstone switches gears back to silver once more.

1919 – Ethel and James Macia purchase the Arcade Hotel (formerly the Cochise Hotel) on the grounds of the old Vizina Mining Company (northeast corner of Fourth and Toughnut Streets), and in 1936 rename it the Rose Tree Inn.

December 13, 1919 – Frederick Bechdolt's Tombstone article (one in a related series) appears in the *Saturday Evening Post*: "Tombstone's Wild Oats."

February 2, 1920 – Bisbee labor strike deportation trials, with Dodge-Phelps (and many other prominent Bisbee residents) as defendant, open in Tombstone's courthouse, and carried by major news organizations across the country, giving Tombstone nonstop (three-month) national attention.

1922 – Bechdolt's significant book, *When the West Was Young*, published.

1922 – Cochise County mine valuation drops $13.5 million compared to 1921. Valuations: Tombstone, approximately $272,192; Bisbee/Douglas, approximately $79 million.[435]

1923 – influential author Frederick Bechdolt persuades Tombstone to officially rename its "Old Cemetery" to "Boothill" and preserve it as a tourist attraction; the process begins.[436]

May 30, 1923 – Treasury Department announces suspension of silver purchases under Pittman Act of 1918. Price of silver dips; many lessees forced out of business, most Tombstone mines cease operations; borrasca (the end of the Fourth Era) looms.

November 12, 1923 – Former Earp O. K. Corral attorney Thomas Fitch, dies in northern California.

March 2, 1924 – Due to significant loss of advertising revenue, Giragi brothers forced to consolidate *Epitaph* and *Prospector* newspapers into one weekly newspaper, the *Epitaph*.

January 24, 1925 – Nellie Cashman dies in Victoria, British Columbia, Canada.

November 28, 1925 – Former Tombstone town marshal and deputy sheriff Dave Neagle dies in Oakland, California.

January 25, 1926 – James Earp at age eighty-four dies of a stroke in the home of Hildreth Halliwell (Virgil's wife Allie Earp's grandniece) in Los Angeles.

March 1, 1926 – The Kelly Printing and Publishing Company, under president W. B. Kelly, purchases the *Tombstone Epitaph* newspaper from the Giragi brothers. His son W. H.

Kelly, grandson of renowned pioneer Arizona publisher G. H. Kelly, takes charge. [437]

1926-1927 – U. S. Highway 80 named, and routes selected; includes Tombstone. The road from Nogales to Tombstone, State Route 82, completed. The almost-ghost town now a highway crossroads, with national and state recognition.

1927-2023 – Tombstone's Fifth Era, "Living on the Legend," final revival/bonanza.

1927 – Walter Noble Burns book *Tombstone: An Iliad of the Southwest* published.

1928 – Breakenridge's *Helldorado* published.

January 13, 1929 – Wyatt Earp dies in Los Angeles.

October 24-27, 1929 – Tombstone's first "Helldorado Days" event, to celebrate town's 50th anniversary, held. Old, closed-down venues such as the Bird Cage Theatre (closed for approximately forty years) cleaned and repaired for the occasion. Celebration a success, but luster/national newsworthiness stolen by same-day stock market crash and its ramifications.

October 24-29, 1929 – Wall Street stock market crashes. Great Depression begins, lasts ten years. Silver and copper prices tank. By the end of 1931, all mining work in Tombstone has ceased.

November 20, 1929 – Bisbee replaces Tombstone as county seat, which, at the time, was one of Tombstone's major two means of subsistence, along with (declining) mining.

1930 – Walter Lombardi buys Crystal Palace.

May, 1930 – Due to dwindling profitability, William H. Kelly sells the *Epitaph* newspaper (to Walter H. Cole) and leaves town for Tucson.

October 25-November 15, 1930 – Stuart Lake's four-part Wyatt Earp/Wild West series appears in consecutive weekly issues of the immensely popular *Saturday Evening Post* for the post-Depression country/world, needing a diversion, to imagine.

February 26, 1931– The emblematic phrase describing Tombstone as the "Town Too Tough to Die," coined by editor/owner Walter Cole, first appears in the *Tombstone Epitaph* newspaper.

October 6, 1931– Stuart N. Lake's seminal book, *Wyatt Earp: Frontier Marshal*, published.[438]

May 2, 1932 – John P. Clum dies in Los Angeles.

1932-Present – Tombstone-related movies begin to appear across the country/world.

February 28, 1932 – *Law and Order*, first movie to portray the Gunfight at the O. K. Corral, released.

January 5, 1933 – George Parsons dies in Los Angeles.

June, 1933 – Phelps Dodge (Bunker Hill Mines) sells all their Tombstone properties to the Tombstone Gold and Silver Mining Corporation (the Tombstone Development Company).

January 19, 1934 – *Frontier Marshal*, the first movie based upon Stuart Lake's Wyatt Earp book, is released.

June, 1935 – Old historic post office on Fremont Street dismantled.

August 21, 1935 – Congress passes Historic Sites Act; federal surveyors search for potential sites to designate as historic landmarks.[439]

May 30, 1938 – Monument erected at Boothill dedicated to the Tombstone pioneers buried there.

July 19, 1938 – Tombstone hits a new low; population down to approximately five hundred, and town offers to sell itself (the entire town, "lock, stock, and barrel") to the Hollywood movie industry for $75,000 after Walter H. Cole, editor of the *Tombstone Epitaph* newspaper, surveyed the townsfolk.[440]

October 6, 1938 – Clayton A. Smith purchases the dying *Tombstone Epitaph* newspaper from Walter H. Cole.

1939-1945 – World War II.

July 28, 1939 – *Frontier Marshal*, the second movie based on the Lake Wyatt Earp book, is released.

November 2, 1940 – Mary Katherine "Big Nose Kate" Harony Fisher Elder Holliday Cummings dies in Pioneers' Home in Prescott, Arizona, and is buried in its cemetery.

1942 – Metal and wooden name markers placed on the old graves in recently restored, renamed Boothill Cemetery, well after Bechdolt's 1923 mandate, and involving the hard work and persistence of many Tombstone stalwarts along the way. Metal for markers provided by H. F. Ohm from his steel factory in Indiana.[441]

June 13, 1942 – *Tombstone, the Town too Tough to Die* movie, based on the 1927 Walter Noble Burns book, is released.

July, 1944 – Mr. and Mrs. H. F. (Harry Fulton) Ohm purchase Bird Cage Theatre from Mrs. C. L. Cummings and renovate it. They have two daughters, one of whom is Mrs. William Hunley (mother of William M. Hunley, Jr.) of Dugger, Indiana.

December 19, 1944 – Josephine Sarah Marcus Earp, wife of Wyatt, having lived to see the books and movies made about him, dies in Los Angeles.

1945 – Emmett and Lela Nunnelley move to Tombstone and begin to clean up and maintain Boothill Cemetery, replacing vandalized markers and identifying graves.

August, 1945 – Tombstone experiences a minor, short-lived population boom after Doctor Peter Paul Zinn, Phelps-Dodge Mining Corporation physician for twenty years, moves up from Bisbee and opens a medical center in the old, abandoned 1890 Bank of Tombstone building, to treat sinusitis, asthma, and arthritis with his "dubious" chlorine gas inhalation therapy. (Building served in 1881 as Agency Pima County Bank and P. W. Smith store, and is the current Visitor's Center.)[442]

December 3, 1946 – *My Darling Clementine* (Tombstone/Earp movie) released to great fanfare.

November 14, 1947 – Alvira "Allie" Packingham Sullivan Earp, the widow of Virgil, dies in Los Angeles in the home of grandniece Hildreth Halliwell (6301 8th Avenue), where she had lived since the death of Virgil in 1905. James Earp was also living with the two at the time of his death in 1926. Ashes buried with best friend and sister-in-law Adelia Earp and brother-in-law James Earp, in San Bernardino's Mountain View Cemetery next to Saint Bernardine's Medical Center.

May 8, 1948 – Restored Crystal Palace reopens.

May 1949 – Tombstone Courthouse gutted/renovated. Plans to convert it to a hotel.

November 3, 1949 – Tombstone Restoration Commission (R. B. Krebs, Walter Lombardi, Sam and Theda Medigovich, Ethel Macia, Mayor John Giacoma, and later *Epitaph* owner/publisher Clayton A. Smith) formed with stated goal of bringing back the original fronts/historic names of buildings, installing boardwalks on Allen Street, defining a "historic district" where all new construction/alterations must first be approved by the zoning commission, and restoring points of allure (historic sites) about the town with placement of historical markers to attract tourism.

1950 – Fort Huachuca decommissioned, leading to a downturn in Tombstone economy after military families move away.

November, 1950 – Wally Foster elected mayor of Tombstone. Would serve in that capacity through 1961.

1952 – Based upon her own research, the original "Boothill Grave Yard" booklet created by cemetery historian/custodian/caretaker Lela B. Nunnelley; distributed (updated version) to this day to tourists of the cemetery.

1953 – U. S. Army reactivates Fort Huachuca, stimulating business in nearby Tombstone.

July, 1953 – Tombstone Restoration Commission starts to put 1949 plans into action. Western dress to be worn by shop owners/residents in historic district. Original 1880s building names to be used. No modern-type signs/advertising. First plan to form "The Vigilantes" reenactment troupe (founded 1946/debuted 1947/incorporated 1954;

still active to this day) to roam the streets in period dress on weekends/holidays to greet the visiting tourists.

April 10, 1954 – City Ordinance Number 146passed, highly advocated for and promoted by *Epitaph* owner/editor Clayton A. Smith. Created a zoning commission and restoration zone requiring all new buildings to convey an "1883 appearance."

October 15, 1954 – The Arizona Bank opens a Tombstone branch, the only bank in the town.

July 17, 1955 – Disneyland, with its Western-themed Frontierland, opens.

September 6, 1955 – *The Life and Legend of Wyatt Earp* TV show starring Hugh O'Brian premieres; runs through 1961.

September, 1956 – *Walk the Proud Land*, starring Audie Murphy, released; movie is based upon the book *Apache Agent*, the 1936 biography of Tombstone mayor, *Epitaph* newspaper founder, and Earp confidant John Clum.

May 30, 1957 – *Gunfight at the O.K. Corral*, starring Burt Lancaster as Wyatt Earp and Kirk Douglas as Doc Holliday, released.

July 7, 1957 – Owing to the immense popularity of the new Wyatt Earp television show and the nonstop string of Tombstone/Earp related movies, Tombstone makes national/worldwide attention once again when Earp's 300-pound headstone is removed from his grave by souvenir/treasure hunters, and the town of Tombstone is wrongly accused of the dastardly deed, owing to prior serious attempts by some local citizens to have Wyatt exhumed and reinterred in their Boothill. Even more publicity generated during the hyped manhunt for the thieves, especially after actor Hugh O'Brian (TV's "Wyatt Earp") offers a reward for the return of the monument and the crook's capture.[443]

October 16, 1957 – Television show *Tombstone Territory* premieres; Tombstone tourism doubles. (Show runs through 1959.)

1958 – Emma Escapule-Main, only daughter of Tombstone pioneer John Escapule, and owner of the O. K. Corral, hires Sid Wilson to restore it to its original state.

January 20, 1959 – Nellie Cashman's Russ House completely gutted by fire. Rebuilt as hotel.

August 1, 1959 – The Tombstone Courthouse becomes Arizona's third state park and receives state funding for repairs/restoration/preservation.

1960 – William M. Hunley, Jr. moves from Indiana to Tombstone to assume ownership of the Bird Cage Theatre, which he purchased from his grandmother.

May 2, 1960 – After fifty-seven years of service to Tombstone, the Southern Pacific Railroad closes its depot on Toughnut Street, which was then taken over by the city for use as a library.

1961 – National Park Service names Tombstone a "National Historic Landmark."

1961 – Restaurateur Steve Goldstein arrives in Tombstone from New York.

September 30, 1962 – Restored Tombstone Courthouse officially reopens after becoming Arizona state's first official historic monument (designated on July 1, 1960).

October 1, 1962 – Tombstone named a Registered National Historic Landmark by the U. S. Department of the Interior under the Historic Sites Act of 1935.[444]

1963/1964 – Consortium ("Historic Tombstone Adventures - H.T.A.") led by Detroit, Michigan attorney Harold O. Love (along with Wallace E. Clayton, Lawrence Fleischman, and William Murray) purchases Tombstone's *Epitaph* newspaper from Mrs. Mabel Smith; Crystal Palace Saloon and the O. K. Corral from Emma Escapule-Main; Schieffelin Hall and other historic landmarks about town, with grand plans for restoration and promoting Tombstone as historical tourist destination. Build Lookout Lodge Motel overlooking Boothill. Consult University of Arizona historian John Gilchriese to advise and assist with authentication. By early 1970s, Love buys out all his partners.

1966 – Passage of the National Historic Preservation Act stimulates preservation activities about town. Wooden awnings placed in front of shops in the historic district on Allen Street, and boardwalks debated.

July 16, 1966 – Opening of the Wyatt Earp Museum on Fifth and Toughnut Streets in Tombstone by John D. Gilchriese; displays his Earp collection. Closes in 1973.

November 1, 1967 – *Hour of the Gun*, Tombstone O. K. Corral/Earp movie, released.

1968 – Tennessee-born Ben T. Traywick moves with his young family to Tombstone from California.

October 25, 1968 – "Spectre of the Gun" episode of Star Trek television show airs. Reenacts Gunfight at the O. K. Corral for a whole new audience—science fiction enthusiasts.

January, 1971 – Ben Traywick establishes the "Wild Bunch" gunfighter's troupe. They disband in 2014 after donating hundreds of thousands of dollars to the city through the years.

August 1, 1971 – *Doc*, a Holliday/Earp/Tombstone/O. K. Corral movie, released.

1972 – "A Plan for the Creation of a Historic Environment in Tombstone, Arizona," preservation proposal published.

February, 1972 – The 1882 city hall placed on National Register.

1973 – Billionaire Hunt brothers purchase millions of ounces of silver in hopes of cornering the market (and hedge against inflation), significantly raising prices. Tombstone mining speculators (mistakenly, as it turned out) hope for a return to its mining glory days.

June, 1974 – The "National Edition" of the *Tombstone Epitaph* introduced, to be produced by Dean Pritchard and published on a monthly basis. Subscriptions increase and paper finally becomes profitable.

1975 – Boardwalks placed in front of businesses on both sides of Allen Street from Third to Sixth Streets.

February 2, 1975 - Owing to continued decreasing circulation, the nonprofitable local weekly *Epitaph* is turned over to the journalism department of the University of Arizona. Publication ceased in 2001.

September, 1980 – Young Gordon Anderson arrives in Tombstone with his parents to run the Larian Motel.

March 21, 1986 – Harold O. Love dies, Wallace A. Clayton succeeds Love as publisher of the *National Epitaph*.

1990 – Cochise Silver Mines, Inc. (established in 1986; Dustin Escapule, vice president), Tombstone's last mining company, shuts down for good owing to increasing miners' salaries, excessive government red tape/burdensome EPA regulations over pollution(cyanide) monitoring. Mining no longer viable/profitable in Tombstone. Old mine shafts fenced/filled in.

July 4, 1991 – After having been married there December 17, 1990, Stephen and Marjorie Elliott move permanently to Tombstone to live. Open the Silver Lady Antiques store and subsequently the Tombstone Western Heritage Museum.

December 25, 1993 – Popular, highly quotable cult favorite *Tombstone* movie, starring Kurt Russell as Wyatt Earp and Val Kilmer as gunfighting dentist Doc Holliday, premieres.

June 24, 1994 – *Wyatt Earp* movie, starring Kevin Costner and Dennis Quaid, released.

1996 – Tombstone "franchise(s) its image" on a new line of foods in exchange for a portion of profits. L. A.-based Tombstone (1877) Prospecting Company sells its products ("Bird Cage Hot Salsa, Boot Hill Extra-Hot seasoning, Big Nose Kate Dijon") locally and nationally.[445]

2000 – Tombstone pioneer family member Dustin Escapule elected as mayor of Tombstone; this would be his first of seven two-year terms.

October 18, 2015 – On the final day of Tombstone's annual three-day Helldorado celebration, a Tombstone "Vigilante Gunfight" reenactor accidently loads live bullets instead of blanks into his gun and shoots five rounds, striking businesses on East Allen Street, another reenactor in the groin (necessitating a flight to Tucson for emergency surgery), and grazing a tourist in the neck during "simulation of a Wild West showdown." Makes national news and prompts new gunfight regulations (ordinance) in town.[446]

August, 2018 – *True West Magazine*'s Mark Boardman hired by Bob Love (son of Harold O. Love) as editor of the "National Edition" of the (monthly) *Tombstone Epitaph.*

2021 – Owing to COVID-19 related employee shortages, Steve and Gloria Goldstein remodel their Russ House from Café Margarita back to hotel (B & B) once again.

November 12, 2021 – Long-time Bird Cage Theatre owner William M. Hunley passes away in Mexico. Buried in Tombstone City Cemetery, after funeral in Sierra Vista and long procession with police escort from there to Tombstone and down Allen Street, with stopover at Bird Cage to pay tribute. Entire vibrant town comes to a complete solemn standstill as hearse saluted along the way by thousands of grieving friends, townsfolk, and visiting town tourists. [447]

June 23-25, 2023 – Tombstone Movie thirty-year (1993-2023) cast reunion conceived and produced by Gordon Anderson, and co-produced by Mark Sankey of Mescal Studios and Hollywood promoters Bob and Julie Ann Ream, who brought back many of the fan-favorite, cult-classic movie's stars; held in Tombstone to great fanfare and record modern-day town crowds.

APPENDIX II

For Some a Final Common Meeting Ground [448]
(Former Tombstoners who met up one last time at the Old Soldiers' Home; Sawtelle, California)

Bradley, William F. Admitted to Sawtelle's Old Soldiers' Home, Los Angeles/Santa Monica, July 1904. Died July 1907. Buried L. A. National Cemetery (Sawtelle). Section 13, Row E, Number 6.

Elkin, James Admitted to Old Soldiers' Home in 1901; died there April 67, 1914; buried in Section 24, Row K, Number 4, L.A. National Cemetery.

Grow, Artemus L. Moved from Tombstone to Sawtelle, adjacent to Old Soldiers' Home for his medical care there, in 1916. Died in Sawtelle on September 19, 1918. Buried in nearby Westwood Memorial Park.

Haggerty, Hugh Died on April 19, 1920, at the Old Soldiers' Home, buried in the Los Angeles National Cemetery adjacent to the Home, section 40, row E, number 9. He first entered the home in 1900.

Herring, Marcus F. Admitted to Old Soldiers' Home in 1891; died there May 22, 1910; buried in section 17, Row F, Number 8, L. A. National Cemetery.

Moses, Thomas Admitted to Old Soldiers' Home in 1895-1896. Died in Seattle March 17, 1896.

Shankland, Dan Admitted to Old Soldiers' Home in April 1897; died on December 4, 1998, buried in section 4, row C, number 8 of the adjacent Los Angeles National Cemetery.

Soule, William H. Admitted to Old Soldiers' Home in 1910, died July 1, 1916, buried in Section 30, Row A, Number 8 of the Los Angeles National Cemetery.

Stout, John H. Admitted to Old Soldiers' Home April, 1912. Admitted to sanitarium in Loma Linda, San Bernardino County, 1922; died there May 14, 1924. Buried Mountain View Cemetery, San Bernardino (where several Earp family members are also buried).

355

Wardwell, David K. Admitted to Old Soldiers' Home in 1906. Died in Arizona in 1908.

Wiser, John Charles Admitted to Old Soldiers' Home November 14, 1905, died there October 6, 1908. He is buried in section 15, row D, number 20 of the adjacent Los Angeles National Cemetery.

ENDNOTES

1 Excerpted from the *Annals of Internal Medicine*, March 2022, Volume 175, Number 3, pp 452 – 453, "On Being a Doctor."

2 James, George Wharton. *Arizona: The Wonderland*, 1917, as excerpted from Lee Silva's *Wyatt Earp: A Biography of the Legend* [Vol. II, Part 1] (Santa Ana, CA: Graphic Publishers, 2010), 150.

3 *The Record-Union* (Sacramento, California), January 16, 1880, as quoted from *The Tombstone Epitaph Monthly Journal*, July 2023, p. 16. Submitted by author/historian James B. Mills.

4 Online dictionary; *Oxford* languages.

5 Good primary sources, in full, are in Silva's *Wyatt Earp: A Biography of the Legend* [Vol. II, Part 1].

6 Lynn Bailey, *Too Tough to Die: The Rise, Fall, and Resurrection of a Silver Camp, 1878 to 1990* (Tucson: Westernlore Press, 2004); William Shillingberg, *Tombstone, A.T.: A History of Early Mining, Milling, and Mayhem* (Norman: University of Oklahoma Press, 1998). Bailey's work is a solid mining history presentation, whereas Shillingberg is a bit heavy on "mayhem." Silva, *Wyatt Earp: A Biography of the Legend* [Vol. II, Part 1].

7 Charles G. Yale, *List of Working Mines on the Pacific Coast* (San Francisco: Geo. Spaulding & Co., 1882).

8 William P. Blake, "The Geology and Veins of Tombstone, Arizona," *Transactions, American Institute of Mining Engineers*, X (1882), 334-45; John A. Church, "Concentration and Smelting at Tombstone, Arizona," *Engineering & Mining Journal*, April 16, 1887; W. P. Blake, *Tombstone and Its Mines* (New York: Chittenden Press, 1902); Lawrence Austin, "Silver Milling at Charleston, Arizona," *Engineering & Mining Journal*, January 27, 1883. An ad for a "Custom Mill" of the Boston & Arizona Smelting & Reduction Co. appeared in most issues of the *Tombstone Epitaph* of 1882.

9 *Tombstone Weekly Epitaph*, December 19, 1881. *Los Angeles Herald*, December 22, 1881.

10 A decent presentation of population is in Eric L. Clements, *After the Boom in Tombstone and Jerome, Arizona* (Reno: University of Nevada Press, 2003).

11 Such incidents and warnings were mentioned in the George Parsons diaries, and there were frequent reports in the Tombstone newspapers of the unwary traveler who was never seen again.

12 John Gregory Bourke, *An Apache Campaign in Sierra Madre* (New York: Charles Scribner's Sons, 1886), devotes several pages to this misnamed "campaign."

13 Lynn R. Bailey, *The Valiants: The Tombstone Rangers and Apache War Frivolities* (Tucson: Westernlore Press, 1999).

14 In 1895 when Joyce was interviewed in San Francisco, he was "Colonel Joyce," and he exaggerated the troubles in Cochise County, the Apache threat, etc.; *San Francisco Examiner*, June 24, 1895.

15   Details on the role of the U. S. Army are in *Mohave County Miner*, August 24, 1884, and *Weekly Arizona Miner*, August 22, 1884.

16   *Tombstone Epitaph*, October 29, 1880. Coauthor DdH email conversation with Australia-based Tombstone researcher/historian Peter Brand, February 16, 2022.

17   There are books galore that examine these town-rural differences. An excellent starting place is Silva, *Wyatt Earp: A Biography of the Legend* [Vol. II, Part 1]. Fattig, *Wyatt Earp: The Biography*. Young, Roberts et al, *Wyatt Earp Anthology*. John Boessenecker, *Ride the Devil's Herd: Wyatt Earp's Epic Battle Against the West's Biggest Outlaw Gang* (Toronto, Ontario, Canada: Hanover Square Press, 2020). William Breakenridge, *Helldorado: Bringing Law to the Mesquite* (Boston, MA: Houghton Mifflin Co, 1928). Regarding Curly Bill, email February 14, 2022, Tombstone researcher/historian Michael Mihaljevich.

18   Lee Silva, *Wyatt Earp: A Biography of the Legend* [Vol. II, Part 1]. Fattig, *Wyatt Earp: The Biography*. Boessenecker, *Ride the Devil's Herd*. Gary L. Roberts, *Doc Holliday: The Life and Legend* (Hoboken, N.J.: John Wiley & Sons, 2006). Breakenridge, *Helldorado: Bringing Law to the Mesquite*. Young, Roberts et al, *Wyatt Earp Anthology*. Larry Ball, *The United States Marshals of New Mexico and Arizona, 1846 - 1912* (Albuquerque: University of New Mexico Press, 1978), examines and role and knowledge of U. S. Marshal Crawley Dake and Territorial Acting Governor John Gosper. See also President Chester A. Arthur's message to the Senate and House regarding the Cochise County cowboys, in *A Compilation of The Messages and Papers of the Presidents* (New York: Bureau of National Literature, 1897). Ann Kirschner, *Lady at the O. K. Corral: The True Story of Josephine Marcus Earp* (New York: Harper Perennial, 2014). For an attorney's comments on the firearms ordinance and other aspects of the event, see Steven Lubet, *Murder in Tombstone: The Forgotten Trial of Wyatt Earp* (New Haven: Yale University Press, 2004).

19   The lower court ruling was clearly explained in *Mining & Scientific Press*, September 23, 1882. This went on appeal to the Arizona Supreme Court as *Tombstone Mill and Mining Company v. Way Up Mining Company*, 25 PAC 794 (1883). The best article on the subject by Dr. James Douglas is "A Remedy for the Law of the Apex," *Mining Reporter*, November 21, 1907.

20   *Engineering & Mining Journal*, December 19, 1885.

21   The Tombstone water problem was well covered in the professional journals as well as in the Arizona and California newspapers. Some interesting comments are in *Mining & Scientific Press*, February 14, 1885; *Arizona Daily Star*, May 2, 1884, December 12, 1885; and *San Diego Union*, February 3, 1883.

22   The Tombstone and Tucson newspapers gave heavy coverage to the labor problems. Some useful material is in *Engineering & Mining Journal*, August 16, 1884; *Weekly Republican*, August 14, 1884; *Arizona Daily Star*, August 2 and August 28, 1884.

23   Specifics for the year appeared in *Daily Tombstone*, October 20, 1885, which pointed out that the community population was 4,000, yet it had been 7,000 in 1883.

24   Some key sources on these points are *Arizona Weekly Citizen*, March 20, 1881, water noticed in the Sulphuret; *Tombstone Epitaph*, December 19, 1881, description of the Girard, the first mill at Tombstone; *Engineering & Mining Journal*, January 21, 1882, Sulphuret, water, and the Girard mill; Thomas C.

Chapman, *The Metallurgy of Silver Chloride Ores from the* in the Tombstone District, (Master's thesis, 1924.) University of Arizona, Tucson, AZ (dated, but still relevant); H. S. Butler, E. D. Wilson, C. A. Razor, *Geology and Ore Deposits of the Tombstone District, Arizona* (Tucson: University of Arizona, 1938), a publication sponsored by the Arizona Bureau of Mines.

25   The report of several columns considers the history of the firm as well as the milling changes; *Daily Tombstone*, September 6, 1886.

26   Baily and Chaput, *Cochise County Stalwarts*, 2000; *Tombstone Epitaph*, August 7, 1898, Pearce restaurant; March 21, 1920, opium incident.

27   *Tucson Citizen*, September 25, 2002, has an article about the search for the grave of "Pie" Allen. Lee Silva, *Wyatt Earp: A Biography of the Legend*, Vol. I (Santa Ana, CA: Graphic Publishers).

28   Don Chaput, *Odyssey of Burt Alvord*, 2000.

29   His ads appear in hundreds of issues of Tombstone newspapers. See in particular *Tombstone Prospector*, October 22, 1887, and for suicide, *Bisbee Daily Review*, July 6, 1905.

30   Unusual material on Babcock is in Lee Silva, *Wyatt Earp Volume II, Part 1: Tombstone Before the Earps*, 2010, 243, 244.

31   Bailey, *Too Tough to Die (Tombstone)*, 2004; Bailey and Chaput, *Cochise County Stalwarts*, 2000.

32   Obituary in *Arizona Republic*, June 12, 1904.

33   There are hundreds of references to Batterman in the mining and legal literature. A decent obituary, with photo, was in the *San Francisco Call*, October 13, 1901. *Arizona Daily Star*, March 25, 1883, dispute with Blake; *Tombstone Epitaph*, March 20, 1882, microscopical society; January 15, 1886, relieved of duty at Head Centre.

34   David D. de Haas, MD. "Revisiting the O.K. Corral Fire Aftermath Photo." *Wild West Magazine*, April 2016. Extended online version available at Revisiting the 'O.K. Corral Fire Aftermath' Photo (historynet.com)

35   Ad, Hooker & Bauer, *Tombstone Epitaph*, October 19, 1881; obituary, *Arizona Republican*, March 18, 1914.

36   Don Chaput, *Virgil Earp: Western Peace Officer* (Norman, OK: University of Oklahoma Press, 1996). Silva, *Wyatt Earp: A Biography of the Legend, Vol. I and II.* Fattig, *Wyatt Earp: The Biography.* Boessenecker, *Wyatt Earp's Epic Battle Against the West's Biggest Outlaw Gang.* Roberts, *Doc Holliday: The Life and Legend.*

37   Lynn R. Bailey and Don Chaput, *Cochise County Stalwarts: A Who's Who of the Territorial Years*, Volumes I and II (Tucson, Arizona: Westernlore Press, 2000). Bob Alexander, *John H. Behan: Sacrificed Sheriff* (Silver City, New Mexico: High Lonesome Books, 2002).

38   Bailey and Chaput, *Cochise County Stalwarts*; Roy B. Young, *Tombstone Epitaph*, May 2021, Ancestry.com. Joseph Williamson, Necrology, *History of the City of Belfast in the state of Maine, Volume II* (Boston, Mass: Houghton Mifflin), 19. *Tombstone Epitaph*, January 23, 1882, for Hearst. Obituary, *Tombstone Weekly Epitaph*, November 11, 1882; *Arizona Weekly Citizen*, November 19, 1882; *Tucson Citizen*, November 16, 1882.

39   Roberts. *Doc Holliday: The Life and Legend.*

40   Bailey and Chaput, *Cochise County Stalwarts.* Roberts, *Doc Holliday*, 2006, 51-53.

41   Don Chaput and David D. de Haas, MD, *The Earps Invade Southern California* (Denton, Texas: University of North Texas Press, 2020).

42   David D. de Haas, MD. "Revisiting the O.K. Corral Fire Aftermath Photo."
Wild West Magazine, April 2016. Please also see extended online version,
Revisiting the 'O.K. Corral Fire Aftermath' Photo (historynet.com).

43   The best sources on the careers of the Bilicke family are in Los Angeles
publications, as well as in pamphlets, advertisements, and books about the
hotel life in Southern California. Bailey and Chaput, *Cochise County Stalwarts*.
See also Roy B. Young, "The Cosmopolitan Touch: The Bilickes – Hoteliers in
Tombstone," *The Tombstone Epitaph*, lead article March 2020. Don Chaput and
David D. de Haas, MD, "The Earp Fellow Sophisticates," *Wild West Magazine*,
October 2021, 64 – 69 Chaput and de Haas, MD *The Earps Invade Southern
California*. de Haas, MD, "Revisiting the O. K. Corral Fire Aftermath Photo." *Wild
West Magazine*, April 2016.

44   Voting registers, censuses, in Nevada, Arizona, California. *Arizona
Weekly Citizen*, 1882 ads, show that his office was with that of Justice Wells
Spicer; *Arizona Daily Star*, December 9, 1880, Pima County deputy sheriff with
Tombstone duties.

45   Chaput and de Haas, MD. *The Earps Invade Southern California*.

46   California Death Index. Blinn owned lumber yards and had investments
in banks and land in more than a dozen Arizona and California counties. He,
and his companies, advertised widely in newspapers and magazines. Chaput
and de Haas, MD, "The Earp Fellow Sophisticates," *Wild West Magazine*, October
2021, 64- 69.

47   Obituary in *El Paso Herald*, November 5, 1925. 1881 Arizona business
directory.

48   There are a few mentions in Young, Roberts, et al, *Wyatt Earp Anthology*.
The *Arizona Sentinel*, August 7, 1886, has a long, negative article on Boyle, who
had just been fired as a guard at Yuma Territorial Prison.

49   William Breakenridge, *Helldorado: Bringing Law to the Mesquite*.

50   *Arizona Weekly Star* (Tucson), January 20, 1881. Many mentions of Curly
Bill are in Young, Roberts et al, *Wyatt Earp Anthology*; some elaboration on
these events are in Bailey and Chaput, *Cochise County Stalwarts*. Detailed local
coverage of the Earp Vendetta, and the Curly Bill curtain call, can be found
in the Tombstone and Tucson newspapers of March and April 1882. For Curly
Bill's close association with the cowboys, and the friendliness of Sheriff John
Behan, see Breakenridge, *Helldorado*. Breakenridge was a deputy sheriff and on
occasion even used Curly Bill as a tax collector. Gary Roberts, *Doc Holliday*, pp
301-304 for Doc (in Denver) re Curly Bill.

51   With Virgil in Prescott, *Arizona Miner*, March 8, 1878; there are several
Bronk entries in Oaths; Claims, of the Cochise County Recorder files; *Morning
Press* (Santa Barbara), June 3, 1892, Bronk being sued. His wife is mentioned
in the Sacramento directories until her death in 1919. *Phoenix Republican*,
March 26, 1899; thank you to author John Boessenecker for this obituary. *Daily
Morning Alaskan*, Feb 21, 1899.

52   The "famed" career of Brooks is easy to follow. His Tombstone
crookedness is summarized well in *Daily Ata California*, December 11, 1884; his
San Francisco arrests are noted in *Weekly Arizona Miner*, January 23, 1885, and
Arizona Silver Belt, January 17, 1885; an interesting tale of his marriage (mail
order bride from England) is in *Tombstone Epitaph*, December 6, 1884; obituary,
Press Democrat (Santa Rosa), June 2, 1923, headed "Death Takes Noted California
Poet."

53   The Brown trail is easily followed in the directories, censuses, and voting registers of Arizona and California. The *Arizona Quarterly Illustrated*, October 1880, has a view of the Tombstone hotel and some comments about Brown. de Haas, MD. "Revisiting the O.K. Corral Fire Aftermath Photo." *Wild West Magazine*, April 2016, 11. See also extended online version.

54   Lynn Bailey, *Tombstone from a Woman's Point of View* (Tucson, 1998).

55   Mountain Maid and Tombstone Townsite sources carry Calhoun material. The Gillett trouble is in *Weekly Arizona Miner*, March 8, 1878; *Arizona Weekly Citizen*, April 11, 1879, filing the Mountain Maid claim; *Arizona Daily Star*, September 1, 1879, shooting up Allen Street; *Tucson Citizen*, May 8, 1881, summons by Tom Fitch; September 4, 1880, arrested by Wyatt Earp; *Coconino Sun*, February 14, 1895, train wreck; Arizona State Board of Health, death certificate.

56   The Tombstone arson charge is easily followed in the *Epitaph* issues of early 1882. The pension claim is in the National Archives. The fraud charge is explained in the *Arizona Daily Star* of March 17, 1921. His death certificate is in the Arizona Board of Health. Bailey and Chaput, *Cochise County Stalwarts: A Who's Who of the Territorial Years*, Vol I, 52. Barron and Lionel Jacobs Collection, University of Arizona, Tucson.

57   His Los Angeles bartender stint shows up in the census of 1900. Bailey and Chaput, *Cochise County Stalwarts*, Vol. I, 53.

58   A typical obituary is in *San Francisco Chronicle*, May 28, 1896. Bailey and Chaput, *Cochise County Stalwarts*, Vol. I, 54.

59   Chaput, Don, *Nellie Cashman and the North American Mining Frontier* (Tucson, Arizona: Westernlore Press, 1995). Chaput and de Haas, MD, "The Earp Fellow Sophisticates," *Wild West Magazine*, October 2021, 64–69.

60   Obituary in *New York Sun* and *Tucson Citizen*, February 13, 1917. One of his best works is the article on Tombstone in *Transactions, American Institute of Mining Engineers*, XXXIII (1902).

61   Details abound in Tombstone histories and anything about Buckskin Frank. Good contemporary accounts are in *Arizona Daily Star*, November 15, 1882, and *Tombstone Epitaph*, November 18, 1882. Don Chaput, *"Buckskin Frank" Leslie* (Tucson, AZ: Westernlore Press, 1999). Jack DeMattos and Chuck Parsons, *They Called Him Buckskin Frank: The Life and Adventures of Nashville Franklyn Leslie* (Denton, Texas: University of North Texas Press, 2018). Ben T. Traywick, *Tombstone's "Buckskin Frank": Nashville Franklyn Leslie* (Tombstone, AZ: Red Bookstore, 2013).

62   Chaput and de Haas, MD. *The Earps Invade Southern California*. Rita Ackerman, *O.K. Corral Postscript* (Honolulu, Hawaii: Talei Publishers, Inc. 2006). Don Chaput, *Virgil Earp: Western Peace Officer* (Norman, OK: University of Oklahoma Press, 1996). Ben T. Traywick, *The Clantons of Tombstone* (Tombstone, Arizona: Red Marie's Bookstore, 1996). Silva, *Wyatt Earp: A Biography of the Legend*. Fattig, *Wyatt Earp: The Biography*. Boessenecker, *Wyatt Earp's Epic Battle Against the West's Biggest Outlaw Gang*. Marshall Trimble, "Ike Clanton," *North/Pleasant Valley Magazine*, May 31, 2019. Roberts, *Doc Holliday: The Life and Legend*.

63   Anything by or about George Parsons will have Clapp information. Detailed obituaries with tough prose on the suicide are in *Los Angeles Times* and *Los Angeles Herald*, both of July 28, 1892.

64   Clark was a heavy advertiser in the Tombstone newspapers. Cochise County Recorder's office, for mining claims, water rights; probate file, Cochise County, in Arizona State Archives.

65   The poverty angle is mentioned in the *Los Angeles Herald,* October 4, 1889, and *Los Angeles Times,* October 6, 1889.

66   Gary Ledoux, *Nantan: The Life and Times of John P. Clum,* 2 vols. (Victoria, BC: Trafford Publishing, 2007/2008). Woodworth Clum, *Apache Agent: The Story of John P. Clum* (Cambridge, Massachusetts: The Riverside Press, 1936). Chaput and de Haas, MD, "The Earp Fellow Sophisticates," *Wild West Magazine,* October 2021, 64-69. Biographical details on the marriage (and divorce) are in *Los Angeles Daily News,* June 18, 1933.

67   David D. de Haas, MD. "Revisiting the O.K. Corral Fire Aftermath Photo." *Wild West Magazine,* April 2016, p 11.

68   For much more on Jones please see Chaput and de Haas, MD. *The Earps Invade Southern California.*

69   *Arizona Quarterly Illustrated,* July 1880, has views and comments about Cook and Vizina; biography in Bailey and Chaput, *Cochise County Stalwarts.* *Tombstone Weekly Epitaph,* February 9, 1902, as fire chief; *Bisbee Daily Review,* October 31, 1915, obituary.

70   It is best to ignore the gun accounts of Cooley, as well as his undercover work, as well as the absurd claim of killing Ringo. Aside from the newspaper accounts in the *Epitaph* and *Prospector,* and the census of 1900, the State of California Death Records seem the most solid to wrap up the Cooley career. Michael Hickey, *John Ringo: The Final Hours* (Honolulu, Hawaii: Talei Publishers, 2001). More of the Cooley intrigue can be found in Silva, *Wyatt Earp: A Biography of the Legend,* Vol. II, Part 1.

71   The doings of the Corbin brothers' massive industrial empire are well covered in merchant and professional publications, especially in New England. An obituary and some information on Philip Corbin is in *Norwich Bulletin,* November 8, 1910.

72   Detailed information about the life and death of Corella are in *Tombstone Weekly Epitaph,* July 15, 1882, and *El Fronterizo* (Tucson), August 4, 1882. His appointment as consul is in *Arizona Weekly Citizen,* May 28, 1882. The Hearst party is mentioned in *Tombstone Epitaph,* February 27, 1882. Judge Lindley died in Major Earle's home later in the year; *Tombstone Weekly Epitaph,* September 19, 1882.

73   *Arizona Daily Star,* November 26, 1889.

74   Don Chaput, *"Buckskin Frank" Leslie* (Tucson, AZ: Westernlore Press, 1999, 55-59). DeMattos and Parsons, *They Called Him Buckskin Frank.* Ben T. Traywick, *Tombstone's "Buckskin Frank"* (Tombstone, AZ: Red Marie's Bookstore, 2013).

75   Obituary, *Arizona Republic,* November 27, 1921.

76   The Crabtree angle can be pursued by delving into the Wyatt Earp and Lotta Crabtree literature.

77   Obituary, *Tombstone Epitaph,* December 6, 1908.

78   Chamberlain, *Journal of Arizona History,* Winter, 1972, for Tombstone saloon details. The voting registers of Cochise and Pima Counties have good coverage of the Danner whereabouts. For the killing of Hicks, see *Arizona Citizen,* July 11, 1879. The *Citizen* and *Star* have many notices of Danner and politics in Total Wreck, in 1882-1883. *Tombstone Weekly Epitaph,* August 30, 1891, back to Tucson from the Grand Canyon. A typical obituary is in *Tucson Citizen,* July 21, 1898.

79   Don Chaput, "Fred Dodge: Undercover Agent, or Con Man?" *NOLA* (National Outlaw and Lawman Association, for outlaw and lawman history), XXV (January-March 2000). Carolyn Lake (ed.), *Undercover for Wells Fargo: The*

Unvarnished Recollections of Fred Dodge (Norman, Oklahoma: The University of Oklahoma Press, 1969). Peter Brand, *The Story of Johnny Tyler*, 2018, 143-144 and endnote 273.

80   *Tombstone Prospector,* Feb. 10, 1888, for move to Clifton. The shooting incident is in *Florence Tribune,* July 16, 1898.

81   Chaput and de Haas, *The Earps Invade Southern California.* Troy Kelley, *The Bisbee Massacre,* self-published. *El Paso Dalyn Herald,* September 5, 1899.

82   Detailed information as well as sources on the Dunbars is in Bailey and Chaput, *Cochise County Stalwarts. Phoenix Tribune,* February 3, 1923.

83   Chaput and de Haas, MD. *The Earps Invade Southern California.* Rita Ackerman. *O.K. Corral Postscript* Chaput, *Virgil Earp: Western Peace Officer.* Silva, *Wyatt Earp: A Biography of the Legend, Vol. I and II.* Fattig, *Wyatt Earp: The Biography.* Boessenecker, *Wyatt Earp's Epic Battle Against the West's Biggest Outlaw Gang.* Roberts, *Doc Holliday: The Life and Legend.*

84   See, for example, the photo and details in *San Francisco Call,* February 3, 1911, obituary.

85   Bailey and Chaput, *Cochise County Stalwarts: A Who's Who of the Territorial Years,* Volumes I and II.

86   For such an important figure in Tombstone's history, his obituary in the local paper seems sort of lukewarm; *Tombstone Weekly Epitaph,* March 14, 1915.

87   The legal and mineral documents of Tombstone are loaded with Allen English material. The Arizona State Board of Health death certificate lists "senility" and "acute alcoholism."

88   There are thousands of Escapule documents in the Cochise County Recorder's files; biography in Bailey and Chaput, *Cochise County Stalwarts;* Wills and Probate, Cochise County, Arizona State Archives. Phone interview and emails between Mayor Dustin Escapule and coauthor David D. de Haas, January 2022, April 2023.

89   Some of this appears in Chaput, *"Buckskin Frank" Leslie.* Her years in Banning can be followed in the census and in an obituary, *Riverside Enterprise,* March 24, 1947. DeMattos and Parsons, *They Called Him Buckskin Frank.* Traywick, *Tombstone's "Buckskin Frank."*

90   *Tombstone Epitaph,* June 3, 1882. de Haas, MD. "Revisiting the O.K. Corral Fire Aftermath Photo." *Wild West Magazine,* April 2016, p. 11. Please see also extended online version.

91   His career can be easily followed in the standard Chicago sources, and his obituary appeared in many of the national newspapers. He also had New Mexican mining interests, and he joined E. B. Gage in the ownership of the Congress Mine in Yavapai County

92   Her marriage to Monks is in *Sacramento Daily Union,* September 30, 1874; to Fallon in *San Jose Mercury-News,* July 1, 1877; divorce from Fallon in *Santa Cruz Weekly Sentinel,* October 19, 1878. John D. Rose, *Tombstone Pioneer Samantha Fallon's Wanton Past* (Sierra Vista: John D. Rose Historical Publications, 2013). Directories and censuses of Arizona and California contain some information. A paragraph about her wedding is in *Tucson Citizen,* December 18, 1880. Her marriage to Logie, in Los Angeles on November 9, 1905, is listed in Ancestry. com. California Death Index. Sources on the San Jose House also have Fallon information. The Lotta Crabtree estate case is well summarized in Bob Boze Bell, "Tombstone vs. Los Angeles," *True West,* August 2015.

93   The public nature of the Farish career makes it easy to follow. Typical obituaries were in *Williams News*, November 14, 1919, and *Mohave County Miner*, November 8, 1919.

94   Fay's career in Western journalism is easy to follow because of his active career, and he appears in the voting registers wherever he lived. California Death Index; he is buried in Belmont Memorial Park, Fresno.

95   His obituary in *Arizona Republican*, May 9, 1903, carries some biographical details.

96   Typical obituaries are *Los Angeles Times*, November 12, 1923, and *Santa Cruz News* of November 15, where he is referred to as "the Silver Tongued." Chaput and de Haas, MD. *The Earps Invade Southern California*, 9 – 11.

97   Good Fly material is available in Napa, California, sources. The Smithsonian Institution has many of the key Fly photographs of Native Americans. Some of his other interests can be seen in such publications as G. E. Goodfellow, "The Sonoran Earthquake," *Science*, August 12, 1887. Mollie's death notice (Mary E. Fly) was in the *Santa Ana Register*, February 20, 1922.

98   He is mentioned frequently in the Tombstone literature of the 1880s. Bailey and Chaput, *Cochise County Stalwarts*; *Arizona Weekly Citizen*, August 8, 1885, Flynn and Vogan in Tucson.

99   An obituary for William Forsyth is in the *Santa Ana Register*, April 17, 1919. The entire Forsyth and Forsythe saga is well covered in an illustrated article, "Victor Clyde Forsythe – Art of the West," HistoryNet.com, by David D. de Haas, MD. See also David D. de Haas MD. "Clyde Forsythe." *Wild West Magazine*; October 2013, 1-2, 22-23; and "Revisiting the O.K. Corral Fire Aftermath Photo," *Wild West Magazine*, April 2016 and online version. Chaput and de Haas, MD. *The Earps Invade Southern California*, 135, 183-184. Mary and David D. de Haas, MD research visits to San Gabriel Cemetery.

100   The obscene language incident is in *Tombstone Epitaph*, April 29, 1881; Chaput and de Haas, MD, *The Earps Invade Southern California*, preface. Boessenecker, *Ride the Devil's Herd*, 262- 267, 276. Silva, *Wyatt Earp: A Biography of the Legend, Vol. I and II*. Fattig, *Wyatt Earp: The Biography*. Roberts, Gary L. *Doc Holliday: The Life and Legend*.

101   Death notices appeared in several California and Arizona newspapers, and detailed obituary appeared in the *Tombstone Weekly Epitaph*, March 16, 1913.

102   *San Diego Union*, May 29, 1878. *The Arizona Sentinel* (Yuma), June 1, 1878. *Weekly Republican* (Phoenix), November 23, 1878. Journal, 11th Leg. Assembly, Terr. of AZ, 1881. *Weekly Arizona Miner*, Feb 4, 1881. *Arizona Daily Star* (Tucson), May 17, 1883. David Grasse, "The Story of Mrs. May Woodman, Murderess," *The Tombstone Epitaph*, June 2022.

103   Grassé, *The Bisbee Massacre*, 201; *Boston Herald*, April 7, 1884, his role at the public hanging; *San Francisco Examiner*, June 3, 1884, Tombstone dumpfight; *Arizona Sentinel*, June 7, 1884, Gallagher plead guilty. "Priest Asks Removal of School Principal," *San Francisco Call*, November 16, 1907; *The Monitor*, April 25, 1958, death date for Fr. Gallagher; this is a publication of the Archdiocese of San Francisco. The Ireland-England aspect of the Gallagher career was uncovered by Southwest historians Roy B. Young and Paul O'Brien, as well as by Raymond Blair of the County Donegal Historical Society. Troy Kelley, *The Bisbee Massacre*, self-published. *Tombstone W. Epitaph*, August 12, 1882, for Gallagher and courthouse.

104   There are dozens of detailed obituaries of Gardiner in the Western press in June 1899; biography in Bailey and Chaput, *Cochise County Stalwarts*.
105   Bailey and Chaput, *Cochise County Stalwarts*. Chaput and de Haas, MD, "The Earp Fellow Sophisticates," *Wild West Magazine*, October 2021, 64- 69.
106   Goldwater family sources abound. The Joseph Goldwater Papers are in the Arizona State University Libraries, presented by Senator Barry Goldwater.
107   His major career is easy to follow in the standard literature. Advertisements for the Boston Mill appeared regularly in the Tombstone newspapers. The article cited here was in *Transactions, American Institute of Mining Engineers*, XVII (1887-88). Blake, *Tombstone and Its Mines*, 1902, has flattering comments on Goodale. Many obituaries of Goodale appeared in Montana and Massachusetts newspapers in April 1929.
108   Donald Chaput, *Dr. George Goodfellow: Physician to the Gunfighters* (Tucson, AZ: Westernlore Press, 1996). Chaput and de Haas, MD, *The Earps Invade Southern California*, and Chaput and de Haas, MD, "The Earp Fellow Sophisticates," *Wild West Magazine*, October 2021, 64- 69.
109   Chaput and de Haas, MD, *The Earps Invade Southern California*, 185. Chaput and de Haas, MD, "The Earp Fellow Sophisticates," *Wild West Magazine*, October 2021, 64- 69.
110   Information on Gray is plentiful because of the townsite controversy. A biography with details and sources is in Bailey and Chaput, *Cochise County Stalwarts*. Linda Wommack, "Relatively Speaking: Colonel Mike Gray of Cochise County," *Journal of the Wild West History Association*, September 2021, Volume XIV, Number 3, 93 – 94.
111   Some information on the Hafford time in Randsburg is in *Los Angeles Herald*, September 17, 1897, and May 9, 1898. Hafford had quite a reputation in Arizona and California as a naturalist, even having space set aside as Hafford's Museum. He put on an exhibit at the Midwinter Fair in San Francisco, which was severely criticized in *Oologist*, April, 1894, p. 151: "No pretense is made to place the birds in a life-like attitude, but half-stuffed they are nailed through the back onto the wall."
112   His military career and stops at the many soldiers' homes are in the National Archives, Homes for Disabled Volunteer Soldiers files. His Tombstone career can be seen in the extensive Earp literature. The court case is *Emma Parker vs. Hugh Haggerty*, MS180 F.657, of 1882, in Arizona Historical Society. Chaput and de Haas, *The Earps Invade Southern California*.
113   Census and voting registers; *Tombstone Weekly Epitaph*, June 3, 1882, office on Allen Street. DdH interviews of Gordon Anderson, longtime owner of Tombstones Larian Motel. Gary S. McLelland, *The Streets of Tombstone* map, 1998. *Tombstone Weekly Epitaph*, June 3, 1882.
114   He is mentioned in most standard Tombstone sources. *Tombstone Weekly Epitaph*, March 9, 1913, obituary. See especially Silva, *Wyatt Earp Volume II, Part 1: Tombstone Before the Earps*, 243, 244.
115   Obituary in *Arizona Sentinel*, June 8, 1904.
116   His name is scattered among thousands of documents in the Cochise County Recorder's office. Many entries in the censuses and voting registers, and dozens of obituaries in the Arizona newspapers. The *Tombstone Epitaph* of October 15, 1916, even had an editorial regarding his career. *Tucson Citizen*, February 22, 1965. Gary S. McLelland, *The Streets of Tombstone* map, 1998.

117   In early November 1965, death notices and brief obituaries about Hattich appeared in more than a dozen California newspapers, pointing out the long California life for this Arizona publisher. Marvin Alisky, "Arizona's First Newspaper, The Weekly Arizonian, 1859," *New Mexico Historical Review,* 34 (No. 2, 1959). A congratulatory editorial appeared in the *Arizona Weekly Star* of May 2, 1895, regarding both Hattich and Bagg. *Tucson Citizen,* February 22, 1965. Obituary, *Arizona Republic,* November 5, 1964. Hattich, *Pioneer Magic,* 1964. *Arizona Daily Star,* August 3, 1913 (for sale of *Tombstone Prospector,* printing press). World War I draft registration.

118   *Tombstone Epitaph,* May 3, 1881, firearms ordinance; *St. Paul Globe,* January 1, 1899, obituary; Roy B. Young, Marcus Hayne: "From Tombstone to the Baseball Diamond," *Tombstone Epitaph National Edition,* March 2021, 14-16. Virgil Earp Spicer hearing testimony. Lubet, *Murder in Tombstone: The Forgotten Trial of Wyatt Earp.*

119   The *Tombstone Epitaph* carried many stories on the Hearst activities; January 16, January 23, February 27, April 17, April 24, 1882. Many authors claim that in January 1882 Wyatt Earp served as a bodyguard for Hearst, but the authors have not been able to find a single contemporary source to back such a claim, which is more than likely only based on myth and not fact. Wyatt had plenty of his own problems to deal with during this time period, with the Cowboy gang on the prowl having recently (December 28, 1881) seriously maimed his brother Virgil in ambush, and threatening even more violence toward the Earp family and their supporters. Email discussions with Earp biographer John Boessenecker (*Ride the Devil's Herd: Wyatt Earp's Epic Battle*). Chaput and de Haas, MD, "The Earp Fellow Sophisticates," *Wild West Magazine,* October 2021, 64-69.

120   The legal and social literature of Arizona in this era has thousands of references to the Herring family. A useful start is *A Historical and Biographical Record of the Territory of Arizona* (Chicago: McFarland& Pool, 1896), and an obituary of Sarah in *Arizona Daily Star,* May 1, 1914. Dental death details in *Tombstone Weekly Epitaph,* November 8, 1891. Herring's first arrival in Tucson, from New York, *Arizona Daily Star,* March 4, 1880. Photos of both Heath's revolver and saddle are in Grasse, *Bisbee Massacre.* The saddle can be seen in the Arizona State Museum in Tucson and the revolver at the Desert Caballeros Museum in Wickenburg, Arizona. Research visit July 2021, Mary and David D. de Haas, MD. *Tombstone Daily Epitaph,* May 22, 1892 (Warnekros in California). *Tombstone Weekly Epitaph,* May 3, 1893 (Warnekros in Mexico). Also, thank you to Australian author and Tombstone historian Peter Brand (email discussions February 1, 2022, with coauthor DdH) for pointing out the proper details of the Warnekros dental mishap and providing this resource; Ron Woggon and Jean Smith, *Cochise County Historical Journal,* Spring-Summer 2021.

121   *Bisbee Daily Review,* December 9, 1917, Copper Queen; *Los Angeles Times,* May 27, 1910, death notice; National Archives, Soldiers' Home files, Herring. Chaput and de Haas, *The Earps Invade Southern California.*

122   Good details appear in *Arizona Sentinel,* July 19, 1879. Ben T. Traywick, *Tombstone's Boothill* (Red Marie's Bookstore), 1971/1994, 8-12.

123   Roberts, *Doc Holliday: The Life and Legend.* Karen Holliday-Tanner, *Doc Holliday: A Family Portrait* (Norman: University of Oklahoma Press, 1998).

124   Ad, Hooker & Bauer, *Tombstone Epitaph,* October 19, 1880. Many Hooker family details and sources can be found in Bailey and Chaput, *Cochise County Stalwarts.* Lynn R. Bailey, *Henry Clay Hooker and the Sierra Bonita* (Tucson, Arizona: Westernlore Press, 1998). Chaput and de Haas, MD, "The Earp Fellow Sophisticates," *Wild West Magazine,* October 2021, 64- 69.

125   Obituary in *Los Angeles Herald,* September 16, 1890. Because of his legal career, and a bitter divorce suit in Los Angeles, the California newspapers carried much news about Howard.

126   Richard Dillon, *Wells Fargo Detective: James B. Hume (*New York: Coward-McCann, 1969). Robert Chandler presents good material on Tombstone and Wells Fargo in Young, Roberts, *Wyatt Earp Anthology,* 2019. For the theft of Hume's revolvers, *Tombstone Epitaph,* January 9, 1882. See also Chaput, "Fred Dodge: Undercover Agent, or Con Man?" *NOLA Quarterly,* XXV (January-March 2000).

127   In addition to the standard legal publications, there are a few interesting Hunsaker letters to, from, and about the Earps in the Stuart Lake Papers, Huntington Library. Chaput and de Haas, MD, *The Earps Invade Southern California.* An obituary of his father, Nicholas, is in the *Tombstone Epitaph,* September 21, 1913. Chaput and de Haas, MD, "The Earp Fellow Sophisticates," *Wild West Magazine,* October 2021, 64-69.

128   Tucson and Tombstone newspapers covered this in detail. Chaput, *Dr. Goodfellow,* 1996; Metz, *Encyclopedia of Lawmen,* 2002. Breakenridge, *Helldorado: Bringing Law to the Mesquite.* Boessenecker, *Ride the Devil's Herd,* 367-370, 378-379.

129   The interesting career of Hurst in the West can easily be followed in National Archives, U. S., Returns from Military Posts. He died on January 24, 1896, and is buried in Camptown, Pennsylvania.

130   Because of the Bird Cage connections, Hutchinson's name appears frequently. A good starting place is Clair Eugene Wilson, *Mimes and Miners: A Historical Study of the Theater in Tombstone* (Bulletin, University of Arizona, January 1935). Jane Eppinga, *Tombstone,* 2010. Ross, *Street Crime in America,* 2013. Agnew, *Entertainment in the Old West,* 2014. Collins, *Arizona on Stage,* 2015. Hendricks, *Haunted Histories in America,* 2020. *Kansas City Times,* July 24, 1882; *Tucson Citizen,* July 24, 1882; *Arizona Daily Star* (Tucson), August 18, 1882; *Tombstone Weekly Epitaph,* September 16, 1882; *The Daily Tombstone,* February 19, 1886; *Arizona Sentinel,* February 27, 1886. Discussions with Bird Cage/Hutchinson biographer Michael Mihaljevich (January 18, 2022; February 14-15, 2022), who has done extensive research over many years on all relating to the Bird Cage Theatre, for his upcoming book on the topic, and has provided the authors with important details here (including correct opening date of Bird Cage); however, he doesn't quite share the authors' assessment of the clientele and acts showcased at the early (1881 – 1882) Bird Cage. Please see his upcoming *WWHA Journal* article and book for much more important detail. Things definitely went downhill after the Hutchinsons sold the theatre in mid-1883.

131   He published *Railway Economics* in 1901, mostly about freight equipment.

132   *Los Angeles Times,* March 24, 1931. Chaput and de Haas, *The Earps Invade Southern California.*

133   There is a useful biographical file on Jackson in the Arizona Historical Society. Matthew Bernstein, "The Buffalo-Bone Cane Mystery," *Wild West Magazine,* Winter 2023, 66–71.

134   The Jacobs family interests can easily be followed in the standard banking and financial literature. Lionel was fluent in Spanish. For example, a full-page ad appeared in *El Tucsonense*, November 16, 1920, containing a list of the services of the Bank of Arizona, as well as some of the history of the Jacobs family. Mary and David D. de HaasMD, with Donna Dycus and Alisha Dycus Long, research visit July 2021. For Tombstone's second bank, Dawn Theresa Santiago, *The Banking Operations of Lionel and Barron Jacobs, Tucson, Arizona, 1867-1913*, Master's thesis, 1988). University of Arizona, Tucson, Arizona; and Safford, Hudson & Co., opened July 1, 1880, source, *Arizona Weekly Citizen*, July 3, 1880; quotes *Nugget*, states Clapp at bank door, July 1.

135   A recent study is by Doug Hocking, *Tom Jeffords: Friend of Cochise* (Helena, MT: Two Dot Books, 2017). Censuses and voting registers. *Arizona Republican*, February 24, 1914, has a three-column obituary, in which there is no mention of Tombstone, but much about the Apaches and Cochise. Shillingberg, *Tombstone, A.T.: A History of Early Mining, Milling, and Mayhem*. Paul Andrew Hutton, *The Apache Wars* (Crown, 1916).

136   Inquest and articles on posses are in the Tombstone and Tucson newspapers of March and April 1882. The best source is Peter Brand, "Wyatt Earp, Jack Johnson, and the Notorious Blount Brothers," *NOLA Quarterly*, October-December 2003. Brand makes the strong argument that Johnson did not go by the name "Turkey Creek" in his Tombstone years. Peter Brand and David D. de Haas email discussions 6/11/2021. Chaput and de Haas, MD, *The Earps Invade Southern California*.

137   The Jones name appears in most O. K. Corral and early Tombstone accounts. His gunplay in Phoenix is in *Weekly Arizona Miner*, May 16, 1879. A good account of the Justice Reilly confrontation is in the *Arizona Daily Star*, August 19, 1880. Details of the ups and downs of Jones are in *The Arizona Champion*, November 1, 1884, and *San Francisco Examiner*, October 11, 1884. The Behan-Jones-Sadie information is in Kirschner, *Lady at the O. K. Corral*. An obituary is in *Colusa Herald*, February 8, 1923.

138   The public nature of his Tombstone years makes it easy to follow. Demattos and Parsons, *They Called Him Buckskin Frank*, have many details regarding Joyce, both in Arizona and California. Multiple discussions with historian and Frank Leslie/Milt Joyce biographer Wayne Sanderson (2019-2021). Peter Brand, *The Story of Johnny Tyler* (Meadowbank, Australia, 2018).

139   He appears in the various voting registers in California, the census of 1920, and the California Death Index. Several of his surveying contracts around Tombstone are in the files of the Bureau of Land Management. His moves to Tucson and Tombstone are in *Arizona Weekly Citizen*, January 24, 1880. *Tombstone Weekly Epitaph*, February 24, 1882, his advice on the sewer situation. Schillingberg, *Tombstone*, 2015, mentions his attitude towards those involved in the Tombstone townsite controversy. Useful obituary in *Long Beach Telegram*, October 24, 1922, which makes no mention of his Tombstone years.

140   *Los Angeles Herald*, May 23, 1878, Lucky Baldwin ad; September 10, 1879, Internal Revenue job; voting register, Tombstone, 1881; *Arizona Daily Star*, August 6, 1880; census of 1880, Tombstone; *Arizona Quarterly Illustrated*, ad, July 1880; biography and illustration, April 1881; *Tombstone Epitaph*, May 1, 1882, house sale to Goodrich; Los Angeles directories, 1890s; *Los Angeles Herald*, May 11, 1897, obituary, biography, death details. The shootout details, and Ike

Clanton in Kelly's Wine House, are well summarized in *Wild West*, October 2006 and in Shillingberg. *Arizona Weekly Citizen*, December 23, 1880, for Kelly's (new) Wine House on Allen Street. *Los Angeles Herald* (from *Tombstone Nugget*), September 14, 1880, for Kelly's sale of his Fremont Street Wine House in favor of his "extensive...large patronage," Allen Street location. See also maps, Rita Ackerman, Gary McLelland.

141   His career is easily followed in the Tucson and Tombstone newspapers. *Tombstone Epitaph*, May 10, 1893, Kinnear divorce, has family information; *Arizona Republican*, September 11, 1916, is a detailed obituary.

142   *Tucson Citizen*, December 11, 1881, Laing losses in Tombstone hotel fire; April 22, 1885, stamp mill in Sonora; *Tombstone Daily Epitaph*, May 28, 1886, Grand Central fire; *Los Angeles Evening Express*, November 7, 1895, legacy from London; *San Diego Union*, August 27, 1889, Laing advertisement. *Hilo Daily Tribune*, February 27, 1906.

143   John D. Rose has written a book and articles on the Le Van shady career, based on solid documentation and research; some of this can be seen in Young, Roberts, et al, *Wyatt Earp Anthology*, 2019. Many works about or treating of the Spicer hearings also carry Le Van information. Much of his mining claims and legal hassles are in the Cochise County Recorder's files; California Death Index.

144   There is a growing literature about Leavy's Western career. The mining and water rights documents are in the Cochise County Recorder's office.

145   DeMattos and Parsons, *They Called Him Buckskin Frank*. Chaput, *"Buckskin Frank" Leslie*. Traywick, *Tombstone's "Buckskin Frank": Nashville Franklyn Leslie*. Chaput and de Haas, MD, "The Earp Fellow Sophisticates," *Wild West Magazine*, October 2021, 64-69. Serious research is still being carried out regarding Buckskin Frank (especially by historian/Leslie biographer Wayne Sanderson), a major Tombstone personality.

146   Obituary in *Mohave County Miner*, April 10, 1897.

147   Census of 1920, Alameda County, California; California Death Index.

148   Robert K. DeArment wrote a dozen articles and books on Masterson's career. The posse information is in Young, Roberts et al, *Wyatt Earp Anthology*, 2019. Robert K. DeArment, *Bat Masterson: The Man and the Legend* (Norman: University of Oklahoma Press, 1979). Chaput and de Haas, *The Earps Invade Southern California*, xv, 191, 192.

149   He has frequent mentions in the Tombstone literature of the 1880s; a biography is in Bailey and Chaput, *Cochise County Stalwarts*.

150   Ads for the foundry business appeared for decades in the Tombstone and Los Angeles newspapers. Funeral service notice for McCone is in *Los Angeles Herald*, October 28, 1920.

151   *Tombstone Weekly Epitaph*, September 30, 1906, May 9, 1909; *Arizona Daily Star*, May 7, 1909. *Arizona Republic*, April 16, 1898, Black Diamond; *Bisbee Daily News*, February 5, 1905, Russelville.

152   The best starting point into the voluminous literature is Paul Lee Johnson, *The McLaurys in Tombstone, Arizona* (University of North Texas Press); Silva, *Wyatt Earp: A Biography of the Legend*. Also Fattig, *Wyatt Earp: The Biography*); Boessenecker., *Wyatt Earp's Epic Battle Against the West's Biggest Outlaw Gang*; Gary L. Roberts, *Doc Holliday: The Life and Legend*. Michael M. Hickey, *Street fight in Tombstone: Near the O.K. Corral* trilogy (Honolulu, Hawaii: Talei Publishers, 1991).

153   Vendetta literature is extensive, and confusing. Anything by Peter Brand is solid; his "Wyatt Earp's Vendetta Posse," *Wild West*, April 2007, is well researched, and there are mentions in Young and Roberts, *Wyatt Earp Anthology*.

154   Thanks to Roy Young for clarifying the documentation of the many John Meaghers. Cowtown Publications has much on the Meagher brothers. Oriental Saloon fire, *Daily Nugget*, October 12, 1881; surety for Doc Holiday, *Weekly Arizona Miner*, July 15, 1881. *Tombstone Epitaph*, April 2, 1886, Anti-Chinese League, April 20, 1886; big bet, *Tombstone Epitaph*, July 7, 1888, swindling; *Tombstone Daily Prospector*, November 14, 1890, Sheriff's Sale, Dr. Goodfellow and details, February 11, 1889, Meagher now in Seattle; *Seattle Post-Intelligencer*, December 13, 1891, bogus checks, July 18, 1895, lottery raid. Detailed information on this John G. Meagher is in his Probate File, King County, Washington, some sixty pages spread out from 1909 through 1911. The Los Angeles newspapers of January 1933 have many articles on son Henry. *The Daily News*, January 24, 1933, headlined "Many Friends at Bootlegger's Rites."

155   Mehan is mentioned in most of the shootout literature. His obituary is in the *Albuquerque Journal* of November 9, 1892. A handy summary of his role in the Warren District legal troubles can be found in *Mining Science*, April 1913. This case eventually went to the U. S. Supreme Court.

156   Census and voting registers; *Weekly Arizona Miner*, July 15, 1881, Doc Holiday; *Tombstone Epitaph*, February 26, 1911, list of chloriders; *Engineering & Mining Journal-Press*, June 16, 1923, end of Tombstone mining; Arizona State Board of Health, death certificate. *Daily Tombstone*, November 16, 1885, assessment work; December 23, 1885, owns the Oriental; *Tucson Citizen*, May 5, 1883, Elite Saloon in Tucson; *Arizona State Miner*, April 10, 1926, son working concentrator.

157   Chaput and de Haas, MD, *The Earps Invade Southern California*, 188.

158   Censuses and voting registers, as well as the widespread hotel literature of California. A photo and decent biography appear in *Los Angeles Herald*, May 11, 1910; see also *Who's Who in the Pacific Southwest*, 1913; California Death Index. For Bilicke in L. A. see Chaput and de Haas, MD, *The Earps Invade Southern California*, and "The Earp Fellow Sophisticates," *Wild West Magazine*, October 2021, 64- 69.

159   His name and the O. K. Corral permeate Tombstone literature. A biography is in Bailey and Chaput, *Cochise County Stalwarts*; *Tombstone Prospector*, May 26, 1909.

160   Census and voting registers of Nevada and Arizona have Moses entries, and Capital Saloon ads appeared in the *Epitaph* throughout 1882. Service on the shootout jury is mentioned in *Tucson Citizen*, November 6, 1881, copied from the *Tombstone Nugget*. National Archives, Soldiers' Home files, sheet for Thomas Moses. Chaput and de Haas, MD, *The Earps Invade Southern California*. Wyatt Earp literature carries mentions of the Clancy-Seattle connections. The Seattle census of 1900 lists the widow Catherine Moses as a member of the John Clancy household. Good example of the "continuum" of life. Good comments on the Moses and Clancy links are in Shillingberg, *Tombstone, A.T.* The *Seattle Post-Intelligencer* of February 1, 1900, mentions both Clancy and Earp in an article regarding gambling houses. The *Evening Statesman* (Walla Walla) of October 29, 1903, had several of the Clancys arrested for gambling in Seattle, still at the old game.

161   Details of the telegram are in *Weekly Republican*, January 22, 1885, and *Weekly Arizona Miner*, January 23, 1885.

162   Sources abound on the Nadeau career. One could start with several works by his namesake descendant, historian Remi Nadeau. Chaput and de Haas, MD, "The Earp Fellow Sophisticates," *Wild West Magazine*, October 2021, 64-69.

163   Frontier, Tombstone, and gambling literature carry many Napa Nick comments. The obituary in *Bisbee Daily Review*, November 2, 1917, also included the phrase "Knight of the Green Cloth."

164   Chaput and de Haas, MD, *The Earps Invade Southern California*, 75. Robert K. DeArment, *Knights of the Green Cloth: The Saga of the Frontier Gamblers* (Norman, Oklahoma: The University of Oklahoma Press, 1982). Chaput and de Haas, MD, "The Earp Fellow Sophisticates," *Wild West Magazine*, October 2021, 64-69.

165   Obituary in *Los Angeles Herald*, February 5, 1910.

166   Obituary in *Los Angeles Herald*, November 19, 1893.

167   Dale Walker, *Rough Rider: Buckey O'Neill of Arizona* (University of Nebraska Press, 1975). Bradley G. Courtney, "The Pride of Prescott," *Tombstone Epitaph National Edition*, March 2021. *Tombstone Epitaph National Edition*, October 2022, p. 2.

168   Fattig, *Wyatt Earp*, 241 – 245. The Tucson and Tombstone newspapers covered the event in detail, and there is no mention of Wyatt. There are some references to the event in Young, Roberts et al, *Wyatt Earp Anthology*. Stuart N. Lake, *Wyatt Earp: Frontier Marshal*, 1931. Breakenridge, *Helldorado: Bringing Law to the Mesquite*. For Allie Earp reference, see Frank Waters, *The Earp Brothers of Tombstone: The Story of Mrs. Virgil Earp* (New York: Clarkson N. Potter, Inc., 1960).

169   The Palmer California doings are well covered in Gold Rush literature. For his early role in Tombstone there is a useful summary in Shillingberg, *Tombstone, A. T.*

170   Most of what is known of her can be found in Bailey and Chaput, *Cochise County Stalwarts*.

171   California Death Index.

172   The important diaries, which also include decades of Los Angeles doings, are in the Arizona Historical Society. He received frequent notices in the press of Tombstone and Los Angeles, as well as in the regional and national mining journals. There are several published editions of the Tombstone-era diaries. Chaput and de Haas, MD, *The Earps Invade Southern California*. Chaput and de Haas, MD, "The Earp Fellow Sophisticates," *Wild West Magazine*, October 2021, 64-69.

173   Sources abound for the Parsons career. Some Tombstone-related comments are in *Engineering & Mining Journal*, December 6, 1884, and Shillingberg, *Tombstone*, 43-44. Two detailed obituaries are in *San Francisco Chronicle*, April 21, 1911, and *Weekly Journal-Miner* (Prescott), April 26, 1911.

174   As an example of his Southern California interests, in 1905 in Los Angeles he incorporated the American Swiss Commercial Company; Incorporation Files, Natural History Museum, Los Angeles.

175   John Boessenecker, *When Law Was in the Holster*, 2012. The best linking of Paul with Tombstone is the article by John Boessenecker in Young, Roberts et al, *Wyatt Earp Anthology*. Roy B. Young, *Robert Havlin Paul: Frontier Lawman, The Arizona Years* (Apache, Oklahoma: Young and Sons Enterprises, 2009).

176   Chaput and de Haas, MD, "The Earp Fellow Sophisticates," *Wild West Magazine*, October 2021, 64-69. S. J. Reidhead, *A Church for Helldorado* (Roswell, New Mexico: Jinglebob Press, 2006).

ENDNOTES

177　California and Arizona censuses and voting registers. *Morning Press* (Santa Barbara), August 15, 1874; *Arizona Daily Star,* November 20, 1879, arrives in Tombstone; *Tucson Citizen,* September 4, 1880, arrested by Wyatt Earp; *Tombstone Epitaph,* April 24, 1882.

178　His name was variously spelled Bryant or Bryan. He is easily followed in the voting registers of Arizona and California. Good details of the murder of his son Martin are in *Arizona Daily Star,* March 31, 1882, and the *Los Angeles Times,* March 28, 1882. The *Los Angeles Evening Express* has a note on Peel's death in Alhambra in the issue of September 28, 1897. Boessenecker, *Ride the Devils Herd: Wyatt Earp's Epic Battle Against the West's Biggest Outlaw Gang,* 367- 370, 378- 379. Breakenridge, *Helldorado: Bringing Law to the Mesquite.*

179　For links between Kelleher and Peel, see detailed obituary in *Los Angeles Herald,* March 28, 1882. A good summary of the botched robbery and the killing of Martin is in Boessenecker, *Ride the Devil's Herd.*

180　*Tombstone Epitaph,* March 16-17, 1881; Chaput, *Dr. Goodfellow.* Orantes dead, *Arizona Sentinel,* August 19, 1882. Brother in from Mexico, *Tombstone Weekly Epitaph,* September 18, 1882.

181　Censuses and voting records; *Arizona Weekly Star,* December 13, 1888, details of the Lincoln assassination; Arizona State Board of Health, death certificate.

182　Funeral details are in *Idaho Daily Statesman,* September 14, 1907.

183　*Los Angeles Herald,* January 5, 1914, funeral notice.

184　*Arizona Daily Citizen,* May 5, 1898, obituary with some biographical details.

185　Biography and sources are in Bailey and Chaput, *Cochise County Stalwarts.* The Tombstone bonanza era sources have considerable mention of Randall.

186　The research problem with Justice Reilly is the abundance of information. All Earp and Tombstone histories have material on this firebrand.

187　The quote is from *Washington Post* (DC), January 31, 1910, and similar articles appeared throughout the country. *Tombstone Epitaph,* July 21, 1901; Arizona State Board of Health, death certificate.

188　Biography and sources are in Bailey & Chaput, *Cochise County Stalwarts,* 2000.

189　DeArment, *Knights of the Green Cloth.* Chaput and de Haas, MD, *The Earps Invade Southern California.* Chaput and de Haas, MD, "The Earp Fellow Sophisticates," *Wild West Magazine,* October 2021, 64- 69. *Arizona Daily Star* (Tucson), September 15, 1885, and *Clifton Clarion,* September 30, 1885, for Tucson gunfight.

190　Several points of view can be found in Young, Roberts et al, *Wyatt Earp Anthology.* Steve Gatto, *Johnny Ringo* (Protar Houser, 2002). Michael M. Hickey, *John Ringo: The Final Hours* (Talei Publishers, 1995). Jack Burrows, *John Ringo: The Gunfighter Who Never Was* (Tucson, Az: University of Arizona Press, 1987). David Johnson, *John Ringo: King of the Cowboys, Second Ed.* (Denton, TX: University of North Texas Press, 2008).

191　Mentioned frequently in the Tombstone newspapers. *Arizona Weekly Star,* July 13, 1893, jailing the jailer; *Tombstone Epitaph,* September 16, 1906, funeral ceremony. de Haas, MD, "Revisiting the O. K. Corral Fire Aftermath Photo," *Wild West Magazine,* April 2016, 11.

192　Early Tombstone literature has extensive coverage of Ritter. *Tombstone Prospector,* April 29, 1899, obituary.

193   Chaput and de Haas, MD, "The Earp Fellow Sophisticates," *Wild West Magazine,* October 2021, 64- 69.

194   The career of this wandering journalist is easy to follow. *Tombstone Prospector,* September 28, 1908, obituary.

195   The sources on this fellow are enormous, including mining, politics, government, high finance, in Arizona Territory and other Western locales, as well as important business and land interests in Florida. For Tombstone's second bank, see Dawn Theresa Santiago, *The Banking Operations of Lionel and Barron Jacobs, Tucson, Arizona, 1867-1913;* and Safford, Hudson & Co., opened July 1, 1880, source, *Arizona Weekly Citizen,* July 3, 1880; quotes *Nugget,* states Clapp at bank door, July 1.

196   The sources on the Schieffelin brothers are many, but the saga is well presented in R. Bruce Craig, *Portrait of a Prospector: Edward Schieffelin's Own Story* (Norman: University of Oklahoma Press, 2017). *Los Angeles Times,* October 14, 1885, for Al's death.

197   The Hearst, Haggin, and Homestake literature has frequent coverage of Sevenoaks. *Tombstone Epitaph,* April 10, 1882, Turquoise District for Hearst; *Arizona Weekly Citizen,* September 17, 1882, "duel." January 25, 1890, drunk in Yuma; *The Californian,* February 27, 1897, obituary.

198   The *Tombstone Weekly Epitaph* of April 10, 1882, had good coverage of the local activities, as did the *Tucson Citizen* of April 16, 1882. The obituary in the *Daily Alta California,* March 1, 1891, is also a useful biography. Chaput and de Haas, MD, "The Earp Fellow Sophisticates," *Wild West Magazine, October 2021,* 64-69.

199   The long public career of Shibbell is easy to follow. For the Harqua Hala excitement see Chaput, *Empire of Sand,* 2015.

200   Luke Short material appears in many gunfighter and gambling publications. For some Tombstone doings, see *Tucson Citizen,* February 27, 1881, and *Arizona Weekly Citizen,* March 6, 1881. Jack DeMattos and Chuck Parsons, *The Notorious Luke Short* (Denton, Texas: University of North Texas Press, 2015). Tombstone/Earp historian/researcher Peter Brand, email conversation February 16, 2022. Peter Brand, *Johnny Tyler: Doc Holliday's Nemesis,* 2018, 162- 172. Please see also Peter's award-winning 2017 *Wild West History Association Journal* article for much more on the Luke Short/Charlie Storms animosity, and Chaput, *Dr. Goodfellow: Physician to the Gunfighters,* 31.

201   The Wells Spicer hearings are available in many formats. Good information about the Sills role is in Young, Roberts et al, *Wyatt Earp Anthology.*

202   Sippy is mentioned in most Tombstone histories. Peter Brand, *Journal of the Wild West History Association,* issues September and December 2020, Volume XIII, Numbers 3/4. Troy Kelley, "Tombstone's Unknown Marshal," *WOLA Journal,* Winter 2003, Volume XI, number 4. Fattig, *Wyatt Earp: The Biography,* 286, 287. Email discussion between Peter Brand and coauthor de Haas, February 1, 2022.

203   His long career in regional and national politics led to considerable coverage in Western newspapers; a good example is his obituary in *Salt Lake Tribune,* April 9, 1924.

204   Obituary, *Arizona Republican,* November 30, 1907.

205   Details of the suit, concerning a hardware store (tools, equipment, etc.) are in *Daily Alta California,* January 15, 1886.

206 Information provided by descendant Jeff Smith and researcher Peter Brand, who surfaced the *Tombstone Nugget* of January 27, 1882; Jeff Smith, *Alias Soapy Smith: Life and Death of a Scoundrel* (Klondike Research, 2009). DeArment, *Knights of the Green Cloth*. Jeff Smith (great grandson of Soapy Smith) via Wild West Collectors Facebook page February 26, 2021, moderated by co-author de Haas, MD.

207 Obituary, *Los Angeles Herald*, December 24, 1901. Roberts, *Doc Holliday: The Life and Legend*. Chaput and de Haas, MD, "The Earp Fellow Sophisticates," *Wild West Magazine*, October 2021, 64- 69.

208 There is considerable coverage of Sorin in many Tucson and Tombstone publications. A biography is in Bailey and Chaput, *Cochise County Stalwarts*. Jane Eppinga, *Southern Arizona Cemeteries* (Charleston, S. C.: Arcadia Publishing, 2014).

209 National Archives, Soule file, Soldiers' Home, Los Angeles; California Death Index. Chaput/de Haas, *The Earps Invade Southern California*.

210 For several decades the Spangenberg career in Seattle can be easily followed, as he advertised widely in several local newspapers. Travel with Schieffelin brothers, *The San Francisco Chronicle*, November 3, 1883, and *The San Francisco Examiner*, October 7, 1883, 8.

211 A key figure in the troubles of 1881-82, Spence gets considerable coverage. *Arizona Silver Belt*, April 2, 1910, marriage; *Arizona Republic*, February 3, 1914, brief obituary. Roy B. Young, *Pete Spence: Audacious Artist in Crime* (Apache, Oklahoma: Young and Sons Enterprises, July 2000). For Clifton saloon gunfight - *Clifton Clarion*, June 20, 1888.

212 Bailey and Chaput, *Cochise County Stalwarts: A Who's Who of the Territorial Years*, Volume II. Chaput and de Haas, MD, *The Earps Invade Southern California*. Lynn R. Bailey, *A Tale of the "Unkilled": The Life, Times, and Writings of Wells W. Spicer* (Tucson, Arizona: Westernlore Press, 1999).

213 The Springer career can easily be followed in the Tombstone newspapers and in banking publications. The *Evening World* (New York), September 12, 1892, carried an article as well as an illustration of Edna.

214 In all Earp and Tombstone literature. Basic details and inquest are in *Arizona Daily Star*, March 25, 1882, and *Tombstone Epitaph*, March 27, 1882. For Morgan Earp murder see above listed Earp books and especially Roy B. Young, "Who Killed Morgan Earp? The Atrocious Assassins," *Journal of the Wild West History Association*, Volume XIII, Number 4, December 2020, 7- 44. See also Young's WWHA YouTube video.

215 Jack's time in Tombstone and Tucson is mentioned in *Arizona Daily Star*, April 30, 1882; a good summary of Jack's career is by Roy Young, "The West's Forgotten Scout," *True West*, March 2015. Roy Young also created an interesting Wild West History Association YouTube video where he clarifies some of the roles of the Stilwell brothers in the Tombstone/Earp saga of the early 1880s, and Frank's murder of Morgan Earp. *Journal of the Wild West History Association*, Volume XIII, Number 4, December 2020, 7- 44.

216 *Arizona Daily Star*, Nov 10, 1882. Roy Young, *William H. Stilwell, Bench & Bar in Arizona Territory* (Apache, OK: Young & Sons, 2011). Roberts, *Doc Holliday*, 241, 245, has good Tombstone details. The court system is explained by Acting Governor Gosper in *Tombstone Weekly Epitaph*, December 19, 1881. The Tombstone Mill & Mining case is 25 PAC 794 (1883). The Tucson incident is in Roy Young, "The Assassination of Frank Stilwell," *WWHA Journal*, August 2008. *Tucson Citizen*,

October 15, 1882. *Democrat and Chronicle* (Rochester, New York), October 28, 1882, for presidential sweep of Arizona officials. Chuck Hornung, *Wyatt Earp's Cowboy Campaign,* 2016, for "mesquite" comment.

217   *Arizona Republican,* September 22, 1908, obituary with photograph. The townsite issue is reported in *Tucson Citizen,* September 19, 1885, and *Tombstone Daily Epitaph,* February 6, 1886.

218   *Daily Tombstone,* February 13, 1886, plaintiff; *Tombstone Daily Prospector,* January 10, 1889, robbery; *Mohave County Miner,* May 28, 1892, her mining claims; details of her death and worth are in *Tombstone Epitaph,* November 21, 1915, *Bisbee Daily Review,* November 17, November 23, 1915.

219   Census of 1920 for San Diego. The *Bisbee Daily Review* of September 16, 1909, mentioned his recent marriage and his past careers around Tombstone.

220   Peter Brand, "Wyatt Earp's Vendetta Posse," *Wild West,* April 2007, and Young/Roberts, *Wyatt Earp Anthology.* The saloon fight and many mentions of Tipton appear in many issues of the Tombstone and Tucson newspapers, but the reports are confusing. Tombstone/Earp historian/researcher Peter Brand, email conversation February 16, 2022. Peter Brand, *Johnny Tyler,* 173.

221   She and her children were occasionally mentioned in the local press. The *Tombstone Epitaph* of March 11, 1886, mentioned the Chinese episode; *Daily Tombstone,* March 5, 1887, she takes over the Russ House again; *Tombstone Daily Prospector,* July 30, 1890, ad for her restaurant in Bisbee. The family history site, Ancestry.com, has a detailed presentation of her family, their weddings and funerals, and places of residence.

222   Early Tombstone literature has many references to the family. Bailey and Chaput, *Cochise County Stalwarts,* contains many sources on the Tribolets.

223   Career is easily followed in the standard political and financial sources. *Arizona Weekly Citizen,* January 22, 1881, Grand Central South; Tombstone *Epitaph,* March 24, 1881, office in Tombstone.

224   A good quick source is Ben Traywick, *Wyatt Earp's Thirteen Dead Men* (Tombstone; Red Marie's Bookstore, 1998), which includes the *Nugget* and *Epitaph* articles. The standard Tombstone, Wyatt Earp, and Doc Holliday literature include the Tyler-Tombstone incidents. Interesting, detailed obituaries are *Spokane Falls Review,* January 22, 1891, and *San Francisco Chronicle,* January 22, 1891. Peter Brand, *Doc Holliday's Nemesis: The Story of Johnny Tyler & Tombstone's Gambler* War (Meadowbank, Australia: Peter Brand, 2018), 182-183 (Earp confrontation), 281- 282 (death). DeArment, *Knights of the Green Cloth* (Norman, Oklahoma: University of Oklahoma Press, 1982), 103. Roberts, *Doc Holliday,* 152- 153. Email discussion coauthor de Haas with Johnny Tyler biographer Peter Brand, January 30, 2022.

225   He is in the various voting registers and censuses of Arizona and California. *Arizona Weekly Citizen,* December 11, 1880, mine agent. Many documents of the Winchester District include the role of Upton. *Tucson Citizen,* March 26, 1882, Morgan Earp inquest. *Los Angeles Evening Post,* December 8, 1896, great success at Randsburg, and role of Goodrich. *Sacramento Star,* March 7, 1912, death notice. *Bakersfield Morning Echo,* December 24, 1912, sale of Upton property.

226   Vendetta literature has many mentions of him. Some specific Vermillion (Texas Jack) notices are in *Tombstone Weekly Epitaph,* March 27, 1882, Florentino Cruz; April 3, 1882, Burleigh Springs (Iron Springs) incident with Curly Bill. Peter Brand, *Wyatt Earp's Vendetta Posse Rider: The Story of Texas Jack Vermillion*

(Meadowbank, Australia: Peter Brand, 2012). E-mail discussions with Vermillion biographer Peter Brand, clarifying the John Oberland Vermillion (the "real" Texas Jack) and John Wilson Vermillion confusion (for years wrongly believed, and wrongly purported by authors to be "Texas Jack"—but not), which has plagued biographers for years; January 29 and 30, 2022. Please see the appendix of his book, and also award winning *WWHA Journal* article (August 2010; Number 4), in which he first published his groundbreaking research findings.

227   *Los Angeles Times*, December 30, 1912, obituary with photo; much is made in the article that Vickers died at home of apoplexy while playing dominoes.

228   Death notice in *San Francisco Call*, April 18, 1907.

229   Obituary, *Arizona Weekly Citizen*, August 5, 1885. *Tombstone Weekly Epitaph*, July 29, 1882. *Tombstone Daily Nugget*, June 1881. For much more detail about the confusing Crystal Palace situation and its iterations ("three different Crystal Palace saloons at three different locations operated by three different owners") please see Silva, *Wyatt Earp: A Biography of the Legend* [Vol. II, Part 1], especially pages 347, 352, 353, and 541 (footnote 54).

230   Although Vosburg gets good coverage in most works about early Tombstone, the best sources for his later decades are in the Los Angeles and Pasadena newspapers, as well as in the Incorporation Records, Natural History Museum, Los Angeles. For George Parsons, see Chaput and de Haas, MD, "The Earp Fellow Sophisticates," *Wild West Magazine*, October 2021; Chaput and de Haas, MD, *The Earps Invade Southern California*.

231   Voting Registers and censuses, California and Arizona. Most literature on Tombstone in the bonanza era will have information on Walker; California Death Index. His role is summarized in Hayostek, *Western Legal History*, 2014.

232   Death notice in *Los Angeles Times*, May 13, 1895.

233   Good biographical information about Ward can be found in David Grasse, *The Bisbee Massacre* (Jefferson, N.C.: McFarland & Co., 2017). Troy Kelley, *Bisbee Massacre*, self-published booklet.

234   Thousands of documents in the Cochise County Recorder's Office; *Los Angeles Times*, July 7, 1912, his Gleeson mining; *Bisbee Daily Review*, November 8, 1922, obituary. Email discussions between Australia based Tombstone historian Peter Brand and coauthor de Haas; February 1 and 2, 2022. Ron Woggon and Jean Smith, *Cochise County Historical Journal*, Spring-Summer 2021 (for brother's dental mishap).

235   *Tombstone Epitaph*, July 23, 24, 28, 1880; *Tombstone Nugget*, July 24, 29, 1880; *Arizona Weekly Citizen*, July 24, 1880; *Weekly Republican* (Phoenix, Arizona), July 23, 1880.

236   Death records in the Arizona Board of Health. The ad for the Watt & Tarbell undertaking business appear in the *Tombstone Epitaph* throughout 1887-1888. A specific contract for the Sonora Copper Company is mentioned in the *Oasis*, June 10, 1911.

237   Obituary, *Bisbee Daily Review*, August 4, 1904. David D. de Haas, MD, "Revisiting the O. K. Corral Fire Aftermath Photo," *Wild West Magazine*, April 2016.

238   This is a key event in the Earp-cowboy feud and was well covered in the Tucson and Tombstone press. Erwin, *The Truth about Wyatt Earp*, 2000, has a decent chapter on the incident. Boessenecker, *Ride the Devil's Herd*, 123.

239   He figures in all early accounts of Tombstone mining history. See also Bailey and Chaput, *Cochise County Stalwarts*; *San Francisco Examiner*, December 31, 1897; *San Francisco Call*, December 20,1898; *Oakland Tribune*, December 30,1898.

240   He died on December 15, 1904, and is buried in Arlington National Cemetery.

241   Cochise County Recorder's Office has many documents related to his mining claims. *Bisbee Daily Review*, July 2, 1910, obituary. Bilicke gunplay: Gus Bilicke and Charles Wilkes were arguing over costs, etc., regarding the Mountain Maid claim. Wilkes drew a revolver; young Albert, approaching the scene, saw this, whipped out his revolver and shot Wilkes in the head (not fatally). Town, etc., understood young Albert's deed and he was exonerated. Summary in Bailey and Chaput, *Cochise County Stalwarts*.

242   *Arizona Daily Star*, February 9, 1882, for the $8,000 comment. Marshall Williams, the Wells Fargo agent, cooked the books, etc. Probably headed towards Pennsylvania. The *Tucson Citizen*, Feb 12, 1882, said Williams left town, leaving folks "in the lurch." Many references to the incident in Young, Roberts et al, *Wyatt Earp Anthology*. Boessenecker, *Ride the Devil's Herd*.

243   A death notice appeared in the *Laredo Times*, April 26, 1890.

244   Obituary, *Sacramento Record-Union*, February 1, 1896.

245   There are a dozen or so articles on her in the May issues of the *Arizona Daily Star*. Other comments can be found in Chaput, *Dr. Goodfellow: Physician to the Gunfighters*. The *Mohave County Miner* of May 18, 1884, reported that May had visited with her mother recently in Tombstone; she was apparently on her way East "to locate permanently." David Grasse, "The Story of Mrs. May Woodman, Murderess," *The Tombstone Epitaph*, June 2022.

246   *Daily Record* (Long Branch, New Jersey), March 3, 1926.

247   The term, pretty much limited to greater Tombstone, probably became common because silver chloride was one of the leading ores of the district. See Thomas Egleston, *Metallurgy of Silver, Gold, and Mercury, Vol. I: Silver* (New York: John Wiley & Sons, 1887).

248   Clements, *After the Boom in Tombstone and Jerome* (2003). The word "chloriding" is usually confined to the American West. Throughout the world in that era, to describe a group of men working out an arrangement with a mining company was referred to as "tribute," e.g., "the mine was worked by tributers." Dozens of examples of this are in Horace J. Stevens, *Copper Handbook* (Houghton, MI: 1900-1912). This covered all copper mines of the world, and was subsequently named *Mines Handbook*, then *Mines Register*.

249   Foster's work is *A Treatise on Ore and Stone Mining* (London: Charles Griffin & Co., Ltd., 1905). The other particulars are from *Engineering & Mining Journal*, December 29, 1883; *Tucson Citizen*, December 22, 1883; *Mining & Scientific Press*, December 13, 1884.

250   Clipping in our possession, "NEW REDUCTION PROCESS," copied from the *Tombstone Democrat* of June 19, 1886. Gary Ledoux, *Nantan: The Life and Times of John P. Clum*, 2 vols (Victoria, BC: Trafford Publishing, 2007/2008). Woodworth Clum, *Apache Agent: The Story of John P. Clum* (Cambridge, Massachusetts: The Riverside Press, 1936).

251   "How Cyaniding Began at Tombstone," *Pacific Coast Miner*, May 2, 1903.

252   *Daily Tombstone*, May 27, 1886; *Tombstone Epitaph*, May 28, 1886; the papers of Tucson, Los Angeles, and San Francisco carried details of the disaster.

ENDNOTES

253 Kevin M. Britz, *The Arizona Mining Career of William F. Staunton, 1883-1931*. (Master's thesis, 1986). University of Arizona, Tucson, Arizona; Robert Fulton, "Millville-Charleston, Cochise County, 1878-1889," *Journal of Arizona History*, Vol. 7 (Spring, 1966).

254 Eric L. Clements, *After the Boom in Tombstone and Jerome, Arizona: Decline in Western Resource Towns* (Reno: University of Nevada Press, 2003). *Arizona Weekly Citizen* (Tucson), January 24, 1885. *The Tombstone Prospector*, April 7, 1887; thank you to Tombstone researcher/historian Michael Mihaljevich for pointing this out to the authors and providing this source.

255 Well-known lumber merchant L. W. Blinn was behind the scheme. Detailed articles on the Blinn Act are in *Tombstone Weekly Epitaph*, March 1, April 5, April 26, and May 3, 1890. Bailey, in *Tombstone, Arizona*, 2004, devotes considerable space to the ins-and-outs of the Blinn Act.

256 The *Annual Report, Director of the Mint* (Washington: GPO, 1897) contains a chart of the silver production of states and territories. The Mint reports from 1888 through 1897 indicate little change for Arizona's ranking, showing minimal impact of the Sherman Silver Purchase Act. Government tampering with metals production was considered in 1939, which led a senate subcommittee to summarize previous efforts, including the fiasco of the 1890s; *To Repeal the Silver Purchase Act of 1934; Hearings before the Subcommittee of the Committee on Banking and Currency* (U. S. Senate, 76th Cong., Washington: GPO, 1939). Thank you to historian Michael Mihaljevich for suggesting we emphasize this point.

257 Issue of November 1, 1900.

258 Don Chaput, *The Odyssey of Burt Alvord: Lawman, Train Robber, Fugitive* (Tucson: Westernlore Press, 2000). On August 27, 2021, Burt Alvord's Colt single-action army revolver sold at the Bonhams' Jim Earle auction in Los Angeles for $8,287.

259 For much more on Jones as one of the founders of Santa Monica, California please see Chaput and de Haas, MD, *The Earps Invade Southern California*. Well covered in Bailey, *Tombstone, Arizona*, 2010. The *Tombstone Prospector* of February 11, 1893, mentions the Aubury success with cyanide at the Mayflower Mine; Prescott's *Weekly Journal-Miner* of October 3, 1898, reports Aubury's organization of the Failings Concentration Co. *Tombstone Weekly Epitaph*, February 12, 1893. *Pacific Coast Miner*, "How Cyaniding Began at Tombstone," May 2, 1903.

260 DeArment, *Knights of the Green Cloth: The Saga of the Frontier Gamblers*. Chaput and de Haas, MD, *The Earps Invade Southern California*. Boessenecker, *Wyatt Earp's Epic Battle Against the West's Biggest Outlaw Gang*, 53-57. Roberts, *Doc Holliday: The Life and Legend*. There are dozens of entries for Bagg in the many voting registers in the counties he lived in Arizona and California. Bailey and Chaput, *Cochise County Stalwarts*. The father of Tombstone's S. C. (Stanley Chipman) Bagg was John Sherman Bagg, a big newspaper mogul in Detroit, Michigan. John's brother was Charles S. Bagg, who was a Mexican War veteran and Montana legislator, who spent his last years in the Old Soldiers' Home in Sawtelle, California. Charles had a son, Charles L. Bagg (a.k.a. the infamous Doc Baggs.

261   He may have mined for decades, but he mostly gets noticed for saloons and entertainment venues. For example, he gets attention in *Michael Rutter, Boudoirs to Brothers: The Intimate World of Wild West Women* (Helena, MT: Farcountry Press, 2014). *Tombstone Daily Epitaph,* January 12, 1886. *Tombstone Daily Epitaph,* February 7, 1886. *Tombstone Daily Epitaph,* March 16, 1886. Email February 14, 2022, Tombstone researcher/historian Michael Mihaljevich.

262   Biographies of both are in Bailey and Chaput, *Cochise County Stalwarts;* see also Ben Traywick, "The Czar of Charleston," *The West,* March 1970. Email discussion Peter Brand with coauthor de Haas; February 1, 2022.

263   Although most modern-day narratives are full of exaggeration and unsourced or based upon secondary sources, the most useful is by Ben Traywick, *Legendary Characters of Southern Arizona* (Tombstone: Red Marie Bookstore Publishers, 1992). The marriage is noted in *Bisbee Daily Review,* March 16, 1906, and some funeral details are in *Tombstone Weekly Epitaph,* December 23, 1906. Death records of China Mary (1906) and Ah Lum (1931) are in the Arizona State Board of Health. She was listed as Ah Lum (female, age 65).

264   *Arizona Republic,* April 12, 1898, appointed postmistress; *Tombstone Weekly Epitaph,* October 25, 1908, marriage.

265   Many of these high-profile cases had extensive newspaper coverage. *Who's' Who in Arizona,* 1913; *Coconino Sun,* October 31, 1924, obituary; Arizona State Board of Health, death certificate.

266   Newspaper mentions of Doyle abound. Some of his more memorable mentions are in Marshall Trimble, *Arizona Oddities* (Charleston, S. C.: History Pub., 2018).

267   His name is found in thousands of documents in the Cochise County Recorder's office; Bailey and Chaput, *Cochise County Stalwarts.*

268   In addition to the sketch in *Cochise County Stalwarts,* the additional data on Fitts is in the Massachusetts marriage records and in the census of 1910.

269   Articles on the suicide can be found in many of the nation's newspapers in May 1890. A typical example is in *Arizona Daily Citizen,* May 12, 1890. The son's suicide is mentioned in *Bisbee Daily Review,* May 10, 1904.

270   There are some comments about him in Young, Roberts et al, *Wyatt Earp Anthology.*

271   The Gees first moved to Tombstone on June 17, 1894, *Tombstone Weekly Epitaph,* June 17, 1894. In voting registers Henry was referred to as a "mining man." *Tombstone Epitaph,* June 24, 1894, Old Guard Mine; December 18, 1898, Schieffelin Hall, Mrs. Gee as pianist; there are dozens of articles and documents about the legal hassles of the estate in the 1906 Tombstone and Bisbee newspapers. *Bisbee Daily Review,* August 11, 1907, with Sunset Telephone Company, Tucson. Wills and Probate, Cochise County, Arizona State Archives.

272   Most major aspects of the Greene mining career can be followed in *Copper Handbook,* which began publishing in 1900, and its successor publications, *Mines Handbook* and *Mines Register.*

273   Literature abundant. The *Arizona Republic,* August 3, 1900, had an "Invitation to a Hanging" article; biographies in Bailey and Chaput, *Cochise County Stalwarts. Halderman v. Territory,* 7 Arizona 120 (1899).

274   Arizona Death Records, as well as the census of 1940 indicate the Pioneers' Home years. Henninger was frequently mentioned in the Tombstone and Bisbee newspapers. The Can Can figures are from *Tombstone Weekly Epitaph,* July 28, 1901.

275   An obituary is in the Nogales *Oasis* of December 4, 1909.

276   The original edition of *Billy King's Tombstone* was printed in Caldwell, Idaho, in 1942, by Caxton Printers. An obituary and photo of King is in *El Paso Herald-Post*, July 1, 1945. *Arizona Republican*, April 17, 1894, their marriage in Phoenix. *Tombstone Weekly Epitaph*, November 9, 1892, constable candidate, and deputy sheriff service. Wills and Probate, Cochise County, Arizona State Archives, details of Dick Clark's many holdings. Although the book is a disaster, Billy King was very active in the ranching and saloon life of Tombstone and Cochise County, and his doings are easily followed in the local newspapers.

277   Chaput, *The Odyssey of Burt Alvord: Lawman, Train Robber, Fugitive*. As a public figure, Land's career is easy to follow. Death record is from the Arizona Board of Health.

278   His career is easily followed in the Tombstone and Bisbee press, especially for the turbulent years of 1900-1903. A useful biography is in Bailey and Chaput, *Cochise County Stalwarts*.

279   His path is easily followed in the census, voting registers, and directories. *Tombstone Epitaph*, May 8, 1892, Kansas pasturage; September 22, 1895, legal suit; Kansas *City Gazette*, August 12, 1892, interview with McClure, from Tombstone. *Los Angeles Times*, March 29, 1913, death notice.

280   The paper trail for Meade is extensive in county, territory, and state records because of his mining and law enforcement connections. *Arizona Republican*, March 15, 1918, obituary.

281   Voting registers; *Tombstone Weekly Epitaph*, September 4, 1892, Maison Doree; September 7, 1902, Bisbee properties; *Cochise Review*, July 14, 1900, Bisbee bakery; *Tombstone Weekly Epitaph*, January 21, 1917, return to Tombstone.

282   The Tombstone, Bisbee, Tucson, and Phoenix newspapers gave the killing and legal action considerable space over these years. A good summary is in Heidi J. Osselaer, *Arizona's Deadliest Gunfight* (Norman: University of Oklahoma Press, 2018).

283   The trials were heavily covered in Arizona newspapers. Arizona State Prison Records; *Tombstone Epitaph*, December 23, 1900, verdict explained; *Tombstone Weekly Epitaph*, July 1, 1900, interview of Ethel regarding her father's firearms. See the Macia and Devere bios in the above pages for further details.

284   There was heavy coverage of the Pearce mining in the Tombstone and Tucson newspapers, as well as in the *Mining & Scientific Press*. *San Francisco Call*, September 18, 1910, obituary; John Jr. died in Oakland on February 23, 1920.

285   National Archives, Mexican War biographical files; *Cochise Review*, February 23, 1901, grand jury affair; *Benson Signal*, August 10, 1918, a typical obituary. The *Wolfville Tales* connection has an extensive literature.

286   She is mentioned in Heidi Osselaer, "On the Wrong Side of Allen Street: The Business Women of Tombstone, 1878-1884," *Journal of Arizona History*, Summer, 2014. Obituary in *Albuquerque Journal*, January 13, 1942. The *Daily Tombstone* and *Epitaph* had dozens of notices and ads for her business and activities, especially in 1885 and 1886. An early notice was in the *Tombstone Weekly Epitaph*, December 2, 1882, for the G.A.R. Ball in Schieffelin Hall, which she and sister Nettie attended.

287   Dated but still useful is Erwin, *The West of John Slaughter*, 1965.

288 Arizona State Board of Health, death certificate; Bailey and Chaput, *Cochise County Stalwarts*; good details appear in the Fort Huachuca newspaper, the *Apache Sentinel,* March 2, March 23, 1945.

289 Scrapbooks can be created on the two Tombstone jail breaks. See also Chaput, *The Odyssey of Burt Alvord*. As a note of further interest, on August 27, 2021, Billy Stiles' Colt single-action army revolver used in the train robbery of the Nogales and Benson, Arizona train, at the Fairbanks railroad depot, on February 15, 1900, sold at Bonhams' Jim Earle auction in Los Angeles for $12,750; please see coauthor de Haas's "Wild West Collectors" Facebook page for much more.

290 Many aspects of his career appear in Scott White, "Bad Men's Nemesis: The Adventures and experiences of an Arizona Sheriff," *Touring Topics*, April 1931.

291 *Tombstone Prospector*, January 3, 1891; Chaput, *Dr. Goodfellow*, and *"Buckskin Frank" Leslie. Tombstone Weekly Epitaph*, November 18, 1882.

292 Voting registers, censuses, and land records. *Bisbee Daily Review,* January 7, 1906, for skipping town; National Archives, Soldiers' Home, Wiser file. Chaput and de Haas, *The Earps Invade Southern California.*

293 His entire career and brief Tombstone stop are covered in Gary Scharnhorst, *Owen Wister and the West* (Norman: University of Oklahoma Press, 2015). Owen Wister, *The Virginian*, 1902.

294 Some of the basics are in the Gage and Staunton biographies in Bailey and Chaput, *Cochise County Stalwarts.*

295 *Los Angeles Herald*, November 30, 1902, has a full page devoted to Cochise County, most of it related to the mining revival and businesses in Tombstone. It is interesting to ponder that at this very same time the Earp family (and many of their former 1880 Tombstone friends) were strongly entrenched in Sawtelle, California (near Los Angeles), and must have seen and been wary of these very same headlines. Please see Chaput and de Haas, MD, *The Earps Invade Southern California: Bootlegging Los Angeles, Santa Monica, and the Old Soldiers' Home* (Denton, Texas: University of North Texas Press, 2020).

296 *Engineering & Mining Journal*, March 1, 1902; *Arizona Republican*, December 17, 1902; *Tombstone Epitaph*, July 20, 1902.

297 *Tombstone in History, Romance and Wealth* (Tombstone: Daily Prospector, 1903).

298 *Mines and Minerals,* March 1907, 371-74.

299 Issue of July 21, 1907.

300 *Mohave County Miner*, September 23, 1905, detailed article from the *Tombstone Prospector; Los Angeles Herald*, August 31, 1908, comments from H. E. Claridge, general manager at Fairbank.

301 *Los Angeles Times*, June 10, 1909.

302 *Bisbee Daily Review,* September 21, 1910.

303 *Tombstone Epitaph,* May 1, 1910.

304 *Mining & Scientific Press*, January 28, 1911.

305 *Los Angeles Times*, June 25, 1911.

306 *Los Angeles Times,* February 5, 1911, in an article headed "Gloom Is Thick at Tombstone."

307 *Oasis*, August 6, 1910; *Mining & Scientific Press*, February 4, 1911; *Mining & Scientific Press*, March 11, 1911.

308 Good details on the sale are in *Bisbee Daily Review*, June 24, 1914, and *Morning Press* (Santa Barbara), June 14, 1914.

309 *Mesa Free Press*, February 23, 1900, move to Benson; *Oasis*, September 8, 1900, describes the Abell farm; *Bisbee Evening Miner*, July 8, 1906, ad for the Tombstone office, Gibson Abstract Co.; *Tombstone Weekly Epitaph*, September 21, 1913, injured while at her ranch; Arizona State Board of Health, death certificate.

310 Censuses and voting registers. *The Oasis*, May 14, 1910, resigns as superintendent; *Bisbee Daily Review*, February 17, 1909, mining interests; World War I and World War II, draft registrations; Arizona State Board of Health, death certificate.

311 Blake's earliest, important work on Tombstone, regarding its geology, appeared in *Transactions of the American Institute of Mining Engineers*, X (1882).

312 *Tombstone Weekly Epitaph*, August 3, 1902, named cashier; *Bisbee Daily Review*, November 3, 1917, December 12, 1917, robbery details and death.

313 The Bravin career is easily followed in standard Tombstone sources. A useful biography is in Bailey and Chaput, *Cochise County Stalwarts*.

314 He is mentioned frequently in the well-covered Alvord-Stiles troubles. *Tombstone Epitaph*, July 21, 1912, move to Globe; *Arizona Republic*, January 25, 1936, obituary.

315 Voting registers and censuses. *Bisbee Daily Review*, August 27, 1922, candidate for superior court judge. *Albuquerque Morning Journal*, December 23, 1925, obituary.

316 *Bisbee Daily Review*, July 28, 1906, as *Prospector* city editor; August 18, 1910, Territorial Fair; *Tombstone Epitaph*, September 7, 1913, move to Douglas. On and after October 11, 1955, obituaries on Goll appeared in many of the nation's newspapers.

317 The Grow years in Tombstone are easy to follow. He was buried in Westwood Memorial Park in Los Angeles County on September 23, 1918. Chaput and de Haas, MD, *The Earps Invade Southern California*.

318 *Telephone Magazine*, August 1901, Tombstone City Council; *Arizona Daily Star*, September 2, 1905, head of Tombstone Telephone Co.; *Tombstone Epitaph*, June 30, 1912, sale of Tucson interests; *Graham Guardian*, December 18, 1917, obituary.

319 *Mining & Scientific Press*, February 26, 1921; *Tombstone Weekly Epitaph*, March 16, 1919, Kelly comments about his birth; April 15, 1906, hidden razor; June 21, 1908, Mendez shootout; death of Kelly in *Arizona Independent Republic*, October 22, 1940, and *Tucson Daily Citizen*, October 23, 1940. Arizona State Board of Health, death certificate. King seems to have been a bad egg. A jury exonerated him, and he even had time to register for the draft in World War II. In the following decades he was arrested and warned several times by federal authorities for violations of mining and other situations on government lands. As late as 1971, "Prospector Admits Cutting Forest Road," *Tucson Daily Citizen*, January 28, 1971.

320 Voting registers and censuses. The careers of the Macias are easy to follow in the Tombstone and Tucson newspapers; Arizona State Board of Health, death certificates. *Arizona Mining Journal*, September 1, 1921, Bert working a claim near Tombstone. Mary and David D. de Haas, MD research visit, July 2021.

321   Magon literature is extensive. The newspapers of Tombstone, Bisbee, Tucson, and Phoenix carried details on the courtroom events, the attorneys and judge, and contained printed versions in full of the charges. The high status of the case is obvious in a story out of Tombstone in the *Arizona Daily Star* of March 10, 1909, suggesting that Clarence Darrow would be hired to defend Magon.

322   The public nature of his work makes his career easy to follow in the thousands of documents in the Cochise County Recorder's office.

323   A dated but solid biography is J. Evetts Haley, *Jeff Milton: A Good Man with a Gun* (Norman: University of Oklahoma Press, 1968). Train robbery details are in Chaput, *The Odyssey of Burt Alvord*. The annual reports of the Department of Commerce and Labor contain information as an inspector. The shooting accident is in *Border Vidette*, April 8, 1916.

324   *Tombstone in History*,1903, includes a Murphy portrait. A full-page obituary, with photograph, appears in *Weekly Arizona Miner*, June 27, 1917. He was referred to as "Empire Builder," an accurate phrase. Tombstone revival sources have much coverage of Murphy's role.

325   There are sources galore on this major figure in the professional literature as well as in the newspapers and popular press. A solid biography is by Britz, *The Arizona Mining Career of William F. Staunton, 1883-1931.*

326   National Archives, Old Soldiers' Home file. The nation's press from 1906 through 1908 was filled with dozens of articles on the plight, wanderings, and troubles of the Wardwells. Chaput and de Haas, MD, *The Earps Invade Southern California*, 100-102.

327   *Tombstone Prospector*, January 2, 1919; obituary, *Bisbee Daily Review*, March 3, 1921; Baily and Chaput, *Cochise County Stalwarts*.

328   The military and court years make it easy to follow the Wilcox careers. *Arizona Republic*, July 4, 1949, obituary.

329   *Boston Globe*, July 14, 1914; *Mining & Scientific Press*, February 26, 1916; *American Mining Manual*, 1920.

330   The Phelps Dodge annual reports are available online and contain details of all production in the firm's various locations. Some "big picture" comments, including mention of Tombstone, are in *Minerals and Metals for War Purposes* [House Resolution 11259] (Washington: GPO, 1918).

331   M. A. Allen and G. M. Butler, "Manganese," *University of Arizona, Bulletin 91* [Bureau of Mines], August 1918. Some chlorider comments are in *Bisbee Daily Review*, September 30, 1917.The important Bisbee role is mentioned in *Engineering & Mining Journal*, February 28, 1920. *Mineral Resources of the United States* (the U. S. Geol. Survey, pub. in 1916).

332   *Arizona Daily Star*, March 23, 1918.

333   The war claims are mentioned in *Tombstone Weekly Epitaph*, May 25, 1919. Some Tombstone and Bisbee rivalry comes through in *Arizona Republican*, April 19, 1918, where the Copper Queen of Bisbee is praised, while the Tombstone large manganese deposit is "of a very low grade."

334   *Mining Code of the State of Arizona* (Yuma: Frank Baxter, 1918); some earlier lease and lien points of Arizona were discussed in *Mining & Scientific Press*, June 15, 1912.

335   Figures are estimates from the U. S. censuses, and from Clements, *After the Boom in Tombstone and Jerome.*

336 Quote from *Engineering & Mining Journal-Press*, April 28, 1923. The Pittman Act is covered in detail in *Hearings before the Committee on Banking and Currency*, United State Senate, 68th Cong., 1st Sess. (Washington: GPO, 1924). A detailed chart on silver production by state is in *Anaconda Standard*, January 30, 1921. A useful article on the impact of the Pittman Act locally is in *Tombstone Epitaph*, April 10, 1921.

337 A useful account of this complicated topic is James W. Byrkit, *Forging the Copper Collar: Arizona's Labor-Management War, 1901-1921* (Tucson: University of Arizona Press, 1982). The nation's press carried many stories of the Tombstone trials; see, for example, the *New York Tribune*, February 2, 1920. Sheriff (or Captain) Wheeler testified on May 29, taking full responsibility for the deportation; his account, and image, are in *Bisbee Daily Review*, March 30, 1920. Bill O'Neal, *Captain Harry Wheeler: Arizona Lawman* (Eakin Press, 2003).

338 A detailed account of Harper is in *Portrait and Biographical Record of Arizona* (Chicago: Chapman Pub. Co., 1901). Mentions of the court action are in *Arizona Silver Belt* (Globe), March 3, 1904; *Williams News*, February 27, 1904; *Bisbee Daily Review*, June 9, June 14, 1904. A brief obituary is in *The St. Johns Herald*, May 9, 1918.

339 Although the Costellos were Tombstoners for years, their big money was from Bisbee copper, and they spent years living in Los Angeles. Bisbee and Los Angeles sources are essential for following this big money trail.

340 There are numerous documents on his activities in the Cochise County Recorder's office; an interesting obituary is in the *Pasadena Post*, December 1, 1930; biography in Bailey and Chaput, *Cochise County Stalwarts. Cummings v. State, 20 Arizona 176* (1919); details also in *Tombstone Weekly Epitaph*, March 30, 1919. Kevin Britz and Roger L. Nichols, *Tombstone, Deadwood and Dodge City: Recreating the Frontier West* (Norman, OK: Univ of Oklahoma Press, 2018). For Gary S. McLelland's YouTube presentation of "Fox News Man Shoots Tombstone" please see *Old West Magazine* 1925 - G.S. McLelland's 1925-1929 Lost Streets of Tombstone Newsreels - Bing video; G.S. McClelland and John Rose (original copy from historian/author John Rose in collection of David D. de Haas, MD). *New York Times*, December 2, 1930 (another obituary). *Deeds of Real Estate Cochise County*, book 3, 521-525, for Cummings purchase of Bird Cage Theatre; thank you to Tombstone/Bird Cage Theatre researcher/historian Michael Mihaljevich for pointing this out and this reference.

341 Information abounds because of their public life. The purchase from Billy Hattich is in *Tombstone Prospector*, August 2, 1913. The *Winslow Mail* of January 15, 1925, has details of the Giragi experiences. Passport Applications, Department of State; Arizona State Board of Health, death certificates. *Coolidge Examiner* (Arizona), April 28, 1933 (for Carmel's death in plane crash). *Tombstone Prospector*, May 12, 1923, for passport for Sarah and her son Louis Giragi.

342 Censuses and voting registers; Arizona State Board of Health, death certificate.

343 Details on the Borderland Route, including road signs, are in *Tombstone Weekly Epitaph*, May 27, 1917, June 10, 1917. A race through downtown Tombstone, Allen and Fremont Streets, is in *Tombstone Weekly Epitaph*, October 19, 1919. *Western Highways Builder*, July 19, 1919, has three articles on Tombstone and Cochise County road projects. A good map of U. S. 80 (known also as the Borderland Route) is in *Douglas Daily Dispatch*, March 4, 1926. Information of Locke meeting with Gardner in *Tombstone Epitaph*, May 11, May 18, 1919. A

detailed article on State Highway 82 is in *Nogales International*, April 25, 1926, authored by A. H. Gardner, "Highway Publicist." A sound summary of these issues is in *Good Roads Everywhere: A History of Road Building in Arizona* (Phoenix: Arizona Department of Transportation, 2003).

344 Please see *Border Vidette* (Nogales), Feb 11, 1928, for an interesting article describing the editor of Pickwick Magazine's research visit to Tombstone motivated by the Burns book. It "...created such a strong desire in him to see Tombstone that he could hardly wait," and it was "his opinion that the Tombstone book will be the means of bringing many tourists to Tombstone..."

345 Phone interview and emails/texts between Gordon and David de Haas, January 16 and 17, 2022. Discussions over a near thirty-year close friendship between Gordon and Mary and David de Haas. In-person discussions during Tombstone visits, July and November of 2021.

346 Bailey, *Tombstone, Arizona*. Census of Ohio, 1920, and California, 1940; voting registers, Cochise County. World War I draft registrations; Arizona State Board of Health, death certificate.

347 Genealogical tree (and family historical discussions) provided by Robert Devere to David D. de Haas, MD in 1996. Phone interview January 23, 2022. Email Devere to DdH, January 25, 2022.

348 Mary and David D. de Haas twenty-five-plus years friendship/conversations with the Elliotts. David D. de Haas, MD phone interview with Marjorie Elliott January 8, 2022, and in-person discussions in July 2021.

349 Phone interview (Dusty Escapule with David D. de Haas, MD), January 23, 2022. Bailey and Chaput, *Cochise County Stalwarts*, Vol. 1, 119. *The Tombstone News*, October 16, 2020. Email Mayor Escapule to DdH, January 24, 2022. As a very interesting aside, it is John Escapule's photo that was misidentified as Doc Holliday many years ago, and to this day is incorrectly labeled as Doc in souvenir shops and books and magazines.

350 Family background information was provided by Gayle Martinson of the Wisconsin State Historical Society, Madison. Details of his move to Tombstone are in *Madison Capital Times*, March 11, 1950. Helldorado program in *Tucson Daily Citizen*, October 19, 1950. Necktie party in *Arizona Silver Belt*, March 2, 1961. His role at the Sierra Vista airport is mentioned in the various *Arizona Blue Books* and in *Douglas Dispatch*, August 30, 1971. There are hundreds of accounts of the flak with President Truman. Easily available is *Harry S. Truman: Containing the Public Messages, Speeches and Statements of the President, 1952-53* (Washington: GPO, 1966). As a brief side note, how well Tombstone itself has succeeded in maintaining Boothill's authenticity is a subject of some debate by modern scholars.

351 He is listed in the census of 1920, 1930, and 1940. Biographical details are in McClintock, *Arizona*, III (1916), and in the obituary in *Tucson Daily Citizen*, October 26, 1942.

352 Voting registers, censuses, and automobile and mining publications carry many references to the brothers. His clash with Tholio is in *Bisbee Daily Review*, September 7, 1922. Anton is listed as a committee member in the Helldorado Days program of 1929. *Arizona Mining Journal*, September 1, 1921, indicates the brothers working a silver manganese claim near the Bunker Hill. John's passport file in 1918 lists a Tombstone address and intent to work a mining property in Lower California. Death certificates for the brothers are in the Arizona State Board of Health.

353   In-person interview in Tombstone November 2021. Phone interviews with David D. de Haas January 15 and 16, 2022. "An Old West Cemetery for Jews Is Rededicated in Tombstone," *New York Times*, February 29, 1984, p. A12.

354   *The Tombstone News*, November 19, 2021. William H. Hunley, Jr. obituary card—Mary and David D. de Haas. *The Tombstone Epitaph* (National Edition), January 2022, 2. Phone interview (Dusty Escapule with David D. de Haas, MD), January 23, 2022. Discussions between Paula Jean Reed and Bill Hunley with Mary and co-author David D. de Haas over a near twenty-five-year warm friendship. Mary and David D. de Haas WWHA/Tombstone research visit July 2022 and discussions with entire surviving family. Phone conversion with Paula Jean, January 12, 2023.

355   His service records in both World Wars are in various files in the National Archives. James J. Hudson, "California National Guard and the Mexican Border, 1914-1916," *California Historical Society Quarterly*, XXXIV (June 1955); *Los Angeles Herald*, August 28, 1916; *Evening Vanguard* (Venice), September 13, October 26, 1916; Radio Broadcast, KSUN, Bisbee, February 7, 1950 (Iszard interview). Good detail on his role with the Tombstone Restoration Commission is in Britz, *Tombstone, Deadwood, and Dodge City*. The censuses and directories of Los Angeles and Santa Monica carry many Iszard entries. California Death Index. Iszard was also a founder and officer in the Hollywood branch of a veteran's organization; *Daily News* (Los Angeles), January 4, 1946. Personal letter from C. M. Palmer, Jr. to artist V. Clyde Forsythe dated July 1, 1952 (after his recent research visit to Tombstone for his painting of the gunfight), and on Tombstone Restoration Commission stationery, original in the collection of coauthor David D. de Haas, MD.

356   Border Vidette, November 16, 1929; obituary of George H. Kelly; *Nogales International*, March 21, 1926, W.H. Kelly takes over the *Tombstone Epitaph*. *Casa Grande Dispatch*, November 14, 1929. *Arizona Daily Star*, June 4, 1930. The Helldorado Days program and publicity in 1929 was mostly Kelly's work. His arrangements and work with Krebs, Macia, and others is detailed in Britz & Nichols, *Tombstone, Deadwood, and Dodge City*. Arizona State Board of Health, death certificate. Original 1929 first Helldorado program in the collection of coauthor David D. de Haas, MD and shared on his "Wild West Collectors" Facebook page (please see).

357   His career is easily followed in the censuses, voting registers, and directories. His move from Bisbee to Tombstone is in *Bisbee Daily Review*, February 24, 1912. The *Tombstone Epitaph* of July 23, 1922, has biographical details at the time he was running for re-election to the state legislature. His role in the Helldorado Days is highlighted in Jane Eppinga, *Tombstone* (Charleston, S.C.: Arcadia Publishing, 2010). Arizona State Board of Health, death certificate.

358   Her name is scattered throughout the newspapers, board minutes, and programs in Tombstone and Tucson. Arizona State Board of Health, death certificates for Thure and Edna Landin. A good summary of her work regarding the courthouse is in Jay M. Price, *Gateways to the Southwest: The Story of Arizona State Parks* (Tucson: University of Arizona Press, 2004). The *Tucson Daily Citizen*, April 2, 1956, contains a lengthy, typical letter from her, detailing why and how the courthouse should be saved.

359   Louis is mentioned as a miner in the *Tombstone Prospector,* March 31, 1888; details of his death are in *Tombstone Epitaph*, August 10, 1913. Walter's prison record, and typical portrait, are in the files of the New Mexico State Penitentiary. The robbery of the Crystal Palace is in Cody Polston, *Haunted Tombstone* (Charleston, S.C.: The History Press, 2018). One account of the cobalt discovery is in *Desert Magazine*, March 1938. Arizona State Board of Health, death certificate.

360   Jane Eppinga, *Southern Arizona Cemeteries* (Charleston, South Carolina: Arcadia Publishers, 2014). January 11, 2022 phone interview, David D. de Haas with Mark Boardman, current editor of the *National Edition of The Tombstone Epitaph Journal. True West*, June 15, 2017, "What History Has Taught Me: Bob Love O. K. Corral Owner." *The Washington Post*, Sara Love obituary, November 2011.

361   Easily followed in the standard Tombstone and postal history sources. Her key FBI informant role is covered in detail in *Investigation, Communist Activities in the Los Angeles Area,* Part I (House, 83rd Congress; GPO, 1953). Obituary, *Arizona Republic,* July 20, 1974; "Grandma Spy" in *Los Angeles Times,* April 17, 1953. She is buried in Melrose Abbey Memorial Park, Prescott.

362   A heavy public record exists for these families. The father's full name (seldom used) was Samuel Christy "Chris" Robertson. The lawman/murderer was Sidney M. Page, whose biography appears elsewhere in these pages. *Arizona Republic,* July 30, 1938, for restoration/remodel of Rose Tree Inn.

363   Medigovich Collection, Arizona Historical Society, twenty-six boxes of manuscripts, ledgers, maps, etc. Censuses, voting registers. An earlier Sam Medigovich in Tombstone, *Tombstone Epitaph,* May 31, 1890; *Tucson Daily Citizen,* April 19, 1977, "Tombstoners go to Germany;" U. S. Naturalization Records (Sam was Savo Vaso Medigovich), Superior Court, Bisbee, March 31, 1933.

364   Copies (updated) of Lela's 1952 pamphlet are still in circulation at Boothill to this day. Original 1952 copy in the collection of coauthor de Haas. For subsequent work and in-depth detail please see Traywick's *Tombstone's Boothill,* especially 4, 5, 171, and 172 on Emmett. The interesting squabble with President Truman is in *Tucson Daily Citizen,* May 7, 1952, and December 12, 1955. On a wider stage, her work is praised in the *Los Angeles Times,* August 5, 1973; obituary in *Arizona Daily Star,* January 28, 1983. The Boothill graveyard itself has recently come under fire from scholars for its many questionable (fictional) characters, markers of purported inhabitants, exaggerated number of burials ("more than 250 graves"), and many sensationalized causes of death (Indian attacks, hangings/lynching, murders); see also Chapter Six and its endnotes. Emmett Nunnelley death certificate November 6, 1946.

365   The role of Smith in the history of Tombstone and Western tourism can be easily followed in the hundreds of pages of the *Tombstone Epitaph* and in the extensive literature on Western tourism. The fatal airplane crash caught the attention of the *New York Times,* January 25, 1964.

366   *The Tombstone News,* October 15, 2010. Discussions over a near twenty-year friendship with Mary and David D. de Haas, MD. Phone interviews of Don Taylor with David January 8 and 9, 2022. Sadly, owing to Covid-19, the number of visitors to Tombstone was down to fewer than 200,000 in 2020.

367   Mary and David D. de Haas twenty-five-plus years dear friendship and dinner conversations with the Traywicks. David D. de Haas, MD phone interview with Mary Traywick, January 8 and 14, 2022. In-person discussions

July and November 2021, July 2022. March 1, 2018, "From Watertown to Tombstone," the *Wilson Post* (Wilson County, Tennessee). *The Tombstone News*, August 15, 2014. *The Tombstone News*, October 15, 2010. Traywick, *Tombstone's Boothill*.

368 In-person interviews Denay with co-author David D. de Haas in Tombstone July 30 and 31, 2022; multiple phone, email, and text interviews, August of 2022. For much more regarding Al Turner's interview of Hildreth Halliwell, which is housed at the Arizona Historical Society in Tucson, and its significance, please see the authors' 2020 book, *The Earps Invade Southern California*.

369 See Baily and Chaput, *Cochise County Stalwarts*, for a Safford biography.

370 *Inter-Ocean* (Chicago), July 5, 1879. The *New York Times* of April 12 and June 18, 1879, mentioned the Safford travels.

371 *Mining & Scientific Press*, October 18, 1879, quote from issue of December 20, 1879.

372 *Mining Industry and Review* (Chicago) November 28, 1896; *Mining* (Spokane), September 1910; *Mining Science* (Denver), December 1914.

373 Silva, *Wyatt Earp: A Biography of the Legend*. Fattig, *Wyatt Earp: The Biography*. Boessenecker, *Wyatt Earp's Epic Battle Against the West's Biggest Outlaw Gang*.

374 There will be no attempt here to list the thousands of potential sources. The best beginning point is Silva, *Wyatt Earp: A Biography of the Legend*; Fattig, *Wyatt Earp: The Biography*; Boessenecker, *Wyatt Earp's Epic Battle Against the West's Biggest Outlaw Gang*. Young, Roberts et al, *Wyatt Earp Anthology*, in addition to many solid articles, includes a detailed bibliography. Roberts, *Doc Holliday: The Life and Legend*.

375 There are books and articles galore on the Bisbee Massacre. Chaput, *Dr. Goodfellow*, has some coverage, and the *Tucson Citizen* of March 19, 1884, has a good contemporary account of the initial robbery, lynching, trials, and hanging. Troy Kelley, *Bisbee Massacre*, self-published.

376 Their feud may be related to Gallagher backing a "new board" in Tombstone affairs; *Arizona Weekly Citizen*, August 18, 1883. Details of the encounter and slander suit are in *Arizona Sentinel*, June 7, 1884, *Arizona Silver Belt*, June 14, 1884, and February 9, 1884.

377 Heavy coverage nationwide and especially in the Arizona and California press, as well as in Canadian newspapers. *Los Angeles Evening Express*, May 28, 1890. The entire affair is interpreted by Roy Young in his article in *Journal of the Wild West History Association*, March 2022. Larry D. Ball, *Tom Horn in Life and Legend* (Norman: University of Oklahoma Press, 2014).

378 Chaput, *Nellie Cashman*.

379 A computer check on Newspapers.com for 1885-1920, for the word "chloride," led to a number of articles: Arizona (400 articles), California (122), Utah (47), Nevada (31), New Mexico (3), and none for Colorado. The word "lease" was sometimes used, but that is a more general word than "chloride."

380 *Gold Hill Daily News*, September 10, 1879, advertisement. Tombstone Mining District recorded in Tucson (Pima County) on April 5, 1878, by Schieffelin (*Arizona Weekly Star*, April 11, 1878).

381 *San Francisco Examiner*, July 4, 1897; *Inter-Ocean* (Chicago), September 12, 1897; *Boston Globe*, October 5, 1897; *The Sun* (New York), September 8, 1897; *Evening Journal* (Ottawa), September 20, 1897.

382   The *Salt Lake Herald* of October 5, 1900, printed the telegram from President McKinley regarding the reprieve. After an earlier reprieve, the *El Paso Herald* of August 18, 1900, stated that, although their sentences would be lessened, the gallows would be "cheated of its victims." The biographies of the brothers are in Bailey and Chaput, *Cochise County Stalwarts*. Chaput, *The Odyssey of Burt Alvord: Lawman, Train Robber, Fugitive*.

383   A foot-thick scrapbook can be created of press clippings of one trial alone. A starting place on these events is in Chaput, *The Odyssey of Burt Alvord*.

384   Chaput, *"Buckskin Frank" Leslie*. DeMattos and Parsons, *They Called Him Buckskin Frank: The Life and Adventures of Nashville Franklyn Leslie*. Traywick, *Tombstone's "Buckskin Frank": Nashville Franklyn Leslie*. Bob Alexander, *John H. Behan: Sacrificed Sheriff* (Silver City, New Mexico: High Lonesome Books, 2002).

385   *Tombstone Epitaph*, January 17, 1892, June 25, 1893.

386   Some of these sanitarium-boosting articles appeared in *Bisbee Daily Review*, April 7, 1904; *Tombstone Epitaph*, November 22, 1908; *Daily Arizona Silver Belt*, January 24, 1909; *Tombstone Epitaph*, April 14, 1912; November 28, 1920.

387   *Southern California Practitioner*, December 1904; this was a leading Western medical publication.

388   Boot Hill mentions: SCOTLAND – *The Courier and Argus* (Dundee), December 16, 1876; ENGLAND – *Western Gazette* (Somerset, England), September 10, 1875; DODGE CITY – *Dodge City Times*, May 6, 1877, October 20, 1877; *Arkansas City Weekly Traveler*, August 15, 1877; HAYS CITY – *Saline County Journal* (Kansas) – March 29, 1877; *Weekly Kansas State Journal*, April 12, 1877; Illinois (Hillsboro) – *St. Louis Globe-Democrat* (Missouri), October 19, 1876; DEADWOOD – *Deadwood Pioneer Times*, June 8, 1876. The *Hays City Sentinel*, February 16, 1878. *Dodge City Times*, May 17, 1878, for Dodge City's Boot Hill School. *Arizona Sentinel* (Yuma), February 24, 1910; *Tombstone Weekly Epitaph*, October 21, 1917 ("converted into a town dump"). Other Boot Hill notices in this era are in *Dodge City Globe*, August 17, 1916; *Daily Progressive Miner* (Ketchikan), October 4, 1917; *Evening Herald* (Albuquerque), October 20, 1917. Details on the significance of Hays, Kansas, is covered in Mike Cox, *Finding the Wild West: The Great Plains, Oklahoma, Kansas, Nebraska, and the Dakotas* (Landham, MD: A Two Dot Book, 2022). Material on both Hays and Dodge City is in Richard and Judy Young, *Outlaw Tales: Legends, Myths and Folklore of America's Middle Border* (Little Rock: August House Pub., 1992).

389   Clement Wood, *Tombstone Epitaph*, February 13, 1947. Bailey, *Tombstone*, 2004. Don Taylor, Rita Ackerman, Kathy Franz; *City of Tombstone/Boothill Graveyard* websites/online. Several interviews conducted with Mayor Dusty Escapule, 2022, and another on April 16, 2023, by co-author de Haas. Also numerous interviews conducted with current Tombstone Town Historian Don Taylor in 2022, and especially April 19, 2023, who also provided the authors with copies of the July 1881 Kelleher map of the city of Tombstone and Boothill cemetery. Traywick (editor), *Minute Book Common Council Village of Tombstone: September 10, 1880 thru January 16, 1882*. For good chronology of these events see Kevin Britz, "'Boot Hill Burlesque' The Frontier Cemetery as Tourist Attraction in Tombstone, Arizona, and Dodge City, Kansas," *Journal of Arizona History*, Autumn, 2003. There is also in circulation an early twentieth-century postcard view of Tombstone from the west (near the area of the current Boothill), looking east towards town with the mining district's second cemetery seen in the foreground. According to Taylor (and Mayor Escapule, who lives in the town), there have been many graves

accidentally unearthed in this location through the years, including by a family who was digging a backyard fountain for their home.

390   This point is well handled in Britz, *Journal of Arizona History*, Autumn, 2003. "Various others" include a few fictional names from the *Wolfville* tales series.

391   For Tombstone's Boothill in the 1950s and 1960s see also Fifth Era biogr phies Emmett and Lela Nunnelley. For Heath lynching in Tombstone, burial in Texas—thank you to author John Boessenecker, email discussions with coauthor DdH, May 12, 13, 16 and 17, 2022. For some of the other dubious Boothill markers (George Johnson—"Hanged by Mistake;" Lester Moore—"No Les No More;" Tom Harper, and more), and an excellent group discussion, see also Boessenecker's Facebook post of July 18, 2020. Boessenecker, *When Law Was in the Holster*; *Kaufman Sun News* (Texas), Feb 28, 1884; Grasse, *Bisbee Massacre*; genealogist Jean Ann Ables-Flatt, December 21, 2008, Terrell, Texas, quotes from *Kaufman Sun*: "His remains were brought to Terrell and interred." For much more, please see the Wild West Collectors Facebook page, discussion May 9, 2022. Likewise, the February 1900 Jesse "Three Fingered Jack" Dunlap burial in Boothill is also somewhat problematic. Most period accounts state that he was taken back to Tombstone and buried in "the cemetery," but do not list which cemetery. By this time, the "Old Cemetery," aka modern day's "Boothill," was closed to further burials (as of 1884) and most subsequent interments were in the current city/"new" cemetery. A search of those buried there does not list Dunlap, though. It is plausible that because "he died with his boots on," he actually was buried in Boothill, but the authors are not able to find any substantiation of that claim. See also Traywick, *Tombstone's Boothill*, 121-127.

392   DeArment, *Knights of the Green Cloth*. Smith, *Alias Soapy Smith*.

393   *Successful American* was a periodical of the Press Biographical Company.

394   Some material on Lewis appears in Chaput, *Dr. Goodfellow*. A statement of the Billy Plaster role is in *Los Angeles Evening Express*, August 1, 1918. Some film presentations are reviewed in *Arizona Republican*, July 14, 1918. A detailed obituary in *New York Times*, December 24, 1914, is useful. Lewis was a major, popular author for several decades.

395   His visits to Arizona and friendship with Harry Wheeler are in the *Tombstone Epitaph*, June 11, 1916, and September 4, 1921.

396   *San Francisco Chronicle*, October 1, 1922.

397   The *Los Angeles Record* of May 25, 1920, report on the wedding party, which included Bechdolt, leaving to visit the Hopi reservation and other sights in the Southwest. The clout of Bechdolt was such that his books were reviewed in the leading newspapers of the nation. The *New York Herald* of September 24, 1922, praised him as the author of a "fascinatingly alive book."

398   *Bisbee Daily Review*, April 7, 1904. *Tombstone Epitaph,* November 22, 1908. *Daily Arizona Silver Belt*, January 24, 1909. *Tombstone Epitaph*, April 14, 1912, and November 28, 1920. *Tombstone Weekly Epitaph*, March 27, 1921.

399   Bechdolt, "Tombstone's Wild Oats," *Saturday Evening Post*, December 13, 1919; *When the West Was Young*, 1922. Britz and Nichols, *Tombstone, Deadwood, and Dodge City*. Britz, "'Boot Hill Burlesque': The Frontier Cemetery as Tourist Attraction in Tombstone, Arizona, and Dodge City, Kansas," *Journal of Arizona History*, Vol. 44 (Autumn, 2003), 211- 42. The current "Boothill Cemetery" (prior name the "Old Cemetery") was not the town's first, but actually its third, with the first in approximately 1878; the second approximately 1879, and the third

approximately mid-1881. The "Old Cemetery" (aka "the Dump," officially renamed "Boothill" after the encouragement provided by author Frederick Bechdolt in 1923), was closed on May 31, 1884, and subsequently used as a garbage dump. Today's town cemetery, the Tombstone Cemetery (aka "New Cemetery") on southwest Allen Street, is actually Tombstone's fourth, the first burial there being on June 30, 1884.

    An article by historian Sharlot M. Hall appeared in *The Arizona Sentinel* (Yuma, AZ) on February 24, 1910, proclaiming, "In the old days of the frontier the burial ground in many a town and mining camp was called "Boot Hill..." and the *Dodge City (Kansas) Globe* on August 17, 1916, claimed that "every Frontier town had its 'Boot Hill,'" mentioning specifically Newton, Hays, Dodge City and Abilene, Kansas, and Deadwood, South Dakota, as being "representative of all the west." Subsequently, the *Daily Progressive-Miner* (Ketchikan), October 4, 1917; the *Evening Herald* (Albuquerque, NM), October 20, 1917; the *Tombstone Epitaph*, October 21, 1917; and the *Nome Daily Nugget*, November 22, 1917, all reproduced an October 3, 1917, national AP dispatch (out of Tombstone) with the earliest mentions the authors can find in the literature describing the "Old Cemetery" in Tombstone as "Boot Hill." Former Mayor John Clum, in an interview quoted in the March 27, 1925 *Epitaph*, stated he "never before heard...any (Tombstone) cemetery referred to as Boot Hill." (Excerpted from Bailey, *Too Tough to Die*, 361, fn 79). It is therefore quite obvious that these (and other latter-day) articles, and the influence of author Frederick Bechdolt, were actually the origin of the 1923 modern day name (which was not the original name), "Boothill," for Tombstone's "Old (third) Cemetery."

    In her May 2013 doctoral thesis (and subsequent book), Kara L. McCormack claims that Tombstone "copied" Dodge City in naming their cemetery "Boot Hill." That may very well be the case, but it appears that Dodge City actually "copied" Hays, Kansas first. They (Hays) claim to have had the very first "Boot Hill;" "the first in the west to be called Boot Hill." Please see the Kansas Historical Society newsletter, *Kansas Memory*, and accompanying Hays Boot Hill 1885 excavation photo. The *Hays City Sentinel* newspaper of February 16, 1878, mentions their old dilapidated "Boot Hill" cemetery. And, according to Richard and Judy Young in their *Outlaw Tales: Legends, Myths, and Folklore from America's Middle Border*, and to Mike Cox in his 2022 book, *Finding the Wild West* (81), "The first Western graveyard...to be called Boot Hill was in Hays City, the earliest burials (there) in 1867 (five years before Dodge City was even in existence). The cemetery was abandoned in 1874...." They also quote the May 14, 1878 issue of Dodge City's newspaper the *Ford County Globe* as mentioning a burial in Hays "Boot Hill." A modern-day tourist placard has now been placed on the Hays site proclaiming it "the Original Boot Hill." Suffice it to say, there is more than enough evidence that the moniker of Tombstone's "Boothill" was not its original, and was actually pilfered in later years (the early twentieth century) from Hays, Kansas' original.

    As we have already alluded to, there is a common modern-day practice of renaming many frontier cemeteries "Boot Hill" for the purpose of making them twentieth-century tourist attractions. Tombstone is actually the only one of such towns which can lay claim to having a "legitimate Boothill" per se. Please see *Tombstone's Boothill*; and *Boothill Grave Yard: A Descriptive List*, by Lela B. Nunnelley (whose husband was one of the last to be buried in Tombstone's

Boothill), 1952; original copy in the collection of coauthor David D. de Haas, MD.
400 Scattered but relevant comment on these authors and their work appears
in Young, Roberts, *Wyatt Earp Anthology*. A major work covering that decade is
Mark J. Dworkin, *Walter Noble Burns and the Legends of Billy the Kid, Wyatt Earp,
and Joaquin Murrieta* (Norman: University of Oklahoma Press, 2015). Please see
Border Vidette (Nogales), Feb 11, 1928.
401 Lorenzo D. Walters, *Tombstone's Yesterday* (Tucson: Acme Printing Co.,
1928). A detailed summary of the many mistakes by Walters can be seen in
Ramon F. Adams, *Burs Under the Saddle: A Second Look at Books and Writing of the
West* (Norman, Oklahoma: University of Oklahoma Press, 1964).
402 Many Western newspapers carried publicity on this first Helldorado;
see, for example, *Oakland Tribune,* November 24, 1929. Original copy of the first
Helldorado Days "official program" in the collection of David D. de Haas, MD
and has been shared on his "Wild West Collectors" Facebook page for those
interested.
403 An interesting summary of this contradiction appeared in the *Tombstone
Times,* November 2021, in which the articles on the celebration and the
change of the county seat were reprinted from November 20, 1929 (*Evening
Star,* Washington DC): "Tombstone Loses Its Last Glory as County Seat: Ghost
Mining Town Skips Still Further Into Forgotten Past." For more of the same, see
also Nassau D. Review (Long Island), December 21, 1929.
404 *Hayward Daily Review*, September 4, 1931.
405 Details of how and why Tombstone moved into this image cultivation
are well covered in Kevin Britz, "A True to Life Reproduction: The Origins of
Tombstone's Helldorado Celebration," *Journal of Arizona History,* Vol. 42 (Winter,
2001).
406 Chaput and de Haas, *The Earps Invade Southern California,* 146 – 147.
407 Published in Norman by the University of Oklahoma Press in 2018.
408 To avoid excessive endnotes and facilitate readability of the appendix
timeline, which is meant to provide a quick overall view, unless otherwise
noted in the entry, one or more of the following sources was used throughout:
Arizona and the West, Vol. 21 (Spring, 1979); Rita Ackerman, *Tombstone: Who,
What, When, Where,* self-published, 2005; Timothy W. Fattig, *Wyatt Earp: The
Biography* (Honolulu, HI: Talei Publishers, 2002); John Boessenecker, *Wyatt
Earp's Epic Battle Against the West's Biggest Outlaw Gang* (Toronto, Ontario,
Canada: Hanover Square Press, 2020); Lynn R. Bailey and Don Chaput, *Cochise
County Stalwarts: A Who's Who of the Territorial Years,* Volumes I and II (Tucson,
Arizona: Westernlore Press, 2000); Lynn Bailey, *Too Tough to Die: The Rise, Fall,
and Resurrection of a Silver Camp,* 1878 to 1990 (Tucson: Westernlore Press, 2004);
William Shillingberg, *Tombstone, A.T.: A History of Early Mining, Milling, and
Mayhem* (Norman: University of Oklahoma Press, 1998); Lee Silva, *Wyatt Earp: A
Biography of the Legend* [Vol. II, Part 1] (Santa Ana, CA: Graphic Publishers, 2010);
Gary S. McLelland, *The Streets of Tombstone 1881,* self-published map, 1998. *Circa
1880 Map of Tombstone and List of Buildings,* Ben T. Traywick and Glenn G. Boyer,
1977 (Red Marie's Bookstore, 1994); *Tombstone, Arizona Territory: Circa 1881- 82,*
John D. Gilchriese (map, 1971. Based on the research of Robert N. Mullin and
his original 1916 sketch); John Gilchriese personal copy in the collection
of coauthor David D. de HaasMD. Paul Andrew Hutton. "Showdown at the
Hollywood Corral: Wyatt Earp and the Movies," *Montana: The Magazine of*

Western History, Summer 1995; Britz & Nichols, *Tombstone, Deadwood, and Dodge City*; Burton Devere, Jr., *Bonanzas to Borrascas*. Jane Eppinga, *Images of America: Tombstone* (Charleston, South Carolina: Arcadia Publishers, 2003).

409 *Arizona Weekly Citizen*, June 20, 1879.

410 *Tucson Citizen*, July 9 and 11, 1879. Traywick, *Tombstone's Boothill*, 8-12.

411 *Tucson Citizen*, November 3, 1879. *Arizona Weekly Star*, November 6, 1879. *The Arizona Sentinel*, November 15, 1879.

412 *Chicago Tribune* reporter Adolphus Henry Noon transcript, cited Silva, *Wyatt Earp Vol. II*, 473, 549.

413 *Daily Arizona Citizen (Tucson)*, January 8, 1880. Original copy in the collection of coauthor David D. de Haas, MD. Also cited in Silva, *Wyatt Earp Vol. II*, 479, 480, 484.

414 *Arizona Daily Star*, April 1, 1880.

415 *Arizona Daily Star* (Tucson), March 2, 1880. *Rhodes Journal*, July 1880. *Tucson Citizen*, July 3, 1880.

416 Peter Brand, "Josephine 'Sadie' Earp's Sordid Secrets & Lies," *Journal of the Wild West History Association*, March 2023, 31.

417 October 19, 1961 letter written by Jeanne Devere and citing city council records.

418 *Weekly Arizona Citizen*, October 30, 1880.

419 *Arizona Weekly Citizen*, March 20, 1881, water noticed in the Sulphuret. Of note is that a year prior to this, in March 1880, a small amount of water seepage had been detected in the Toughnut mine.

420 *Tucson Citizen*, April 10, 1881.

421 A good handy source are some Cochise County statements by Judge J. F. Duncan, *Tombstone Weekly Epitaph*, May 21, 1911. *Arizona Weekly Miner*, Aug 12, 1881, Tombstone to have a Mining Exchange; San Francisco operators are congregating there. *Arizona Weekly Citizen*, Aug 7, 1881, the new Mining Exchange, Tombstone, now occupied by city and county officials on top floor; lower floor being turned into a courtroom.

422 George W. Parsons diary. Entry for May 30, 1882. *Florence Western Enterprise* of May 27, 1882 (Saturday issue). *Tombstone Weekly Epitaph*, June 3, 1882. David D. de Haas, MD, "Revisiting the O.K. Corral Fire Aftermath Photo," *Wild West Magazine*, April 2016.

423 *Tombstone Weekly Epitaph*, July 15, 1882. Although felt to be a bit undercounted, and probably closer to six thousand-plus by end of 1882, this is likely the population peak.

424 *Tombstone Weekly Epitaph*, July 29, 1882. *Tombstone Daily Nugget*, June 1881 for Vogan.

425 Peter Brand, *Journal of the Wild West History Association*, March 2023, 31-32.

426 Ibid., 32.

427 *Weekly Republican* (Phoenix), June 14, 1883.

428 *Tombstone Weekly Epitaph*, February 22, 1890.

429 Roy B. Young, *Journal of the Wild West History Association*, March 2022, 21-44.

430 *Arizona Daily Star*, June 2, 1900; *Los Angeles Evening Express*, June 19, 1900.

431 *Arizona Republic* (Phoenix), March 25, 1903, interview with W. F. Staunton (general manager of Tombstone Consolidated Mines). *Arizona Daily Star* (Tucson), March 28, 1903.

432 *Bisbee Daily Review*, June 24, 1914.

433 Thomas K. Marshall, *The First Six Months of Prohibition in Arizona and its Effect Upon Industry, Savings and Municipal Government*, Tucson, Arizona, 1915.

434 *Bisbee D. Review*, July 3, 1915. *Tombstone Epitaph*, July 4, 1915.

435 *Tombstone Epitaph*, July 2, 1922.

436 Bechdolt, "Tombstone's Wild Oats.," *Saturday Evening Post*, December 13, 1919; *When the West Was Young*. Britz & Nichols, *Tombstone, Deadwood, and Dodge City*. See epilogue and especially its associated endnote above for much more.

437 *Douglas Daily Dispatch*, March 6, 1926, 8. *Winslow Daily Mail*, November 13, 1929.

438 Mayor John Clum's personal copy, from the day of book's first release, autographed, personalized, and dated by author Stuart Lake, in collection of coauthor David D. de Haas, MD.

439 *The Tombstone News*, October 14, 2022.

440 *New York Times*, July 20, 1938, "Tombstone for Sale to Movies."

441 See *Arizona Republic*, October 3, 1937, for interesting discussion on controversy regarding dilapidated "Boot Hill graveyard" and missing/misplaced grave markers ("Boot Hill Controversy Brings Order To Buy Grave Markers") which culminated in its restoration. Traywick's *Tombstone's Boothill*. Please also see epilogue and its detailed endnote for full explanation and timeline of events.

442 *Time Magazine*, November 19, 1945. *Arizona Republic*, January 18, 1946. *Tombstone Times*, January 2015.

443 Chaput and de Haas, *The Earps Invade Southern California*, 146-147.

444 *The Tombstone News*, October 14, 2022.

445 Britz and Nichols, *Tombstone, Deadwood and Dodge City*.

446 See *Arizona Central*, October 20, 2015, for details and reaction and comments from Mayor Dusty Escapule. For interesting follow-up, see *Herald-Review* (Sierra Vista), March 26, 2016.

447 David and Mary de Haas in attendance November 2021.

448 Chaput and de Haas, MD, *The Earps Invade Southern California*. Washington DC National Archives, "Registers of Veterans at the National Home for Disabled Volunteer Soldiers, Pacific Branch in Sawtelle, California, 1888-1933," files, data sheets.

BIBLIOGRAPHY

PRIMARY

Bisbee. Cochise County Recorder's Office. Deeds of Mines. Mining Locations. Water Rights. Real Estate Deeds. Power of Attorney.

Los Angeles. Natural History Museum. Incorporation Records. William S. Hart Papers (Hart-Earp correspondence). Register of Voters.

San Marino, California. Huntington Library. Stuart Lake Papers (a Wyatt Earp collection).

Tucson. Arizona Historical Society. George W. Parsons Diaries; Biographical Files.

Washington, DC National Archives, Soldiers' Home (National Homes for Disabled Volunteer Soldiers), file on each veteran admitted. U. S., Returns from Military Posts.

U. S. Censuses, 1850-1930.

GOVERNMENT DOCUMENTS

Register of Voters

BOOKS

Ackerman, Rita K.W. *O.K. Corral Postscript: Death of Ike Clanton*. Honolulu: Talei Publishers, 2006.
 Tombstone: Who, What, When, Where. Self-published, 2005.
Ainsworth, Ed. Foreword by John Wayne, *The Cowboy in Art*. Cleveland: The World Publishing Company, 1969.
 Painters of the Desert. Palm Desert, CA: Desert Magazine, Inc., 1960.
Alexander, Bob. *John H. Behan: Sacrificed Sheriff*. Silver City, NM: High Lonesome Books, 2002.
Babcock, Kendric Charles. *The Published Writings of William Phipps Blake*. Tucson: University of Arizona, 1910.
Bailey, Lynn R.:
 Tombstone, Arizona: "Too Tough to Die." Tucson: Westernlore Press, 2004.
 Henry Clay Hooker and the Sierra Bonita Ranch. Tucson: Westernlore Press, 1998.

Tombstone from a Woman's Point of View: The Correspondence of Clara Spalding Brown July 7, 1880, to November 14, 1882. Tucson: Westernlore Press, 1998.

A Tale of the "Unkilled": The Life, Times, and Writings of Wells W. Spicer. Tucson: Westernlore Press, 1999.

The Valiants: The Tombstone Rangers and Apache War Frivolities. Tucson: Westernlore Press, 1999.

Tombstone, Arizona: "Too Tough to Die." Tucson: Westernlore Press, 2004.

Bailey, Lynn R., and Don Chaput. *Cochise County Stalwarts*, 2 vols. Tucson: Westernlore Press, 2000.

Ball, Larry D. *Tom Horn in Life and Legend.* Norman: University of Oklahoma Press, 2014.

Bechdolt, Frederick R. *When the West Was Young.* New York: The Century Company, 1922.

Bell, Bob Boze. *The Illustrated Life and Times of Wyatt Earp.* Phoenix: Tri Star Boze Publications, 1993.

Boessenecker, John. *When Law Was in the Holster: The Frontier Life of Bob Paul.* Norman: University of Oklahoma Press, 2012.

Boessenecker, John. *Ride the Devils Herd: Wyatt Earp's Epic Battle Against the West's Biggest Outlaw Gang.* Toronto: Hanover Square Press, 2020.

Blake, William P. *Tombstone and its Mines.* New York: n. p., 1902.

Brand, Peter. *Wyatt Earp's Vendetta Posse Rider: The Story of Texas Jack Vermillion.* Meadowbank, Australia: Peter Brand, 2012.

Brand, Peter. *Doc Holliday's Nemesis: The Story of Johnny Tyler & Tombstone's Gambler War.* Meadowbank, Australia: Peter Brand, 2018.

Brand, Peter. *The Life and Crimes of Perry Mallon.* Meadowbank, Australia: Peter Brand, 2006.

Breakenridge, William M. *Helldorado: Bringing the Law to the Mesquite.* Boston and New York: Houghton Miflin Co., 1928.

Britz, Kevin and Nichols Roger L. *Tombstone, Deadwood and Dodge City: Recreating the Frontier West.* Norman: Univ of Oklahoma Press, 2018.

Burrows, Jack. *John Ringo: The Gunfighter Who Never Was.* Tucson: University of Arizona Press, 1987.

Carmony, Neil (ed.). *Tombstone's Violent Years, 1880-1882, As Remembered by John Plesent Gray.* Tucson: Trail to Yesterday Books, 1999.

Cataldo, Nicholas R. *The Earp Clan: The Southern California Years.* San Bernardino: Back Roads Press, 2006.

Cataldo, Nick, and Fred Holladay. *The Earps of San Bernardino County.* San Bernardino: City of San Bernardino Historical & Pioneer Society, 2001.

Carr, John. *Pioneer Days in California.* Eureka: Times Pub. Co., 1891.

Chafin, Earl: *Wyatt Earp in Alaska: The Story of Wyatt and Josephine Earp from 1897 to 1901 in Rampart, St. Michael, and Nome, Alaska.* Riverside, CA: The Earl Chafin Press, 1999.

Final Hours of Wyatt Earp: His Last Years, Funeral, Burial Place and Getting His Story Told. Riverside, CA: Earl Chafin Press, 2001.

Sincerely Your Friend, Wyatt S. Earp: The Letters of Wyatt Earp. Riverside, CA: The Earl Chafin Press, 2001.

Chaput, Donald:
> *Dr. Goodfellow: Physician to the Gunfighters.* Tucson: Westernlore Press, 1996.
> *Nellie Cashman and the North American Mining Frontier.* Tucson: Westernlore Press, 1995.
> *The Odyssey of Burt Alvord: Lawman, Train Robber, Fugitive.* Tucson: Westernlore Press, 2000.
> *Virgil Earp: Western Peace Officer.* Norman: University of Oklahoma Press, 1996.
> *The Earp Papers.* Encampment, WY: Affiliated Writers of America, 1994.
> *"Buckskin Frank" Leslie.* Tucson: Westernlore Press, 1999.
> *Empire of Sand: The Ehrenberg-Quartzsite-Parker Triangle.* Santa Ana, CA: Graphic Publishers, 2015.

Chaput, Don and David D. de Haas, MD. *The Earps Invade Southern California: Bootlegging Los Angeles, Santa Monica, and the Old Soldiers' Home.* Denton, TX: University of North Texas Press, 2020.

Clements, Eric L. *After the Boom in Tombstone and Jerome, Arizona: Decline in Western Resource Towns.* Reno: University of Nevada Press, 2003.

Cox, Mike. *Finding the Wild West, the Great Plains: Oklahoma, Kansas, Nebraska, and the Dakotas.* Lanham, MD: Two Dot.

Craig, R. Bruce. *Portrait of a Prospector: Edward Schieffelin's Own Story.* Norman: University of Oklahoma Press, 2017.

DeArment, Robert K. *Knights of the Green Cloth: The Saga of the Frontier Gamblers.* Norman: University of Oklahoma Press, 1982.

DeArment, Robert K. *Bat Masterson: The Man and the Legend.* Norman: University of Oklahoma Press, 1979.
> *Broadway Bat: Gunfighter in Gotham: The New York City Years of Bat Masterson.* Honolulu: Talei Publishers, 2005.

DeMattos, Jack. *The Earp Decision.* College Station, TX: Creative Publishing Company, 1989.

DeMattos, Jack, and Chuck Parsons. Foreword by John Boessenecker. *They Called Him Buckskin Frank: The Life and Times of Nashville Franklyn Leslie.*
Denton: University of North Texas Press, 2018.
> *The Notorious Luke Short: Sporting Man of the Wild West.* Denton, TX: University of North Texas Press, 2015.

Devere, Jr., Burton. *Bonanzas to Borrascas: The Mines of Tombstone, Arizona.* Tombstone: Rose Tree Museum, 2010.

Dodge, Fred. Edited by Carolyn Lake. *Undercover for Wells Fargo: The Unvarnished Recollections of Fred Dodge.* Boston: Houghton Mifflin Company, 1969.

Dolph, Jerry, and Arthur Randall. *Wyatt Earp and Coeur d'Alene Gold: Stampede to Idaho Territory.* Post Falls, ID: Eagle City Publications, 1999.

Dworkin, Mark J. *American Mythmaker: Walter Noble Burns and the Legends of Billy the Kid, Wyatt Earp, and Joaquin Murrieta.* Norman: University of Oklahoma Press, 2015.

Earp-Edwards, Adelia. *Wild West Remembrances (1861–1941).* Riverside, CA: Earl Chaffin Press, 1998.

Earp, Josephine S. Edited by Earl Chafin. *Wyatt's Woman: She Married Wyatt Earp: The Life and Times of Josephine Sarah Marcus*.1938. Reprint, Riverside, CA: The Earl Chafin Press, 1998.

Earp, Wyatt S. Collected and Introduction by Glenn G. Boyer. *Wyatt Earp: A Peace Officer of Tombstone*. Sierra Vista, AZ: Yoma V. Bissette, October 26, 1981. Personal copy of author Al Turner.

Earp, Wyatt. Edited by John Richard Stephens. *Wyatt Earp Speaks: My Side of the O. K. Corral Shootout, Plus Interviews with Doc Holliday*. Cambria Pines by the Sea, CA: Fern Canyon Press, 1998.

Erwin, Richard E. *The Truth About Wyatt Earp*. Carpinteria, CA: The O.K. Press, 1992.

Erwin, Allen A. *The Southwest of John H. Slaughter, 1841-1922*. Glendale, CA: Arthur C. Clark Co., 1965.

Eppinga, Jane: *Tombstone: Images of America*. Charleston: Arcadia Publishing, 2003.
Around Tombstone: Ghost towns and Gunfights. Charleston: Arcadia Publishing, 2009.
Tombstone: Postcard History Series. Charleston: Arcadia Publishing, 2010.
Southern Arizona Cemeteries. Charleston: Arcadia Publishing, 2014.

Fattig, Timothy W. *Wyatt Earp: The Biography*. Honolulu: Talei Publishers, 2002.

Fischer, Ron W. *Nellie Cashman: Frontier Angel*. Preface by Jane Candia Coleman, introduction by Ben T. Traywick, foreword by Glenn G. Boyer. Honolulu: Talei Publishers Inc., 2000.
The Last Great Frontier Marshall: A Biography of William "Bill" Tilghman. Tombstone: Ron W. Fischer Enterprises, 2001.

Fisher, Truman Rex, ed. *Correspondence Between Wyatt S. Earp and William S. Hart et al., from 1920 to 1929*. Newhall, CA: William S. Hart Museum, 1984. Incl. photos of Earp's L. A. residences.

Flood, Jr., John Henry. *Wyatt Earp*. Edited by Don Taylor. Tombstone: Old West Research & Publishing, 2011.

Flood Jr., John Henry. *Biography of Wyatt Earp: Gunfighter of the Old West (1926)*. Edited by Earl Chafin. Riverside, CA: Earl Chafin Press, 1988.

Forrest, Earle R. *Arizona's Dark and Bloody Ground*. Caldwell, ID: Caxton Printers, 1936.

Gatto, Steve:
John Ringo: The Reputation of a Deadly Gunman. Tucson: San Simon Publishing Company, 1995.
Wyatt Earp: A Biography of a Western Lawman. Tucson: San Simon Publishing Company, 1997.
The Real Wyatt Earp: A Documentary Biography. Silver City, NM: High Lonesome Books, 2000.
Johnny Ringo. Lansing: Protar House, 2002.
Curly Bill: Tombstone's Most Famous Outlaw. Lansing: Protar House, 2003.

Gilchriese, John D. *The Odyssey of Virgil Earp*. Tucson, 1968. Gilchriese's personal annotated copy of the original manuscript (edited version subsequently published in *The Tombstone Epitaph*, National Edition, Fall 1968) in collection of coauthor David D. de Haas.

Grasse, David. *The Bisbee Massacre: Robbery, Murder and Retribution in the Arizona Territory 1883–1884*. Jefferson, NC: McFarland & Co., 2017.

Haley, J. Evetts. *Jeff Milton: A Good Man with a Gun*. Norman: University of Oklahoma Press, 1968.

Hand, George. *Whiskey, Six-guns and Red-light Ladies: George Hand's Saloon Diary, Tucson, 1875–1878*. Edited and with an introduction by Neil Carmony. Silver City, NM: High-Lonesome Books, 1994.

Hattich, William. *Tombstone: In History, Romance and Wealth*. Foreword by John D. Gilchriese. Oklahoma: University of Oklahoma Press, 1981. Reprint, originally published Tombstone, Arizona: *Tombstone Daily Prospector*, April 1903.
　Pioneer Magic: Adventurous Tales of Turbulent Arizona. New York: Vantage Press, 1964.

Hickey, Michael M.:
　The Street Fight Trilogy: Street Fight in Tombstone Near the O.K. Corral; Los Dos Pistoleros Earp, The Two Earp Pistoleers; The Cowboy Conspiracy to Convict the Earps. Honolulu: Talei Publishers, 1992, 1993, 1994.
　The Death of Warren Baxter Earp: A Closer Look. Honolulu: Talei Publishers, 2000.
　John Ringo: The Final Hours. Honolulu: Talei Publishers, 2001.
　History of Arizona Territory. San Francisco: Wallace W. Elliott & Co., 1884.

Hooker, Forrestine Cooper. *An Arizona Vendetta: The Truth About Wyatt Earp— and Some Others*. Los Angeles: The Munk Library of Arizona Southwest Museum, ca. 1919. See also retyped copy Neil B. Carmony, 2000.

Hornung, Chuck. *Wyatt Earp's Cow-boy Campaign*. Jefferson, NC: McFarland & Co., 2016.

Hutton, Paul Andrew. *The Apache Wars*. New York: Crown Publishing, 1916.

John's Western Gallery and William B. Shillingberg. *Wyatt Earp, Tombstone and the West (Parts I, II, and III)*. John D. Gilchriese Collection Auction Catalogues. San Francisco: John's Western Gallery, 2004/2005.

Johnson, David. *John Ringo: King of the Cowboys, 2nd Ed.* Denton: University of North Texas Press, 2008.

Johnson, Paul Lee. *The McLaurys in Tombstone, Arizona: An O.K. Corral Obituary*. Denton, TX: University of North Texas Press, 2012.

Kelly, Troy (comp.)). *From Tombstone to Their Tombstones*. Self-published.

Kintop, Jeffrey, and Guy L. Rocha. *The Earps' Last Frontier: Wyatt and Virgil Earp in the Nevada Mining Camps, 1902-1905*. Reno: Great Basin Press, 1989.

Kirschner, Ann. *Lady at the O.K. Corral: The True Story of Josephine Marcus Earp*. New York: Harper Collins Publishers, 2013.

Lake, Stuart N. *Wyatt Earp: Frontier Marshal*. Cambridge, MA: Houghton Mifflin Company, 1931. Tombstone Mayor John P. Clums's personal copy in collection of David D. de Haas, MD.

Lake, Carolyn, ed. *Undercover for Wells Fargo: The Unvarnished Recollections of Fred Dodge*. Norman: The University of Oklahoma Press, 1969.

Ledoux, Gary. *Tombstone: A Chronicle in Perspective*. Victoria, BC: Trafford Publishing, 2002.

Ledoux, Gary. *Nantan: The Life and Times of John P. Clum* (2 vols.). Victoria, BC: Trafford Publications, 2007-2008.

Lewis, Alfred Henry:
The Sunset Trail. New York: A. L. Burt Company, 1905.
Wolfville (series). New York: Grossett & Dunlap, 1897-1908.

Lubet, Steven. *Murder in Tombstone: The Forgotten Trial of Wyatt Earp.* New Haven: Yale University Press, 2004.

Marks, Paula Mitchell. *And Die in the West: The Story of the O.K. Corral Gunfight.* New York: William Morrow and Company, 1989.

Marshall, Thomas K. *The First Six Months of Prohibition in Arizona and its Effect Upon Industry, Savings and Municipal Government.* Tucson, 1915.

McCormack, Kara L. *Imagining Tombstone: The Town Too Tough to Die.* Lawrence, KS: University Press of Kansas, 2016.

O'Neal, Bill.: *Encyclopedia of Western Gunfighters.* Norman: University of Oklahoma Press, 1979.
The Arizona Rangers. Austin: Eakin Press, 1987.
Captain Harry Wheeler: Arizona Lawman. Austin: Eakin Press, 2003.

Parsons, George W. *A Tenderfoot in Tombstone: The Private Journal of George Whitwell Parsons: The Turbulent Years, 1880–82.* Edited by Lynn R. Bailey. Tucson: Westernlore Press, 1996.

Parsons, George W. *The Devil Has Foreclosed: The Private Journal of George Whitwell Parsons, Volume II: The Concluding Years, 1882–87.* Edited, trans. by Lynn R. Bailey. Tucson: Westernlore Press, 1997.

Palenske, Garner A. *Wyatt Earp in San Diego: Life After Tombstone.* Santa Ana, CA: Graphic Publishers, 2011.

Reidhead, S.J. *Travesty: The Story of Frank Waters and The Earp Brothers of Tombstone.* Roswell, NM: Jinglebob Press, 2005.

Reidhead, S.J. *A Church for Helldorado: The 1882 Tombstone Diary of Endicott Peabody.* Roswell, NM: Jinglebob Press, 2006.

Roberts, Gary L. *Doc Holliday: The Life and Legend.* Hoboken, NJ: John Wiley & Sons, 2006.
"'Suppose…Suppose…': Wyatt Earp, Frontier Violence, Myth and History." Epilogue in *A Wyatt Earp Anthology: Long May His Story Be Told.* Denton: University of North Texas Press, 2019.

Roy Young, et al. *A Wyatt Earp Anthology: Long May His Story Be Told.* Denton: University of North Texas Press, 2019.

Ross, Thom. *Gunfight at the O.K. Corral: In Words and Pictures.* Golden, CO: Fulcrum Publishing, 2001.

Silva, Lee A.: *Wyatt Earp: A Biography of the Legend.* Vol. I, *The Cowtown Years.* Santa Ana, CA: Graphic Publishers, 2002.
Wyatt Earp: A Biography of the Legend. Vol. II, *Tombstone Before the Earps.* Santa Ana, CA: Graphic Publishers, 2010.

Shillingberg, William B. *Tombstone, A. T.:*
A History of Early Mining, Milling, and Mayhem. Spokane: Arthur C. Clark Company, 1999.
Dodge City: The Early Years, 1872-1886. Norman, OK: The Arthur H. Clark Company, 2009.

Sonnichsen, C.L., ed. *Billy King's Tombstone: The Private Life of an Arizona Boom Town.* Tucson: University of Arizona Press, 1972.

Smith, Jeff. *Alias Soapy Smith: The life and Death of a Scoundrel.* Juneau: Klondike Research, 2009.

Taylor, Don. *Tombstone: The First Fifty Years (1879 – 1929).* Old West Research & Publishing, L.L.C., 2010.

Tanner, Karen Holliday. *Doc Holliday: A Family Portrait.* Norman: University of Oklahoma Press, 1998.

Traywick, Ben T.: *Historical Documents and Photographs of Tombstone.* 1971. rev. ed., Tombstone: Red Marie's Bookstore, 1994.

John Henry (The "Doc" Holliday Story). Tombstone: Red Marie's Bookstore, 1996.

The Clantons of Tombstone. Tombstone: Red Marie's Bookstore, 1996.

Wyatt Earp's Thirteen Dead Men. Tombstone: Red Marie's Bookstore, 1998.

Wyatt Earp: Angel of Death. Honolulu, HI: Talei Publishers, 2007.

Tombstone's "Buckskin Frank": Nashville Franklyn Leslie. Tombstone: Red Marie's Bookstore, 2013.

Minute Book Common Council Village of Tombstone: September 10, 1880 thru January 16, 1882. Edited/self-published by Ben T. Traywick.

1879 *Census Tombstone, as taken by Pima County Sheriff Charles A. Shibell on September 18, 19, and 20, 1879.* Edited/self-published by Ben T. Traywick, 1999.

Tombstone's Boothill. Tombstone: Red Marie's Bookstore, 1971, second ed. 1994.

Trimble, Marshall. *Wild West: Heroes and Rogues.* Vol. 1, *Wyatt Earp: Showdown in Tombstone.* Phoenix: Golden West Publishers, 2008.

Turner, Alfred, ed:

The Earps Talk. College Station, TX: The Early West/The Creative Publishing Company, 1980.

The O.K. Corral Inquest. College Station, TX: The Early West/The Creative Publishing Company, 1981.

Waters, Frank, *The Earp Brothers of Tombstone: The Story of Mrs. Virgil Earp.* New York: Clarkson N. Potter, Inc., 1960.

Walters, Lorenzo D. *Tombstone's Yesterday.* Tucson: Acme Printing Co., 1928.

Wister, Owen. *The Virginian: A Horseman of the Plains.* New York: The Macmillan Company, 1902.

Young, Richard Alan and Judy Dockrey. *Outlaw Tales: Legends, Myths, and Folklore from America's Middle Border.* Little Rock: August House Publishers, Inc.

Young, Roy B.: *Cochise County Cowboy War: "A Cast of Characters."* Apache, OK: Young & Sons Enterprises, 1999.

Pete Spence: "Audacious Artist in Crime." Apache, OK: Young & Sons Enterprises, 2000.

James Cooksey Earp: Out of the Shadows. Apache, OK: Young & Sons Enterprises, 2006.

Robert Havlin Paul: Frontier Lawman, The Arizona Years. Apache, OK: Young & Son Enterprises, 2009.

Foreword by Gary L. Roberts and Robert E. Palmquist. *Judge William H. Stilwell: Bench and Bar in Arizona Territory.* Apache, OK: Young & Sons Enterprises, 2011.

Gary L. Roberts et al, eds., *A Wyatt Earp Anthology: Long May His Story Be Told.* Denton: University of North Texas Press, 2019.
Newton Jasper Earp: Mystery Brother of the Famous "Fighting Earps," Apache, OK: Young & Sons Enterprises, 2022.

ARTICLES

Bechdolt, Frederick R. "Tombstone's Wild Oats." *Saturday Evening Post* (December 13, 1919).
Bell, Bob Boze. "Wyatt Earp in Hollywood." *True West Magazine* (October 2015).
Blake, William P. "The Geology and Veins of Tombstone, Arizona." *Transactions, American Institute of Mining Engineers*, X (1882): 334-45. "The Geology and Veins of Tombstone." *Engineering & Mining Journal* (March 18, 1882):145.
Brand, Peter. "Josephine 'Sadie' Earp's Sordid Secrets & Lies." *Wild West History Association Journal* (March 2023): 10-34.
Britz, Kevin. "Boot Hill Burlesque: The Frontier Cemetery as Tourist Attraction in Tombstone, Arizona, and Dodge City, Kansas." *Journal of Arizona History* 44 (Autumn 2003): 211-42.
Chaput, Don. "Fred Dodge: Undercover Agent, or Con Man?" *National Outlaw and Lawman Association Quarterly* XXV (January-March, 2000).
Chaput, Don. "The Earp Brother's Body Count." *National Outlaw and Lawman Association Quarterly* (April-May 2000): 33-39.
Chaput, Don and de Haas, MD, David D. "The Earp Fellow Sophisticates." *Wild West Magazine* (October 2021): 64 – 69.
Chaput, Don and de Haas, MD, David D. "Tumbling Dice, Blind Pigs and Brothels: The Earps' Last Stand in Los Angeles Was More Bust Than Bonanza." *True West Magazine* (November 2022): 26-31.
de Haas, David D. "Clyde Forsythe Painted California Deserts; and One Little Vacant Lot in Tombstone." *Wild West Magazine* (October 2013): 1, 2, 22-23. Full extended online version: <https://www.historynet.com/victor-clyde-forsytheand-the-gunfightatcorrala-new-perspective.htm>. "Revisiting the 'O.K. Corral Fire Aftermath Photo'." *Wild West Magazine.* (April 2016): 11. Extended online version: <https://www.historynet.com/revisitingthe-ok-corral-fire-aftermath-photo.htm>. "My Best Friend Lee." *Wild West History Association Journal* (October 2014): 8-19. "Collectors Roundup." C.T. Hayden: Tempe, Arizona. *Wild West History Association Journal* (February 2012): 49-52. Letter to the editor re: Follow up to "Collectors Roundup:" U.S. Senator Carl Hayden and the Graham/Tewksbury Feud. *Wild West History Association Journal* (August 2012): 3-4. Letter to the Editor re: "Albert B. Fall and his Teapot Dome Scandal." *Wild West History Association Journal* (February 2012) 4-5.
Dyke, Scott, and Bob Palmquist. "Adelia Earp's Dubious Memoir." *Wild West Magazine* (October 2016).
Fisher, Truman Rex. "Wyatt Earp's Multitudinous Tombstones." *True West Magazine* (April 1997): 26-29.

Gilchriese, John D. "Wyatt Earp's Personal Diagrams of Prominent Historical Events." McLean, VA: United States Marshals Foundation, Inc. (1989).

"Goldfield, The New Eldorado," *Putnam's Monthly* (March 1907): 658–72.

Hutton, Paul Andrew. "Showdown at the Hollywood Corral: Wyatt Earp and the Movies." *Montana: The Magazine of Western History* (Summer 1995).

Lee, Jane Matson, Mark Dworkin, and H.F. Sills. "Mystery Man of the O. K. Corral Shootout." *WOLA Journal* (Spring 2004).

Palmquist, Bob. "Justice in Tombstone." *Wild West Magazine* (October 2015).

Peterson, Roger S. "Wyatt Earp: Man Versus Myth." *American History Magazine* (August 1994): 54-61.

Roberts, Gary L. "Allie's Story: Mrs. Virgil Earp and the 'Tombstone Travesty.'" *WOLA Journal* (Fall 1999).

Silva, Lee A. "The Mysterious Morgan Earp." *Wild West Magazine* (October 2010): 28-35.

"In a Brother's Shadow." *Wild West Magazine* (December 2009): 26-33.

"Did Tom McLaury Have a Gun?" *Wild West Magazine* (October 2006): 34-41.

Silva, Susan L., and Lee A. Silva. "The Killing of Dora Hand." *Wild West Magazine* (December 2009): 40-47.

White, Scott. "Bad Men's Nemesis: The Adventures and Experiences of an Arizona Sheriff." *Touring Topics* (April, 1931).

NEWSPAPERS

Arizona Citizen (Tucson)
Arizona Daily Star (Tucson)
Arizona Republican (Phoenix)
Arizona Sentinel (Yuma)
Arizona Silver Belt (Globe)
Bisbee Daily Review
Border Vidette (Nogales)
Brooklyn Daily Eagle
Clifton Clarion (Graham County, Arizona)
Daily Progressive Miner (Ketchikan)
Daily Record (Long Branch, New Jersey)
Dodge City Globe
Dodge City Times
El Paso Herald
Evening Herald (Albuquerque)
Evening Statesman (Walla Walla)
Hays City Sentinel
Leavenworth Times
Los Angeles Herald
Los Angeles Times
Mohave County Miner
New York Times
Oasis (Nogales)
Sacramento Record-Union
San Francisco Call
San Francisco Chronicle
San Francisco Examiner
Santa Fe New Mexican
Seattle Post-Intelligencer
Tombstone Epitaph
Tombstone Nugget
Tombstone Prospector

BIBLIOGRAPHY

OTHER

Bonhams Auction catalogue, *The Early West: The Collection of Jim and Theresa Earle*, Los Angeles, CA, August 27, 2021.

de Haas, David D. MD. "Victor Clyde Forsythe—Art of the West." HistoryNet. com.

Gilchriese, John D. *Tombstone, Arizona Territory: Circa 1881-82*, map, 1971. Based on the research of Robert N. Mullin and his original 1916 sketch; John Gilchriese's personal copy in the collection of coauthor David D. de Haas, MD.

Halliwell, Hildreth, September 21, 1971, interview with Al Turner, recordings in her home in Valley Center, California; Tucson: University of Arizona, 1971; copy in collection of David D. de Haas, MD.

McCormack, Kara L. *"Imagining the Town Too Tough to Die": Tourism, Preservation, and History in Tombstone, Arizona.* Doctoral Dissertation. Albuquerque: The University of New Mexico, May 2013.

McLelland, Gary S. *The Streets of Tombstone: Territory of Arizona on October 26, 1881.* Self-published map, 1998.

Newspapers.com

Rousseau, Sarah Jane. Rousseau diary: Across the Desert to California From Salt Lake City to San Bernardino in 1864. San Bernardino County Museum Association. Vol. VI, No. 2, Winter 1958.

Santiago, Dawn Theresa. (1998). *The Banking Operations of Lionel and Barron Jacobs, Tucson, Arizona, 1867-1913.* (Master's thesis). University of Arizona, Tucson, Arizona.

Taylor, Don. Map *Tombstone Arizona, 1881 – 1882*, Old West Research, 2005. "Texas Jack" [James Wright]. "Texas, by God" and the Twin Territories. (New Mexico & Arizona). Internet Wild West discussion board.

Facebook, "Wild West Collectors. de Haas, MD, David D. and de Haas, Mary D., moderators. <https://www.facebook.com groups/261849524484480/>.

ILLUSTRATIONS

ILLUSTRATIONS

ACKNOWLEDGMENTS

Don Chaput

David D. de Haas, MD

DAVID WOULD ALSO LIKE TO ACKNOWLEDGE THE FOLLOWING individuals for their assistance, support, friendship/camaraderie, inspiration, and encouragement during the writing of this, Don and David's second book together: Lance de Haas and Rachel Wagner (technical support; congratulations March 2024!); Ed Chaput (technical support; help salvaging the manuscript from a Microsoft hacker; illustrations); Verena Coutts (and her wonderful parents Stephen and Loyella); Bill (two-term State Historian of Texas) and Karon (RIP) O'Neal; John Boessenecker (manuscript critique; wrote the foreword; *New York Times* best-selling author); Ben Harleman (a fine human being and loyal friend), and Peter Brand (manuscript critique); Asher and Levi Marcos; Marjorie Elliott (of Tombstone's Silver Lady Antiques and Western Heritage Museum); Don Taylor (current official Tombstone town historian); Mark (and Patty) Boardman (editor of *Tombstone Epitaph* newspaper and features editor of *True*

West magazine; manuscript critique); Ben and Mary Traywick (prolific author and retired official Tombstone town historian); Steve Goldstein (owner, Tombstone's Longhorn Restaurant, Big Nose Kate's Saloon, Nellie Cashman's Bed and Breakfast); Gordon Anderson and Linda (owner of Tombstone's Larian Motel; thirty-year trusted friend); Dustin Escapule (mayor of Tombstone; pioneer Tombstone family); Mary de Haas (editing); Robert Devere (pioneer Tombstone family); all members of the Wild West Collectors Facebook page; Linda Wommack (manuscript critique; contributing editor, *True West* magazine, *Wild West* magazine, and the *Tombstone Epitaph Journal*; prolific author); Stuart Rosebrook, Ph.D. (editor, *True West* magazine); Marshall and Vanessa Trimble (manuscript critique; official Arizona state historian; *True West* magazine's "Ask the Marshall" monthly columnist/contributing editor; vice president, Wild West History Association; author); and wonderful artist (the second amazing dustjacket he has now painted for us) Gary Zaboly. Ron Clark (desert artist Bill Bender estate); Ronald Chrisman (manuscript review/critique); Lee and Susan Leiser Silva (RIP); Mike Mayberry; Denay Turner Valenzuela; Cheryl Leavere Honeycutt; James and Margaret Bailey; Clell and Arlene Furnell; Hollywood promoters Julie Ann and Bob Ream; James "Texas Jack" and Carrla (RIP) Wright; Roy and Charlotte Young; Chuck and Pat Parsons; Dr. Gary L. Roberts; Tom Gaumer; Garth Gould; Kenneth (K.t.K.) Vail; Alan Blanchette; Jeff Wheat; Tom Moy; Ron Woggon; Chuck and Jean Smith; Troy Kelly; Lisa Lach Chiles; Jim and Lynda (RIP, June 2023) Groom; Jeffrey and Cindy Roth; Michael Bell; Doug and Rita Ackerman; Elaine Patterson Bennett; Rita and Daniel (RIP, my good buddy) Patterson; Peter Sherayko (a true gentleman and Tombstone movie's "Texas Jack"); William (RIP) and Paula Jean Hunley (owners of Bird Cage Theatre); Billy Hunley; Felicia Valdez and Arabella Martinez (Hunley granddaughters); Kevin and Bev Mulkins; Greg Lalire (former editor of *Wild West* magazine), Brian Carlin (my long-term CPA) and Teri Meissner (for their friendship and support through some very difficult times during the writing of this book); Medhat Mikhael, MD (for keeping me out of pain), Gad Heilweil, MD, Ralf Reuland, MD; Larry (and Kelly) Kaban, DDS; Phyllis Eccleston; J.P. Synnott (CVCS senior student athlete); my gym buddies who have given me encouragement, support, and advice for the book as we all daily sit in the sauna together debating life: Scott Malin, Rocco Falabella, Frank Micucci, Mark Bauer, Anthony DiCenzo, Michael Gleason, MD, James Seide, Ray Soria, Luis Enriquez, Steve "Gil" Gillan, Peter Hampson, Mark and Roseana Kuczynski, and Byron Collins.

Also, Tombstone/Earp researcher and author Garner Palenske; Anne Collier; Michael Hickey (RIP); Donna Dycus and Alisha Long; Karen Holliday Tanner and John Tanner (who have both passed—RIP); Mario and Jeremy Ficarola; Ron Lawson; Naomi and Marlin Wertman; Mary and Paul Johnson; artist Joe Cesario; the wonderful Libert family of Chicago – Marshall, Lou, Michael, newlyweds David and Jess, Steven and Lauren; Christine Rhodes (former Cochise County recorder – who more than likely holds the world's record for most "acknowledgements" in Tombstone/Earpiana-related books); Dale Hector; Mark Wilhelm; Rick (RIP) and Shelby Mosolf; Jim Schiffer; Sharon Cunningham; Bob Pugh; Steve Gatto (RIP); Donna, Madison, and Louis Harrell; Norman Wayne Brown (RIP); Terry Ike and Mary Ann Cosby Clanton; Irisse and Richard Lapidus; Wayne and Laura Sanderson; Bob Cash; Richard Ignarski (Tombstone's Gunfighters Hall of Fame); Gary and Rachel Ledoux; Michael Pitel; David Lauterborn (editor, *Wild West* magazine); John (J. R.) and Rose Sanders; Mark Warren; Erik Wright; Barb, Dave, and Paul (my Godson) Chiero; Robert Keith; Dave Snowden; Jeff Broome; Brad Courtney (the "Whiskey Row historian"); Ken Hess; Michael Lanning; Albert Jennings IV and Billie Fountain; David and Wenda Wagner; Brazil's Long Branch Beltrao; Richard and Sherry Green; Steven and Linda Ridnor; Douglas and Laura Ridnor; Candice Harding and Vince Brocato; Jake and Miranda Green (May 12, 2023 congratulations!); Rachel Ridnor, Patrick and Kelli Page Krabeepetcharat; Jeremy Ridnor, and Sara and Kelsey Ridnor; Nicholas Cataldo; Paul Cool (RIP); Mark (RIP) and Harriet Dworkin; Rose and Robert (RIP) DeArment; Suzanne and Michael Wallis; Paul Marquez; Billy Clanton Naylor; Jan Devereaux and Bob Alexander; Jeff Millet; Robert McDearmon; Larry and Ruth Ball; Thom Ross; Jane Eppinga (RIP); Bob Paul (great grandson of the legendary lawman); Dennis and Mary Lee McCown; Dick Derham; Jerry Fields; Leah Jaswal; Walt and Vickie Ross; Joe Gallagher; Corey Recko; Eli Lizzie (France's Tombstone historian); rare book collector William Nicholas; Nicholas Narog; Dr. Paul Andrew Hutton; Gary McLelland; Peter Vourakis; Billy Reed; David Wright; Gail Allan; Kurt House (Wild

West collector extraordinaire); Jim and Jodi MacGregor; Shawn Bordine; Randy Edwards; the hardworking, enthusiastic Rebecca Larsen (marketing, City of Tombstone); Pat Pattison; Mark Sankey (Mescal Studios); Randy Lish; our amazing copy editor Tish Thornton; Scott Gipson (president, Caxton Press); Wayne Sorenson; Kirby White. Last, but not least, I acknowledge all my new Tombstone Movie buddies who have now re-inspired me: John Philbin (Tom McLaury in the movie); Wyatt Earp (Billy Claiborne), and his charming sister, Denise Earp-Halliburton; Robert Burke (Frank McLaury); Dana Wheeler-Nicholson (Wyatt's wife Mattie); the delightful Lisa Collins (Louisa Earp); Christopher Mitchum (Hooker's Ranch Foreman and son of movie narrator and Hollywood legend Robert Mitchum); Joanna Pacula (Doc's "Big Nose" Kate); and Chris Swinney (Tombstone movie medic, who was on scene more than any other—every single day of shooting).

About the cover artwork: *Tombstone Mystique* by Gary Zaboly. Time passes from bottom right to upper left corner (modern day 2023) of dust jacket with renowned townsfolk/scenarios which all play a part in the story and represent the five eras studied throughout the book. On August 1, 1877, the ecstatic Ed Schieffelin admires his first discovery of silver (glowing in his left hand) in the harsh barren southeastern Arizona desert, soon to become known as the Tombstone Hills and Mining district. Surrounded by desert cacti and at his side his trusty burro. Below to the left in the depiction is his future partner Dick Gird. Next to them the Boothill Graveyard with a tarantula, rattlesnake, skull, and howling coyote. Above that are famed Apache Indians Geronimo and the Apache Kid, Mayor John Clum, and above them the Earp brothers and Doc Holliday on the way to their legendary gunfight at the OK Corral. Coming off Schieffelin's miners pick lightning simultaneously erupts as he makes his silver strike and a tornado/whirlwind (engulfing the entire painting) of time/events which unbeknownst to him will follow in the ensuing 146 years, all set in motion by this initial discovery. Nellie Cashman holding a copy of the celebrated Tombstone Epitaph newspaper and below her Cowboy gunman Johnny Ringo and Schieffelin Hall. Moving on in time and to the left is Fort Huachuca with a Buffalo Soldier and scorpion and to the far left Wells Fargo stagecoach representing not only its mythical past, including storied Tombstone area holdups, but its current status as a tourist attraction ride in modern Tombstone. Above them is George Hearst, China Mary, Texas John Slaughter, and George Parsons mining, all of them legends who contributed to the aura of Tombstone. A mill/mine representing Tombstone's mining resurgence in 1901 and again in 1914 (eras 3 and 4) and to the left of that the modern Crystal Palace Saloon. As time passes in 1929 is the original first Helldorado event program. Further to the left is the old Agency Pima County bank which is currently the visitors center as shown. Above that, the tourists begin to appear in Tombstone (the book's "era # 5") at its celebrated Bird Cage Theatre. Here co-authors David D. de Haas (and wife Mary) and Don Chaput are greeted by current Tombstone townsfolk as they arrive in their blue Suburban ("Tombstone-mobile;" behind them), including (shaking hands with David) emeritus official Tombstone Town Historian Ben (and his wife, Mary, center with

411

long-term close friend Mary de Haas) Traywick. Also emerging to greet them (to the far left) are dear friends (and Bird Cage Theatre owners) Bill and Paula Jean Hunley.

INDEX

428